C000146033

Equality in the Sec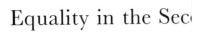

**Also available from Continuum**

*Equality in the Primary School*, Dave Hill and Leena Helavaara Robertson

*Education and Community*, Diane Gereluk

*Values in Education*, Graham Haydon

*Educational Attainment and Society*, Nigel Kettley

# Equality in the Secondary School

## Promoting Good Practice across the Curriculum

Edited by Mike Cole

continuum

**Continuum International Publishing Group**

The Tower Building
11 York Road
London
SE1 7NX

80 Maiden Lane
Suite 704
New York
NY 10038

www.continuumbooks.com

**British Library Cataloguing-in-Publication Data**
A catalogue record for this book is available from the British Library.

ISBN: 9781847061010 (hardcover)

**Library of Congress Cataloging-in-Publication Data**
Equality in the secondary school: promoting good practice across the curriculum/edited by Mike Cole.
     p. cm.
   Includes bibliographical references.
   ISBN 978-1-84706-101-0 (hardback)
  1. Discrimination in education–Great Britain. 2. Educational equalization–Great Britain.
3. Education, Secondary–Great Britain. I. Cole, Mike, 1946–

  LC213.3.G7E79 2009
  379.2'60941–dc22
2009020708

Typeset by BookEns, Royston, Herts.
Printed and bound in Great Britain by

# Contents

# Notes on Contributors

**Pura Ariza** worked in inner-city Liverpool for eight years, teaching French and Spanish and later special educational needs (SEN). She is currently working in education at Manchester Metropolitan University, mainly in Initial Teacher Education (ITE) programmes. Her research interests include promoting equality between languages, and she is a member of The National Centre for Languages (CILT) advisory group on community languages. Pura is an active trade unionist.

**Wayne Au** is an assistant professor in the Department of Secondary Education at California State University, Fullerton, US, and former co-chair of the now defunct National Coalition of Education Activists. He writes regularly on issues of social justice and critical educational theory, is an editorial board member for the progressive education journal *Rethinking Schools*, and is author of the book *Unequal by Design: High-Stakes Testing and the Standardization of Inequality* (Routledge 2009).

**Dr Mark Boylan** is a Senior Lecturer in Mathematics Education at Sheffield Hallam University, working in ITE, teacher professional development and educational research. Before this he taught mathematics in comprehensive schools. He is also a movement teacher and uses a variety of creative action methods in his work. As part of his concern for social justice, his work as an educator involves creating learning environments which support the development of participants' embodiment, critical awareness and personhood.

**Matthew Bury** is a Senior Lecturer in Education, Middlesex University, responsible for the Postgraduate Certificate of Education (PGCE) D&T, also contributing to MA Teaching, BA Product Design and Engineering, BA Education Studies, and is a moderator for the Graduate Teacher Programme. Prior to this he was head of three design and technology departments in

London, Essex and Hertfordshire and taught D&T, ICT, science and art for 12 years. During this time he taught in a French technical school as joint organizer of a European project, as a supply teacher at British secondary and primary schools, and worked as a New Opportunities Fund (NOF) ICT trainer in secondary science and D&T.

**John Clay** taught science in both secondary and middle schools before moving into science teacher education in what is now the University of Greenwich and the University of Brighton. He then worked as a Local Authority Adviser on raising the achievement of pupils/students from minority ethnic backgrounds. He is currently working as a Senior Policy Adviser for the General Teaching Council (England).

**Professor Mike Cole** is Research Professor in Education and Equality and head of research at Bishop Grosseteste University College Lincoln. He has published extensively in the field of education and equality. His latest books are *Education, Equality and Human Rights: Issues of Gender, 'Race', Sexuality, Disability and Social Class* (Routledge, 2nd edn, 2006), *Marxism and Educational Theory: Origins and Issues* (Routledge 2008) and *Professional Attributes and Practice: Meeting the QTS Standards* (Routledge, 4th edn, 2008). He is the author of *Critical Race Theory and Education: A Marxist Response* (Palgrave Macmillan 2009).

**Valerie Coultas** is a Principal Lecturer in the School of Education at Kingston University. She taught in London secondary schools for over two decades as an English teacher, head of English and Senior Teacher. She is the author of *Constructive Talk in Challenging Classrooms* (Routledge 2007).

**Dr Paul Dash** is course Programme Leader for the Artist Teacher MA at Goldsmiths, University of London and MA module leader for Diaspora, Race and Culture in Education. He is co-editor of *IJADE* (*International Journal of Art & Design Education*) and Assistant Director of the Centre for the Arts and Learning. Dash has had papers published in a number of books and journals, and has contributed to conferences in both the UK and overseas. In 2005 he co-edited with Professor Dennis Atkinson *Social and Critical Practices in Art Education*. His PhD thesis, entitled 'African Caribbean pupils in art education', is published as a book in 2009. Dash is a practising artist.

**Debs Gwynn** taught French, English and SEN in Greater Manchester for eight years, and is currently working as a Special Educational Needs Coordinator (SENCO) in Salford. She is Equal Opportunities Officer in her local trade union branch and an active campaigner against academies.

**Jo Hardman** is currently a Principal Lecturer in the Faculty of Sport, Health and Social Care at the University of Gloucestershire. She teaches modules in Adapted Physical Activity, Inclusive Physical Activity, Sport Pedagogy and practical modules at the university. Prior to her university work Jo taught in variety of teaching establishments in the UK and the US. Her particular interest is in disability sport and inclusion issues related to PE in the National Curriculum.

**Peter Hick** is Senior Lecturer in Inclusive Education at Manchester Metropolitan University. His previous posts were at the universities of Birmingham and Manchester; his background is as an Educational Psychologist and further education teacher. Peter's research projects are in developing more inclusive practices with ICT; his wider interests are in inclusion and diversity in urban education. He is co-editor of *Psychology for Inclusive Education: New Directions in Theory and Practice* (Routledge 2008) and *Inclusion and Diversity in Education* (Sage, 4 vols, 2008).

**Dr Gillian Hilton** has worked in teacher education for many years and is now head of education at Middlesex University, London. She has a keen interest in education in Europe, particularly teacher education in the Baltic States. These European connections have aided her specific research interests in teacher education, gender and education and in PSHE, in particular sex education. Gillian has undertaken a considerable amount of fieldwork research in the area of Sex and Relationships Education (SRE), particularly related to the needs of boys.

**Dr Dina Kiwan** is an Academic Fellow/Senior Lecturer in Citizenship Education at Birkbeck College, University of London. Her areas of expertise include citizenship, diversity, education, immigration and nationality. She was a member of the Crick Home Office Life in the UK Advisory Group, and is a member of the Lord Goldsmith Review of Citizenship Advisory Board. Dina's book *Education for Inclusive Citizenship* (Routledge 2008) examines the policy development of citizenship education based on first-hand accounts from interviews with key policy-makers. She is also co-author of 'Diversity and citizenship: curriculum review' (the Ajegbo report).

**Julie Ann Light** is a teacher of humanities and Learning Leader for Religious Education and citizenship in a school on the south coast of England. Coming from a working-class background she was quickly converted by her father James Light to the wisdoms of socialism. During the *blue* years of Conservatism she became one of the 'thorns in Margaret Thatcher's side' by becoming a single parent. Entering the world of education in the late 1990s she quickly found an interest in the Labour government's proposals for the Education of the future 2008 to 2014 White Papers. Light is an advocate of student equality believing that all her students have something to learn, and teach to others.

**Leila Marr** is an Advanced Skills Teacher (AST) of design and technology. She is currently responsible for graphic products at a Hertfordshire secondary school where she has taught for the past nine years. Through her AST outreach work with several schools in challenging circumstances she is committed to promoting design and technology as a way forward to enthuse and inspire students to become young designers and entrepreneurs.

**Brian Matthews** taught science in secondary schools in London for 19 years before joining Goldsmiths, University of London where he was Head of the Secondary PGCE course. He has always been interested in finding ways of increasing school students' interest in science and incorporating equal opportunities issues. Brian has researched ways of developing emotional literacy in science classrooms and is author of *Engaging Education: Developing Emotional Literacy, Equity and Co-education* (McGraw-Hill/Open University Press 2006) He is the Director of the Engaging Education Consultancy (www.engagingeducation.co.uk).

**Martin Milner** is a community musician, composer and education consultant. He studied history at Sussex University in the school of African and Asian Studies and jazz at Chichester FE college (with Bobby Wellins among others). He did a Music PGCE at Leeds University and taught for two years in a large comprehensive school in Essex before becoming Education Director at Band on the Wall, a jazz and world music venue in Manchester, where he helped set up the Greater Manchester Music Action Zone. Martin taught music practice to Community Arts degree students and 'dis/abled' artists at the Liverpool Institute for Performing Arts (LIPA), and delivers training for musicians working in community contexts. He has worked with babies, children and young people in a variety of formal and non-formal settings. Consultancy clients include Creative Partnerships Greater Manchester. Articles and chapters for various publications include 'Community music and new technology' (LIPA 1999), *Sounding Board* and *Community Music: A Handbook* (Russell House Publishing 2005). He has been Chair of Sound Sense, the UK development agency for community music, and since 2008 has been teaching music at the Berlin Brandenberg International School.

**Maurice Nyangon** is a Senior Lecturer at the University of Greenwich, London and leads the PGCE Secondary ICT/Applied ICT courses. He is in the final year of his Doctorate in Education and is due to publish his thesis, a theory of planned behaviour study of the under-representation of female students in ICT and the impact group work has on their attitudes and behaviour. He has published widely on both his ongoing research into ICT and gender and current best practice in ICT teaching. Before specializing in ICT, Maurice Nyangon spent 20 years leading geography departments in a number of diverse schools both in England and abroad.

**Professor Hilary Povey** worked for many years in the field of secondary school mathematics, both as a teacher and in curriculum development. She is now Professor of Mathematics Education at Sheffield Hallam University, where she researches equity issues in mathematics education and teaches undergraduate mathematics to ITE students. Throughout her working life, she has had a commitment to promoting social justice in and through the mathematics classroom.

**Jo Shire** is currently a Senior Lecturer in the Faculty of Sport, Health and Social Care at the University of Gloucestershire and is Subject Leader for the PGCE secondary PE course. She teaches modules which focus on pedagogic practice including: Curriculum Dimensions, Contemporary Issues, Special Populations and various practical modules at the university. Prior to her university work Jo was head of PE for ten years at a school in Gloucestershire, and taught in Wiltshire. Jo's particular interests are in issues relating to pedagogy, equality and sexuality.

**Dr Ian Woodfield** has been a head of social studies, head of history and head of the faculty of humanities in a large comprehensive school on the south coast of England where he currently holds the post of Learning Leader. He has served for many years as a Senior Examiner and worked on the introduction of the GCSE examination system. He wrote three chapters in *Professional Attributes and Practice: Meeting the QTS Standards* (Routledge, 4th edn, 2008), on 'Innovation and improvement', 'Coaching and mentoring' and 'Teaching, learning and behaviour strategies', respectively. His book *The Damaging Effect of Recent British Educational Reforms on Secondary School Teachers* was published by Mellen Press in 2008.

**Dr Terry Wrigley** has worked for many years as a secondary school teacher and various other roles, and is now Senior Lecturer in Education at the University of Edinburgh. His teaching, research and writing span and connect diverse fields of interest: school development, pedagogy, curriculum reform, social justice and education for citizenship. He edits the journal *Improving Schools* and his publications include three books: *The Power to Learn* (Trentham Books 2000), *Schools of Hope* (Trentham Books 2003) and *Another School Is Possible* (Bookmarks 2006).

# Acknowledgements

I would like to acknowledge the help and advice of Dave Hill, Alpesh Maisuria, Peter McLaren, Alpesh Maisuria and Richard Woolley.

# Preface

## Mike Cole

Like its predecessor, Hill and Cole (eds) (1999), this book aims to find spaces in all the subjects of the secondary/high-school curriculum to promote equality for all. While the subjects covered pertain to the UK, the issues are relevant to all those who believe that equality should be one of the central focuses of schools. As well as dealing with the issues on a subject-by-subject basis, the book also looks at equality issues in US high schools, and at the way this can be promoted through pedagogy and policy. A new sister volume dealing with equality issues in primary schools, taking inspiration from Cole *et al.* (1997), has also been published by Continuum, edited by Hill and Helavaara Robertson (2009).

## References

Cole, M., Hill, D. and Shan, S. (eds) (1997), *Promoting Equality in Primary Schools*. London: Cassell.

Hill, D. and Cole, M. (eds) (1999), *Promoting Equality in Secondary Schools*. London: Cassell.

Hill, D. and Helavaara Robertson, L. (eds) (2009), *Equality in the Primary School: Promoting Good Practice across the Curriculum*. London: Continuum.

# Part One

# The Wider Context

Chapter 1

# The Condition of Equality in the US

Wayne Au

In this chapter, I offer an overview of issues of power and inequality in US schools. I begin with a framing of the US educational policy context and its reliance on systems of high-stakes testing, paying particular attention to how such systems contribute to 'race-' and class-based educational inequalities. This chapter further explains the links between US educational policy and the capitalist system of production and profit, and then moves on to explore issues of 'race' and class, disability, gender and sexual orientation within the US educational system. I conclude with a discussion on ways in which US educators and activists are working for equality in schools and society.

The US has long advanced a rhetoric of individual equality and individual opportunity for success both within education and in society more generally. Indeed, this idea that the US is a meritocracy, that is, that here is a land where success is the result of hard work and individual merit (Lemann 1999; Sacks 1999), is a fundamental presumption underlying the model of education (Au 2008). When compared to the reality of the conditions of equality in secondary schools in the US, however, it becomes clear that meritocracy is a myth, simply because so much inequality exists among different groups there.

## The US Education Policy Landscape

It is virtually impossible to understand the conditions of equality in the US without also understanding the major policy structure that shapes education there: the use of high-stakes testing. Such testing was codified on a national level when the No Child Left Behind (NCLB) Act was passed into law by the federal government in 2002.[1] Since then, high-stakes, standardized testing has become the central mechanism for school reform, where such tests are used to hold schools accountable to external audits by government officials and taxpayers and have become the single measure of educational quality, success, and funding (Karp 2006). In addition to the high-stakes testing associated with reforms like NCLB, as of 2004, over twenty-four states required high-school exit exams, with all but six withholding diplomas based on the test scores (Emery and Ohanian 2004). The over-reliance on standardized test scores in education policy ensures that such testing plays a determining role regarding issues of equality in the US today.

## 'Race' and Class in US Secondary Education

By most indicators, there are vast inequalities among different 'races' and classes in US secondary schools.[2] For instance, scores in the 2005 National Assessment of Educational Progress show white students outscoring African American and Latino/Latina students by 23 and 26 points in eighth-grade reading scores respectively (Ladson-Billings 2006). High-school exit exams produce similar gaps in performance (Darling-Hammond *et al.* 2006; Zabala 2007), and research analysing data across 18 states finds that 62 per cent of states with high-school exit exams saw an increase in drop-out rates when they implemented their exams (Amrein and Berliner 2002). Given that, according to the National Center for Educational Statistics, African American and Latino/Latina students are twice as likely as white students to drop out of school, and students from low-income families are five times more likely to drop out than students from high-income families (Laird *et al.* 2006), these findings would seem to support a relationship between high-stakes testing, drop-out rates, and a disproportionate impact on low-income students and students of colour (Roderick and Nagaoka 2005; Nichols and Berliner 2007). Such test-related outcomes point to the reality that standardized tests in the US have produced unequal results since their inception in the late 1800s, raising the spectre that they are unequal by design (Au 2008).

## The Example of Texas

The state of Texas, whose state-level educational policy became the blueprint for NCLB, provides a particularly illustrative example of how such focus on high-stakes, standardized testing contributes to inequality. The high-stakes testing and accountability movement in public education in Texas witnessed conservatively estimated school drop-out rates of 40 per cent in 2001. This translates into Texas public schools losing between 90,000 and 95,000 students a year, the vast majority of which are African American and Latino/Latina (McNeil 2005). Darling-Hammond (2004) tells the story of the 'Texas miracle', where highly publicized gains in test scores were discovered to be the product of disappearing students, most of whom were students of colour. For instance, Darling-Hammond explains how at Sharpstown High School in Houston, 'a freshman class of 1,000 dwindled to fewer than 300 students by senior year – a pattern seen in most high-minority high schools in Houston, including those rewarded for getting their test scores "up" ' (*ibid.*, p. 21). The miracle is that in Houston, not a single drop-out was reported. This impossibly low drop-out rate came through the designation of missing students as incarcerated, transferred (with no follow-up address), returned to Mexico, or having received a General Educational Development certificate, any of which would keep them from officially counting as drop-outs, while simultaneously keeping these students, often low test scorers, from counting against the schools on the tests (McNeil 2005).

## Disability in US Secondary Schools

Students with disabilities, often placed in 'special education' programmes, are also feeling a particularly sharp impact from current educational reforms. One central cause is that standardized, high-stakes tests do not have the capacity to accurately measure the performance of students with high-incidence disabilities (Ward and Au 2008). Hence, students with disabilities regularly do not meet US states' performance standards in reading (Schulte *et al.* 2001) and are regularly blamed for their low performance on high-stakes tests (Heubert 2001; Madaus and Clarke 2001; Darling-Hammond 2004; Thomas 2005). They are now also being over-identified as having learning disabilities because of current policy. In New York state, for instance, Allington and McGill-Franzen (1992) find that, 'The rate of increase [of special education designation] was three times greater in schools with historically lower but improving . . . reading achievement than in schools with historically higher . . . reading achievement' (p. 409). Further, educational diagnosticians are being pressured to identify more students for special education based on low standardized test scores (Fielding 2004; Harry and Klingner 2006), and in the state of Texas, students have been placed in special education as a means of keeping them from taking standardized tests altogether (Booher-Jennings 2005).

Such a focus on test score achievement in the US has created specific burdens for students in special education, who feel both pressured to pass the tests (Ysseldyke *et al.* 2004) and embarrassed if they perform a lower level than their peers (Nelson 2002). In one study, a teacher of students with disabilities remarked how her students with mild to moderate disabilities not only randomly answered test questions out of frustration but also got physically sick taking the tests. Further, because students in special education tend to have lower than average test score achievement, schools and teachers are increasing pressure on them to raise test scores – particularly because current US education policy requires that sanctions will be triggered if scores do not increase (Darling-Hammond 2004; McNeil 2005).

Perhaps more appalling is that the high-stakes testing is directing resources away from programmes that support students in special education. Research in the US has found that schools and teachers essentially teach to the tests by focusing mainly on tested subjects such as maths and reading (e.g. Au 2007). While such redirection of resources has led to loss of time spent in the teaching of such non-tested subjects as science, social studies, art, music and PE, it has also meant that students with disabilities have also seen a loss of resources, including those committed to small-group instruction in special education classes (Harry and Klingner 2006). Further, as a result of high-stakes testing, elective courses that may be more easily constructed to meet the needs of students with disabilities, as well as vocational programmes to provide job training for students in special education, are also being cut (Nelson 2002). Finally, with lower chances to pass exit exams and reduced post-high-school opportunities increasingly limited due to cuts in high-school programmes themselves (Ysseldyke *et al.* 2003), research has found that students with disabilities are, in some cases, ten times more likely to drop out of school than those in 'regular' education (MacMillan *et al.* 1990).

## US Education and Capitalism

In addition to contributing to inequality in US secondary schools, current education policy also illustrates the increasing inroads of capitalist privatization in public education. Fundamentally, policies like NCLB create conditions where schools compete with each other in the 'free market' of education. Under such policies, failing schools will be shut down or reorganized under new management, and successful schools will attract more customers/students. As former US President George W. Bush asserted (5 October 1999) in a presidential campaign speech delivered to the conservative US think-tank, the Manhattan Institute:

> Federal funds will no longer flow to failure. Schools that do not teach and will not change must have some final point of accountability. A moment of truth, when their Title 1 funds are divided up and given to parents, for tutoring or a charter school or some other hopeful option. In the best case, schools that are failing will rise to the challenge and regain the confidence of parents. In the worst case, we will offer scholarships to America's neediest children. (np)

Thus, schools become like any other business enterprise where the rules of efficiency and free-market competition apply (Sacks 1999). In this neo-liberal model, Adam Smith's invisible hand of capitalism will ensure that 'weaker' educational producers will go out of business and be removed from the market while 'stronger' educational producers will survive the private competition (Brosio 1994). It is plainly an expression of the capitalist notion of 'free', individual choice and production in the competitive marketplace.

One of the most profound examples of the structuring of US educational policy to create private markets that draw from public monies can be found in the standardized testing industry, which benefits from policies like NCLB. As Burch (2006) observes:

> Test development firms have sought to use NCLB mandates to attract new business. Major suppliers of test development and preparation firms explicitly reference the No Child Left Behind Act on their Web pages, and several named the law as spurring revenue in their recent financial statements. In addition, they all have links to the Department of Education's Web site on No Child Left Behind, and include in their marketing materials references to how their products can help districts comply with NCLB. (p. 2590)

The Education Sector, an independent education think-tank in Washington, DC, reports that during the 2005–6 school year alone, the 23 states that had not fully implemented NCLB's testing requirements would administer 11.4 million new tests in reading and maths to meet the federal mandate. Additionally, by the 2007–8 school year, when states would be required to test in science as well, another 11 million new tests would also be needed. This is in addition to the estimated 45 million tests required under NCLB generally (Toch 2006).

The broader testing market in the US has likewise reached incredible heights. Sales of test-related printed materials rose from $211 million in 1992 to $592 million in 2003 (Burch 2006). Eduventures Inc. estimates the total value of the tests, test-prep materials and testing services in 2006 to be $2.3 billion. This total includes $517 million for all NCLB-related test development, publishing, administering, analysing and reporting during the 2005–6 school year alone. Eduventures Inc. also estimates that 90 per cent of the revenues generated by state-wide testing is collected by only a few companies, including Pearson Educational Measurement, CTB/McGraw-Hill, Harcourt Assessment Inc., Riverside Publishing (a subsidiary of Houghton Mifflin Co.) and ETS (Jackson and Bassett 2005).

Education policies, like NCLB, which focus on high-stakes testing also create test-related secondary markets (Burch 2006). For instance, National Computer Systems Inc. (NCS) received $12 million a year from Harcourt Brace to handle and process the massive amounts of test data that would be produced by their contract with California. In direct response to NCLB, one leading firm in the area of test-based technological solutions for districts and states grew by nearly 300 per cent (*ibid.*). Regimes of high-stakes testing associated with NCLB have also increased profits for remediation and professional development programmes (both content and services) aimed at increases in test scores. For-profit tutoring companies did $4 billion in business in 2003, expecting this figure to have risen to $5 billion by 2005. Further, even though the market is nearly equally shared with non-profit companies, for-profit companies offering NCLB-related content and services to school districts saw revenues of nearly $1.62 billion in 2003 (*ibid.*).

The fact that US education policies demonstrate a particular debt to the wishes of big capital should come as no surprise considering that groups like the Business Round Table, established in 1972 and made up of Chief Executive Officers of major US corporations, have had considerable influence in the structuring of education policy reforms generally, NCLB included (Emery and Ohanian 2004). Further, it is important to remember that, within the mass of facts and figures outlined above, all of these monies are essentially public funds generated by taxpayers being funnelled into the coffers of private industry.

## Gender in US Secondary Schools

In recent years, similar to what has happened in Australia, Canada and Great Britain (Frank *et al.* 2003), a 'boy crisis' has been declared by many mainstream US media outlets, political groups and education policy-makers (Mead 2006). Girls are popularly portrayed as moving ahead of boys in areas of standardized test score achievement, secondary school graduation rates and college entrance rates, and as a result, public education reforms such as single-sex classrooms have resurfaced (Barnett and Rivers 2007). However, analysing 30-year data from the National Assessment of Educational Progress (NAEP), a standardized test given by the US Department of Education to a large, representative sample of students, policy analyst Sara Mead (2006) provides a different picture of the 'boy crisis'. She finds that in general,

> with a few exceptions, American boys are scoring higher and achieving more than they ever have before. But girls have just improved their performance on some measures even faster. As a result, girls have narrowed or even closed some academic gaps that previously favored boys, while other long-standing gaps that favored girls have widened, leading to the belief that boys are falling behind. (p. 3)

Indeed, eighth-grade boys (around the age of 13) have only improved in both reading and maths scores since 1992. Interestingly, as Mead makes light of, in the 1970s, 13-year-old girls actually outscored 13-year-old boys in NAEP maths testing, but in the 1980s and 1990s, boys moved ahead of girls in the same tests, leading Mead to comment that 'It's telling that even though younger boys are now doing better than girls on the long-term NAEP in math, when they once lagged behind, no one is talking about the emergence of a new "girl crisis" in elementary- and middle-school math' (*ibid.*, p. 6).

In addition to test scores, there are other gender-related issues in US secondary schools. For instance, there is still increased gender segregation based on school subjects, where secondary-level boys gravitate towards the subjects of maths and science, and girls gravitate towards language and arts. Girls are also at much higher risk for sexual abuse and harassment than boys, and teachers still favour boys in classroom interactions (Sadker 2000). In one study of middle-school students, researchers found that 'boys and girls continued to have disturbingly different experiences in the classroom, with girls feeling greater pressure to conform, behave and perform, and boys evidencing greater freedom and acceptance of mistakes as an expected and accepted part of the learning process' (Spencer *et al.* 2003, p. 1800). Thus, there is still reason to believe that girls continue to face inequitable treatment in US classrooms.

To say all of this, however, is not to disregard the fact that boys in US schools do face certain issues. For instance, the intersection of boy's issues and of students with disabilities is substantial. As Mead (2006) explains:

> Boys make up two thirds of students in special education – including 80 percent of those diagnosed with emotional disturbances or autism – and boys are two and a half times as likely as girls to be diagnosed with attention deficit hyperactivity disorder (ADHD). The number of boys diagnosed with disabilities or ADHD has exploded in the past 30 years, presenting a challenge for schools and causing concern for parents. (p. 9)

Additionally, once we consider the intersection of 'race' and class with gender, it is clear that some groups of boys are doing particularly poorly in secondary schools because African American and Latino boys have the lowest test score achievement. But, as Mead (*ibid.*) points out, the 'race' and class gaps in test score achievement (discussed above) are two to five times bigger than any gender gaps, suggesting that a focus on these issues might be more pragmatic for immediate impact on educational equality. Unfortunately, in the US, disparities in 'race' and class seem so commonplace that they are deemed less newsworthy than middle-class parents worrying about their boys (Barnett and Rivers 2007).

## Sexual Orientation in US Schools

According to a Human Rights Watch (Bochenek and Brown 2001) report, roughly 5 to 6 per cent of school age children identify as either lesbian, gay, bisexual, questioning or transgender (LGBQT). This translates to there being almost two million LGBQT students in US schools. Unfortunately, while welcomed in some schools, they are often targeted for harassment and violence. According to the report, they are three times more likely to be physically assaulted and three times more likely to be threatened or injured with a weapon at school relative to their heterosexually identified peers. Further, LGBQT students are four times more likely to skip school because of feeling unsafe. Making things more difficult is that racial intolerance in schools is regularly disciplined, but intolerance of LGBQT students and their sexual orientation is regularly overlooked as not being that serious.

Fortunately, in response to the existence of homophobia in US schools, many LGBQT students, as well as their heterosexual allies, have led local reform efforts regarding their rights and safety. As Human Rights Watch (*ibid.*) reports, students, in the states of California and Utah for instance, have led successful fights against conservative school boards and school districts which have sought to ban school-based student gay–straight alliance organizations and other student run groups that operate to support LGBQT youth. In the state of Illinois, as another example, students struggled with the Naperville school district to include discrimination based on sexual orientation in their official anti-discrimination policies.

## Working Towards Equality in US Secondary Schools

Despite the relatively dreary picture of the conditions of equality in US secondary schools I've painted in this chapter, there are significant efforts working towards educational equality (e.g. Apple and Beane 2007), and it is important to mention some of them here. Grassroots organizing efforts to counter educational inequality have been growing in recent years. A few examples include Teachers 4 Social Justice (2006), a San Francisco collective of teachers, which holds an annual conference that drew well over 1,200 educators in 2007 and 2008, and continues to offer study groups and teacher work groups that focus on issues of equity and equality in education; Chicago Teachers for Social Justice (Teachers for Social Justice 2005), a collective of Midwestern teachers very similar to their San Francisco counterparts; and the New York Collective of Radical Educators (2006), which holds regular meetings and study sessions, organizes around social justice issues, and develops critical curricula in both New York City and the northeastern US. Additionally, there are groups of teachers in the Seattle, Washington and

Portland, Oregon (Portland Area Rethinking Schools 2006) areas that unite around the social-justice-oriented, progressive publication, *Rethinking Schools* (2008).

Indeed, Rethinking Schools, an organization where I admittedly hold a position as an editorial board member, is a prime example of efforts to increase educational equality in the US. Rethinking Schools is a non-profit magazine and publishing house that was started by public school teachers in the city of Milwaukee, Wisconsin, over twenty years ago. These teachers sought to develop the magazine (then newspaper) as a tool for disseminating practices that promote social justice, antiracism and educational equality, as well as an organ for sharing more critical perspectives on education policy in the US. *Rethinking Schools* has since become a leader in publications on social-justice-oriented, classroom-friendly books, including *Rethinking Our Classrooms: Teaching for Equity and Justice* (Au et al. 2007) and *Rethinking Columbus* (Bigelow and Peterson 1998), which have sold over 175,000 and 250,000 copies respectively. These publications, as well as many others not mentioned here, are united by their collective focus on classroom practice and a firm belief that teachers, as active resisters of the forces of inequality in society and education, can make a significant and powerful difference in the lives (and futures) of students and the world (Au and Apple 2004). Other organizations like FairTest (2005) and the Rouge Forum (Gibson et al. 2007) have also played roles in critiquing both high-stakes testing and the NCLB legislation while simultaneously offering alternative visions of what more equitable education can look like. Additionally, in academia, for instance, the work of McNeil (2000), Lipman (2004), Smith (2004), Sleeter (2005), Valenzuela (2005) and Apple (2006) represent critical scholarly interrogations of NCLB and educational inequality. Thus, despite the amount of inequality that may exist in secondary schools in the US (and within US education generally), considerable educational organizing and community struggle for a more equitable educational system continues to take place today.

## Postscript

Since this chapter was originally written, two potentially significant shifts have happened. Economically, the US, along with much of the world, has fallen into a deep recession sparked by crashes in the housing market, the stock market and the banking system more generally. Also, politically, the Bush–Cheney regime has finally come to an end, giving many some semblance of hope that the new administration will be different in some key ways (e.g. supporting more democratic healthcare reforms). While it is impossible to tell right now, these two shifts will likely have some impact on conditions of equality in US secondary schools.

The economic recession is currently devastating public education funding at all levels, from kindergarten to college, in many US states. Both tax revenues and university endowments invested in the financial markets have fallen precipitously. This has meant that not only are budgets for spending on public education shrinking (including districts and schools being asked to make mid-year expenditure cuts), but also the financial supports for secondary students to graduate and pay for college education are disappearing. In the midst of such conditions, we can only expect educational inequality to increase.

On a more positive note, the political change may see some improvement in conditions of equality in US secondary schools. While not guaranteed, the end of the Bush–Cheney era in American politics may also mean the end of the No Child Left Behind era in education policy. At the very least, some education reformers in the US are expecting a shift away from the current focus on high-stakes testing. Considering that this testing generally reproduces social and educational inequality, such a shift could result in more equitable treatment of secondary students and would be a welcome change.

## Notes

[1] Due to political instability in the US, including the 2008 presidential elections, it is unclear if NCLB will be reauthorized as a law without any changes, if it will be revised before being reauthorized, or if it will possibly be tossed out due to the law's negative effects.

[2] I want to be clear, however, that even though I will be using the term 'race' to discuss African American, Latino/Latina, Asian American, white, Native American, etc. students, my intent is not to reinforce the idea that 'race' exists as an immutable or even valid biological category. Rather, my use of these racial identifications is to recognize that scientists have long established that 'race' is not biological at all, and is in fact a completely social construction that humans often use as a category of difference to justify social, cultural and economic inequalities (Gould 1996; see also Cole, Chapter 2 of this volume). In contrast, I do not use the term 'class' in the same manner, for class position under capitalism does not merely exist as a social construction in the same sense as 'race'. Rather, class exists as category for describing a very concrete position relative to economic production and accrued economic and social status (Allman *et al.* 2000; Cole 2008).

## References

Allington, R. L. and McGill-Franzen, A. (1992), 'Unintended effects of educational reform in New York'. *Education Policy*, 6, (4), 397–414.

Allman, P., McLaren, P. and Rikowski, G. (2000), 'After the box people: the labour–capital relation as class constitution – and its consequences for Marxist educational theory and human resistance'. Available at http://www.ieps.org.uk.cwc.net/after-thebox.pdf (accessed 1 May 2004).

Amrein, A. L. and Berliner, D. C. (2002), 'An analysis of some unintended and negative consequences of high-stakes testing'. Tempe, AZ: Arizona State University, College of Education, Language Policy Research Unit, Educational Policy Studies Laboratory.

Apple, M. W. (2006), *Educating the 'Right' Way: Markets, Standards, God, and Inequality* (2nd edn). New York: Routledge.

— and Beane, J. A. (eds) (2007), *Democratic Schools* (2nd edn). Portsmouth, NH: Heinemann.

Au, W. (2007), 'High-stakes testing and curricular control: a qualitative metasynthesis'. *Educational Researcher*, 36, (5), 258–67.

— (2009), *Unequal by Design: High-Stakes Testing and the Standardization of Inequality*. New York: Routledge.

— and Apple, M. W. (2004), 'Interrupting globalization as an educational practice'. *Educational Policy*, 18, (5), 784–93.

— Bigelow, B. and Karp, S. (eds) (2007), *Rethinking Our Classrooms: Teaching for Equity and Justice* (revised and expanded, 2nd edn, Vol. 1). Milwaukee, WI: Rethinking Schools.

Barnett, R. C. and Rivers, C. (2007), 'Gender myths and the education of boys'. *Independent Schools*, 66, (2), 92–103.

Bigelow, B. and Peterson, B. (eds) (1998), *Rethinking Columbus: The Next 500 Years* (2nd edn). Milwaukee, WI: Rethinking Schools, Ltd.

Bochenek, M. and Brown, A. W. (2001), *Hatred in the Hallways: Violence and Discrimination against Lesbian, Gay, Bisexual, and Transgender Students In U.S. Schools*. New York: Human Rights Watch.

Booher-Jennings, J. (2005), 'Below the bubble: "educational triage" and the Texas accountability system'. *American Educational Research Journal*, 42, (2), 231–68.

Brosio, R. A. (1994), *A Radical Democratic Critique of Capitalist Education*. New York: Peter Lang.

Burch, P. E. (2006), 'The new educational privatization: educational contracting and high stakes accountability'. *Teachers College Record*, 108, (12), 2582–610.

Bush, G. W. (1999), 'The future of educational reform'. Available at http://www.manhattan-institute.org/html/bush_speech.htm (accessed 11 February 2006).

Cole, M. (2008), *Marxism and Educational Theory: Origins and Issues*. London: Routledge.

Darling-Hammond, L. (2004), 'From "separate but equal" to "no child left behind": the collision of new standards and old inequalities', in D. Meier and G. Wood (eds), *Many Children Left Behind: How the No Child Left Behind Act Is Damaging Our Children and Our Schools*. Boston: Beacon Press, pp. 3–32.

— , McClosky, L. and Pecheone, R. (2006), *Analysis and Recommendations for Alternatives to the Washington Assessment of Student Learning*. Palo Alto, CA: School Redesign Network, Stanford University School of Education.

Emery, K. and Ohanian, S. (2004), *Why Is Corporate America Bashing Our Public Schools?* Portsmouth, NH: Heinemann.

FairTest (2005), Available at http://www.fairtest.org (accessed 11 July 2005).

Fielding, C. (2004), 'Low performance on high-stakes test drives special education referrals: a Texas survey'. *The Educational Forum*, 68, (2), 126–32.

Frank, B., Kehler, M., Lovell, T. and Davison, K. (2003), 'A tangle of trouble: boys, masculinity, and schooling – future directions'. *Educational Review*, 55, (2), 119–33.

Gibson, R., Queen, G., Ross, E. W. and Vinson, K. D. (2007), '"I participate, you participate, we participate ... they profit": notes on revolutionary educational activism to transcend capital: the Rouge Forum'. *Journal for Critical Education Policy Studies*, 5, (2). Available at http://www.jceps.com/index.php?pageID=article&articleID=97 (accessed 2 November 2007).

Gould, S. J. (1996), *The Mismeasure of Man* (revised and expanded. edn). New York: Norton.

Harry, B. and Klingner, J. (2006), *Why Are So Many Minority Students in Special Education? Understanding Race and Disability in Schools*. New York: Teachers College Press.

Heubert, J. P. (2001), 'High stakes testing and civil rights: standards of appropriate test use and a strategy for enforcing them', in G. Orfield and M. L. Kornhaber (eds), *Raising Standards or Raising Barriers? Inequality and High-Stakes Testing in Public Education*. New York: Century Foundation Press, pp. 179–94.

Jackson, J. M. and Bassett, E. (2005), *The State of the K-12 State Assessment Market*. Boston: Eduventures.

Karp, S. (2006), 'Leaving public education behind: the Bush agenda in American education'. *Our Schools/Our Selves*, 15, (3), 181–96.

Ladson-Billings, G. (2006), 'From the achievement gap to the education debt: understanding achievement in U.S. schools'. *Educational Researcher*, 35, (7), 3–12.

Laird, J., Lew, S., DeBell, M. and Chapman, C. (2006), *Dropout Rates in the United States: 2002 and 2003* (No. NCES 2006-062). Washington, DC: U.S. Department of Education, National Center for Education Statistics.

Lemann, N. (1999), *The Big Test: The Secret History of the American Meritocracy*. New York: Farrar, Straus, and Giroux.

Lipman, P. (2004), *High Stakes Education: Inequality, Globalization, and Urban School Reform*. New York: RoutledgeFalmer.

MacMillan, D. L., Balow, I. H., Widainan, K. F. and Hemsley, R. E. (1990), *A Study of Minimum Competency Tests and Their Impact: Final Report (grant G008530208)*. Washington, DC: Office of Special Education and Rehabilitation Services, U.S. Department of Education.

Madaus, G. F. and Clarke, M. (2001), 'The adverse impact of high-stakes testing on minority students: evidence from one hundred years of test data', in G. Orfield and M. L. Kornhaber (eds), *Raising Standards or Raising Barriers? Inequality and High-Stakes Testing in Public Education*. New York: Century Foundation Press, pp. 85–106.

McNeil, L. M. (2000), *Contradictions of School Reform: Educational Costs of Standardized Testing*. New York: Routledge.

— (2005), 'Faking equity: high-stakes testing and the education of Latino youth', in A. Valenzuela (ed.), *Leaving Children Behind: How 'Texas-Style' Accountability Fails Latino Youth*. Albany, New York: State University of New York, pp. 57–112.

Mead, S. (2006), *The Evidence Suggests Otherwise: The Truth about Boys and Girls*. Washington, DC: Education Sector.

Nelson, R. J. (2002), 'Closing or widening the gap of inequality: the intended and unintended consequences of Minnesota's basic standards tests for students with disabilities' (unpublished doctoral dissertation, University of Minnesota).

New York Collective of Radical Educators (2006), Available at http://www.nycore.org/ (accessed 4 March 2006).

Nichols, S. L. and Berliner, D. C. (2007), *Collateral Damage: How High-Stakes Testing Corrupts America's Schools*. Cambridge, MA: Harvard Education Press.

Portland Area Rethinking Schools (2006), Available at http://web.pdx.edu/∼bgds/ PARS/ (accessed 4 March 2006).

Rethinking Schools (2008), Available at http://www.rethinkingschools.org (accessed 1 January 2008).

Roderick, M. and Nagaoka, J. (2005), 'Retention under Chicago's high-stakes testing program: helpful, harmful, or harmless?' *Educational Evaluation and Policy Analysis*, 27, (4), 309–40.

Sacks, P. (1999), *Standardized Minds: The High Price of America's Testing Culture and What We Can Do to Change It*. Cambridge, MA: Perseus Books.

Sadker, D. (2000), 'Gender equity: still knocking at the classroom door'. *Equity and Excellence in Education*, 33, (1), 80–3.

Schulte, A. C., Villwock, D. V., Wichard, S. M. and Stallings, C. F. (2001), 'High-stakes testing and expected progress standards for students with learning disabilities: a five-year study of one district'. *School Psychology Review*, 30, (4), 487–506.

Sleeter, C. E. (2005), *Un-Standardizing Curriculum: Multicultural Teaching in the Standards-Based Classroom*. New York: Teachers College Press.

Smith, M. L. (2004), *Political Spectacle and the Fate of American Schools*. New York: RoutledgeFalmer.

Spencer, R., Porche, M. V. and Tolman, D. L. (2003),'We've come a long way – maybe: new challenges for gender equity in education'. *Teachers College Record*, 105, (9), 1774–1807.

Teachers for Social Justice (2005), Available at http://www.teachersforjustice.org/ (accessed 4 March 2006).

— (2006), Available at http://www.altrue.net/site/t4sj/ (accessed 4 March 2006).

Thomas, R. M. (2005), *High-Stakes Testing: Coping with Collateral Damage*. Mahwah, NJ: Lawrence Erlbaum Associates.

Toch, T. (2006), *Margins of Error: The Education Testing Industry in the No Child Left Behind Era*. Washington, DC: Education Sector.

Valenzuela, A. (ed.) (2005), *Leaving Children Behind: How 'Texas Style' Accountability Fails Latino Youth*. New York: State University of New York Press.

Ward, S. and Au, W. (2008), 'Civic responsibility and the challenge of high-stakes testing: exercising our right to an equitable education system'. Paper presented at the Annual Meeting of the American Educational Research Association, New York, 24–28 March.

Ysseldyke, J., Dennison, A. and Nelson, R. J. (2003), *Large-Scale Assessment and Accountability Systems: Positive Consequences for Students with Disabilities (Synthesis Report 51)*. Minneapolis, MN: University of Minnesota, National Center of Educational Outcomes.

— , Nelson, R. J., Christensen, S., Johnson, R. D., Dennison, A., Triezenberg, H.,

Sharpe, M. and Hawes, M. (2004), 'What we know and need to know about consequences of high-stakes testing for students with disabilities'. *Exceptional Children*, 71, (1), 75–94.

Zabala, D. (2007), *State High School Exit Exams: Gaps Persist in High School Exit Exam Pass Rates – Policy Brief 3*. Washington, DC: Center on Education Policy.

Chapter 2

# Conceptual and Practical Issues for the Teacher[1]

## Mike Cole

This chapter is in two parts. The first part deals with the conceptual issues of 'race' and racism; gender; disability; sexual orientation; and social class and capitalism. In the second part I look at practical issues, specifically strategies we might use to overcome what I refer to as 'ism/phobia'. In this part of the chapter, I address personal issues and institutional issues, and how the two might be connected. The chapter is based on the premise that we should develop the learning of all students without limits rather than entertain vague notions of 'to their full potential'; that we should reject ideas of fixed ability; enable students to make rational and informed decisions about their own lives; enable them to make rational and informed decisions about the lives of others; that we should foster critical reflection, with a view to transformative action; and help empower students to be in a position to take transformative action.

## Part One: Conceptual Issues

### 'Race' and racism

There is a consensus among certain geneticists and most social scientists that 'race' is a social construct rather than a biological given. That this is the case is explained succinctly by Steven Rose and Hilary Rose (2005). As they note, in 1972, the evolutionary geneticist Richard Lewontin pointed out that 85 per cent of human genetic diversity occurred *within* rather than *between* populations, and only 6 to 10 per cent of diversity is associated with the broadly defined 'races' (*ibid.*). As Rose and Rose explain, most of this difference is accounted for by the readily visible genetic variation of skin colour, hair form and so on. The everyday business of seeing and acknowledging such difference is not the same as the project of genetics.

For genetics and, more importantly, for the prospect of treating genetic diseases, the difference is important, since humans differ in their susceptibility to particular diseases, and genetics can have something to say about this. However, beyond medicine, the use of the invocation of 'race' is increasingly suspect. Rose and Rose conclude that '[w]hatever arbitrary boundaries one places on any population group for the purposes of genetic research, they do not match those of conventionally defined races'. For example, the DNA of native Britons contains traces of multiple waves of occupiers and migrants. 'Race', as a scientific concept, Rose and Rose conclude, 'is well past its sell-by date' (*ibid.*). For these reasons, I would argue that 'race' should be put in inverted commas whenever one needs to refer to it.

Racism, however, is, of course, self-evidently real enough, and, indeed, like inequalities associated with the other conceptual issues discussed in this chapter, a major worldwide problem. In order for teachers to deal with racism, they need to have an awareness of what it means. My view is that we should adopt a wide-ranging definition of racism, rather than a narrow one based, as it was in the days of the British Empire, for example on biology. Racism can be institutional or personal; it can be dominative (direct and oppressive) as opposed to aversive (exclusive and cold-shouldering) (Kovel 1988); it can be overt or covert; intentional or unintentional; biological and/ or cultural. Attributes ascribed to ethnic groups can also be seemingly positive, as, for example, when whole groups are stereotyped as having strong cultures or being good at sport. Such stereotypes may well be followed up, respectively, with notions that 'they are taking over', or 'they are not so good academically'. The point is to be wary of attributing any stereotypes to ethnic groups. All stereotypes are *at least potentially* racist.


### Non-colour-coded racism and religious hatred

Racism directed at white people is not new and has a long history; for example, anti-Irish racism in Britain (Mac an Ghaill 2000) and, of course, anti-Jewish and anti-Slavonic racism are predominant factors in twentieth-century history. The continued persecution of Gypsy Roma Travellers in Britain is also a factor (Office of Public Sector Information 2006). In addition, Sivanandan has identified a new form of racism, primarily directed at people from the NJCEU coming to the UK: xeno-racism. He defines it as follows: 'it is a racism ... that cannot be colour-coded, directed as it is at poor whites as well ... [it] ... bears all the marks of the old racism' (Sivanandan 2001, p. 2). There has been evidence in the media of xeno-racism directed at NJCEU people (e.g. *Belfast Today* 2006; *BBC News* 2007), and of racism of NJCEU students directed at Asian and black students in the UK (Glenn and Barnett 2007). Certain tabloids (in particular the *Sun*) have in recent years unleashed anti-Polish rhetoric on a regular basis. Xeno-racism and xenoracialization: the process of falsely categorizing people from the NJCEU (Cole 2008b, pp. 124–6) thus need careful attention from antiracists in the UK and elsewhere.

Islamophobia, which has greatly increased in a number of countries worldwide, is also not necessarily based on skin colour. Moreover, though often triggered by (perceived) symbols of the Muslim faith, Islamophobia is not necessarily religion based, and, though a form of racism, needs to be addressed as a discrete phenomenon. However, more generally, discrimination on religious grounds also needs serious attention. In this regard, it is important and significant that The Racial and Religious Hatred Act was passed in the UK in 2006 (Office of Public Sector Information 2006), making provision about offences involving stirring up hatred against persons on racial or religious grounds.

The implications are as follows. Education plays a role in reproducing racism (monocultural and much multicultural education), but also has a major role to play in undermining racism (antiracist education). Monocultural education in the UK is to do with the promotion of so-called British values;[2] multicultural education is about the celebration of diversity and has often been tokenistic and patronizing; antiracist education focuses on undermining racism (Cole 1998; Cole and Blair 2006).

Modern technology has major implications for delivering antiracist multicultural education, in that it allows people to speak for themselves, via websites and email. It is highly likely that xeno-racism will filter down into schools in the UK, and impact on day-to-day student interaction. How this will affect intra- and inter-ethnic relations is largely unforeseen. What is clear is that anti-xeno-racist multicultural education must feature largely in UK schools' priorities. Unfortunately, antiracist multicultural education appears to be under threat from the Education and Inspections Act (2006), which came into effect in September 2007. The Act introduced a duty on the governing bodies of maintained schools to promote 'community cohesion'. Following Wetherell, Lafleche and Berkeley (2007), Andy Pilkington (2007, p. 14) distinguishes between 'hard' and 'soft' versions of community cohesion, the former viewing community cohesion and multiculturalism as ineluctably at loggerheads and insisting that we abandon the divisiveness evident in multiculturalism and instead should adhere to British values. The hard version of 'community cohesion' is thus monocultural. The 'soft' version, on the other hand, views community cohesion as complementing rather than replacing multiculturalism. In addition, the 'soft' version recognizes that the promotion of community cohesion requires inequality and racism to be addressed. Unsurprisingly, the former New Labour Secretary of State for Communities, Ruth Kelly, favours the hard version (for a discussion, see Cole 2009, pp. 74–5). The resolve of antiracist educators to keep antiracism as the priority is thus more important than ever.

## Gender

Generally speaking, a distinction is made between 'sex' and 'gender', with sex being biological and gender being constructed. These essentialized categories of male and female have important consequences in society, for you are either 'in' the category or 'outside' of it (Woodward 2004). Within a patriarchal society the male is the norm and women are the 'other' (Paechter 1998). However, it is argued that gender roles are learned and are relative to time and place. In other words, what are considered 'acceptable modes of dress' or body language for males and females vary dramatically through history and according to geographical location (which is not to say, of course, that everyone in a given society conforms to such norms – there are many examples throughout history, and of course today, of people who have refused to conform).

Davies (1993) has shown that from their earliest years children hold strong views about their gender positioning and that gender identities are constructed and learned throughout schooling. Schools have traditionally reproduced gender categorization and, as Francis (1998) suggests, children work hard at constructing and maintaining their gender identities. However, she also points out that gender constructions are only one part of children's identities and that, for example, 'race', ethnicity (e.g. Connolly 1998; Archer 2003) and social class (see Reay 2006) are also part of their identities and these can compete with or reinforce gender stereotypes. For example, there are undoubtedly differences between boys' and girls' development and progress in reading and writing. However, there is sometimes an over-simplification in the debate about gender and achievement in English as it is not all boys per se who are underachieving but particularly those from lower socioeconomic groups (Francis and Skelton 2005; Coultas 2007; Hill 2008).

Many schools today are aware of their role in providing a curriculum free of bias and a curriculum that is emancipatory. Many schools are also aware of the power that the structures, rules and regulations can have in promoting sexism. The curriculum, actual and hidden, can be non-sexist, or it can be anti-sexist (George 1993). In other words, schools can make sure that they do not promote sexism, or they can actively promote anti-sexism. Traditionally, there has been concern among feminists and their supporters about the way in which schooling has reproduced gender inequalities, particularly with respect to female subordination. More recently, since the late twentieth century, now that it has become apparent that many boys are now being outperformed academically by girls, there has been more general media and government concerns about boys. It is important to note that for many years girls had been disadvantaged by the education system with very little media attention being given to the problem. Indeed, in the 1950s and 1960s in the UK it was acknowledged that girls' literacy and numeracy skills were superior to those of boys and that, as a consequence, to achieve a grammar school place girls had to score far higher than boys in the 11+ (Gaine and George 1999; George 2004). In England and Wales, it has only been with the compulsory assessment and testing following the introduction of the National Curriculum that girls' superior achievement has become visible, provoking a minor 'moral panic'. In fact, boys are actually improving year on year. Head (1999) points to a much more serious issue in relation to a number of adolescent boys which is their alienation from not only schooling but from society in general.[3] He notes the disproportionate number of boys who are excluded from schools, are deemed dyslexic, suffer from ADHD and attempt suicide. It is not all plain sailing for girls either. Much of the recent work, which focuses on girls, indicates that they are now caught between two competing discourses. They are valued for being caring and selfless, putting the concerns of their friends first, but at the same time they have to be competitive and individualistic in order to maintain their current successes in school (e.g. George 2007).

If many boys are now being outperformed by girls, this is not to say, of course, that schooling does not continue to reproduce other forms of sexism, of which females are at the receiving end. For example, boys often still dominate space and talk in mixed-sex classrooms, and schools and university education departments suffer from an over-representation of men in higher positions, which is a reflection of wider society. Women despite their 'schooling success' still occupy the low ranks in most areas of work and their earning potential is still far worse than it is for men, with women in the UK earning approximately 80 per cent of a man's wage. Indeed, nearly forty years after the first Women's Liberation Conference, held at Ruskin College, Oxford, in 1970, as Jane Kelly (2006, p. 7) argues, women are still far from having achieved equality. This is with respect to the demands made at that conference, which included equal pay, the availability of childcare facilities for women at all times, free contraception, and abortion on demand (Kelly's chapter provides a comprehensive Marxist analysis of gender; for discussions on the way in which sexism impacts on schooling, on differential achievement and what can be done about it; see also Gaine and George 1999; Hirom 2001; Martin 2006; Skelton *et al.* 2006).

## Disability

Richard Rieser (2006a, pp. 135–7) has made a distinction between what he calls the 'medical model' and 'social model' of disability. The 'medical model' views the disabled person as the problem. Disabled people are to be adapted to fit into the world as it is. Where this is not possible, disabled people have historically been shut away in some specialized institution or isolated at home. The emphasis is on dependence, and calls forth pity, fear and patronizing attitudes (*ibid.*, p. 135). Rather than the focus being on the person, it tends to be on the impairment (*ibid.*). With the 'medical model', people's lives are handed over to others (*ibid.*). The 'medical model' creates a cycle of dependency and exclusion from which is difficult to break free (*ibid.*).

The 'social model' of disability, on the other hand, views the barriers that prevent disabled people from participating as being that which disables them (*ibid.*). This model was first developed by Mike Oliver (1990) to counter what he refers to as 'the personal tragedy theory of disability' (p. 3). The 'social model' makes a fundamental distinction between *impairment* and *disability*. Impairment is 'the loss or limitation of physical, mental or sensory function on a long-term, or permanent basis' (Rieser 2006a, p. 135), whereas The Disabled People's International (2005) defines disability as 'the outcome of the interaction between a person with an impairment and the environmental and attitudinal barriers he/she may face'. Supporters of this model are of the view that the position of disabled people and the oppression they face is socially constructed (Rieser 2006a, p. 135). It is up to institutions in society to adapt to meet their needs. This is the model favoured by disabled people.

The educational implications for each of these are the 'fixed continuum of provision' and the 'constellation of services' (Rieser 2006b, pp. 159–67). Under the former, associated with the 'medical model', the disabled person is slotted and moved according to the assessment of (usually non-disabled) assessors. This model is based on segregation (*ibid.*, p. 159). With respect to the 'constellation of services', associated with the 'social model', provision is made for the disabled child in mainstream school. The child and the teacher under this model are backed up by a variety of support services (*ibid.*, p. 167).

Currently, there is a wide consensus among disability activists, many educational institutions and the British government that the way forward is inclusion, which, of course, relates to the 'social model' and the 'constellation of services'. Rieser (*ibid.*, p. 174) commends the London Borough of Newham as a 'useful indicator of how such moves towards inclusion can occur in a poor, multi-cultural, inner-city area'. Newham's (undated) aims for an inclusive education are:

- A policy of welcoming all children and young people whatever special educational needs or disability they have
- Governors and staff trained in disability awareness issues
- A policy which ensures recruitment and training of staff who will support and are committed to inclusion
- An inclusion policy which is an integral part of the school development plan
- A special needs policy which is rigorously implemented and reviewed

We aim to promote high levels of achievement for all children and young people by:

- Offering a wide range of learning and teaching experiences
- Developing and implementing Individual Education Plans
- Valuing the contribution of all children and young people
- Having high expectations of all children and young people
- Training staff to equip them to teach all children and young people

We aim to include all children and young people in all the activities of the school by:

- Fostering supportive friendships among children and young people
- Having clear codes of behaviour that take account of the particular difficulties that certain children and young people face
- Working to enable children and young people to become more independent
- Finding ways to overcome any difficulties caused by the physical environment, school rules or routines
- Promoting diversity, understanding difficulties, recognising and respecting individual differences
- Taking positive steps to prevent exclusions, especially of children and young people with statements of special educational needs

We aim to work in partnership with parents and carers by:

- Welcoming parents and carers into the school
- Making written and spoken language accessible
- Dealing with parents and carers with honesty, trust and discretion
- Taking time, sharing information, listening and valuing contributions in meetings

For more information, see London Borough of Newham 2007.

There is an urgent need for all mainstream state schools to follow Newham's lead, and for major investment, both financial and social, to make genuine inclusion a reality.


## Sexual orientation

Sexual orientation has often been ignored in education. There are a number of reasons why it should be central. First, sexual orientation is an issue for every teacher, primary as well as secondary; for example, there is evidence that some children identify as gay or lesbian in the primary years (National Union of Teachers 1991, p. 7; Epstein 1994, pp. 49–56; Letts IV and Sears 1999). For this reason and to militate against the normalization of homophobic attitudes, it is important that sexualities education starts at an early age. In this respect, an important project is No Outsiders: Researching Approaches to Sexualities Equality in Primary Schools, a 28-month research project based in primary schools and funded by the UK-based Economic and Social Research Council. It involves a team of primary teachers from three areas of the UK, who have developed ideas and resources to address lesbian, gay, bisexual and transgender equality in their own schools and their communities. The outcomes are being disseminated via the Teacher Training Resource Bank, a documentary film and an edited book of teaching ideas.[4]

Second, in most schools, lesbians, gay men and bisexuals will be members of the teaching and other staff. In some schools, there will be transgender members of staff. Some parents/carers will be lesbian, gay, bisexual or transgender (LGBT), and some students will be open about their sexual orientation. Virtually all children will be aware of issues of sexual orientation. To this end, a project at Bishop Grosseteste University College Lincoln (Morris and Woolley 2008), undertaken by academic and support staff and undergraduate students, has produced the *Family Diversities Reading Resource*, an annotated bibliography of over one hundred quality children's picture books showing diverse families (including single parent, two and three parent, lesbian and gay parent and extended families). These texts explore ways of valuing difference in families and among children. Making such resources available to children in schools is essential if they are not to feel that their own family background is undervalued or even invisible within the formal learning environment.

Third, ignoring sexual orientation and homophobia is unprofessional and illegal in the UK. Harassment on the grounds of sexual orientation is unprofessional conduct. New equalities regulations will outlaw discrimination towards LGBT people in the provision of goods and services as well as in employment.

Homophobia is an unacceptable feature of society and there is evidence that lesbian and gay young people experience bullying at school, including physical acts of aggression, name calling, teasing, isolation and ridicule (see Ellis with High 2004; see also Forrest 2006; and the Stonewall website: http://www.stonewall.org.uk/stonewall). There is also evidence that young people who experience homophobic violence are likely to turn to truancy, substance abuse, prostitution or even suicide. Lesbian, gay and bisexual students should be listened to and should be encouraged to seek parental/carer advice and/or encouraged to refer to other appropriate agencies. Their experiences of homophobia and harassment should not be dismissed as exaggerated or exceptional. Homophobic 'jokes', remarks or insults should always be challenged.

It should be pointed out here that, given growing research into boys, girls and heterosexualities, and the links between homophobia and misogyny, sexual bullying (from homophobia to heterosexual harassment) encompasses more than issues connected to LGBT identities (Renold 2000a; 2000b; 2005; 2006).[5]

The curriculum should tackle homophobia and transphobia[6] as well as other forms of discrimination; just to give some examples, in order to promote equality for lesbians, gays, bisexuals and transgendered people, a range of family patterns and lifestyles can be illustrated in fiction used in English lessons, while drama can help to examine feelings and emotions. Reference can be made to famous LGBT writers, sports personalities, actors, singers and historical figures. (For a fuller discussion of sexual orientation, see Forrest and Ellis 2006; for fuller discussions of sexual orientation and education, see Williamson 2001; Forrest 2006; Ellis 2007; for a discussion of transphobia, see Whittle *et al.* 2007.)

## Social class and capitalism

Social class defines the social system under which we live. For this reason, among others, social class has tended to be left out of teacher education programmes, except in the narrow though nonetheless fundamentally important sense of more opportunities for working-class children. This is because discussion of social class and capitalism poses a threat to the status quo, much more profound than the other equality issues discussed in this chapter.

There are two major ways in which social class is classified. First, there is 'social class' as based on the classification of the Office for Population Census Studies (OPCS), first used in the census of 2001. Based on occupation, lifestyle and status, it accords with popular understandings of social-class differentiation; in particular, the distinctions between white-collar workers, on the one hand, and blue-collar workers and those classified as long-term unemployed, on the other. However, it is not without its difficulties:

- It masks the existence of the super-rich and the super-powerful (the capitalist class and the aristocracy).
- It glosses over and hides the antagonistic and exploitative relationship between the two main classes in society (the capitalist class and the working class).
- It segments the working class and thereby disguises the ultimate common interests of white-collar, blue-collar and long-term unemployed workers. (Hill and Cole 2001, pp. 151–3; Kelsh and Hill 2006)

Thus, while for sociological analyses, in general, it has its uses, its problematic nature should not be forgotten.

The other way to conceive social class is the Marxist definition, in which those who have to sell their labour power in order to survive are the working class, *whatever their status or income*, and those who own the means of production and exploit the working class by making profits from their labour are the capitalist class (see Cole 2008b for an analysis; see also Hickey 2006).

In post-Second World War Britain, the economic system was generally described as a mixed economy; that is to say, key sectors (e.g. the railways, gas, water, electricity and the telephones) of the economy were owned by the state and other sectors were owned by private capitalist enterprises. This is no longer the case and not only is globalized neo-liberal capitalism nearly universal, but also it is openly exalted as the only way the world can be run, even if, with the 2008–9 'credit crunch', there is some recognition that neo-liberal capitalism needs a degree of regulation.

With respect to education, it is my view that instead of commodifying knowledge in the interests of global capitalism, education should be about empowerment, where visions of an alternative way of running the planet (Venezuela is a good example; see Cole 2008c) become part of the mainstream curriculum. As Peter McLaren (2002) concludes his book *Life in Schools*, schools should cease to be defined as extensions of the workplace or as front-line institutions in the battle for international markets and foreign competition. Paulo Freire (1972) urged teachers to detach themselves and their students from the idea that they are agents of capital, where *banking education* (the teacher deposits information into an empty account) is the norm and to reinvent schools as democratic public spheres where meaningful *dialogue* can take place. No space is provided for a discussion of *alternatives* to neo-liberal global capitalism, such as world democratic socialism (see Cole 2008b for a discussion; see also Hill 2009). Discussing socialism in schools may be seen as one of the last taboos (Cole 2008d). It is time to move forward and bring such discussions into the classroom.

## Part Two: Practical Issues

Educators, in my view, should:

- develop the learning of all students without limits rather than entertain vague notions of 'to their full potential'[7]
- reject ideas of fixed ability
- enable students to make rational and informed decisions about their own lives
- enable students to make rational and informed decisions about others' lives
- foster critical reflection, with a view to transformative action
- help empower students to be in a position to take transformative action.

Equality and equal opportunity issues have both an institutional and legislative dimension and an individual dimension.

## The personal challenge

It needs to be stressed that people's positions vis-à-vis the equality issues outlined in this chapter are not *natural*, but reflect particular social systems. Inequalities are not *inevitable* features of any society; they are social constructs, crucial terrains between conflicting forces in any given society. In other words, societies do not *need* to be class based; to have racialized hierarchies; to have one sex dominating another. I do not believe that people are *naturally* homophobic or transphobic, or prone to marginalizing the needs of disabled people. On the contrary, we are socialized into accepting the norms, values and customs of the social systems in which we grow up. This is a very powerful message for teachers. If we *learn* to accept or to promote inequalities, we can also *learn* to challenge them. Schools have traditionally played an important part in socializing students to accept the status quo. They have also played and continue to play a major role in undermining that process (e.g. Hill 2009).

In the personal challenge it is important first to distance oneself from the notion of 'political correctness', a pernicious concept invented by the Radical Right, and which, unfortunately, has become common currency. The term 'political correctness' was coined to imply that there exist (left-wing) political demagogues who seek to impose their views on equality issues, in particular appropriate terminology, on the majority. In reality, nomenclature changes over time. To take the case of ethnicity, in the twenty-first century, terms such as 'negress' or 'negro' or 'coloured', nomenclatures which at one time were considered quite acceptable, are now considered offensive. Antiracists are concerned with *respect* for others' choice of nomenclature and, therefore, are careful to acknowledge changes in it, changes which are decided by oppressed groups themselves (bearing in mind that there can be differences of opinion among such groups). The same applies to other equality issues. Thus, for example, it has become common practice to use 'working class' rather than 'lower class';[8] 'lesbian, gay, bisexual and transgender' rather than 'sexually deviant'; 'disability' rather than 'handicap'; and 'gender equality' rather than 'a woman's place'. Using current and acceptable nomenclature is about the fostering of a caring and inclusive society, not about 'political correctness' (Cole and Blair 2006).

Haberman (1995, pp. 91–2) suggests five steps which he considers to be essential for beginning teachers to overcome prejudice. I have adapted and considerably expanded Haberman's arguments and replaced his psychological concept of prejudice with the more sociological concept of 'ism/phobia'[9] in order to encompass racism, xeno-racism, sexism, disablism, classism and homophobia/transphobia/Islamophobia/xenophobia. I have also provided my own examples of how each step might develop. It is important to point out that these steps apply to all members of the educational community, as well as beginning teachers, as specified by Haberman. I have also created a sixth step.

The first step is a thorough self-analysis of the content of one's ism/phobia. What form does it take? Is it overt or covert? Is it based on biology or is it cultural? Is it dominative (direct and oppressive) or aversive (excluding and cold-shouldering) (Kovel 1988)? Is it intentional or unintentional?[10] Are my attitudes patronizing? This is, of course, a *process* rather than an event. In many ways, this is the most crucial and difficult of the steps.

The second step is to seek answers to the question of source. How did I learn or come to believe these things? Did I learn to be ist/phobic from my parents/carers? Did I become ist/phobic as a result of experiences at primary school or at secondary school? Was it in further education or in higher education? Did I pick up ism/phobia from my peers; from the media: from newspapers; from magazines; from the internet? Was it a combination of the above? Why was I not equipped to challenge ism/phobia when I came across it?

Step three is to consider to what extent I am on the receiving end of, or how do I benefit from, ism/phobia. How does it demean me as a human being to have these beliefs? On the other hand, how do I benefit psychologically and/or materially from holding these beliefs?

Step four is to consider how one's ism/phobia may be affecting one's work in education. Am I making suppositions about young people's behaviour or attitudes to life based on their social class, ethnicity, impairments, gender, sexual orientation, religion or belief, or nationality? Am I making negative or positive presumptions about their academic achievement? If there is evidence of low achievement, am I taking the necessary remedial actions? Am I making assumptions about the parents/carers of the young people in my care? Am I making assumptions about other members of the school community, based on the above?

Step five is to lay out a plan explicating what one aims to do about one's ism/phobia. How do I propose to check it, unlearn it, counteract it and get beyond it? This can involve reading a text or texts and/or websites which address the issues. It should mean an ongoing update on equality/equal opportunities legislation.[11] It must certainly mean acquainting oneself with differential rates of achievements, and a critical analysis of the various explanations for this, centring on the explanations given by those who are pro-equality. It should mean acquainting oneself with various forms of bullying related to ism/phobia, and their effects. It might mean going on a course or courses.

It is not being argued that these five steps will necessarily occur in an individual's psyche (although they might) or spontaneously. Indeed, they can often be better addressed in group situations. I am suggesting that encouragement should be given for individuals to take these steps. Such encouragement could be done in the form of an introductory session for student or beginning teachers (and other educational workers). Also it is not being suggested that this is *merely* an individual process. It could be followed up with the sharing of questions and answers in groups and publicly. This could then progress (in practice) to an exploration of how a shared analysis of the five steps relates to the work of the school and the community: local, national and international.

### The personal and the institutional

After or during these five steps, the sixth step should be to connect the personal with the institutional, in order to undermine ism/phobia, and to promote equality. This might involve becoming active in one's school and/or community and/or becoming a trade union activist.[12] It might involve joining and working for a socialist/Marxist political party. It might also involve becoming active in local, national or international lobby groups. It should involve making the combating of ism/phobia and the promotion of equality central to one's work in educational institutions, in both the actual curriculum (what is on the timetable) and the hidden curriculum (everything else that goes on in educational institutions). It might involve writing and lecturing about ism/phobia and equality.

## Conclusion

In this chapter, I have outlined the main conceptual issues with respect to equal opportunity and equality issues in schools. Schools and other educational institutions should be places where personal and group reflection on *and action on* equality issues is central, and an integral part of the institutions' ethos. If we are to relate to and empower our students, if we are to engage in meaningful and successful teaching, we need to begin with the students' comprehension of their daily life experiences, whether in pre-school or university. From their earliest years, children's self-concepts are tainted by cultures of inequality. By starting from *their* description of these experiences, we are able to ground our teaching in concrete reality, then to transcend common sense and to move towards a critical scientific understanding of the world. This is the process by which teachers can support the process of the self-empowerment of tomorrow's children and young people. As stressed above, I firmly believe that we are not born ist/phobic. The way we think is a product of the society in which we live.[13] We can make important changes in societies as they are. However, in order to fully eradicate oppression of all forms, we need to change society, and indeed the world.

## Acknowledgements

I would like to thank Viv Ellis, Rosalyn George, Emma Renold and Krishan Sood for their very helpful comments on an earlier draft of this chapter. As always, responsibility for any inadequacies remains mine.

## Notes

[1] This is an updated version of a chapter that appeared in expanded form as the Introductory chapter in Cole 2008a.

[2] There are a number of problems with the notion of 'British values'. First, it assumes a parity of circumstance for all Britons, whereas the populace is deeply unequal in terms of ethnicity, social class and gender; second, it implies a consensus of values, when in fact these vary considerably according to ethnicity, social class and gender; third, it renders the economic system of global neo-liberal capitalism and imperialism unproblematic – 'we all believe in this, because we are British' (see the discussion on social class below).

[3] In a social class-based society, where there is little hope for millions of young working-class people, such alienation often leads to anti-social behaviour. Young people need hope for the future, and expectations of a decent and fulfilling life, something apparent in countries such as Venezuela, but severely lacking in Britain (e.g. Cole 2008c).

[4] The project was led by Elizabeth Atkinson and Renée DePalma at the University of Sunderland, in collaboration with researchers at the University of Exeter and the Institute of Education (University of London) and a team of three research assistants. It started on 1 September 2006 and ran until 31 December 2008. For further details, see http://www.nooutsiders.sunderland.ac.uk/.

[5] However, it is not all bad news. Renold 2005 has explored the ways in which some young boys are playing around with homoerotic discourses in fun and pleasurable ways (in contrast to the vast literature on homophobic talk) and girls queering heterosexuality through 'tomboyism'. The ability to queer normative gender and sexuality, however, remains restricted to the middle classes.

[6] Transphobia has been defined as 'an emotional disgust towards individuals who do not conform to society's gender expectations' (Hill and Willoughby 2005, p. 91, cited in *Whittle et al.* 2007, p. 21). Transphobia (by analogy with homophobia) refers to various kinds of aversions towards transsexuality and transsexual or transgendered people.

- It often takes the form of refusal to accept a person's new gender expression.
- Whether intentional or not, transphobia can have severe consequences for the targeted person; also, many transpeople experience homophobia as well, from people who associate gender identity disorder as a form of homosexuality.
- Like other forms of discrimination such as homophobia, the discriminatory or intolerant behaviour can be direct (e.g. harassment, assault, or even murder) or indirect (e.g. refusing to take steps to ensure that transgender people are

treated in the same way as cisgender (non-transgender) people). (Action Against Homophobia and Transphobia, undated)

[7] The book *Learning Without Limits* aims to challenge notions of fixed ability, and 'to build a new agenda for school improvement around the development of effective pedagogies that are free from ability labelling' (Hart *et al.* 2004, p. 21). For a critical Marxist appraisal of the *Learning Without Limits* paradigm, see Cole 2008d; 2008e; Yarker 2008.

[8] As a Marxist, I recognize, of course, that the working class are structurally located in a subordinate position in capitalist societies, and, *in this sense*, are a 'lower class'. However, the nomenclature 'working class' is used to indicate respect for the class as a whole, a class which, as noted above, sells its labour power to produce surplus for capitalists in an exploitative division of labour.

[9] For grammatical clarity, I have put 'ism/phobia' in the singular. Clearly, for many people it will be 'isms/phobias'. I also recognize that there are a number of positive 'isms' – Marxism, socialism, feminism, trade unionism among them.

[10] These considerations are adapted from my definition of racism (see the '"Race" and racism' section of this chapter).

[11] I do not deal with equalities legislation in this chapter, but see Nixon 2008; for ongoing information about equalities legislation in England, see the Equality and Human Rights Commission (http://www.equalityhumanrights.com/en/Pages/default.aspx); for Wales, which has some particularly progressive features, see Welsh Assembly Government: Equality and Diversity (http://new.wales.gov.uk/topics/equality/?lang=en); see also Chaney *et al.* 2007. My trade union, University and College Union (UCU), has a very good website on such legislation (http://www.ucu.org.uk/index.cfm?articleid=1742).

[12] It should be pointed out here that, as a matter of principle, all socialists and Marxists join trade unions, and honour strikes and do not cross any picket lines, believing that industrial action is essentially a struggle over surplus value appropriated from workers' labour (for a discussion, see Cole 2008b, pp. 24–27).

[13] Having visited Cuba on three occasions, I became even more convinced of the importance of socialization. Nearly fifty years of socialization in socialist values has had a dramatic effect all over the island. The selfish Thatcherite values abundant in the West are generally not apparent. They are apparent, however, in the tourist resorts and hotels, and in some of the *casas particulares* (private rented accommodation). With respect to Venezuela, with the projected programme for socialist values to be promoted in schools and workplaces, we are likely to see a further consolidation of socialist values and attitudes in that country.

# References

Action Against Homophobia and Transphobia (nd), 'What is transphobia?' Available at http://www.homophobia.org.uk/ (accessed 20 December 2008).

Archer, L. (2003), *Race, Masculinity and Schooling*. Buckingham. Open University Press.

BBC News (2007), 'Poles in Redditch hit by racism'. Available at http://www.bbc.co.uk/herefordandworcester/content/articles/2007/03/22/breakfast_polish_racism_feature.shtml (accessed January 2008).

Belfast Today (2006), 'Polish man hurt in vicious attack'. Available at http://www.belfasttoday.net/ViewArticle2.aspx?SectionID=3425&ArticleID=1532979 (accessed 24 July 2006).

Callinicos, A. (2000), *Equality*. Oxford: Polity.

Chaney P., Mackay, F. and McAllister, L. (2007), *Women, Politics and Constitutional Change*. Cardiff: University of Wales Press.

Cole, M. (1998), 'Racism, reconstructed multiculturalism and antiracist education'. *Cambridge Journal of Education*, 28, (1), 37–48.

— (2008a), 'Introductory chapter: education and equality – conceptual and practical considerations', in M. Cole (ed.), *Professional Attributes and Practice: Meeting the QTS Standards* (4th edn). London: Routledge.

— (2008b), *Marxism and Educational Theory: Origins and Issues*. London: Routledge.

— (2008c), 'The working class and the State Apparatuses in the UK and Venezuela: implications for education'. *Educational Futures*, 2, 2008. Available at http://www.educationstudies.org.uk/materials/vol_1_issue_2_cole_black.pdf (accessed September 2009).

— (2008d), '*Learning Without Limits*: a Marxist assessment'. *Policy Futures in Education*, 6, (4), 453–63. Available at http://www.wwwords.co.uk/pfie/content/pdfs/6/issue6_4.asp (accessed 27 February 2008).

—(2008e), 'Reply to Yarker'. *Policy Futures in Education*, 6, (4), 468–9. Available at http://www.wwwords.co.uk/pdf/validate.asp?j=pfie&vol=6&issue=4&year=2008&article=8_Yarker_PFIE_6_4_web (accessed 21 December 2008).

— (2009), *Critical Race Theory and Education: A Marxist Response*. New York: Palgrave Macmillan.

— and Blair, M. (2006), 'Racism and education: from Empire to New Labour', in M. Cole (ed.), *Education, Equality and Human Rights: Issues of Gender, 'Race', Sexuality, Disability and Social Class* (2nd edn). London: Routledge.

Connolly, P. (1998), *Racism, Gender Identities and Young Children*. London: Routledge.

Coultas, V. (2007), *Constructive Talk in Challenging Classrooms*. London: Routledge.

Davies, B. (1993), *Shards of Glass*. Sydney: Allen Unwin.

Disabled People's International (2005), 'Position paper on the definition of disability'. Available at http://v1.dpi.org/lang-en/resources/details.php?page=74 (accessed 27 February 2008).

Ellis, V. (2007), 'Sexualities and schooling in England after Section 28: measuring and managing "at risk" identities'. *Journal of Gay and Lesbian Issues in Education*, 4 (3), 13–30.

— with High, S. (2004), 'Something more to tell you: gay, lesbian or bisexual young people's experiences of secondary schooling'. *British Educational Research Journal*, 30, (2), April, 213–25.

Epstein, D. (1994), 'Introduction', in D. Epstein (ed.), *Challenging Lesbian and Gay Inequalities in Education*. Buckingham: Open University Press.

Forrest, S. (2006), 'Straight talking: challenges in teaching and learning about sexuality and homophobia in schools', in M. Cole (ed.), *Education, Equality and Human Rights: Issues of Gender, 'Race', Sexuality, Disability and Social Class* (2nd edn). London: Routledge.

— and Ellis, V. (2006), 'The making of sexualities: sexuality, identity and equality', in M. Cole (ed.), *Education, Equality and Human Rights: Issues of Gender, 'Race', Sexuality, Disability and Social Class* (2nd edn). London: Routledge.

Francis, B. (1998), *Power Plays: Primary School Children's Construction of Gender Power and Adult Work*. Stoke-on-Trent: Trentham Books.

— and Skelton, C. (2005), *Reassessing Gender and Achievement: Questioning Contemporary Key Debates*. London: Routledge.

Freire, P. (1972), *Pedagogy of the Oppressed*. Harmondsworth: Penguin.

Gaine, C. and George, R. (1999), *Gender, 'Race' and Class in Schooling: A New Introduction*. London: Falmer Press.

George, R. (1993), *Equal Opportunities in Schools: Principles, Policy and Practice*. Harlow, Longman.

— (2004), 'The importance of friendship during primary to secondary school transfer', in M. Benn and C. Chitty (eds), *A Tribute to Caroline Benn*. London: Continuum.

— (2007), *Urban Girls' Friendships: Complexities and Controversies*. Rotterdam: Sense Publications.

Glenn, J. and Barnett, L. (2007), 'Spate of racist complaints against Polish pupils'. *The Times Educational Supplement* (30 March).

Haberman, M. (1995), *Star Teachers of Children in Poverty*. West Lafayette, IN: Kappa Delta Pi.

Hart, S., Dixon, A., Drummond, M. J. and McIntyre, D. (2004), *Learning Without Limits*. Maidenhead: Open University Press.

Head, J. (1999), *Understanding the Boys: Issues of Behaviour and Achievement*. London: Routledge.

Hickey, T. (2006), 'Class and class analysis for the twenty-first century', in M. Cole (ed.), *Education, Equality and Human Rights: Issues of Gender, 'Race', Sexuality, Disability and Social Class* (2nd edn). London: Routledge.

Hill, D. (2008), 'Caste, Race and Class: A Marxist Critique of Caste Analysis, Critical Race Theory; and Equivalence (or Parallellist) Explanations of Inequality', *Radical Notes*. Delhi, India. Online at http://radicalnotes.com/component/option,com_front-page/Itemid,1/.

— (ed.) (2009), *Contesting Neoliberal Education: Public Resistance and Collective Advance*. London and New York: Routledge.

— and Cole, M. (2001), 'Social Class', in D. Hill and M. Cole (eds) *Schooling and Equality: Fact, Concept and Policy*. London: Kogan Page.

Hirom, K. (2001), 'Gender', in D. Hill and M. Cole (eds) (2001), *Schooling and Equality: Fact, Concept and Policy*. London: Kogan Page.

Kelly, J. (2006), 'Women thirty-five years on: still unequal after all this time', in M. Cole (ed.), *Education, Equality and Human Rights: Issues of Gender, 'Race', Sexuality, Disability and Social Class* (2nd edn). London: Routledge.

Kelsh, D. and Hill, D. (2006), 'The Culturalization of Class and the Occluding of Class Consciousness: The Knowledge Industry in/of Education'. *Journal for Cricial Education Policy Studies*, 4(1). Online at http://www.jceps.com/index.php?page ID = article&articleID = 59 ~ .

Kovel, J. (1988), *White Racism: A Psychohistory*. London: Free Association Books.

Letts IV, W. J. and Sears, J. T. (eds) (1999), *Queering Elementary Education: Advancing the Dialogue about Sexualities and Schooling*. Lanham, MD: Rowman and Littlefield.

London Borough of Newham (nd) 'Inclusive education – our aims'. Available at http://www.newham.gov.uk/Services/InclusiveEducation/AboutUs/inclusiveeducationouraims.htm (accessed 27 February 2008).

—(2007) 'Inclusive education strategy 2004–7. Available at http://www.newham.gov. uk/NR/rdonlyres/27813CF3-A71F-4235-8F58-94C7C4FF492F/0/IES_Booklet.pdf (accessed 27 February 2008).

Mac an Ghaill, M. (2000), 'The Irish in Britain: the invisibility of ethnicity and anti-Irish racism'. *Journal of Ethnic and Migration Studies*, 26, (1), 137–47

Martin, J. (2006), 'Gender, education and the new millennium', in M. Cole (ed.), *Education, Equality and Human Rights: Issues of Gender, 'Race', Sexuality, Disability and Social Class* (2nd edn). London: Routledge.

McLaren, P. (2002), *Life in Schools* (4th edn). Boston, MA: Pearson Education.

Morris, J. and Woolley, R. (2008), *Family Diversities Reading Resource*. Lincoln: Bishop Grosseteste University College (copies available from Dr. Richard Woolley: Richard.Woolley@bishopg.ac.uk).

Nixon, J. (2008), 'Statutory frameworks relating to teachers' responsiblities', in M. Cole *(ed.) Professional Attributes and Practice: meeting the QTS standards*, 4th edn. London: Routledge.

NUT (National Union of Teachers) (1991), *Lesbians and Gays in Schools: An Issue for Every Teacher*. London: National Union of Teachers.

Oliver, M. (1990), 'People with established locomotor disabilities in hospitals'. Paper presented at a joint workshop of the Living Options Group and the Research Unit of the Royal College of Physicians. Available at http://www.leeds.ac.uk/disability-studies/archiveuk/Oliver/in%20soc%20dis.pdf (accessed 27 February 2008).

OPSI (Office of Public Sector Information) (2006), 'The Racial and Religious Hatred Act 2006 (Commencement No. 1) Order 2007'. Available at http://www.opsi.gov. uk/si/si2007/uksi_20072490_en_1 (accessed 20 December 2008).

Paechter, C. (1998), *Educating the Other: Gender, Power and Schooling*. London: Routledge.

Pilkington, A. (2007), 'From institutional racism to community cohesion: the changing nature of racial discourse in Britain'. Inaugural professorial lecture, University of Northampton, 29 November.

Reay, D. (2006) 'Compounding inequalities: gender and class in education', in C. Skelton, B. Francis and L. Smulyan (eds), *The SAGE Handbook of Gender and Education*. London: Sage.

Renold, E. (2000a), 'Coming out: gender, (hetero)sexuality and the primary school'. *Gender and Education*, 12, (3), 309–27.

— (2000b), 'Presumed innocence: heterosexual, homophobic and heterosexist harassment in the primary school'. *Childhood*, 9, (4), 415–34.

— (2005), *Girls, Boys and Junior Sexualities: Exploring Children's Constructions of Gender and Sexuality in the Primary School*. London: Routledge.

— (2006), 'They won't let us play "unless you're going out with one of them": girls, boys and Butler's "heterosexual matrix" in the primary years'. *British Journal of Sociology of Education*, 27, (4), 489–509.

Rieser, R. (2006a), 'Disability equality: confronting the oppression of the past', in M. Cole (ed.), *Education, Equality and Human Rights: Issues of Gender, 'Race', Sexuality, Disability and Social Class* (2nd edn). London: Routledge.

— (2006b), 'Inclusive education or special educational needs: meeting the challenge of disability discrimination in schools', in M. Cole (ed.), *Education, Equality and Human Rights: Issues of Gender, 'Race', Sexuality, Disability and Social Class* (2nd edn). London: Routledge.

Rose, S. and Rose, H. (2005), 'Why we should give up on race: as geneticists and biologists know, the term no longer has any meaning'. *Guardian* (9 April). Available at http://www.guardian.co.uk/comment/story/00,,1455685,00.html (accessed 8 August 2006).

Sivanandan, A. (2001), 'Poverty is the new Black', *Race and Class* 43 (2), 2–5.

Skelton, C., Francis, B. and Smulyan, L. (eds) (2006), *The SAGE Handbook of Gender and Education*. London: Sage.

Whittle, S., Turner, L. and Al-Alami, M. (2007), *The Engendered Penalties: Transgender and Transsexual People's Experience of Inequality and Discrimination*. London: The Equalities Review. Available at http://www.theequalitiesreview.org.uk/upload/assets/www.theequalitiesreview.org.uk/transgender.pdf (accessed 25 April 2007).

Williamson, I. (2001), 'Sexuality', in D. Hill and M. Cole (eds) *Schooling and Equality: Fact, Concept and Policy*. London: Routledge.

Woodward, K. (2004), *Questioning Identity: Gender, Class, Ethnicity*. London: Routledge.

Yarker, P. (2008), '*Learning Without Limits* – a Marxist assessment: a response to Mike Cole'. *Policy Futures in Education*, 6 (4), 464–468.

Chapter 3

# Promoting Equality: Pedagogy and Policy

## Terry Wrigley and Peter Hick

This chapter reclaims the Enlightenment concept of *pedagogy* as broader than 'teaching methods'; it is contextual, dynamic and concerned with identities and democratic citizenship. In its critique of current policies, this chapter highlights the origins of 'special' education for those who could not be constrained into the disciplinary structures of mass elementary education required by a capitalist class structure. Bringing this up to date, it points to the contradiction between high-stakes accountability regimes and inclusion.

The chapter also re-examines and critiques historic attempts to understand attainment differences (IQ, language deficit, etc.). It outlines a theory of learning based on the dialectic of experience and symbolic representation. It argues that theoretical knowledge, built on the secure foundation of experience, helps us see beyond everyday 'common sense' assumptions, but also that more sensory-rich activities such as simulations and the arts can help us envision alternative futures. Both of these are important in inclusive education for democratic citizenship and social responsibility.

Finally, the chapter introduces three 'open architectures' (project method, storyline and design challenges) in which a diversity of students can successfully participate and which provide dynamic opportunities for constructing a critical understanding of a troubled world.

## Pedagogy and Equality

The word *pedagogy* is quite new in English-speaking countries. Recently its use has become almost a fashion statement, often with limited understanding. In most European languages and education systems, the concept of pedagogy means more than just teaching methods; it requires an articulation of educational aims and processes in social, ethical and affective as well as cognitive terms, and involves reflection about the changing nature of society or the value of human existence. The current political environment of

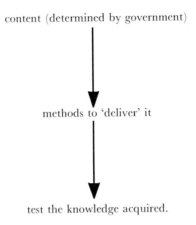

content (determined by government)

methods to 'deliver' it

test the knowledge acquired.

**FIGURE 3.1**

accountability and surveillance has strengthened the position of simple linear models (Figure 3.1).

A more rounded *pedagogical* understanding connects teaching and learning to social and cultural context and to the need to debate and discuss curriculum and educational aims, rather than simply complying with government demands (Figure 3.2). It situates teaching and learning within a more complex, dynamic and contradictory interplay between:

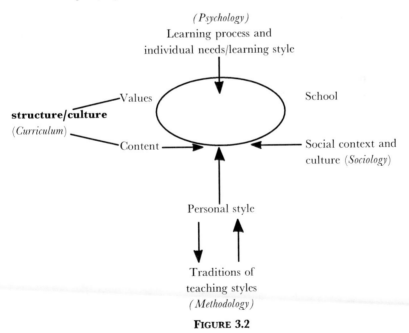

*(Psychology)*
Learning process and
individual needs/learning style

**structure/culture**
*(Curriculum)*

Values

School

Content

Social context and
culture *(Sociology)*

Personal style

Traditions of
teaching styles
*(Methodology)*

**FIGURE 3.2**

- curriculum (values as well as content)
- inherited teaching repertoires, along with the individual teacher's personality and preferred styles
- the school ethos and environment, interacting with the culture of the wider society
- a general theory of learning, and particular learners' characteristics and habits.

As Robin Alexander (2004) has argued, this broader understanding, which is both philosophical and situated, offers important protection against the simplistic demands of government policies, which lack a coherent values base:

> Ministers and DfES have elevated the quintessentially pragmatic mantra 'what works' to the status of ultimate criterion for judging whether a practice is educationally sound. (p. 9)

> Clearly, pedagogy is a somewhat more complex enterprise than may be recognised by those who reduce effective teaching to 'what works', or 'best practice' lessons downloaded from government websites. (*ibid.*, p. 13)

Pedagogy is inherently an optimistic concept. Born of the European Enlightenment in the late eighteenth century,

> the early development of the field is closely connected with political, economic, religious and scientific developments, as well as reflection in philosophy, social theory, literature and art. In particular, the radical critique by Enlightenment philosophy of inherited dogmas, and the struggle for a rational and free shaping of life ... If human beings are gifted with reason and are good by their nature, and if everything that is truly human is what humans know, want and can do, then in the end these can be cultivated by education. Education, therefore, helps to overcome the spiritual and intellectual restraints and clear away archaic ways of living ... A pedagogy was developed which was free from theology and ethical dogmatism, and which could contribute to the perfection of individual and community life. (Schaub and Zenke 1995, p. 260)

At the same time, as these authors point out, the development of school systems is entangled with state formation, modernity and national unification. Consequently, pedagogy is forced to deal with highly contradictory developments and values. To understand the roots of equality issues in pedagogy, we need to address the development of a competitive education system.

The introduction of mass compulsory schooling in the latter part of the nineteenth century can be understood as fundamentally a product of industrialization. Restrictions were placed on the funding of anything more than an 'elementary' level of education; anything beyond this was restricted to those who could pay. Schooling for the working class was largely instruction in the 3Rs (reading, writing and arithmetic – since renamed 'literacy and numeracy'), along with socialization into obedience and a pride in the British Empire. In providing this different education for working-class children, the development and maintenance of a coercive and competitive system required a sanction for failure, a process for separating out and disadvantaging those who presented particular difficulties. This involved, for example, the development of the technology of IQ testing as a means of labelling children as failures and as locating difficulties in learning within the individual. The construction of the ideology of special education has arguably played an important role in this process since that time: 'the problem of school failure was reframed ... in the new field of special education, which emerged as a means to remove and contain the most recalcitrant students' (Skrtic 1991, p. 152).

Special education has been based in large part on a notion of specialist pedagogy, an assumption that children who have been singled out as having 'special needs' learn in a qualitatively different way to others. The evidence for this assumption has recently been challenged, on the basis that there is little evidence to support it and that the use of specialist equipment or teaching approaches does not constitute a specialist pedagogy (Norwich and Lewis 2007). A developing concept of inclusive or 'connective' pedagogy (Corbett and Norwich 2005) locates disability issues within the wider inclusion agenda by emphasizing the social context of schooling.

This is not to suggest that there should be no attempt to adapt teaching to meet the particular needs of different learners. Rather, we wish to argue that such adjustments are quantitative rather than qualitative; they amount to methodological adaptations rather than a fundamentally different pedagogical theory or model. Thus bilingual students may need a relatively greater use of visually based materials, but connecting up abstract theory with experience is important for all learners within a constructivist pedagogy. Equally, students on the autism spectrum experience particular problems in English secondary schools when moved around every 50 minutes from room to room and teacher to teacher, but this fragmentation of learning and belonging can be damaging to many other students too.

The rhetoric of inclusion and 'inclusive pedagogy' has been appropriated under New Labour to subvert the meaning of equity in education. Indeed, New Labour politicians are generally careful to speak of 'equality of opportunity' rather than equity or equality, while sustaining conditions which undermine even that.

There is a tendency to speak in one breath about inclusive education, but to fail to acknowledge the policy context that presses us relentlessly towards educational exclusion in the other. Here we refer to the marketisation of schooling. (Allan and Slee 2001, p. 179)

Most of the architecture of marketization established by the Thatcher and Major governments has been continued and extended under New Labour; from Ofsted, Standard Assessment Tasks (SATs) and league tables to tuition fees, academies, and private sector partnerships. The impact of these pressures has continually 'entailed the generation of a more competitive, selective, and socially divisive series of policies and practices' (Barton 2004, p. 64). Inevitably it is the disadvantaged, the minoritized, and the disempowered who are the losers in the education marketplace. Unsurprisingly, students identified as having special educational needs have sustained a disproportionately high rate of disciplinary exclusion throughout this period (Hick *et al.* 2007). Ball (1993, p. 8) points out that 'excluded students have their market "choice" taken away from them'. Indeed, Nes (2004, p. 122) poses the question aptly: 'what is the market value of people with special needs?' The same can be said for black boys, for example, who continue to suffer disproportionate levels of exclusion, and also for young people growing up in poverty.

The relocation of inclusive education within the New Labour rhetoric of 'social exclusion' has involved a downplaying of the role of material inequality and disadvantage, in favour of an individualized and internalized discourse of 'poverty of aspiration' and self-esteem (Hick *et al.* 2007). It has shifted the onus of social change from the institution to the individual, so that: 'special educational needs continues to be a legitimating label for the failure of the system to address itself to the aspirations, dignity and human worth of so many young people' (Armstrong 2005, p. 147). Along with this psychologistic shift, the responsibility has been pushed downwards from the political to the school level, blaming schools located in the poorest neighbourhoods for being 'ineffective'.

Young people who cannot reconcile their life histories or physical characteristics with the rigours of a standardized, fast-delivery curriculum are categorized as personally deviant. This finds new forms, including the epidemic-level diagnosis of 'ADHD'. It is a strange 'disease' whose official symptoms are a list of classroom misbehaviour. As well as being highly profitable for pharmaceutical companies and temporarily convenient for teachers struggling to control behaviour, this medical framing of a social problem diverts attention from both the cultural pressures upon today's young people (poor nutrition, fast media, anxiety about the future, etc.) and the rigidity of our schools. It is easy for teachers under pressure from unnecessarily large class sizes, for example, to collude with the notion that a particular student 'has ADHD', rather than questioning why he or she is expected to sit still and passively for hours on end (see, for example, Lloyd *et al.* 2006 for a convincing argument that 'ADHD' as a medical entity is a myth).

A further way in which government rhetoric now attempts to 'paint out' equality issues in pedagogy is through the discourse of 'personalization' of learning. Here there is no longer a need to address, for example, processes of institutionalized racism evident in systematic inequalities in educational outcomes for students from some black and minority ethnic communities. Instead, the issue becomes reframed as one of setting and monitoring progress towards individual learning targets. This can all too easily become transposed to a *de*-personalized experience of individualized learning tasks, presented through a Virtual Learning Environment. The rhetoric of 'personalization', and the lack of any clear definition, provides cover for an even stronger emphasis on segregation and social selection.

Similarly, government prescriptions of teaching methods which are supposedly evidence based and distorted by neither values nor educational theory have done little to promote social justice. Indeed, they have often proved incompetent in assisting the most disadvantaged young people. Because they isolate the transmission of knowledge and skills from socio-cultural issues, they tend towards simplistic fixes. One recent example is the official response to 'boys' underachievement'. A failure to question either the validity of assessment data or their longer-term importance (men subsequently win out), or the intersections with 'race' and class, quickly led to a moral panic and demands for a quick-fix. This solution, in its crudest form, consisted of pandering to (culturally formed) male interests – give the boys war comics to read – thus reflecting and strengthening those macho versions of masculinity which helped cause the underachievement in the first place (see Martino and Meyenn 2001 for further discussion).

Another current example is the recourse to highly regulated phonics teaching to improve literacy test scores. This strategy, particularly applied to schools in the most deprived areas, fails to consider that their students might be poorly motivated to read because they have not enjoyed pleasurable engagement with texts. Ironically, in its more fundamentalist versions, the emphasis on phonics has the effect of squeezing out enjoyable reading even more.

## Constructing Learner Identities

Nancy Fraser (1997) has argued that social justice requires attention both to recognition and to redistribution. In the educational context, our hypothesis is that one cannot be achieved without the other. A mechanistic attempt to raise attainment levels is unsustainable without a reworking of learner identities; conversely, any curriculum which seeks to raise the (self-) esteem of marginalized students will ultimately fail if they are unable to gain socially recognized knowledge, skills or qualifications.

Learner identities are formed on three levels: neighbourhood/society, school and classroom. Young people pick up messages and develop attitudes and habits in each of these contexts. A girl may acquire messages of worthlessness from the derelict condition of her housing or her mother's menial occupation; from the culture (environment, behaviour code, teachers' use of language, etc.) of her school; and from tedious classroom routines which require compliance rather than thinking and creativity. All three are important sites of learning, but each intersects with the others. An authoritarian regime may work tolerably well in elite schools, but in deprived neighbourhoods it simply reinforces a sense of worthlessness and powerlessness. Neo-conservative attempts to transfer codes of behaviour from selective private schools to non-selective or comprehensive state secondary schools are usually counter-productive. In *The Motivated School* Alan Mclean (2003) emphasizes three themes – autonomy, agency and affiliation – which need building into school relationships but equally into classroom learning; it is also clear that negative features of the wider social context will constantly interfere.

Bourdieu (1997 (1986)) coined the terms 'cultural capital' and 'social capital' to explain how upper-class families are able to use more than their material wealth to transfer advantage to their children. Others have reified these terms, for example Robert Putnam's followers, who believe they can quantify and measure the social capital of a neighbourhood. It is important to understand that Bourdieu used these terms dialectically, in a dynamic of *exchange*. It is a deep mistake to speak of a particular community suffering from 'low cultural capital'; in Bourdieu's sense, the problem lies substantially in the school devaluing and failing to recognize the cultural assets of that community. To read cultural or social capital as a quantifiable entity contained or possessed by families or a neighbourhood is inevitably to fall into discourses of deficit and denigration.

This was fundamentally the error of Basil Bernstein (e.g. 1972), who, in his attempt to discover causes of class-related underachievement in family language patterns, failed to problematize classroom discourse. His argument was that working-class (i.e. manual worker) families used a 'restricted code' which was appropriate to describing immediate and present circumstances, but left children ill-prepared for the more abstract discourses of school. Bernstein's description of working-class language was strongly contested at the time (e.g. Labov 1969; Rosen 1972; Edwards 1976). Labov (*ibid.*) argued that this 'illusion of verbal deprivation' arose from a 'poor understanding of the nature of language' and of 'the logic of nonstandard English'.

## Language and Experience

Language deficit theories, as an explanation of attainment differences, took different forms on the two sides of the Atlantic. In the US they were mainly linked to 'race'– the supposed illogicality of Black American English – but in England to class. However, as Britain's population became ethnically more diverse, the language repertoire of bilingual/multilingual families was seen as a prime source of underachievement.

We have made substantial gains in recent decades. It is quite rare nowadays to hear teachers refer to 'non-English speakers' in their class. The preferred terminology is 'bilingual pupils', and support given for 'English as an Additional Language'.

Second, thanks largely to the work of Jim Cummins (e.g. 1984; see also www.iteachilearn.com), the linguistic development of bilingual pupils is much better understood. Based on substantial international research, Cummins argues that it takes some years to progress from everyday transactional/conversational language (contextualized but normally cognitively simple) to academic language (abstract but cognitively complex). Teachers tend to give pupils who are struggling with academic language simple written exercises to complete, but this is a move in the wrong direction – a discourse which is abstract but lacking in cognitive challenge. He proposes instead forms of learning which are cognitively challenging but well grounded in experience (Figure 3.3).

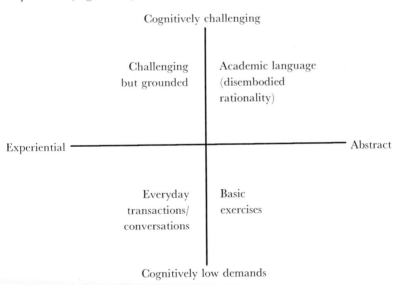

**FIGURE 3.3**

We may also usefully apply this to other students who struggle with academic language and literacy. To take a social constructivist position, some students, because of their upbringing, will have acquired the experiences needed to make sense of teacher talk; they will readily connect the teacher's words with pictures in their heads. They may, for example, have visited medieval cathedrals or have discussed nature documentaries with their parents. Others will not. Rather than develop deficit arguments based on class, 'race' or language, or ascribe students' difficulties in understanding to low 'intelligence' or 'ability', we would do better to develop pedagogies which ground theory in real and in simulated experiences.

Howard Gardner's (1993) notion of multiple intelligences and the simplified version represented by visual, auditory and kinaesthetic (VAK, see Smith 2003) have been a popular attempt to reduce reliance on abstract theoretical language. However, the versions presented to teachers have often been oversimplified: 'The idea that children may be "visual", "auditory" or "kinaesthetic" learners, for instance, translates the mutual process of dynamic, multimodal communication to a fixed characteristic and capacity of each child involved' (Kershner 2008). In reality children may prefer different modes of learning for different kinds of learning tasks; their preferences may change over time or in different contexts; classroom activities may not be readily classified as 'V, A or K', and they may not be perceived by students in the way intended by teachers. These simplifications have brought problems, however, due to the wider policy context as well as their unclear formulation:

- In a policy climate which emphasizes testing, labelling and segregation, many teachers have used questionnaires to identify students as either visual, auditory or kinaesthetic. In some classrooms, students even have coloured cards or labels on their desks. This begs the question: even if a student did have a leaning towards one or the other, what should one do about it? Should the young David Beckham's teachers have advised him to avoid visual or auditory learning? 'Just forget about Spanish, son. You're never going to need it.' Whereas Gardner sought to expand modes of teaching and learning, adoption of such ideas in the current policy environment leads to a narrowing of opportunities and takes us away from inclusion.
- Although considerably more sophisticated than VAK, Gardner's theory tends to view intelligences, albeit multiple, as biological facts. His 'multiple intelligences' are as innate as the previous concept of IQ as a measure of generalized intelligence. By ascribing strengths to individual learners such as language, visualization or interpersonal understanding, he underplays the importance of developing all of these as fundamental channels and processes we need in order to become successful learners and human beings (for further discussion, see Franklin 2006).

More recent theoretical understandings of *situated cognition*, building broadly on Vygotsky (1978; 1986), embed cognition as an integral aspect of activity or practice. Thinking is (generally at least) not something which happens 'inside' an individual's head, but rather is stretched between human beings, the resources and environment they use for an activity, and inherited cultural tools such as language and other symbolic systems: '"Situated cognition" expresses the idea that ... some aspects of knowledge and certain cognitive strategies are closely connected to the situation in which they are learned, used and assessed' (Kershner 2008, p. 57). Within this school, Wertsch (1990) questions the predominance of 'decontextualised rationality', a voiceless register which silences and conceals conflicting perspectives and interests beneath the pseudo-objectivity of academic discourse. This is not to fall in the trap of arguing that students who find this register alien should simply be steered towards 'practical subjects'. The current attempt in England to segregate many students into a vocational track from age 14 is tantamount to disenfranchisement; it denies them the knowledge to become mature citizens or the ability to express their ideas in an increasingly complex and troubled world.

Social justice requires a pedagogical search for forms of learning which are simultaneously challenging and accessible. Theory is important to all learners, as a way of transcending immediate realities and moving beyond 'common sense'. As Vygotsky (1986) argued, taking the example of mathematics, algebra is more powerful than arithmetic since it enables us to see general patterns. Conversely (*ibid.*), he also argued that words which are not rooted in experience remain an empty shell rather than a concept. We need learning activities which ground theorization in experiences. Similarly, Bruner points out the loss when schools overemphasize the 'logico-scientific' mode and neglect the 'narrative' mode. Stories have their own way of explaining the world, and a connectedness with our activities and emotions.

The philosopher of science Wartofsky (1973, pp. 208–9), discussing the role of models in theory-building, points to the value of forms of representation which are closer to lived experience. He speaks of 'micro-worlds' or 'imagined worlds' such as pictures, novels or simulations as in play and drama. Such activities are sensory rich, rather reflecting aspects of lived reality than more abstract forms of representation such as scientific formulas or academic explanation. However, they are not to be mistaken for reality itself, and this is a virtue. He sees them as 'off-line' activity which is not constrained by economic necessity and which allows scope for creativity. We are able to imagine, that is, create mental images of what we have not actually experienced. In the realm of play, simulations and virtual reality, as well as the arts, we are able to imagine the world different from what it is. We can transcend necessity. Here, there is an alternative.

When we speak of 'relevance' in the context of a search for socially just schooling, we cannot be constrained by vocationalist versions of 'relevance'. These may be 'inclusive', in the sense of giving some direct satisfaction and a sense of maturity, but when vocational training dominates the curriculum and eliminates critical and creative thinking, we are trapping young people in particular social positions. Rather than schools being emancipatory, we have a cycle of reproduction whereby the children of low-paid workers are themselves channelled into low-paid work. Our concept of the 'practical' needs to be expanded into experiential activities which allow learners to play with alternatives. Play, simulations and the creative arts enable us to explore the world as it is and how it could be, in sensory-rich, affective and social ways; they can also provide a platform from which we can easily move into more theoretical registers, as in the debriefing after a simulation, or a discussion with friends after seeing a film.

## Identity, Imagination and Social Justice

The present policy climate not only reduces every learning activity which is not precisely measurable, but it does so more drastically for students who are already disadvantaged. Andy Hargreaves (2003) points to the danger of an apartheid model of school development in countries like England. While schools in more advantaged areas are being granted greater flexibility to develop as learning communities which prepare their students for the 'knowledge society', others will instruct their students for limited short-term gains in preparation for a low-level service role:

> Schools and teachers in poor communities in the desolate sprawl of housing estates ... struggle in the shadow of impending failure – watchful of test scores, fearful of intervention and with a bellyful of imposed restrictions and requirements ... They teach the basic skills of maths and literacy that get their students to improve up to a point in primary school only to see their achievements plateau in the high-school years ... Students learn not to create knowledge, develop ingenuity or solve unfamiliar problems in flexible formats; their destiny is to be literate and numerate enough to serve and support the 'weightless work' of their affluent superiors in restaurants, tourist hotels, health spas, and other service work where understanding instructions, communicating obsequiously and urging others to have a nice day, have far greater importance than inventiveness or ingenuity. (*ibid.*, p. 191)

A restricted notion of 'basic skills' not only leads to boredom and disaffection, it also trivializes and limits learning. It consigns young people to habits and identities which deny voice and agency:

> When we frame the universe of discourse only in terms of children's deficits in English and in phonological awareness (or deficits in any other area), we expel culture, language, identity, intellect, and imagination from our image of the child. Similarly, these constructs are nowhere to be found in our image of the effective teacher of these children, or in policies that might guide instruction. The positivistically correct seem to believe that identity and imagination can't be relevant because they can't be measured. (Cummins 2003, p. 57)

Cummins argues that such approaches to teaching and learning are based on a deficit view of both learners and teachers.

> Clearly, for teachers, the top-down imposition of scripts represents an attempt to teacher-proof the curriculum. It reflects a profound distrust of teachers and an extremely narrow interpretation of the teaching-learning process. Nowhere in this anemic instructional vision is there room for really connecting at a human level with culturally diverse students; consigned to irrelevance also is any notion of affirming students' identities and challenging coercive power structures, by activating what they already know about the world and mobilizing the intellectual and linguistic tools they use to make sense of their worlds ... No role is envisaged for teachers or students to invest their identities (affect, intellect, and imagination) in the teaching/learning process. (*ibid.*, p. 56)

Cummins argues that such teaching methods are particularly damaging to minority and bilingual learners. They work with wider discourses of denigration, serving to 'constrict the interpersonal space such that total assimilation to the dominant culture and language is the only identity option offered to any student who aspires to academic success' (*ibid.*, p. 54). Thus, rather than literacy expanding horizons and possibilities, it is reduced to a technical skill which forecloses on personal and cultural development. This is not to suggest a lesser role for literacy teaching in schools serving disadvantaged neighbourhoods; rather, that enjoyable, engaging and critical literacies need to be connected with the breadth of scientific, historical, environmental and cultural learning.

## More Open Architectures for Learning

Traditional teaching first excludes the learner and his or her world from curriculum, and then seeks to compensate by adding 'motivation' in the form of extrinsic rewards. Learners are given little say in what they will learn. The 'selective tradition' (Lawton 1978, drawing on Williams 1961) of curriculum content is not only presented as something alien to everyday human activity, but tends to exclude particularly the experiences of female, gay, disabled, black or working-class students. It is too simplistic, however, to argue this point simply at the level of representation; though some groups are invisible in texts and curricula, others may be present in forms which tokenize or essentialize. Thus, the abolition of slavery is represented as a result of white philanthropy; cultural diversity is acknowledged but not racism; Muslims are demonized. Above all, a sense of injustice and resistance is missing.

It is difficult to overcome this when teaching methods are focused on individual lesson plans, each 40-minute block subdivided into short sections for more intensive transmission of knowledge. We need to rediscover more open structures of learning which give time and opportunity to the learner to explore, critique and imagine. These more open patterns were frequently to be found before the National Curriculum and its tests were introduced. While rejecting the New Labour myth that the 1970s were some kind of educational Dark Age with neither standards nor innovation (Drummond 2005), we also need to acknowledge the limitations of some thematic or project work as practised at that time. At their worst, 'projects' became an individualized curriculum based on collection rather than problem-solving or problematization.

First, learning theory was dominated by the individualized constructivism of Piaget (1952); Vygotsky's social constructivist psychology (1978; 1986) was little known at the time. Second, 'doing a project' was seen as an individual activity, and at its worst could be based more on collecting data than on addressing problems. Thus, students might choose to study Victorian fashions or 1930s cars, but not be steered to connect the phenomena with cultural or technological or political change. Following Vygotsky (*ibid.*), social constructivism draws on cultural tools such as language in order to build concepts and models. It espouses a dialogic relationship between teachers and learners. It does not assume a simple derivation of ideas from perceptions; the immediate 'common sense' conclusions and beliefs are an important starting point but may be erroneous and in need of skilful challenge.

Principles of social constructivism can and should be applied to social learning as well as scientific. The starting point must be an openness towards the perceptions and lives of young people in all their diversity. Our pupils/ students must be enabled to reflect upon that experience, but in ways which open up the possibility of a different future. This is a pedagogical approach which emerged in the course of case studies of successful urban schools (Wrigley 2000); *cultural reflection and repositioning* seemed a useful summary. For example, girls of South Asian heritage in an East London school were studying *Romeo and Juliet*; in threes, they improvised the scene Shakespeare didn't write, namely an encounter between Juliet, her mother and her nurse immediately after her father has threatened to throw her out on the street if she refuses his choice of husband. This provides a safe space in which the students can discuss many forms and degrees of parental/carer involvement in their children's relationships. Another class were asked to explore religious texts for guidance on modern environmental issues, bearing in mind the possibility of inferring from broader values what is not explicitly stated. Pat Thomson (2006) has described similar activities such as a class which used the village war memorial as the starting point for research into the experience and significance of the world wars for local people; thus began a process of critically rethinking assumptions about patriotism and war. Learning of this quality cannot be achieved through supposedly 'effective teaching' based on rapid memorization and recall in tests.

The pedagogies of social justice need to be inclusive of diverse identities and experiences, and open to alternative futures. One of us, at a conference involving students and teachers from different Balkan countries and American states, introduced a simulation whereby different interest groups devised five 'rights', for example for old people, a religious minority or teenage girls, before presenting these to an assembly for debate and ratification. School students need fewer 'four-part lessons' and much more engagement in role-play and simulations, fieldwork, research, real-life problem-solving and so on.

More extended models need to combine a recognizable structure and coherence with sufficient room for autonomous decisions and activity, for which a useful metaphor is *open architectures* (see Wrigley 2006, pp. 105–9; 2007). These include project method, in a sense deriving from Dewey and his colleagues (see Kirkpatrick 1918), and common in much of Europe; storyline (a Scottish invention now flourishing in Scandinavia); and design challenges (see www.criticalskills.co.uk).

**Project method** frames individual/small-group research within plenary discussion, presentation and often real-life outcomes. For example, using a model borrowed from the Danish curriculum for social studies (Undervisningsministeriet 1995), a project on asylum seekers begins with a simulation of a future military coup, leading families to uproot and seek refuge in neighbouring countries. A discussion follows in which students contribute their different levels of knowledge and awareness. Some choose to research more factual questions, such as where asylum seekers currently come from or the procedures they undergo, whereas others, with more prior knowledge, may choose more challenging issues such as national identity, xenophobia and xeno-racism (see Chapter 2, p. 17 of this volume). Participants then present their findings to each other, not as finalized knowledge but to stimulate further discussion. A further stage can include various forms of community action. Project method has many variants internationally, including forms known as *inquiry* in North America.

**Storyline** (Bell *et al.* 2007) is a form of interdisciplinary work with a narrative-based structure. It was invented in Scotland for young children, but is commonly used for all ages in Scandinavia and elsewhere. It begins with a situation, into which participants locate themselves by inventing characters for themselves; the teacher triggers steps in a loose narrative, each of which stimulates a particular type of activity such as writing, drama, research. A Norwegian example, Rainbow Street, involves a rural secondary school class imagining they are a multi-ethnic community living in east Oslo. They paint pictures of their houses and stick them round the walls; one day they arrive to find some racist graffiti. A visitor in the role of a fundamentalist Christian preacher scowls when any of them identify as Hindu or Muslim. Two Iranian refugees seek permission from the local council to use their front room as a small mosque.

**Design challenges** present problems involving investigation and leading to solutions. Teams work within a clearly defined time frame towards a final product or presentation. A version designed by student teachers in Scotland was based historically on the Highland Clearances (the mass eviction of peasants to make way for large-scale cattle and sheep farming, which led to relocation on more barren land and to emigration – see Marx 1965 (1887), pp. 728–33). An updated scenario involved the fiction of a media tycoon buying Scotland and seeking to turn it into a theme park; the population face the choice of emigration, working in the theme park or resistance. This scenario has considerable resonance in an era of neo-liberal globalization, with remote financiers radically transforming whole ways of life and mass migration in the face of war and environmental disaster (see Cole 2008a, Chapter 7 for a discussion; see also Feldman and Lotz 2004).

## Concluding Thoughts

Developing a pedagogy for social justice requires an understanding of teaching and learning which is well informed by Marxist and sociological theories of social division, power relationships and cultural change (see Chapter 2 of this volume). It requires curriculum thinking which focuses on ethics as well as content, and psychological theories which relate specific learning needs to identity and social positioning. It is worlds apart from the discourse of 'effective teaching', that is, the rapid transmission of inert knowledge which dominates the current policy agenda.

A recent education White Paper *Higher Standards, Better Schools for All* (DfES 2005) scandalously divided the school population into 'gifted and talented', those who are 'struggling', and the 'just average'. As David Gillborn (2005) pointed out, this is based on a view of 'ability' as fixed and generic, which inevitably reinforces disadvantage. It leaves out of account the many young people whose gifts and talents remain undiscovered. It presents those who are struggling as a separate category, unlike the 'average' rest (aren't we all struggling at something?). It does not recognize that each and every student has an identity/identities which is/are never purely individual, but part of wider divisions and configurations of power and disadvantage (for arguments against notions of 'fixed ability', see Hart *et al.* 2004; see also Cole 2008b; 2008c; Yarker 2008). Divisions and identities of gender, sexuality, 'race', religion and language intersect in complex ways with physical and sensory characteristics, emotional patterns and social class.

This word *class* is further complicated by its double significance. Much educational sociology focuses on the division between manual workers on the one hand, and white collar and professional on the other. This is important, given the various cultural and linguistic explanations of differential school achievement built on a disjunction between schools and manual workers. Within this, the impact of absolute and relative poverty has received increasing attention. However, class has a wider pedagogical significance in terms of social justice. Marx's analysis that the world was increasingly dividing into two classes, a small but very powerful class of capitalists, and a large and diverse class of workers employed in all manner of manual, clerical and intellectual occupations, raises crucial issues for anyone concerned about the future of education and social justice (see Hill and Cole 2001, pp. 150–3). In our neo-liberal age, the rich and powerful have sought to redefine all sectors of education in terms of economic competitiveness (Sears 2003; Ball 2008), reducing the spaces in which critical questions about the world can be asked and answered, as well as opportunities for personal, social and cultural development. In our age of globalized disaster – poverty at home and internationally, climate chaos, and war – social justice and equality require a struggle for a broad, engaged and socially critical education which is truly open to all.

It is worth reiterating Fraser's (1997) reminder that social justice involves both recognition and redistribution. We would add the importance of resistance – at the same time the development of agency needed to transform power relationships, and a crucial part of identity formation for all subordinated groups. A pedagogy aimed at addressing inequalities in educational outcomes 'cannot escape challenging or supporting a status quo that patently produces different outcomes for different groups ... it is unavoidably a "pedagogy of the oppressed"' (Dyson and Hick 2004, p. 202, following Freire 1972).

Curriculum policy in England in particular over the past two decades, since the introduction of the National Curriculum, has been marked, paradoxically, both by standardization and by hierarchical segregation. Indeed, the former has been the condition for the latter. Social justice could never be achieved by expecting those at the bottom of the ladder simply to speed up their ascent. Different routes to learning have to be made available, including the chance to negotiate and redefine what learning might be important and satisfying. At present, this is only being offered in terms of consumer choice – heavily tied, in practice, to social origins – between an academic and a vocational curriculum. We need to argue for more opportunities in which young people are themselves able to determine what is valuable, both as specific individuals and as groups growing up in a particular place and time (Bangladeshi girls in London or bi white male New Yorkers, perhaps), and as part of a global humanity subjected by capitalism to poverty and insecurity, consumerism, war and climate chaos.

Critical pedagogy is nothing if not situated. Unlike some versions of 'thinking skills', critical literacy is not a box of tricks with which to interrogate texts, but strategies to enable readers to gain a new perspective by counter-positioning their own experience and identity to the text and author. We have much to learn still from Freire (1972), for whom 'reading the word' was also 'reading the world'; and for whom the breakthrough to literacy was simultaneously an access to wider cultural meanings, the unveiling of hidden power, and the emergence of people reborn into identities of resistance and revolt.

# References

Alexander, R. (2004), 'Still no pedagogy? principle, pragmatism and compliance in primary education'. *Cambridge Journal of Education*, 34, (1), pp. 7–33.

Allan, L. and Slee, R. (2001), 'Excluding the included: a reconsideration of inclusive education'. *International Studies in Sociology of Education*, 11, (2), 173–92.

Armstrong, D. (2005), 'Reinventing "inclusion": New Labour and the cultural politics of special education'. *Oxford Review of Education*, 31, (1), 135–51.

Ball, S. (2008), *The Education Debate*. Bristol: Policy Press.

Ball, S. J. (1993), 'Education markets, choice and social class: the market as a class strategy in the UK and the USA'. *British Journal of Sociology of Education*, 14, (1), 3–19.

Barton, L. (2004), 'The politics of special education: a necessary or irrelevant approach?', in L. Ware (ed.), *Ideology and the Politics of (In)Exclusion*. New York: Peter Lang, pp. 63–75.

Bell, S., Harkness, S., and White, G. (eds) (2007), 'Storyline – past, present and future'. Glasgow: University of Strathclyde (Enterprising Careers)

Bernstein, B. (1972), 'Social class, language and socialisation', in P. Giglioli (ed.), *Language and social context*. Harmondsworth: Penguin, pp. 157–178.

Bourdieu, P. (1997 (1986)), 'The forms of capital', in A. H. Halsey *et al.* (eds), *Education: Culture, Economy, Society*. Oxford: Oxford University Press, pp. 46–58.

Cole, M. (2008a), *Marxism and Educational Theory: Origins and Issues*. London: Routledge.

— (2008b), '*Learning Without Limits*: a Marxist assessment'. *Policy Futures in Education*, 6, (4), 453–63. Available at http://www.wwwords.co.uk/pfie/content/pdfs/6/issue6_4.asp (accessed 27 February 2008).

—(2008c), 'Reply to Yarker'. *Policy Futures in Education*, 6, (4), 468–9. Available at http://www.wwwords.co.uk/pdf/validate.asp?j = pfie & vol = 6 & issue = 4 & year = 2008 & article = 8_Yarker_PFIE_6_4_web (accessed 21 December 2008).

Corbett, J. and Norwich, B. (2005), 'Common or specialised pedagogy?', in M. Nind, J. Rix, K. Sheehy and K. Simmons (eds), *Curriculum and Pedagogy in Inclusive Education*. Abingdon: RoutledgeFalmer, pp. 13–30.

Cummins, J. (1984), *Bilingualism and Special Education: Issues in Assessment and Pedagogy*. Clevedon: Multilingual Matters.

Cummins, J. (2003), 'Challenging the construction of difference as deficit: where are identity, intellect, imagination, and power in the new regime of truth?', in P. P. Trifonas (ed.), *Pedagogies of Difference: Rethinking Education for Social Change*. London: RoutledgeFalmer, pp. 41–60.

DfES (2005), *Higher Standards, Better Schools for All*. London: The Stationery Office. Available at www.dfes.gov.uk/publications/schoolswhitepaper (accessed 15 April 2008).

Drummond, M. J. (2005), 'Professional amnesia: a suitable case for treatment'. *Forum*, 47, (2–3), 83–90.

Dyson and Hick (2004), 'Low attainment', in A. Lewis and B. Norwich (eds), *Special Teaching for Special Children: A Pedagogy for Inclusion?* Maidenhead: Open University Press, pp. 192–205.

Edwards A. D. (1976), *Language in Culture and Class*. London: Heinemann.

Feldman, P. and Lotz, C. (2004), *A World to Win: A Rough Guide to a Future without Global Capitalism*. London: Lupus Books.

Franklin, S. (2006), 'VAKing out learning styles – why the notion of "learning styles" is unhelpful to teachers'. *Education 3-13*, 34, (1), 81–7.

Fraser, N. (1997), *Justice Interruptus: Critical Reflections on the 'Postsocialist' Condition*. London: Routledge.

Freire, P. (1972), *Pedagogy of the Oppressed*. Harmondsworth: Penguin.

Gardner, H. (1993), *Frames of Mind: The Theory of Multiple Intelligences*. London: Fontana.

Gillborn, D. (2005), *Written Evidence on the Education White Paper (2005)*. London: Institute of Education. Available at www.ioe.ac.uk/schools/efps/GillbornRace EqualityandTheWhitePaper.doc (accessed 15 April 2008).

Hargreaves, A. (2003), 'Professional learning communities and performance training cults: the emerging apartheid of school improvement', in A. Harris *et al.* (eds), *Effective Leadership for School Improvement*. London: RoutledgeFalmer, pp. 180–195.

Hart, S., Dixon, A., Drummond, M. J. and McIntyre, D. (2004), *Learning Without Limits*. Maidenhead: Open University Press.

Hick, P., Visser, J. and MacNab, N. (2007), 'Education and social exclusion', in D. Abrams, J. Christian and D. Gordon (eds), *Multi-Professional Handbook of Social Exclusion*. Chichester: John Wiley & Sons, pp. 95–114.

Hill, D. and Cole, M. (2001), 'Social class', in D. Hill and M. Cole (eds), *Schooling and Equality: Fact, Concept and Policy*. London: Routledge, pp. 137–160.

Kershner, R. (2008), 'Learning in inclusive classrooms', in P. Hick, R. Kershner and P. Farrell (eds), *Psychology for Inclusive Education: New Directions in Theory and Practice*. London: Routledge, pp. 52–65.

Kirkpatrick, W. H. (1918), 'The project method'. *Teachers College Record*, 19, (4), 319–35.

Labov, W. (1969), 'The logic of non-standard English'. *Georgetown Monographs on Language and Linguistics*, 22, 1–31 (Washington, DC: Georgetown University Press).

Lawton, D., Gordon, P., Ing, M., Gibby, B., Pring, R. and Moore, T. (1978), *Theory and Practice of Curriculum Studies*. London: Routledge.

Lloyd, G., Stead, J. and Cohen, D. (2006), *Critical New Perspectives on ADHD*. London: RoutledgeFalmer.

Martino, W. and Meyenn, B. (eds) (2001), *What about the Boys? Issues of Masculinity in Schools*. Buckingham: Open University Press.

Marx, K. (1965 (1887)), *Capital, Vol. 1*. Moscow: Progress Publishers.

McLean, A. (2003), *The Motivated School*. London: Sage.

Nes, K. (2004), 'Quality versus equality? Inclusion politics in Norway at Century's end', in L. Ware (ed.), *Ideology and the Politics of (In)Exclusion*. New York: Peter Lang, pp. 125–40.

Norwich, B. and Lewis, A. (2007), 'How specialised is teaching children with disabilities and difficulties?' *Journal of Curriculum Studies*, 39, (2), 127–50.

Piaget, J. (1952), *The Origins of Intelligence in Children*. London: Routledge & Kegan Paul.

Rosen H. (1972), *Language and Class: A Critical Look at the Theories of Basil Bernstein*. Bristol: Falling Wall Press.

Schaub, H. and Zenke, K. (1995), *Wörterbuch Pädagogik*. Munich: DTV.

Sears, A. (2003), *Retooling the Mind Factory: Education in a Lean State*. Aurora, ONT: Garamond Press.

Skrtic, T. M. (1991), 'The special education paradox: equity as the way to excellence'. *Harvard Educational Review*, 61, (2), 148–206.

Smith, A. (2003), *Accelerated Learning: A User's Guide*. London: Continuum.

Thomson, P. (2006), 'Miners, diggers, ferals and show-men: school-community projects that affirm and unsettle identities'. *British Journal of Sociology of Education*, 27, (1), 81–96.

Undervisningsministeriet – Folkeskoleafdelingen (1995) Samfundsfag (Faghæfte 5).

Vygotsky, L. S. (1978), *Mind in Society: The Development of Higher Psychological Processes* (eds M. Cole, V. John-Steiner, S. Scribner and E. Souberman). Cambridge, MA: Harvard University Press.

Vygotsky, L. (1986), *Thought and Language*. (ed. A. Kozulin). Cambridge, MA: MIT Press.

Wartofsky, M. (1973), *Models*. Dordrecht: D. Reide.

Wertsch, J. (1990), 'The voice of rationality in a sociocultural approach to mind', in L. Moll (ed.), *Vygotsky and Education*. Harvard, MA: Cambridge University Press, pp. 111–126.

Williams, R. (1961), *The Long Revolution*. London: Chatto and Windus.

Wrigley, T. (2000), *The Power to Learn: Stories of Success in the Education of Asian and Other Bilingual Pupils*. Stoke-on-Trent: Trentham Books.

— (2006), *Another School Is Possible*. London: Bookmarks.

— (2007), 'Projects, stories and challenges: more open architectures for school learning', in S. Bell, S. Harkness and G. White (eds), *Storyline – Past, Present and Future*. Glasgow: University of Strathclyde (Enterprising Careers), 166–81.

Yarker, P. (2008), '*Learning Without Limits* – a Marxist assessment: a response to Mike Cole' *Policy Futures in Education*, 6 (4), 464–468.

# Part Two

# The Subjects

Chapter 4

# Art and Design

## Paul Dash

This chapter problematizes[1] the teaching and learning of white working-class, female, lesbian, gay, bisexual and transgender (LGBT), and non-white learners in the art and design classroom. While looking at the process by which such groups are marginalized, the chapter exposes areas of exclusion with a relevance to all disadvantaged groups. An analysis of the centrality of capital to art-making practices in classrooms is also provided. It is hoped that teachers will find value in this text when planning and apply it to their own teaching schemes.

## The Background to Inclusion and the National Curriculum

Concern for the plight of children from different disadvantaged groups in education was provoked by the implementation of comprehensive education in the 1960s in English and Welsh secondary schools. In such schooling children of different abilities and social backgrounds were taught alongside one another. But comprehensive teaching while supported by some was viewed with suspicion by others. Melissa Benn, daughter of Tony and Caroline Benn,[2] in speaking of her own experience of such schooling, reflects on the horror of comprehensive education in the minds of some members of the middle classes:

> I am the child of a dream. Born in the late 1950s, at the very time when the fledgling comprehensive ideal was taking root, my three brothers and I were mostly educated at local state schools. Nothing particularly unusual about that – except that all four of us had been taken out of the private sector in order to 'do comprehensive', a decision made on the grounds of principle, not pragmatism, and one which at the time, provoked considerable public and private comment and, often, enormous consternation. (Benn and Chitty 2004, p. 21)

Comprehensive schooling threw into relief areas of need that were not so clearly apparent in selective education policies, which, until then, dominated educational provision in England and Wales. How, for example, could teachers comfortably operate in classroom environments where some secondary students were on course for Oxford entry examinations while others were struggling to cope with basic literacy (see John 2006)? With mass migration to Britain from the Caribbean and South Asia in the 1950s, to 1970s, the need for progressive pedagogies to better accommodate the differentiated learning needs of all pupils became even more urgent.

Recognition of the difficult circumstances faced by some disadvantaged groups in education was acknowledged in the publication in 1991 of the National Curriculum for art. Two sections in the document, entitled 'Art and the whole school curriculum' and 'Art for all', highlighted areas of teaching and learning with a bearing on specific, often under-represented groups in school communities. They listed 'Multicultural education', 'Education for minorities', 'Special educational needs' and 'Gender' as categories requiring enhanced resources. In a similar light the revised National Curriculum for England and Wales, published in 1999, placed great emphasis on equality of opportunity for learners. The section entitled 'Inclusion: providing effective learning opportunities for all children' is the longest in the document. Under the subheading 'Responding to pupils' diverse learning needs', it makes explicit recommendations for teaching young people from different social and political worlds, indicating that,

> When planning, teachers should set high opportunities for all pupils to achieve, including boys and girls, pupils with special educational needs, pupils with disabilities, pupils from all social and cultural backgrounds, pupils of different ethnic groups including travellers, refugees and asylum seekers, and those from diverse linguistic backgrounds. (p. 25)

It further emphasized the challenges children from different cultural contexts take into schools, calling on teachers to be mindful of the assessment strategies employed when working with children from diverse backgrounds. The art and design Programme of Study (POS) for Key Stage 3 (KS3) (11–14 year olds), the statutory order used in schools from September 2008, is far less prescriptive than previous national curricula. As in earlier versions, however, it requires teachers and schools to organize their teaching to take account of difference. It is apparent therefore that inclusion and equity should form a central plank in school art and design activity in England and Wales. To better engage these concerns, this chapter provides a historical background to the politics inherent to the educational experience of each of the listed groups and provides a brief overview of pertinent issues with relevance to their teaching in the present-day classroom. It starts with the politics of difference constructed by some in the project of white working-class alienation from the locus of power, an alienation that impacts on working-class pupil performance.

## White and Working Class – A Belated Recognition of an Invisible Minority

Critical voices with an interest in the plight of working-class learners today problematize concerns rooted in the history of rejection and marginalization that influences their performance in the classroom (see Willis 1990; John 2006; Cole 2008). In 'The forgotten people', a preview of BBC television's 'White' season, Sarfraz Manzoor (2008) highlighted issues pertinent to white working-class disaffection. He noted that, 'In the past few years ... with the orthodoxy on multiculturalism unravelling, and the arrival of a new wave of immigrants from eastern Europe, their grumblings have begun to be noticed' (p. 9, col. 1, *Media Guardian*). Quoting the commissioning editor for the series, Richard Klein, Manzoor continued, 'the aim of the season is to "question what has happened to Britain's white working class during a sustained period of great change which has swept the country ... there is a clear mood that their voices are not being heard"' (*ibid.*).

The underperformance of white working-class boys in school examinations has served only to emphasize the challenges that many working-class pupils face in present-day school settings. If the voices of such pupils are to be heard in the art and design classroom, teachers should devise pedagogies that present opportunities for them to share their views from their own subject positions. As such, it is in critical and contextual studies, the discourse of learning to question through practice, that contemporary art could play a key role in white middle-class pupil learning.

Burgess and Addison (2004) assert that contemporary art often refuses classification (see also Dawe Lane 1996) while Adams (2005) contends that contemporary practices 'inevitably elide the boundaries between author, spectator, producer, and participant, and call into question individual agency itself' (p. 24). Downing and Watson (2004) circumvent a clear description of such approaches, asserting instead that 'The definition of what constituted contemporary art practice, or of a school that demonstrated a commitment to this, was left entirely to those identifying the schools' (p. 5). In providing a framework for postmodern art education from 1990 to the present, Efland *et al.* (1996) state that such practices:

- Recycle contents and methods from modern and premodern forms of instruction.
- Feature the mini-narratives of various persons or groups not represented by the canons of master artists.

- Explain the effects of power in validating art knowledge.
- Use arguments grounded in deconstruction to show that no point of view is privileged.
- Recognize that works of art are multiply coded within several symbol systems. (p. 72)

In keeping with this Downing and Watson (2004) contend that contemporary art provides an opportunity 'for the exploration of social, moral and political issues and recognition of art as a visual communication tool' (p. 5). Pedagogies that draw on such artistic practices test conventions of creative engagement in classrooms and traditional means of assessment. Many may have an overt or implicit political dimension that delegate the power of voice to each individual participant or group of collaborators. It is this democratization of practice that problematizes previous givens regarding social and aesthetic values, alongside notions of self and other, truth and untruth.

As argued here, progressive pedagogies in art that empower young people's critiques of visual artworks, literature and the present-day media could offer white working-class and other marginalized learners a voice for debating issues with relevance to their lives. But in exploring issues of marginalization in the classroom, concerns about the power of capital and its position at the heart of visual art practices must also be acknowledged.

## Capitalism and Art Practice

The arts in the West have traditionally been associated with wealthy patrons and powerful organizations. The Medici family in fifteenth- and sixteenth-century Florence were models of such artistic patronage (Cronin 1969). They commissioned important artworks and maintained the careers of some of the greatest artists of the period. Similarly, the Catholic Church, arguably the most powerful of all patrons, contracted Michelangelo, Raphael, Titian, Leonardo da Vinci and other leading artists of the day to produce work, much of which have become icons in the history of Western art. Today, wealthy institutions and individuals such as the Rothschild banking family, Saatchi and John Paul Getty III continue the practice of arts sponsorship by the rich. It can be seen therefore that the history of art in Europe is indivisible from Western financial success and power. But artists, even in our capitalist environment, while benefiting from the patronage of the wealthy, frequently use their art as a medium with which to highlight social inequalities and corporate exploitation.

Several Pop artists in the 1960s and 1970s made pieces that interrogated the culture of mass production: 'The act of purchasing ... modern hunting and gathering' (Grundenberg and Hollein 2002, p. 13). Tom Wesselmann, Roy Lichtenstein, Claus Oldenburg among others problematized Western consumerist culture in work that foregrounded issues of material gain and waste and the chicanery commensurate with modern-day advertising. I think, too, of Andy Warhol's look at the ostentatious world of Hollywood pop idolatry, exemplified in the representation of Marilyn Monroe as 'product' (Batchelor 1996). Through their eyes we looked again at the world of production, the use of the media as a form of social control, the demand for greater and greater sales and profits (see also Grundenberg and Hollein 2002).

Today, in many contexts, the wheels of production turn on the spending power of the young. On MTV gyrating pop icons dripping with glitzy jewellery engage the camera from a fantasy world to which their fans and admirers aspire. In contradistinction to this, socially grounded artists such as Banksy[3] pay little regard to mainstream patronage or the power of capital. Banksy's art, in emerging from the street to the respectability of the high-art establishment, parallels the achievements of Jean-Michel Basquiat (Wilkinson 2008). It demonstrates how ordinary artists, often untrained, can have an impact in exclusive environments where the wealthy have sway. Other graffiti art in New York, Barcelona and elsewhere reveal a similar grounded aesthetic which can play an important part in the lives of the wider populace, outside the realm of gallery displays.

John Johnston (2005) reveals the important role public murals can play in troubled, often impecunious social settings. A Catholic, his account of working with Protestant youth in Northern Ireland highlights the politics of representation inherent to socially generated artefacts in polarized communities. Tim Rollins' youth arts collective Kids of Survival (KOS), in which disadvantaged young people are empowered to make artwork about key issues that impact on their lives, could in this regard be a model of good practice for young people elsewhere (see Rollins 2005). 198 Gallery in South London is also doing groundbreaking work in schemes for marginalized youth in the London Borough of Lambeth (Bayode and Davies 2005). Equally significant is the work generated by the young contributors to Room 13, an enterprise run entirely by children, in which the young people involved speak of their experience in pieces that have attracted worldwide critical acclaim (Adams 2005) (for more on these initiatives see Atkinson and Dash 2005). Work at these centres evolved from the commitment of visionary educators determined to liberate young people's creativity and personal voice. In a similar vein, the people of Haiti, though living in a deeply impoverished State, make murals that are a popular response to local imperatives. Theirs is an art that gives voice to the hopes, fears and aspirations of a community subsisting in conditions of enormous challenge. Such initiatives and contexts, which (with the possible exception of Room 13) lay outside the realm of large-scale capitalist influence, demonstrate that by contributing to issues with a bearing on the community, and by celebrating the voice of the participants themselves, popular artistic activity can empower 'ordinary' people including school students. The next section, while exploring gender concerns, particularly with reference to the marginalization of girls, also reminds the reader of the linkage between education, gender, capital and power.

## Girls in Art and Design Education

In the nineteenth and even much of the twentieth century the education of girls in art classrooms was shaped by perceived differences in gender roles and attitudes to class (Swift 1999). With the emergence of the women's liberation movement in the latter part of the twentieth century, and the growing popularity of critical and contextual studies in art education, women artists and critical voices in the women's liberation movement have highlighted the objectification of women in wider society and the degree to which this impacts on teaching and learning concerns. But in order to better appreciate the significance of this critical work, we need to be acquainted with the way in which the marginalization and objectification of women were at times subsumed into wider organizational frameworks both in the world of work and in education.

Dalton (2001) quotes Thistlewood (1993), who summarized a perceived division in art education in which:

> There was a tacit distinction between the 'higher' discipline of teaching drawing and design and the 'lower' discipline of teaching art. The former was associated with national economic purposes and aspired to academic respectability; the latter connoted 'play' and rather modest learning. The National Society of Art Masters encouraged its members to pursue high levels of technical accomplishment as measured by its own examination system ... The Art Teachers Guild on the other hand was much more concerned with tactical approaches necessary for encouraging an essential creativity ... in children not specifically destined for an aesthetic way of life. (Dalton 2001, p. 59)

In analysing this text Dalton suggests that 'What Thistlewood did not make explicit was that this division of teaching Art was clearly gendered: the National Society of Schoolmasters, as its name suggests, was a male institution, while the Art teachers Guilds recruited women of "modest learning"' (*ibid.*). This viewpoint was presaged the previous year in Section 11 of the National Curriculum, which stated that:

A study of the subject matter of art can contribute significantly to helping pupils challenge traditional attitudes towards issues of marginalisation such as gender concerns. They can consider how masculinity and femininity are pictured, both in fine art and in popular culture. They can look for similarities and differences and examine any recurrence of stereotypical forms; for example, by exploring the extent to which men are frequently portrayed as active while women are portrayed as passive; men are surveying, women being surveyed. (p. 60, col. 2)

Since the 1970s much has gone on in the struggle for acceptance of women's voices in fine art arenas. Harris (1996) acknowledges this in asserting that

by 1970 groups and alliances of women working as artists, critics and historians had sprung up on both sides of the Atlantic Ocean. In New York for instance, an ad hoc committee of Women Artists was formed in 1970to protest at the marginalised five per cent of women exhibited in the annual survey exhibition of art held at the Whitney Museum of American Art. (pp. 149–150)

Barber (1996) contends that changing attitudes in art appreciation in the West has provided new opportunities for women to make work about their own identities, even in environments where women still suffer an imbalance of opportunity. She argues that 'the shift towards previously marginalized forms of representation has provided a language for the exploration of their own identities as culturally marginal' (p. 156, col. 2).

Cindy Sherman's take on the gaze in photographic pieces, over-layered with concerns of objectification and desire, sheds new light on how we view works of art from different sexualized and social standpoints (see *Untitled* 1982 in the Tate Modern collection). Similarly, Tracy Emin's depictions of sexual exploitation in images such as *I've Got It All* (2000) highlights the way women are positioned by male desire and power. Such politically committed artists expose the structures through which stereotypes are produced with a bearing on women's representation. A balanced education should ensure that children engage with such practices in order to disrupt the givens through which they and the rest of us in society are produced as subjects.

The politics of resistance mounted by women activists and artists in the arts from the 1970s to the present day has resonances for lesbian, gay, bisexual and transgender (LGBT) learners. As Harris contends, 'Campaigns for equal rights and pay for women, along with the call for free abortion on demand and adequate child care facilities, became linked to emergent gay and lesbian political struggles' (1996, p. 149). With this in mind, I will now look at the representation of LGBT groups in art and design educational discourses.

# Lesbian, Gay, Bisexual and Transgender (LGBT) Students in Education

Few learners experience greater hostility or uncertainty about schooling than LGBT students (Addison 2007; Stanley 2007). Hetero-normative environments exert a pressure to conform that can stifle or deny their difference. McKenzie-Bassant (2007) articulates this sense of isolation in a paper culled from her experience at a teachers' in-service training (INSET) day. During the training day she proposed that 'homophobia' should 'be included on a list of words being compiled as part of a discussion about attitudes that hinder teamwork among teachers' (p. 55, col. 1). She suggests that

> The overwhelming response of my colleagues was to leap to the defence of heterosexism by concluding that I must be a lesbian, since the teachers who raise homophobia as an issue must themselves be lesbian or gay, and therefore not normal. (*ibid.*)

Many LGBT learners in schools are similarly isolated and fearful of disclosure in environments where being perceived as lesbian, gay, bisexual or transgender can have serious consequences (Stanley 2007). Yet it is in the art and design classroom that teachers should offer a context where such young people can talk about their identities, and share perspectives on issues with a vital bearing on their well-being. But teachers of art, themselves conditioned by exposure to heterosexist 'normative' values, are reluctant, fearful or simply lack the skill to address these issues confidently or meaningfully (McKenzie-Bassant 2007; Stanley 2007). Addison (2007), however, opines that homophobia in classroom discourses can be successfully tackled by 'engaging students in discussion and investigative practices' (p. 15, col. 1). He argues for a pedagogy in which learners explore notions of identity that are fluid and boundary crossing. These encode 'identities based on age, class, disability, ethnicity, gender, nationality, politics, religion, sexual orientation' (*ibid.*). Such fluid boundary-crossing pedagogies, which position diversity and difference as normative and non-discriminatory, lend themselves, I argue, to issues-based approaches in art and design classrooms. As such they raise concerns about teaching styles and even the availability of appropriate media for making. From Stanley's (2007) viewpoint, 'lesbian and gay art education necessarily involves many different media, and in particular conventions and approaches derived from cinema' (p. 7, col. 2). He regards irony and parody as key elements in the building of meaningful schemes with a bearing on lesbian and gay experience, citing the 'epigrams of Mae West and Oscar Wilde ... the bite in their humour' and the 'upturning of taken-for-granted sexual mores' (p. 4, col. 1). Lens-based activities in school classrooms are at the cutting edge of relevant present-day art educational practices. Immersed in such technologies, young people naturally take to them in classroom activities. Whether employing mobile phones or camcorders for movie-making, engaging in computer-based practices or merely reflecting on the significance of television in their lives, they have potentialities that would be liberated through engagement with such technologies that should transform the possibilities for talking about difficult issues. These new approaches and the re-alignments they could promote, both in the use of media and in our attitude to difference, should be central to the challenge to all discriminatory practices in teaching and learning arenas including multicultural pedagogies.

## Multicultural Education – A Platform for Inclusive Teaching

Several experts in the field have listed categories of teaching in art and design that could be described as multicultural (among them Grigsby 1977; Mason 1985; Troyna 1992; Efland *et al.* 1996; McFee 1998; Moore 1999; Emery 2002, Dash 2005; Richardson 2005). In referencing Zimmerman and Stuhr, Chalmers (1996) posits five models of multicultural teaching:

- The first approach is simply to add lessons and units with some ethnic content.
- The second approach focuses on cross-cultural celebrations, such as holiday art, and is intended to foster classroom goodwill and harmony.
- The third approach emphasizes the art of particular groups – for example, African American art or women's art – for reasons of equity and social justice.
- The fourth approach tries to reflect socio-cultural diversity in a curriculum designed to be both multiethnic and multicultural.
- The fifth approach, decision-making and social action, requires teachers and students to move beyond acknowledgement of diversity and to question and challenge the dominant culture's art world canons and structures. In this approach, art education becomes an agent for social reconstruction, and students get involved in studying and using art to expose and challenge all types of oppression. Although this last approach may not be multicultural per se, students will probably be dealing with issues that cross many cultural boundaries. (p. 45)

When planning projects that build on approaches from other traditions, teachers of art often draw on the first two models, which correlate with Troyna's (1992) definition of assimilationist and integrationist policies (see also Swift 1996). Evidence of this can be seen in schemes where cultural materials from the backgrounds of students in the classroom are used to foster goodwill (Efland *et al.* 1996, p. 79), a policy described by Troyna (1992) as 'the 3Ss interpretation of multicultural education (Saris, Samosas, and Steel bands)' (see also Mirza 2005). The third approach will often engage students in study that draws on practices from another tradition in in-depth enquiry. Such approaches would question long-standing viewpoints and assumptions by meaningful exposure to the work of others. Benin bronzes, Egyptian art, Indian rickshaws, artefacts generated by the Mexican 'Day of the Dead' and Aboriginal paintings are resources frequently used in such approaches, pedagogies described by Efland *et al.* (1996) as 'a haphazard inclusion of various cultures' (p. 43). The fourth approach, as I understand it, draws on materials produced by people from different cultural heritages, without necessarily challenging societal structures and 'norms' that under-gird ethnic division. It is an approach that places at the forefront of teaching and learning, the celebration of differences in religious activity, cuisine, the use of language, the literature and arts of a people. Such teaching styles would therefore offer more holistic approaches to the type of 'multicultural' activities represented in the first three models. They have at their core a notion of radical reconstruction that could have critical implications for all students. Antiracism, a radical movement for change which has emerged from this discourse, by its project of meaningful access and fair representation for black learners, throws a spotlight on other forms of exclusion.

## Antiracist Education

Antiracism, despite its more militant profile, is at times subsumed into multiculturalism (see Gillborn 1995). In assessing antiracist strategies in education, John (2006) opines that 'Antiracism concerns itself with structural issues in a way that multicultural education does not. Moreover, it seeks to challenge institutional practices and individual acts which derive from an ideology of racism' (p. 106). Indeed, as he contends, the curriculum itself needs to be transformed if antiracism is not to be perceived as 'clinical sanitizing of existing nasties' and a useful tool 'of conflict management and little more' (*ibid.*, p. 107). Redesigning the curriculum to better celebrate the central contributions of non-European subjects to world civilizations and more especially to the West, therefore, would require a complete re-conceptualization of how teaching and learning is done (see also Cole 2008 for a discussion of the history of 'race' and education, and arguments for the promotion of both antiracism and antiracism multiculturalism). As a pedagogical approach in art education, deconstruction offers the teacher of art opportunities for making even the most culturally discordant material relevant to the lives of children from different groups. As such it presents opportunities for antiracist teaching. The next section will look in greater depth at the politics of teaching for inclusion through the adoption of techniques of deconstruction.

# Deconstruction: A Strategy for Teaching and Learning in the Present-Day Art and Design Classroom

Deconstruction as a mode of artistic enquiry in contemporary arenas, when student-centred, draws on individual interpretations of a given subject which could be used by creative teachers to encourage personal responses to a theme, concept or artefact. Emery (2002) states that 'deconstruction is a tool for examining texts and images to reveal the meaning systems upon which the work is based' (p. 49), while Efland *et al.* (1996) see 'deconstruction' as action 'to unearth hidden, oppressive elements in democratic society' (p. 28). They further assert that

> Deconstruction was developed by Derrida to reveal the multiple meanings, especially the contradictions, of literary texts ... In some cases, deconstruction involves a 'turning upside down' of old myths that have been taken-for-granted and the 'unpacking' of social constructs that have become so embedded in society as to appear natural. This process can be helpful in illustrating the fragility of meaning and the relation of truth to power. (*ibid.*)

Taken literally, the unpicking of meanings embedded in Manet's *Olympia* (1863) that problematizes the gaze and the symbolic system of codes inherent to it, would constitute a critical act of deconstruction (see Boime 1990). I think of Keith Piper's analysis of the politics of the Slave Trade in *An English Queen* (1991), or Georgia Belfont's *Re-Evaluating Olympia* (1987–8), a work which posits a re-positioning of the black woman's presence in Manet's 'Olympia' (1865) (for more on the Black Art movement in the UK, see Chambers 1989). Similarly, analyses of Tracey Moffatt's *Homemade Hand-Knit*, which engages issues of exclusion and difference (1958) (see website details), could provide teachers with wonderful opportunities to address almost any form of discrimination. Such activity should aid understanding of what it means to be ostracized and subjected to prejudice of any sort. It is by the adoption of such methods, possibly in discourses of contemporary practices, that important work could be done to promote respect for all through a celebration of difference.

## Conclusion

This chapter looked at the historical background to exclusion with a bearing on the learning of marginalized communities in the art classroom. It also raised the issue of teaching styles and the types of pedagogic approaches that could bring benefits to all young people in art and design classrooms. Several approaches were analysed, and I concluded that issues-based pedagogies that allowed students a voice in determining lesson content had the potential to engage all learners in progressive classroom-based activity. To this end, five multicultural frameworks listed in Chalmers (1996) were analysed. The last, decision-making and social action, I contend, offers a rationale for pedagogies that challenges the boundaries of multiculturalism per se and is a model for teaching that places all children at the centre of learning.

In seeking ways of making the teaching of art and design relevant to the spread of children in the modern-day classroom, teachers of art could therefore draw on contemporary issues-based artwork in designing frameworks for making. Such work offers a potpourri of voices and approaches from traditionally marginalized groups. It is for teachers committed to meaningful representation of students in art to devise pedagogies that would allow such teaching and learning to take place. Their solidarity with excluded subjects, exemplified in their pedagogic style, is essential if diverse identities are to be acknowledged and suitable teaching methods formulated to accommodate the pupils' rights to social justice.

## Notes

1   Problematize, as I use it, means to distinguish as an issue.
2   Tony Benn is from an aristocratic family. A socialist and senior British politician who became a cabinet minister in the Wilson and Callaghan government (see Benn and Chitty 2004), he and his late wife Caroline, herself a leading socialist, broke with tradition by sending their children to the local comprehensive school rather than a private school.
3   Banksy is something of a phantom figure who makes witty graffiti murals in public places but is rarely seen making them. His work is celebrated for its wit, irony and high technical accomplishment.

## References

Adams, J. (2005), 'Room 13 and the contemporary practice of artist-learners', in *Studies in Art Education*, 47, (1), Fall 2005, National Art Education Association.

Addison, N. (2007), 'Identity politics and the queering of art education: inclusion and the confessional route to salvation', in N. Stanley (ed.), 'Lesbian and gay issues in art, design and media education'. *JADE*, 26, (1), 10–20.

Art and Design (1999), *The National Curriculum for England*. London: QCA.

— (2008), *The National Curriculum for England*. London: QCA.

Art for Ages 5 to 14 (1991), 'Proposals of the Secretary of State for Education and Science and the Secretary of State for Wales'. *The National Curriculum*. DES and COI, HMSO.

Atkinson, D. (2002), *Art in Education: Identity and Practice*. Klewer Academic Publishers: Dordrecht, Boston and London.

— and Dash, P. (eds) (2005), *Social and Critical Practices in Art Education* (eds D. Atkinson, and P. Dash). Stoke-on-Trent and Sterling, USA: Trentham Books.

Barber, F. (1996), 'Shifting practices: new trends in representation since the 1970s', in *Investigating Modern Art* (eds L. Dawtrey, T. Jackson, M. Masterton, P. Meecham and P. Wood). The Open University.

Batchelor, D. (1996), 'Modernity and tradition: Warhol and Andre', in *Investigating Modern Art* (eds L. Dawtrey, T. Jackson, M. Masterton, P. Meecham and P. Wood). Yale University Press.

Bayode F. and Davies, L. (2005), 'The 198 Gallery', in D. Atkinson, and P. Dash (eds), *Social and Critical Practices in Art Education*. Stoke-on-Trent and Sterling, USA: Trentham Books.

Benn, M. and Chitty, C. (eds) (2004), *A Tribute to Caroline Benn: Education and Democracy*. London and New York: Continuum.

Boime, A. (1990), *The Art of Exclusion: Representing Blacks in the Nineteenth Century*. London: Thames and Hudson.

Burgess, L. and Addison, N. (2004), 'Contemporary art in schools: why bother?', in *Art Education 11-18: Meaning, Purpose and Direction* (ed. R. Hickman). London and New York: Continuum.

Chalmers, G. (1996), *Celebrating Pluralism: Art, Education and Cultural Diversity*. Los Angeles: The Getty Education Institute for the Arts.

Chambers, E. (1989), *Black Art: Plotting the Course*. Wolverhampton Leisure Services and Oldham Leisure Services.

Cole, M. (2008), 'Antiracist education', in G. McCulloch and D. Crook (eds), *The Routledge International Encyclopedia of Education*. Routledge: London.

Cronin, V. (1969), *The Flowering of the Renaissance*. London: History Book Club with Collins Publishers.

Dalton, P. (2001), *The Gendering of Art Education: Modernism, Identity and Critical Feminism*. Buckingham and Philadelphia: Open University Press.

Dash, P. (2005), 'Cultural demarcation, the African Diaspora and art education', in *Social and Critical Practices in Art Education* (eds D. Atkinson and P. Dash). Stoke-on-Trent and Sterling, USA: Trentham Books.

Dawe Lane, L. (1996) 'Using contemporary art', in L. Dawtrey *et al* (eds), *Critical Studies and Modern Art*. Yale University Press in Association with The Open University, the Arts Council of England and the Tate Gallery London.

Downing, D. and Watson, R. (2004), *School Art: What's in It?: Exploring Visual Arts in Secondary Schools*. NFER: Berkshire.

Efland, A., Freedman, K. and Stuhr, P. (1996), *Postmodern Art Education: An Approach to Curriculum*. Virginia: The National Art Education Association.

Emery, L. (2002), *Teaching Art in a Postmodern World*. Altona, Victoria: Common Ground.

Gillborn, D. (1995), *Racism and Antiracism in Real Schools*. Buckingham and Philadelphia: Open University Press.

Grigsby Jr, J. (1977), *Art and Ethnics: Background for Teaching Youth in a Pluralistic Society*. Arizona: Wm. C. Brown Company, Arizona State University.

Grundenberg, C. and Hollein, M. (eds) (2002), *Shopping: A Century of Art and Consumer Culture*. Frankfurt: Hatje Cantz Publishers.

Harris, J. (1996), 'Visual cultures of opposition', in *Investigating Modern Art* (eds L. Dawtrey, T. Jackson, M. Masterton, P. Meecham and P. Wood). Yale University Press.

John, G. (2006), *Taking a Stand: Gus John Speaks on Education, Race, Social Action and Civil Unrest 1980 – 2005.* Manchester: Gus John Partnership.

Johnston, J. (2005), 'Art in contentious spaces', in D. Atkinson and P. Dash (eds), *Social and Critical Practices in Art Education.* Stoke-on-Trent and Sterling USA: Trentham Books.

Manzoor, S. (2008), 'The forgotten people'. *Guardian* (3 March).

Mason, R. (1985), *Art Education and Multiculturalism.* Bristol: NSEAD.

— (1996), 'Beyond tokenism: towards criteria for evaluating the quality of multicultural curricula', in L. Dawtrey (ed.) (1996), *Critical Studies and Modern Art.* Yale University Press in Association with The Open University, the Arts Council of England and the Tate Gallery London.

McFee, J. K. (1998), *Cultural Diversity and the Structures and Practice of Art Education.* Oregon: National Art Education Association.

McKenzie-Bassant, C. (2007), 'Lesbian teachers walking the line between inclusion and exposure', in N. Stanley (ed.), 'Lesbian and gay issues in art, design and media education'. *JADE*, 26, (1), 54–62.

Mirza, H. (2005), 'The more things change, the more they stay the same: assessing black underachievement 35 years on', in B. Richardson (ed.), *Tell It like It Is: How Our Schools Fail Black Children.* London: Bookmarks Publications and Trentham Books.

Moffatt, T. (nd), Roslyn Oxley9 Gallery. Available at www.roslynnoxley9.com/artists/26/tracey_moffatt/60/32659/.

Moore, A. (1999), *Teaching Multicultured Students, Culturism and Anti-Culturism in School Classrooms.* London and New York: Falmer Press.

Richardson, B. (ed.) (2005), *Tell It Like It Is: How Our Schools Fail Black Children.* London: Bookmarks Publications and Trentham Books.

Rollins, T. (2005), 'One's joy in one's labour', in D. Atkinson and P. Dash (eds), *Social and Critical Practices in Art Education.* Stoke-on-Trent and Sterling, USA: Trentham Books.

Stanley, N. (2007), 'Preface: "Anything you can do": proposals for lesbian and gay art education', in N. Stanley (ed.), 'Lesbian and gay issues in art, design and media education'. *JADE*, 26, (1), 2–9.

Swift, J. (1996), 'Critical studies: a Trojan Horse for an alternative critical agenda?', in L. Dawtrey (ed.), *Critical Studies and Modern Art.* New Haven and London: Yale University Press and The Open University.

Swift, J. (1999), 'Women and art education at Birmingham's art schools 1880–1920: social class, opportunity and aspiration'. JADE, 18, (3), 317–26.

Troyna, B. (1992), 'Can you see the join? An historical analysis of multicultural and antiracist education policies', in D. Gill, B. Mayor and M. Blair (eds), *Racism and Education Structures and Strategies.* London, Newbury Park and Delhi: SAGE Publications.

Wilkinson, C. (ed.) (2008), *The Observer Book of Art.* London: Observer Books.

Willis, P. (1990), *Common Culture.* Milton Keynes: Open University Press.

Chapter 5

# Citizenship

## Dina Kiwan

This chapter provides a brief historical background to the statutory introduction of citizenship at Key Stage 3 (KS3) (ages 11–14) and Key Stage 4 (KS4) (ages 14–16) in England, before examining issues of ethnic and religious diversity, gender and sexuality, age and disability, as well as social class, and environmental issues in relation to citizenship. Relevant policy and curriculum documentation are critically analysed using these frames of reference, with some case study material used to exemplify some of these issues. The chapter concludes with some theoretical recommendations, and recommendations for practice.

## A Brief Historical Background

By definition citizenship has historically been an exclusionary concept with only a certain subset of people within society considered to be citizens (Heater 1990). For example, ancient Greek conceptions of citizenship were conceived of as a privilege, not just excluding women, but also excluding various other categories of men – the very young, the very old, and those of certain occupations (*ibid.*). With the relatively recent expansion of citizenship to include all members of society, it has become increasingly pertinent to examine citizenship and diversity in a theoretically more explicit and integrated way (e.g. Kymlicka 1995; Parekh 2000).

Citizenship education in England can typically be traced back to the nineteenth-century Victorian context where education in general had clear social and moral purposes: private schools playing a role of preparing the upper classes for leadership in England and the Empire, in contrast to education for the poor serving a quite different purpose – in effect, teaching them to accept their position in society, with a clear moral purpose (Batho 1990; Lawton 2000).

Throughout the twentieth century, there have been ongoing debates about the best way to teach citizenship. In the 1920s, it was widely thought that citizenship should be taught through traditional school subjects such as history, geography and religious knowledge, referred to as the 'indirect training' approach (Lawton 2000). But by the 1930s, a 'direct training' approach was being advocated, with a more traditional 'civics' curriculum involving a study of British institutions and outlining related rights and duties, rather than teaching citizenship in context.

The Council for Curriculum Reform used this approach in its recommendation of 'social studies' as a compulsory subject; however, throughout the 1950s and 1960s, social studies had low status, associated with lower achievers (Batho 1990). Up until the 1960s, the focus had been on teaching social studies or citizenship to older students, but some advocated much earlier teaching, for example Bernard Crick – who was involved in the Programme for Political Education (PPE) in the 1970s (Davies 1999; Lawton 2000). The focus of this programme was to develop critical knowledge and promote skills for active participation (Crick and Porter 1978). However, this political literacy project did not come to fruition with the Conservatives coming into power in 1979. Throughout the 1980s, a range of new grassroots education programmes broadly committed to social justice developed, for example peace education, anti-sexist education and antiracist education, reflecting wider public debates (Davies 1999).

After the 1988 Education Reform Act introducing the National Curriculum, the National Curriculum Council (NCC) proposed citizenship as one of a number of cross-curricular themes. But as this was non-statutory, it got squeezed out of the curriculum (Lawton 2000). In the 1990s, Nick Tate, Chief Executive of the Schools Curriculum and Assessment Authority (SCAA) (later to become the Qualifications and Curriculum Authority (QCA)), argued that the National Curriculum should play a key role in fostering a national identity and 'social cohesion' (Beck 1998). With traditionalists expressing concerns that religion no longer provided an agreed morality framework in multicultural Britain (*ibid.*), SCAA set up the National Forum for Values in Education and the Community in order to discover what society's shared values might be.

A key turning point occurred with the 1998 policy review of citizenship education carried out by the Advisory Group on Education for Citizenship and the Teaching of Democracy in Schools, chaired by Sir Bernard Crick. This group was set up by David Blunkett (then Secretary of State for Education) in 1997, and managed by QCA, following the decision to strengthen the teaching of citizenship in schools, as outlined in the 1997 education White Paper 'Excellence in schools' (Kerr 2000). The advisory group was made up of practitioners, teachers, members of relevant organizations, as well as those with political expertise.

The Crick Report recommended that citizenship education be a statutory 'entitlement', and also that it would be a separate subject in the curriculum (QCA 1998). Citizenship was defined in terms of three strands – social and moral responsibility, community involvement, and political literacy, making reference to T. H. Marshall's conceptualization of citizenship as being made up of three elements – civil, political and social citizenship (Marshall and Bottomore 1992). The earlier emphasis on 'shared values' – the primary focus of the National Forum for Values, was subsequently downplayed in the Crick Report (QCA 1998). The proposed learning outcomes in the curriculum materials, the Programmes of Study, and Schemes of Work are presented in terms of three categories: 'knowledge and understanding', 'skills of enquiry and communication', and 'skills of participation and responsible action' (QCA 2000; 2001). The key recommendations of the Crick Report were accepted by government, and 'citizenship' was introduced as a new statutory foundation subject in secondary schools, and part of the non-statutory framework within Personal, Social and Health Education (PSHE) in primary schools in September 2002.

As was the case in the 1990s, it is of note that discourses of 'shared values', national identity and community cohesion continue to be dominant, although framed in relation to the UK's ethnic and religious diversity, and linked to discourses on immigration, naturalization and security concerns (Kiwan 2008). In 2006, reflecting these concerns, the Department for Education and Schools (DfES) (now Department for Children, Schools and Families (DCSF)) commissioned a review of diversity and citizenship, which the government framed in terms of concerns with community cohesion, and linked to discourses on identity and diversity, 'shared values' and 'Britishness' (Rammell 2006). This report, which I co-authored with Sir Keith Ajegbo and was published in January 2007, recommended the addition of a fourth strand, entitled 'Identity and diversity: living together in the UK' (Ajegbo *et al.* 2007). This has been incorporated into the newly drafted QCA Programmes of Study (QCA 2007a; 2007b), introduced in schools from September 2008. The following section on ethnic and religious diversity examines the changing constructions of citizenship with regard to issues of ethnic and religious diversity over the past decade, explicated in relation to the broader social and political context.

## Ethnic and Religious Diversity

The dominant conception of citizenship in the original Crick Report (QCA 1998) is one that emphasizes active participation. This contrasts with the relatively underplayed 'identity-based' conceptions of citizenship addressing issues of antiracism, multiculturalism, nationality, and global and European aspects of citizenship (Kiwan 2008). Ethnic and religious diversity in relation to citizenship was typically presented as politically problematic. According to Tony Breslin, head of the Citizenship Foundation, the downplaying of issues of ethnic and religious diversity was due to political sensitivities at the time. Proposing citizenship education as a statutory requirement in secondary schools was deemed to be already controversial enough – with fears of political indoctrination in schools – without in addition introducing potentially sensitive or controversial issues relating to ethnic and religious diversity in the context.

In conceptual terms, Crick's reticence with regard to the accommodation of ethnic and religious diversity into a conception of citizenship is perhaps paradoxical given that he defines the nature of politics in terms of: 'Politics arises from accepting the fact of the simultaneous existence of different groups, hence different interests and different traditions, within a territorial unit under a common rule' (Crick 2000, p. 18). One explanation is that while Crick recognizes political diversity or indeed differences in social class, he does not recognize ethnic or religious diversity as relevant in his civic republican understanding of citizenship – where ethnic and religious identities are seen to be private identities to be kept out of the public sphere.

In the Crick Report (QCA 1998), diversity is conceived as a potential barrier to citizenship, rather than as an integral aspect of it. The report proposes a 'common citizenship' to create 'common ground' in the context of such ethnic and religious diversity. There is an emphasis on integration into a shared *political* culture, with a focus on shared commitment to political institutions and laws proposed: 'minorities must learn and respect the laws, codes and conventions as much as the majority ... because this process helps foster common citizenship' (*ibid.*, pp. 17–18). Yet the presentation of integration as a one-way process has been criticized for assuming a deficit model of minorities (Osler 2000). In addition, reference to the binary conceptualization of diversity as majority–minority might suggest that the political integration of 'minorities' into the mainstream 'majority' is relatively unproblematic and is mainly an issue of minorities acquiring political knowledge and abiding by the law (Kiwan 2008).

While diversity was primarily perceived to be a problem in relation to the outlined conception of citizenship in the Crick Report (QCA 1998), this is not so apparent in the Programmes of Study (QCA 2000) and the Schemes of Work (QCA 2001). For example, in the KS3 Programmes of Study, diversity is presented in terms of 'the need for mutual respect and understanding' (QCA 2000). However, in terms of pedagogical approach, diversity is only explicitly addressed under the 'knowledge and understanding' learning outcome with students being 'taught about' such 'diversity of ... identities', rather than in terms of acquiring skills (*ibid.*). This suggests a rather passive acceptance of a description of the status quo, rather than an active engagement with the issues (Kiwan 2008).

Of note, there are no references linking antiracism to citizenship in the Crick Report (QCA 1998). In addition, there is no explicit reference to antiracism in the KS3 and KS4 Programmes of Study (QCA 2000). In the KS3 Schemes of Work, antiracism is referred to in Unit 4: 'Britain – a diverse society?', although this is not developed substantively. The learning expectations in Unit 4 for 'most pupils' do not contain any explicit reference to antiracism; instead, there is the concept of 'the importance of respect for all' (QCA 2001, Unit 4, p. 1). Antiracism is included implicitly in recommended resources, through references to websites such as 'Kick racism out of football campaign', 'Show racism the red card', and the QCA 'Respect for all' – where diversity and antiracist education through the curriculum are listed.

As noted in the background section of this chapter, the citizenship education curriculum has recently undergone a review. The remit for the DCSF Diversity and Citizenship Review was to 'review the teaching of ethnic, religious and cultural diversity across the curriculum to age 19, and in relation to Citizenship, explore particularly whether or not "modern British social and cultural history" should be a fourth pillar of the Citizenship curriculum' (Ajegbo *et al.* 2007, p. 14). This was launched publicly in May 2006, by minister Bill Rammell, and linked to issues of 'community cohesion', identity and diversity and 'shared British values'.

In our report, we recommended a fourth strand, entitled 'Identity and diversity: living together in the UK'. Five sub-themes are highlighted as important areas to include:

1. understanding that the UK is a 'multinational' state, made up of England, Northern Ireland, Scotland and Wales
2. immigration
3. Commonwealth and the legacy of Empire
4. European Union
5. extending the franchise (e.g. legacy of slavery, universal suffrage, equal opportunities legislation).

With regard to pedagogical approaches, we emphasized the importance of the processes of communication and dialogue in relation to contemporary issues with regard to 'shared values' and 'Britishness', as opposed to trying to 'teach' or inculcate an abstract list of values. In addition, we stressed the importance that the active participative nature of citizenship education be retained, but that this also be explicitly linked to issues of identity, and where appropriate, drawing on relevant historical material.

The government welcomed the recommendations of the report and QCA has since produced revised Programmes of Study for Citizenship at KS3 and KS4 (QCA 2007a; 2007b), in practice in secondary schools from September

2008. 'Identity and diversity: living together in the UK' is one of three key concepts along with 'democracy and justice' and 'rights and responsibilities'. In addition, a 'Who do we think we are?' week, a recommendation from the Diversity and Citizenship Curriculum Review, exploring identity, diversity and citizenship across the curriculum, was launched in secondary schools in June 2008. There is also a requirement for schools to actively promote community cohesion, inspected from September 2008. This emphasis on the privileging of 'shared values' or 'unity' at the expense of diversity (Kiwan 2008) is seen by some (see Chapter 2 of this volume) as a threat to multicultural and antiracist education.

## Gender and Sexuality

A number of feminist writers (e.g. Mouffe 1993; Young 2000; Arnot 2003) have argued that traditional liberal conceptions of citizenship have been exclusive, given that citizenship is conceived of as relating to the public sphere whereas women were historically associated with the private sphere. As a consequence, feminist discourses have problematized the public/private sphere distinction, and it has been argued that in order to actively participate as citizens, it must be recognized that experiences are necessarily gendered in a context of unequal power relations between men and women and historically embedded structural inequalities. However, there are tensions between calling for equality (with men) yet also calling for the recognition of difference (Benhabib 1995). While early feminists believed that by achieving formal equality with respect to the vote and achieving equal rights in the workplace would result in women being able to exercise equal citizenship, others have instead argued that it is critically important to recognize difference for this formal equality to translate into practice. While on paper, women may have equal rights, institutional structures, processes and practices may actually hinder their full participation. What must be done is to ensure that the voices of women and other marginalized groups, such as those in lesbian, gay, bisexual and transgender (LGBT) communities, can be heard in order to be able to influence and change systems and the status quo.

It is relevant and important to examine how citizenship education should explore 'the hegemonic dominance of heterosexuality' (Arnot and Dillabough 2000, p. 15). In addition, the role that sexuality plays out in different contexts, for example that women experience violence, bullying and harassment in the workplace and within the family, is another area of pertinence in examining how inclusive dominant (male/heterosexual) constructions of citizenship are. Yet how sexuality relates to citizenship is a relatively underplayed dimension in citizenship education.

This can be understood partly in terms of how citizenship has come to be defined and distinguished from PSHE. In the original Crick Report, Crick was concerned to differentiate topics to be addressed within the citizenship education curriculum from those in PSHE, warning that citizenship must not 'become simply issues based on moral education, revolving around key concepts such as drugs, health education, housing and homelessness, careers development and employability etc' (QCA 1998, p. 20). The Programmes of Study for PSHE (QCA 2005) include learning about physical and emotional changes and puberty, sexual activity and behaviour and related health, which were seen to be primarily personal matters. While these issues can be taught in terms of personal identities and choices, it is too simplistic to ignore the political dimensions of gender and sexuality of relevance to an interrogation of inclusive understandings of citizenship. What is critical is the approach to the topic, rather than categorizing one topic the domain of one curriculum subject versus another. For example, while careers education addresses personal development issues, it can also entail a critical examination of prejudices about stereotypical gendered job roles.

A case study example from a North London school[1] illustrates how a lesson on teenage pregnancy has relevant citizenship education learning objectives. These include: 'to understand that teenage pregnancy has health, social, economic and political implications', and to understand the 'role of the local authority and PCT (Primary Care Trust) in welfare service provision'. The lesson also examines issues such as the public cost to communities and society of high teenage pregnancy rates, all illustrating how gender and sexual choices have public and political implications – clearly of relevance to citizenship education. This lesson is situated in background work on differences in perceptions about boys' and girls' sexuality, and critically evaluating norms of behaviour and attitudes including the legal age of consent, from a range of different and international perspectives.

A second example is the development by the students themselves of an anti-homophobic bullying charter. This was an outcome from a series of lessons for Year 11 on sexuality, consisting of eleven bullet points including statements welcoming and respecting all students and staff of all sexualities, ensuring all students and staff feel safe, that everyone has a voice and is listened to without abuse, that discrimination and bullying against lesbians and gays is combated, that training, advice and guidance for staff and students are provided, and that disciplinary procedures are implemented if the charter guidelines are broken.

## Disability and Age

Theories of citizenship are based on an assumption of individuals as 'rational' actors, so that those categorized as 'sub-normal' are excluded (Barbalet

1993). Yet at least 10 per cent of the world's population have significant, long-term physical or mental impairments, and are impeded from taking part in education, social and economic activity, due to barriers in attitudes, the built environment and how society is organized (Rieser 2006). Disability has been conceptualized predominantly as illness or deviance, framed in terms of a medical model (Barton 1996) and also individualized (Oliver 1996). Those with disabilities experience social differentiation and discrimination within society. In this section, I also make some reference to age, where there are some striking commonalities in the dominant conceptualizations of youth and those with disabilities. Children and young people have also typically been constructed as incompetent, vulnerable and incomplete (Weller 2007), although also constructed as politically apathetic, in moral crisis and in danger of slipping into crime (Beck 1998). What is also of note is that public institutions within society, for example the media, play a significant role in shaping public perceptions and framing the status (often in negative ways) of both those with disabilities and of children and young people.

Over the past decade, we have started to witness shifts in the conceptualization of those with disabilities (as well for children and young people) where they are recognized to have their own perspective and expertise and therefore considered worth consulting with, evidenced in the development of policy, and in the domain of rights and active participation. There has been a shift from thinking about those with disabilities in terms of need, to one of rights, where individuals and groups are empowered to challenge power relations, structures and practices within society (Oliver 2001; Rieser 2006).

Unfortunately, this is not the dominant construction for disability in the KS3 Scheme of Work. In Unit 18: 'Developing your school grounds' (QCA 2001, Unit 18, p. 1), under the theme 'How can you meet the needs of people using the school grounds?', the emphasis of the curriculum is on promoting sensitivity to the needs of others; however, this is not the same as ensuring that there are mechanisms to enable those 'others' (e.g. those with special needs) to participate so that they themselves are empowered to bring about change, and 'speak' for themselves. Indeed, it has been argued that thinking about social justice only in terms of distribution obscures issues of oppression and domination (Young 1990). The focus in this Scheme of Work is on the practicalities and skills of students' 'planning, devising and implementing ways', to make improvements in their school. However, in pedagogical terms, it is important to go beyond 'learning about' diversity and being aware of the needs of others to actually ensuring that those 'other' voices can talk for themselves and be heard.

Rieser (2006) argues for a 'social' model, as opposed to a medical model, which continues to dominate the education system. Rather than locating the disability in the individual, such a model views barriers from participating as being what disables them (see Chapter 2 of this volume). The new Programmes of Study at KS3 and KS4, which focus on developing skills for active participation linked to the focus on identity, have the potential to provide a more inclusive curriculum where all students can become actively involved in real situations dealing with issues of concern to them. Rieser (*ibid.*) proposes a number of practical recommendations, including diversifying curriculum delivery and curriculum content, with positive portrayal of those with disabilities, developing a whole-school ethos on accepting difference, with attention to language, developing empowerment, self-respect and self-esteem, employing disabled staff, ensuring that there is ongoing training in disability issues, ensuring governing body representation, and consulting and involving parents and carers.

So what are the implications for citizenship? This in part depends on the model. So, for example, a 'legal' model of citizenship understood primarily in terms of eligibility to vote is constructed around competence. Those with severe disabilities will not legally be allowed to vote, as under common law, legal capacity is required in any transaction leading to a legal effect (Vorhaus 2005). Children, in this model, are seen as 'citizens-in-waiting', who will become 'competent' at 18. It has been argued that the possible introduction of citizenship ceremonies as recommended in Lord Goldsmith's review of citizenship report would reinforce this arbitrary boundary that defines children as non- or incomplete citizens (Weller 2007).

In contrast, a participatory model of citizenship where those with disabilities are empowered to actively participate and shape decisions in domains of their lives that have an impact on them does not assume a conception of incompetence. Similarly, such a model has similar implications for children. The Crick Report, in highlighting the important role of education in promoting active participation, implicitly relies on 'cognitive engagement theory' (*Pattie et al.* 2004), which hypothesizes that participation depends on access to information. However, this does not address what motivates people to participate. It is crucial to consider people's identities in order to understand what might act as a barrier to participation or reversely what might facilitate or encourage it.

## Social Class

Those arguing for more inclusive conceptions of citizenship advocate raising awareness of structural discrimination that operates within society, fighting against inequalities based on class, as well as gender and ethnicity. It has been argued that liberalism ignores such power structures in society that facilitate the participation of some while acting as a barrier for others. Barber (1998) has argued that private companies dominate government, and that this can undermine democracy. Similarly, Faulks (2000, p. 10) has argued that liberal conceptions of citizenship have been 'subordinated to market principles and the interests of political and economic elites'. As with feminists, those arguing for a less class-differentiated citizenship have criticized the public/private sphere distinction.

It has been argued that class 'no longer matters' and is no longer a feature of our contemporary landscape – in terms of acting as an explanatory factor with regard to social and political outcomes. Partly this debate may relate to defining what 'class' actually refers to, with those declaring the 'death of class' prescribing an overtly economistic conception of it (Marsh *et al.* 2007). While the term 'class' may be less frequently used in everyday language, it certainly seems difficult to come to the conclusion that class has no significant influence in shaping people's lived experiences or life-chances. Indeed Marsh *et al.*'s (*ibid.*) research on young people and participation in the UK shows that while the young people they interviewed rarely talked about class, they were very much aware of how it affected their lives. For many of the less privileged respondents, politics was seen as something often negatively affecting their everyday lives, and they saw clear links between economic, social and cultural forms of capital. They argue, following Bourdieu's approach, that class is a structured lived experience, rather than a fixed category (*ibid.*).

The Crick Report takes T. H. Marshall as its starting point for its conceptualization of citizenship (QCA 1998) – a social democratic citizenship, consisting of civil, political and social rights developed within the socialist tradition in the context of class struggle (Marshall and Bottomore 1992). Although Marshall's primary concern was with social inclusion, the Crick Report does not substantively address the issue of social inclusion and it also lacks Marshall's focus on rights (Marshall and Bottomore 1992). It has been argued that (New) Labour's approach to citizenship with its focus on active participation and volunteering emphasizes duties at the expense of rights, thus corroding the Marshallian construction of citizenship (Beck 2008).

So, to what extent does 'class' feature in the most recent developments of the citizenship curriculum? It is clearly arguable that class is not currently of primary concern, but rather issues relating to ethnic and religious diversity, as discussed in the earlier section of this chapter, have been imbued with a heightened sense of urgency, given the current socio-political context and political concerns. As the co-author of the DCSF 'Diversity and citizenship' curriculum review (Ajegbo Report), I have often been asked why other forms of diversity were not addressed – the answer to which lies in the government's focus on integration and community cohesion, in the context of increased immigration and security concerns.

Looking at the new Programmes of Study at KS3 and KS4, the introductory section 'The importance of citizenship' makes reference to encouraging students to challenge injustice, inequalities and discrimination (QCA 2007a; 2007b). However, there is no explicit reference to issues relating to class. In addition, how social class relates to citizenship is not addressed at all under 'key concepts', in contrast to detailed explication of ethnic and religious diversity. There is scope for issues relating to class to be addressed at KS4 in that the last item under 'range and content' proposes that the study of citizenship should include 'the development of, and struggle for, different kinds of rights and freedoms' (QCA 2007b, p. 46). Economic issues are addressed at both KS3 and KS4, to the extent that it is proposed that students learn how economic decisions are made in relation to public money; in addition, at KS4, it suggests that this should include 'the role of the individual in the economy and the right to representation in the workplace' (*ibid.*, p. 47). It will be particularly important for students to learn about social class in relation to citizenship, given its key historic role in extending the franchise in the UK context, and its continued relevance in contemporary Britain today. While there is scope for addressing such issues within citizenship education, it may be necessary for a more explicit focus on these issues, and the development of suitable teaching resources in this domain (see Chapter 2 of this volume for a discussion of social class and socialism; see also Cole 2008).

## Environmental Issues

Addressing environmental issues in citizenship education often tends to be located both at a more global level – in relation to global conceptions of citizenship – and at a more local level. It is of note that environmental concerns do not tend to be coupled with discourses on national citizenship, but instead framed in relation to discourses of postmodernity or 'institutional reflexivity', where forms of governance and citizenship operate outside the traditional spheres of government (Marsh *et al.* 2007). Terms like 'expert citizen' and 'everyday maker' have been coined to reflect a growing trend of self-organization and the importance of networks in combating exclusion (Bang 2005) – a more bottom-up rather than the traditional top-down politics.

For example, the KS3 Programmes of Study (QCA 2000) refer to the European and global community under the 'Knowledge and understanding' heading (1i), where it is proposed that students be taught about 'the world as a global community, and the political, economic, environmental and social implications of this, and the role of the European Union, the Commonwealth and the United Nations'. Unit 10: 'Debating a global issue' is an example of a unit in the KS3 Schemes of Work, which is devoted to global dimensions of citizenship, with a specific focus on environmental issues (the consequences in the Amazon rainforest given as the example). Students are expected to 'make connections between their own actions and choices and the effects these have on other communities locally, nationally and globally' (QCA 2001, Unit 10, p. 9).

While the relationship between the local and global is referred to in the Crick Report, where students' experiences acting at a local level may help to enable them 'to make the connection between learning and acting locally to thinking globally' (QCA 1998, p. 37), the relationship between the national and global level, or indeed local and national, is not explicitly addressed. There seems to be an implicit and unquestioned assumption that learning and participating at the local level somehow 'trickles up' to the national and then global level, as is illustrated on interviewing one of the original members of the Crick group: 'I think we all felt that actually if you start local, it would filter out, and I'm sure that's got to be right. Local ought to be the school' (interview with Marianne Talbot, member of Crick Advisory Group). However, there is evidence that this kind of linear transfer does not necessarily occur in such a straightforward manner, with examples from democratic 'multicultural' societies where the different groups have relatively minimal contact between one another, yet exhibit a 'cosmopolitan interculturalism', where individuals of these groups develop skills for participation at a more global level, rather than at the local or national level (Kymlicka 2003). It has been argued that such global forms of citizenship, including environmental citizenship, must acknowledge that individuals operate from within the legal and political structures of the nation state, and economic, social and political inequalities between citizens both within and between nation states must be addressed (Demaine 2002).

In the new Programmes of Study at KS3 (QCA 2007a), the environment is identified under 'Range and content' framed actively in terms of 'actions individuals, groups and organizations can take to influence decisions affecting communities and the environment'. The term 'environment' is also listed under 'explanatory notes', where it states that this provides an opportunity for students to 'evaluate individual and collective actions that contribute to sustainable practices' and how this can link to other curriculum work in science and geography. The environment is also referred to under the section 'Curriculum opportunities' at both KS3 and KS4, which highlights that it is important to take account of 'environmental dimensions[2] of different political problems and issues' (QCA 2007a, p. 34; 2007b, p. 48). At KS4, under 'Range and content' there are two items that reference the environment. First, students are expected to learn about 'policies and practices for sustainable development and their impact on the environment'(QCA 2007b, p. 47), which contains further details under 'explanatory notes' – emphasizing an active approach – 'the ways in which individuals and groups can influence these policies through action'(*ibid.*). In addition, students are expected to learn about the challenges facing the global community, including issues relating to 'sustainability and the use of the world's resources' (*ibid.*). In teaching and learning about the environment in the context of citizenship, it will be important to consider the interconnected sites of political action at local, national and global levels.

## Concluding Thoughts

This chapter has considered the issue of promoting more inclusive conceptions of citizenship – encompassing ethnic and religious diversity, gender and sexuality, age and disability, social class and environmental issues. We have seen how the Crick Report implicitly relies on 'cognitive engagement theory' – which hypothesized that participation depends merely on access to information (Pattie *et al.* 2004) – and so that if young people are equipped with the necessary knowledge and skills, then it will follow that they will actively participate as citizens. However, what is missing in this rationale is that it does not consider what actually motivates people to participate. This chapter has shown that different forms of identity are clearly important in understanding what motivates and what hinders participation. In order to be motivated to participate, young people must be able to identify or relate their own personal identity/ies with those reflected in the larger community or society. Similarly, just as a sense of belonging or identity may promote participation, the experience of participating can enhance a sense of belonging. This challenges civic republican conceptions of citizenship which typically rely on preserving the public/private sphere distinction, in contrast to the aim of promoting equality and diversity, which calls for 'inclusiveness rather than neutrality' of the public sphere (Modood 2005, p.20).

The focus of the original Crick Report (QCA 1998) and subsequent Programmes of Study and Schemes of Work (QCA 2000; 2001) on the accessibility to information and developing participatory skills is certainly necessary, but it is not sufficient, as it does not address the impact of differential power between groups, which can lead to disempowerment and lack of motivation to participate for those historically marginalized groups. It is positive that the QCA's revised Programmes of Study for Citizenship at KS3 and KS4 (QCA 2007a; 2007b) go some way towards addressing issues of identity. However, it will be important to go beyond the reactive emphasis of 'shared values' for community cohesion in the context of security concerns, not only in terms of a more nuanced consideration of ethnic and religious identity, but also in other forms of identity – gender and sexuality, social class, age and disability – which have been considered in this chapter. If not, citizenship education may fail to achieve a more substantive participation of young people from a range of different backgrounds and identities.

# Notes

[1] My thanks goes to Michele Lambert from the Hornsey School for Girls in North London for kindly providing me with exemplar materials relating to gender, sexuality and citizenship.

[2] As well as other listed dimensions including moral, economic, historical and social (QCA 2007a; 2007b).

# References

Ajegbo, K., Kiwan, D. and Sharma, S. (2007), *Curriculum Review: Diversity and Citizenship*. London: DfES.

Arnot, M. (2003), 'Citizenship education and gender', in A. Lockyer, B. Crick and J. Annette (eds), *Education for Democratic Citizenship: Issues of Theory and Practice*. Aldershot: Ashgate Publishing Ltd, pp. 103–119.

— and Dillabough, J.-A. (2000), 'Introduction', in M. Arnot and J.-A. Dillabough (eds), *Challenging Democracy: International Perspectives on Gender, Education and Citizenship*. London and New York: Routledge, pp. 1–18.

Bang, H. (2005), 'Among everyday makers and expert citizens', in J. Newman (ed.), *Remaking Governance: Peoples, Politics and the Public Sphere*. Bristol: The Policy Press, cited in D. Marsh, T. O'Toole and S. Jones (2007), *Young People and Politics in the UK*. Basingstoke: Palgrave Macmillan.

Barbalet, J. (1993), 'Citizenship, class inequality and resentment', in B. Turner (ed.), *Citizenship and Social Theory*. London: Sage, pp. 35–56.

Barber, B. (1998), *A Place for Us*. New York: Hill and Wang, cited in D. Marsh, T. O'Toole and S. Jones (2007), *Young People and Politics in the UK*. Basingstoke: Palgrave Macmillan.

Barton, L. (1996), 'Sociology and disability: some emerging issues', in L. Barton (ed.), *Disability and Society: Emerging Issues and Insights*. Harlow, Essex: Addison Wesley Longman Ltd., pp. 3–17.

Batho, G. (1990), 'The history of the teaching of civics and citizenship in English schools'. *The Curriculum Journal*, 1, (1), 91–100.

Beck, J. (1998), *Morality and Citizenship in Education*. London: Cassell.

— (2008), *Meritocracy, Citizenship and Education*. London: Continuum.

Benhabib, S. (1995), 'From identity politics to social feminism', in D. Trend (ed.), *Radical Democracy: Identity, Citizenship and the State*. New York: Routledge, pp. 27–41.

Cole, M. (2008), *Marxism and Educational Theory: Origins and Issues*. London: Routledge.

Crick, B. (2000), *In Defence of Politics* (5th edn). London and New York: Continuum.

— and Porter, A. (eds) (1978), *Political Education and Political Literacy*. London: Longman.

Davies, I. (1999), 'What has happened in the teaching of politics in schools in England in the last three decades, and why?' *Oxford Review of Education*, 25, (1 and 2), 125–140.

Demaine, J. (2002), 'Globalisation and citizenship education'. *International Studies in Sociology of Education*, 12, (2), 117–28.

Faulks, K. (2000), *Citizenship*. London: Routledge, cited in D. Marsh, T. O'Toole and S. Jones (2007), *Young People and Politics in the UK*. Basingstoke: Palgrave Macmillan.

Heater, D. (1990), *Citizenship: The Civic Ideal in World History, Politics and Education*. London: Longman.

Kerr, D. (2000), 'Changing the political culture: The Advisory Group on Education for Citizenship and the Teaching of Democracy in Schools'. *Oxford Review of Education*, 25, (1–2), 275–84.

Kiwan, D. (2008), *Education for Inclusive Citizenship*. London and New York: Routledge.

Kymlicka, W. (1995), *Multicultural Citizenship*. Oxford: Oxford University Press.

— (2003), 'Multicultural states and intercultural citizens'. *Theory and Research in Education*, 1, (2), 147–69.

Lawton, D. (2000), 'Overview: citizenship education in context', in D. Lawton, J. Cairns and R. Gardner (eds), *Education for Citizenship*. London: Continuum, pp. 9–13.

Marsh, D. O'Toole, T. and Jones, S. (2007), *Young People and Politics in the UK*. Basingstoke: Palgrave Macmillan.

Marshall, T. H. and Bottomore, T. (1992), *Citizenship and Social Class*. London: Pluto Press.

Modood, T. (2005), *Multicultural Politics: Racism, Ethnicity and Muslims in Britain*. Edinburgh: Edinburgh University Press.

Mouffe, C. (1993), *The Return of the Political*. London: Verso.

Oliver, M. (1996), 'A sociology of disability or a disabilist sociology?', in L. Barton (ed.), *Disability and Society: Emerging issues and insights*. Harlow, Essex: Addison Wesley Longman Ltd., pp. 18–42.

— (2001), 'Disability issues in the postmodern world', in L. Barton (ed.), *Disability, Politics and the Struggle for Change*. London: David Fulton Publishers Ltd., pp. 149–159.

Osler, A. (2000), 'The Crick Report: difference, equality and racial justice'. *The Curriculum Journal*, 11, (1), 25–327.

Parekh, B. (2000), *Rethinking Multiculturalism*. Basingstoke and London: MacMillan Press Ltd.

Pattie, C., Seyd, P. and Whiteley, P. (2004), *Citizenship in Britain: Values, Participation and Democracy*. Cambridge: Cambridge University Press.

QCA (1998), *Education for Citizenship and the Teaching of Democracy in Schools* (Crick Report). London: QCA.

— (2000), *KS3 Citizenship Programmes of Study*. Available at http://www.nc.uk.net/ (accessed 30 October 2000).

— (2001), *KS3 Schemes of Work*. Available at http://www.standards.dfes.gov.uk/local/schemes/citizenship/schemes.html (accessed 9 September 2001).

— (2005), *KS3 PSHE Programmes of Study*. Available at www.nc.uk.net/nc/content/PSHE-3-POS.html (accessed 13 January 2005).

— (2007a), *Citizenship: Programme of Study for KS3*. London: QCA.

— (2007b), *Citizenship. Programme of Study for KS4*. London: QCA.

Rammell, B. (2006), Speech to community cohesion event, Southbank University, 16 May. Available at www.dfes.gov.uk/speeches/search_detail.cfm?ID = 340 (accessed 16 February 2007).

Rieser, R. (2006), 'Disability equality: confronting the oppression of the past', in M.

Cole (ed.), *Education, Equality and Human Rights: Issues of Gender, 'Race', Sexuality, Disability and Social Class* (2nd edn). London: Routledge, pp. 134–156.

Vorhaus, J. (2005). 'Citizenship, competence and profound disability'. *Journal of Philosophy of Education*, 39, (3), 461–75.

Weller, S. (2007), *Teenager's Citizenship: Experiences and Education*. London: Routledge.

Young, I. M. (1990), *Justice and the Politics of Difference*. Princeton, NJ: Princeton University Press.

— (2000), *Inclusion and Democracy*. Oxford: Oxford University Press.

Chapter 6

# Design and Technology

Matthew Bury and Leila Marr

The five material areas taught within secondary design and technology have at various times been taught as combined qualifications, or separate examinations and coursework assessments. Their historical derivation from craft subjects is traced, and the incorporation of the ever-changing element of modern manufacturing processes are explored and linked to the skill set of an advanced technological nation. Various examples are given to demonstrate how the design and technology curriculum provides plenty of opportunities to promote social inclusion and engagement by incorporating global historical perspectives and responsible citizenship. This chapter will briefly cover each equality issue with respect to both subject content and pedagogy. The historical place of design and technology within the education system is seen against the background of the internationalization of manufacturing, social consequences and education policy. The interdependent issues of 'race', class and the continuing debate around vocational as well as academic education are considered.

## Introduction

Design and technology (D&T) has its antecedents in craft trades: woodwork and metalwork, village rafiawork, home economics, needlework and cookery. In the 1980s the subject became craft, design and technology (CDT). The 1984 Technical and Vocational Education Initiative (TVEI) programme offered courses of technical and vocational education for students between 14 and 18 years old. This was a large government investment inspired by the success of German technical schools. The non-traditional exam boards BTEC, RSA and C&G developed relevant examinations, but the TVEI funding stopped as the National Curriculum began to be designed. (Penfold 1988, p. 145; Cross and McCormick 1986, p. 218).

The National Curriculum (NC) order for technology of 1990 included within the subject business studies and ICT, as well as materials (including textiles); food; structures; control systems and energy. The NC divided schooling into Key Stage 1 (KS1) (5 to 7 years old), Key Stage 2 (KS2) (7 to 11 years of age), Key Stage 3 (KS3) (11 to 14) and Key Stage 4 (KS4) (14 to 16 years of age).

As a result of concerns over the magnitude and vagueness of the content, the NC was rationalized and slimmed down by the Dearing review of 1995, removing business studies and ICT from technology. The 1997 National Strategies in Literacy and Numeracy at primary level reduced curriculum time for D&T at KS1 and KS2. Another revision produced Curriculum 2000, with KS3 covering all areas and KS4 food technology (FD), textiles (TX), resistant materials (RM), systems & control (S&C), graphic products (GP), with the possibility to disapply D&T at KS4 for students undertaking work-related learning or the pursuit of excellence in areas of talent. The KS3 National Strategy came in 2003, after which D&T became optional at KS4 except in schools with specialist technology college status.

Having replaced many of the non-academic craft subjects, the NC did not offer alternatives to students who were not 'good' at English, maths and science. The GCSEs retained their paperwork-based assessments (McCormick 2002).

The new 2008 NC for D&T has broadly continued the existing KS3 but with the requirement to offer only three out of FD, TX, RM and S&C. The cooking entitlement guarantees 25 hours of cookery for all KS3 students. At KS4 some ninety-six Local Authorities pilot five 14–19 diplomas and a new secondary curriculum will be introduced, raising the school leaving age to 17 in 2013 or 18 in 2015. KS4 D&T remains a popular option with large numbers of GCSE entries annually. Students can take more than one technology option for GCSE. Vocational GCSEs and diplomas are discussed below.

Existing curriculum time provision at KS3 varies from two hours per week in FD and TX, two hours in RM and S&C, to one hour per week in technology as a whole. Depending on whether single or double periods are timetabled, the suggestions for teaching found below can be incorporated as time allows at KS3, though wider, more in-depth treatment is feasible at KS4 due to the greater proportion of curriculum time.

This chapter will briefly cover each equality issue with respect to both subject content and pedagogy.

## Gender

D&T was split along gender lines from the days when boys did woodwork and metalwork and girls did needlework and home economics. Under the

1990 NC orders, girls and boys studied all D&T subjects, including electronics and food. However, this was not the case in many single-sex schools. Since 2003 when D&T became a foundation subject which students opted for at KS4, the gender lines are back. While it could be argued that all male electronics groups and all female food groups reflect students' interests, this is seen as an issue not least because careers in scientific and technical areas are better paid than the majority of those in hospitality, catering, and the food and clothing industries.

In order to encourage girls into scientific and technical subjects it is important to modify learning materials to balance gender bias in content or style. The contribution of women inventors to technology is not highlighted in textbooks and this can have a negative effect on girls' interest in traditionally male subjects. Listed 'http' addresses in the References to this chapter are only a few of the many women inventors' websites. Some examples follow:

- Ada Lovelace, daughter of the poet Lord Byron, collaborated with Charles Babbage, the inventor of the first mechanical thinking and calculating machine. Her 40-page appendix to a French paper on Babbage's 'analytical engine' proved mathematical universality in 1843. She devised a method of using punch cards to calculate Bernoulli numbers, thus becoming the first computer programmer.
- Hedy Lamarr, the Hollywood actress, patented in 1941 a device which manipulated radio frequencies between transmission and reception to develop an unbreakable code so that top-secret messages could not be intercepted.
- Stephanie Kwolek's Kevlar, patented in 1966, is used in bulletproof vests.
- Lillian Gilbreth was a pioneer in ergonomics, patented many kitchen appliances including an electric food mixer and is also known for the concept of arranging equipment to reduce the time spent walking while at work. (inventors.about.com, undated)

The social focus of many women's inventions has meant their development often occurred outside corporations and patent applications (McClellan and Dorn 1999, p. 254).

Ways to promote gender equality might include:

- talks by visiting speakers from organizations such as Women into Science, Engineering and Construction (WISE) in order to challenge views about these careers
- having prepared responses to 'laddish' behaviour and seeking to reduce bullying, sexual harassment and swearing
- listening to girls to make them feel valued and respected

- explaining concepts in a way that makes them relevant to wider social issues.

Over the past 20 years, many efforts have been made to address the lower attainment of girls, particularly in mixed schools. To a large degree success has been achieved, with the consequence that boys are now seen as underachieving with respect to girls. When CSE coursework was combined with O level exams in 1986 to produce GCSEs, both coursework and exams formed the assessment of D&T. Boys of 15 are less keen on disciplining themselves to complete paperwork for long-term goals. The proportion of marks for the made artefact is less than half of the coursework, accounting for less than a quarter overall. This raises the question of whether GCSE assessment is a disadvantage to boys. Historically boys did well in the craft subjects in which skills were emphasized (Spendlove 2002).

Currently, initiatives to raise boys' achievement have come to be viewed as increasingly important. Using Assessment for Learning to promote boys' achievement can involve composing 'levels ladders' for each KS3 project, the aim being to make clearer, through the simplification of the language, what the students need to do to raise the quality of their work. Other strategies are suggested below:

- 'Chunking' work, i.e. breaking up the learning and giving short-term, achievable targets. Use of concept ladders (Penny 1998, p. 101).
- Structuring talk time using focused conversation prior to writing or peer assessment.
- Giving positive, specific feedback and advice on how to improve. Giving public praise and private rebukes (Bleach 1998, p. 77).
- Providing folders and a secure store for these within the department to push boys to organize their work more effectively.
- Explaining concepts in a way that makes them relevant to the boys' outside lives (Swan 1998, p. 168).
- Starters which are quick, sharp and interesting, e.g. visual cues, matching, sequencing or thinking about prior learning in a new way.
- Frequent changes of activity and lesson format, busy, purposeful movement, small, self-directed groups. Projectable timers and countdown clocks can be found on the internet and also in software for the interactive whiteboard (IAWB). Adding theme tunes from TV shows and films tends to be well received.
- WALT (We are learning to . . .) and WILF (What I am looking for is . . .) as lesson objectives and outcomes. It is important that boys are clear how the learning links to previous and future lessons.
- Product analysis by rolling a dice with printed prompts on the sides of a cube, then picking one of the questions under the different category

headings, transferring it to their sheet and writing down the answer. The active nature of the task and a ban on one-word responses should produce more detailed answers.

- Other fast-moving kinaesthetic techniques use 'post-it' notes in response to projected questions or mini-whiteboards made from laminated photo-copies. Students circulate around a collection of products.

When teaching boys and girls GCSE GP, it is apparent that boys underachieve in this subject area. From experience boys can be slower to acquire organizational skills but this can also be the case for girls. It is the teachers' responsibility to manage and guide students in how to succeed while promoting individual responsibility. Making both students and parents/carers aware of how to manage deadlines is half the battle.

It is important to promote a subject from KS3 if you want to gain strong candidates at GCSE and A level whatever gender they are. Any technology subject is demanding due to the high percentage of coursework involved but some students thrive on this in comparison to examinations. In GP it is important to teach students about flair, creativity, style, presentation and to introduce different methods of communication in both designing and making a product of a high standard.

It is essential to display examples of current and previous students' work, celebrating achievement to make students aware of standards. It is also important to use existing products that have relevance to the students' gender, background and lifestyle to keep them motivated to learn more about the design process.

## Sexual Orientation

D&T can contribute to promoting equality with respect to sexual orientation.

Students may be the victims of homophobic bullying, which may be contributing to the reluctance of many boys to choose FD or TX subjects at KS4, even though the majority of top chefs and fashion designers are men. Fear of sexist or homophobic name calling is a factor in students' choices at this age.

Implementation of the Every Child Matters agenda, stopping verbal abuse, particularly the use of homophobic language, is part of the broader, whole-school approach to preventing homophobic bullying. Introducing famous male chefs or fashion designers and linking this with women engineers or building surveyors or professors of electronics are useful strategies. Links can also be made to other curriculum areas. For example, gender-specific sports can be discussed. What happens when a boy is good at dancing or gymnastics? What happens when a girl is good at football?

While Section 28 has now been abolished, homophobia is common, with homophobic language used regularly, often casually. It is very important to confront the use of certain words if homophobic bullying is to be seriously challenged (Salend 2000; Booth and Ainscow 2002; Campbell 2002; teachernet.gov.uk 2005).

When dealing with incidents of insulting terms used by students in the classroom or workshop it is advisable to refer to the content of PSHE and citizenship lessons in which students discuss the difficulties faced by lesbian, gay, bisexual and transgender people in society today. By questioning based on the four themes below students can be encouraged to reconsider attitudes which may lie behind the use of inappropriate language:

1. Question the language used to describe sexual practices. It can be made clear that all forms of name calling are included in school policies on bullying and that the D&T department will take action as necessary.
2. Examine their attitudes towards sexual relationships. Would they stop buying or playing the music from a particular band if one of the group was gay?
3. Debate the reasons for homophobia and transphobia. A link can be made with sectors of industry; there is less persecution of LGBT workers in some sectors such as fashion, film and TV. If it is unacceptable to be victimized in one's place of work, we should do something about this to make all workplaces safe.
4. Think about the emotional and physical consequences of homophobic bullying. We should encourage students to respond in the same way to this form of bullying as to all the other forms of bullying.

## Ethnicity

History can be the favourite haunt of ideology. The march of technological progress has been seen from a worldview confined solely to the West. However, the more recent history of Chinese, Indian, Indo-American and African technological development is now more accessible in terms of published works, and promotes students' involvement in an inclusive curriculum (Griswold *et al.* 1986; Sizemore 1987; McPartland and Slavin 1990; Sewell 1997; Blair and Bourne 1998; McKenley *et al.* 2003; Geer 2005; Hall 2005; Henry and Williams 2007; blackinventor.com 2008).

The distant past is less documented, but there are some examples. The first smelting of copper was around 5000 BC in Iran and Afghanistan; the first alloying of this with tin to form bronze took place in the Middle East around 3800 BC; and it passed to China before 1500 BC (Bronowski 1974, p. 126). The first evidence for iron smelted from ores is a piece of a tool stuck in one of the Egyptian pyramids around 2500 BC. The wide use of iron by the Hittites around the Black Sea dates from 1500 BC (Derry and Williams 1993, pp. 126, 145).

In Africa, the Egyptians used blue Lapis Lazuli stone from Badakshan in Afghanistan around 2000 BC (Coenraads and de Bon 2000), while five hundred years later, they adopted bronze working, sourcing their copper locally and their tin from other countries (Lucas and Harris 1962; Meyer and Bir Umm Fawakhir 1997; Wesler 1998; Dollinger 2000). In Nigeria the Nok civilization in the Jos region was smelting iron by 500 BC (Sutton 1983; Wai Andah 1981, p. 611). Nearer to Egypt, large-scale iron smelting in Meroe, Sudan is found from the same period (Riad 1981, p. 204).

Many historians now accept that the ancient African empires of Ghana, Mali and Songhay were urbanized with developed scientific societies. In AD 900 camel traders brought gold from medieval Ghana in the Sahel to the Almoravid Berbers of Morocco and Spain. From AD 1200 gold from the empire of Mali was traded to the Europeans across the desert, the Malian city of Timbuktu passing into familiar colloquial usage in England as signifying a faraway place (Coleman 1999, p. 21). The wealth of Mali was recorded by the Arab historian Ibn Battuta, who travelled much of the continent (Levitzion and Hopkins 1981; Hrbek 1992; ki-Zerbo and Niane 1997). However, Timbuktu's long-lasting contribution to Islamic and world civilizations is scholarship. From AD 1300, important books were written and copied in the University of Sankore in Timbuktu, establishing the city as the centre of a significant written tradition in Africa (Hamdun and King 1994).

Located in the south central African nation of Zimbabwe are the ruins of monuments and cities built of stone. These ruins extend around the well-preserved Great Zimbabwe site by a radius of 100 to 200 miles, a diameter almost as great as the nation of France. Built by Africans from AD 1000 to 1400, they are evidence of a thriving culture. The wealth of Great Zimbabwe lay in cattle production and gold. There are a number of mines to the west of Great Zimbabwe, about 40 kilometres away. The wall of the great enclosure measures 244 metres in length, is 5 metres thick at its greatest point, and 10 metres high. There is a tall beehive-shaped stone tower within.

External trade existed between Great Zimbabwe and Sofala on the southern coast of what is now Mozambique, an important port where goods from India, China and the Islamic world were imported and then sent into the interior, which in turn exported products from inner Africa. Gold and copper were the main exports. Imports were primarily cloth, glass beads and ceramics. Items found at Great Zimbabwe include a glazed Persian bowl from the thirteenth or fourteenth century, Chinese celedon dishes, shards from a Chinese stoneware vessel, and fragments of engraved and painted Near Eastern glass (Beach 1980). From 1405 to 1419, the Ming Emperor of China ordered Admiral Zheng He to launch seven great maritime expeditions in the largest wooden ships ever built, with 20,000 men. The countries visited were Vietnam, Thailand, Java, Sri Lanka, India, Persia, Arabia, Somalia, Kenya and Tanzania. A giraffe was brought back from Malindi in Kenya (McClellan and Dorn 1999, p. 126). Hundreds of blue and white porcelain bowls lined the domes of Kilwa and thousands of shards of jade-green Sung dynasty pots have been turned up by archaeologists at another Tanzanian site. These date from AD 1000, at which time China was producing 125,000 tons of steel, mostly for military purposes. The monsoon trade winds allowed Omani ships to travel from Zanzibar or Sofala on the East African coast to India and then on to Java and Sumatra (Coleman 1999, p. 109). With respect to South Asia, prior to AD 900 most of the Indian subcontinent practised Hinduism and Buddhism, the modern-day states of Pakistan, India, Sri Lanka and Bangladesh being made up of various kingdoms and principalities. Historically ancient India refers to the entire region, which traded with the spice islands of Indonesia bringing about a rich cross-fertilization, producing many of the Southeast Asian and South Asian dishes which are eaten at home by large numbers of schoolchildren and often introduced in food lessons. Small quantities of spices used to reach Europe via the Middle East until the voyages of Da Gama and Magellan from 1488 to 1519. A shipload of cloves and cinnamon was brought back by the survivors of Magellan's crew (*ibid.*, pp. 108, 120).

By 1000 BC steel of very high quality was made in India (Bronowski 1974, p. 131), which eventually reached Rome via Abyssinia from southern India and was highly prized by the Romans as wootz or seric iron (Derry and Williams 1993, pp. 126, 145).

Western decimal numbers come from ancient India, including the invention of zero and assigning a place value to the digits. The Arabs carried this system to Africa and Fibonacci carried it from North Africa to Europe (Bronowski 1974, pp. 155, 168).

Indian astronomers were working at the Astronomical Bureau in Nang'an China in AD 600, introducing the nine digits and zero, although the Chinese had their own decimal place value system from 400 BC. Contacts with India also brought knowledge of saltpetre chemistry which contributed to the Chinese invention of gunpowder (Chant and Goodman 1999, p. 271; Coleman 1999, p. 25; McClellan and Dorn 1999, p. 213).

The spread of Hinduism to Indonesia took place from 500 BC via south Indian traders. Buddhism's influence came later, around AD 400. Trade with Hindu kingdoms such as the Khmer (AD 800 to 1400) allowed Chinese artefacts into Indonesia. Textiles technology allows students to research the history of different techniques from other cultures which promotes respect and understanding. A selection of these are listed below:

- Batik, which was practised in China as early as AD 581, using silk, was also found in Nara, Japan in the form of screens from AD 710. Frescoes in the

Ajunta caves of India show head wraps and garments like batiks. In Java and Bali temple ruins show figures whose garments are patterned in a way suggestive of batik.

- In West Africa resist dyeing using cassava and rice paste has existed for centuries in Nigeria and Senegal. (batikguild.org.uk, undated; McClellan and Dorn 1999, p. 151).
- Students can also collect research on the Mayans; mola blouse designs are often inspired by modern graphics such as political posters, labels, pictures from books and TV cartoons, as well as traditional themes from Kuna legends and culture (Parker and Neal 1977; Patera 1995).
- Other projects based on respect for historical cultures which introduce students to quilting and careful hand stitching can be inspired by the textiles of the Indus Valley and the Torres Strait islanders.

## The special case of Gypsy, Roma and Traveller students

European initiatives to tackle social inclusion identify the Gypsy, Roma and Traveller communities as minority ethnic groups. According to the UK schools minister, Lord Adonis, many Gypsy, Roma and Traveller pupils are among the lowest-achieving in UK schools, and the situation is not improving. Fear of xeno-racism (see Chapter 2 of this volume) and bullying means that many children and families are too afraid to identify themselves (Owen 2008). This makes it all the more important for the presence of Gypsy, Roma and Traveller students in schools to be acknowledged, and for their cultural heritages to be made known.

The various Traveller communities encountered in British schools come from three broad groups in terms of cultural heritage: English Gypsies and European Roma, Irish Travellers, English Showfolk. Many circumstances can cause these children to be primary carers. They are used to learning in mixed age groups, alongside adult extended family members, and making mistakes. On reaching puberty they are treated as adults and involved in the childcare of younger siblings. Many parents prefer their own monocultural model and can also be resistant to revealing their children's ethnicity in school, often as a result of hostility from the local community. Attendance is more usual at primary school than at secondary. There can be resistance to children revealing the Romani and Gammon languages to children or teachers outside the community (Derrington and Kendall 2004; O'Hanlon and Holmes 2004).

Families travel seasonally and there is often a winter base school and dual registration; communication via the schools is by the National Association of Teachers of Travellers (NATT) 'red book'. Learning resources have been created, derived from local Traveller associations. There is also the DfES (2001) *Are We Missing Out* video for parents (Tyler 2004).

- Issue work packs for particular subjects, FD, TX, RM, S&C, GP. The work packs can be recorded in the red book, postcards and emails used to keep in touch, and any assessed work recorded and dispatched to the base school. Laptops can also be issued.
- The appointment of older teenage girls from the Traveller community as TAs in East London primary schools promoted the attainment of Traveller children in classes. It is difficult for teenagers to attend secondary school when their presence in or near the primary classroom is often demanded by parents and younger siblings, as they are usually charged with their care.
- Withdrawal for intensive reading and numeracy can mean students will not appear in D&T.
- Visit (whole group) a 'vardo' (trailer), where students try out craft skills, musical instruments, cookery, embroidery, woodcarving and storytelling led by Travellers. The technological ingenuity in the community is breathtaking, particularly mechanical engineering among showfolk. S&C projects such as levelling devices for trailers, and TX projects on clothes making, can be set as work packs to Traveller students. (Derrington and Kendall 2004; O'Hanlon and Holmes 2004; Tyler 2004; Pugh 2007)

# Disability

## Hearing impairment

Particular issues relevant to D&T which confront students with hearing impairment are listed below:

- Check with pastoral staff if a hearing aid should be worn. Many students will be reluctant to wear them as a result of other children's comments.
- Be conscious of the effects of strain and tiredness – the more echoey the room and the more people talking, the more effort to filter out words. A 1-metre range with a hearing aid is optimal, 3 metres for lip reading.
- The effect of high-frequency loss is filtered hearing, e.g. the disappearance of s, th, ch, t, k sounds.
- Face the student to allow lip reading. Standing in front of a light source, like a window, makes it hard for them to lip read.
- Avoid shouting at other students; instead, cross the room quickly to deal with behaviour at a normal voice level. Avoid exaggeration of mouth movements when speaking.
- Give visual cues to topics being discussed, notes and pictures on the board. Children cannot lip read words they do not know.
- Repeat questions from other students.

- All videos and DVDs must have subtitles. If possible, this needs to be checked before educational visits.

Messages from school to hearing impaired parents/carers can be sent by phoning Typetalk. If calling a meeting at school for a hearing impaired parent/carer, a signer should to be paid to attend.


## Visual impairment

Partial visual impairment may not preclude a student taking part in D&T, but Health & Safety has to be a priority and a risk assessment should be done by the Mobility Officer. Alternative means of providing information through tactile and auditory channels involve a considerable time commitment in adapting resources. It may be useful to consider how blind and partially sighted adults employed in precision engineering depend on voice-synthesized numerical readouts as they set up and adjust computer numerical controlled (CNC) machines to cut materials into products. Tactile information is used to train divers to disassemble, repair and reassemble machinery underwater. Visual impairment (VI) Units in Local Authorities (LAs) train students entering mainstream schools in the use of a variety of devices which are described below:

- Braille grade 1 is letter for letter; grade 2 is a form of shorthand.
- The Braille Note machine talks, produces a tactile readout and translates word processor text, but not diagrams, into Braille.
- Special Tactile Diagrams are produced by VI Units in LAs. These can be easily made using thin plastic on a vacuum former, or by CNC routers driven by Image Relief or Lithoplane software which convert a bitmap image into relief by engraving an acrylic sheet (cadinschools.org 2008).
- The Perkins Braille Embosser is used for columns of text.
- Diagrams can be drawn by the student on German film, which is a plastic sheet placed on a rubber mat and inscribed with a stylus, raising any pictures drawn so they can be felt again.
- Ridged lined paper is used for writing slowly.

Suggestions for good practice include:

- Talk to students, use their name first, say who you are, and say when the conversation is at an end. This avoids other students observing them talking to someone who is no longer there.
- Don't talk to students in the corridor; they're using auditory information to navigate.
- Assess their independence: can they pick up things they've dropped? Can they line up for dinner?

- Assess their concept formation, e.g. descriptions of snowflakes and chimneys may attest to less visual impairment in childhood.

Access to curriculum:

- Say what you write on the board, spell all surnames, say 'Look, see' and give students objects to hold.
- Read out what is on any displays referred to.
- Set books on tape to 2.5 times normal speed with the pitch lowered.
- Tell students what to do with their work at the end, e.g. print off work from your laptop and hand it in to me at my desk.

## Social Class and Capitalism

Before GCSEs quite a complicated situation existed in British schools. During the 1960s and 1970s most local education authorities (LEAs) had abolished selection by the 11 +, and combined secondary modern and grammar schools into comprehensives, producing economies of scale. Many schools had thus expanded, from 600 to 2,500 students in some cases. As a result many had become fairly expert in differentiating the curriculum to suit the aspirations of their local communities.

Examples would be found of children opting for courses such as motor vehicle mechanics, allowing those who considered themselves practically minded to accelerate their cognitive development through problem-solving with materials and also train in something which held out a promise of financial reward earlier in life than the academic route via university. Examples like AEB's Engineering Workshop Theory and Practice were popular with large uptakes (Archer and Bruce 1978; 1980; 1982; Penfold 1988).

The collapse of manufacturing industry in the 1980s has imposed huge changes on school leavers. Manufacturing currently directly employs around 3.7 million people in the UK, with millions more in the service sector dependent on it (britishdesign.co.uk 2007). It accounts for over 60 per cent of UK export earnings but around 20 per cent of overall income (GDP) (esrc.ac.uk 2007; defra.gov.uk 2008). However, in the 1950s it accounted for 80 per cent of GDP (statistics.gov.uk 2007).

Much has been written about unskilled work outside the building trade and the skill demands of the knowledge economy. There are seven world-class industries common to most of the G11 countries: microelectronics, biotechnology, telecommunications, civil aviation, new materials, robots and machine tools, computers & software. These relate to the school curriculum areas of maths, science, ICT and D&T.

Many students have benefited from the upgrades to their school facilities delivered under the specialist schools programme as there are currently 2,502 designated specialist schools: 408 arts, 217 business and enterprise, 47 engineering, 72 humanities, 216 language, 222 mathematics and computing, 18 music, 282 science, 345 sports, 583 technology colleges, 12 SEN and 80 schools with combined specialisms (standards.dfes.gov.uk 2007).

Britain still has a large economy and is still part of the G11. However, social mobility has declined to lower levels than it had been under the 11+ system and is lower than most European states. Fewer directors of companies come from the shop floor; at the same time, there has been a boom in private education which has produced many state schools no longer able to claim a comprehensive intake.

However, for young people in these schools, there are few opportunities to train in the vocational way, where their skills are not measured by paper-based examinations, but by a series of competences signed off by an assessor, or where they are put in real-life situations which allow them to fail and learn from their mistakes.

During the 1970s the Youth Opportunities Scheme (YOPS) inadvertently put an end to the older system of apprenticeship. A firm was funded for one year to take a trainee, but to attract another grant of money, the firm had to take on someone else and let the first trainee go. In contrast, apprentices had been taken on for very little pay and the firm would absorb the costs of training, in the hope that later the apprentice would be a reliable and cheap employee. Some trades could apprentice for up to seven years. There were opportunities to learn by doing and to talk procedures through with an expert. The number of different situations encountered developed a sound knowledge base, so that if people eventually struck out on their own, they could quote accurately on jobs and ensure they made enough money to pay themselves and their workers.

Since 1944 the British education system had not spent as much on technical and vocational schools as other competing industrialized nations. The removal of the apprenticeship route further closed off the opportunities available to young people. The compulsory school leaving age had been raised to 16 but with the removal of diversity at 14–16, many students fitted uneasily into academic GCSEs and secondary schools.

The NC produced a standardized subject content across all schools, making D&T a subject at KS4 with 10 per cent curriculum time. One element was the amount of paperwork necessary to provide the evidence that students could make objects. The CSE coursework had been retained in a form which required good levels of written expression and also the ability to draw. However, the exam boards' mark schemes credited the paperwork more than the practical. Ryle's concept of 'knowing how', like Polangi's or Layton's 'tacit knowledge', had to be made explicit via pages of writing and diagrams (Chidgey 1994; Jones 2002).

The 1992 introduction of NVQs as a work-based learning route foundered as the employers' requests for schoolteachers' training records ran into legal problems. Many schools then offered the school-based GNVQs as being at least somewhere on the way to a work-related learning environment.

Vocational GCSEs were launched in 2002, with many schools latching onto these as a way of differentiating KS4. The courses, however, had not been written to employ the methods of work-based training with a series of competences signed off by an assessor. This meant practically minded students did not do well without substantial teacher support with the documentation.

The 2004 Tomlinson Report on the 14–19 curriculum resulted in a new variety of vocational routes such as diplomas and proposed an equivalence between academic and vocational qualifications. The level 1 Engineering Diploma, equivalent to five GCSEs grades D to G, has an emphasis on practicality, with one written exam. The level 3 Engineering Diploma, equivalent to three GCE A levels, has substantial written coursework.

Many schools keen to pursue vocational 14–19 routes found work placements for only one or two weeks. Consortia were established with further education (FE) colleges but supervision, transport and attendance issues quickly emerged. The close personal supervision which was a strength of technician taught modules at FE colleges could be frustrated by the attitudes of 14 year olds used to challenging authority figures within the school environment. The one-to-one relationship with adults was noted in the Bullock Report as important in language development, necessary in learning (Bullock 1975).

- Schoolchildren thoroughly enjoy independent learning, working with modern technologies and materials to develop knowledge, skills and awareness to support their designing and making activities.
- To teach technology subjects it is crucial that a department has the right resources to do this. Students have excelled due to the experience of using programs like Photoshop, ProDESKTOP, Speedstep, Nutrient and Crocodile Clips, providing them with advanced knowledge linked to industry, therefore connecting education to the real world (cadinschools. org 2008).
- D&T subject content changes every year as industrial practices advance. Students have the experience to explore the creative process developing new ideas and modifying old ones. The rewards of teaching include witnessing the progression of students taking pride in their own achievements and building skills for workplace technologies that lie 5 years in the future. (Ofsted 2002)

# The Environment

*Technology education is not just an instrumental activity, giving students the knowledge, skills and resources to be able to make things, but should be encouraging students to harness their creative abilities towards goals that they have consciously chosen and evaluated, with growing sensitivity to the needs of other people and the environment, and responsible decision-making.*

*(Conway 1990, p. 22)*

Environmental issues have become more urgent each year, for instance raw material extraction and processing, disposal of products, deforestation, air- and water-borne effluents. The suggestions below look at D&T materials/ ingredients teaching from a sustainability perspective:

- Materials which are currently economic to recycle in the UK are metals; products like bottles or packaging, made of a single common thermo-softening plastic; glass but not ceramics. Melting and re-forming is usually employed. Pure timber, paper and card are also recycled via pulp.
- Much old furniture is recycled to make melamine faced chipboard and modern flatpack furniture. The glue UF and the surface melamine are not reyclable or biodegradable. Disposal requires landfill or energy reclamation with smoke scrubbing.
- In past centuries hot melt protein glues derived from cattle hooves and fish bones were used, which meant broken wooden parts could be detached and replaced. This furniture was made entirely of biodegradable materials.
- Monomaterial textiles like polyamide are recyclable; cotton, silk, wool, even viscose are biodegradable. Polyesters are often thermosets and mixed fibres can't be recycled, so disposal requires landfill or burning. However, cotton production involves poisons and pesticides (sda-uk.org 2006).
- Food waste which is buried in landfill sites is subject to anaerobic breakdown, producing methane gas, which is explosive. For this reason many UK landfill sites burn off the gas to produce $CO_2$.
- Agricultural waste in China has been collected in large fermenters producing methane which is piped and used as biogas fuel. The $CO_2$ released is recently fixed carbon unlike that released from the burning of fossil methane or natural gas (Tentscher 2004).
- Deforestation depletes tropical soils as all the nutrients are in the biomass. Without roots to hold the Himalayan hillsides together, heavy rains produce mudslides and block rivers, causing flooding in Bangladesh.
- Most snow and rain forms in chilly conditions high in the sky and the condensation is often seeded by bacteria that are discharged into the atmosphere by forests. The water transpired from forest leaves also contributes significantly to atmospheric moisture (Christner et al. 2008).

- Life cycle analysis looks at the cost of extracting and processing the raw material, manufacturing and distributing it, collection and disposal (Cresswell *et al.* 2003, p. 227).
- The consequences of throwaway consumer electronics can be demonstrated online at websites www.independent.co.uk, www.macworld.co.uk (Daniel 2007).
- Encouraging the use of fair trade ingredients in FD – in organic, local, in-season ingredients – discourages out-of-season, air-freighted goods, genetically modified ingredients.
- The use of renewable resources, Forest Stewardship Council softwood plantations, the Programme for Endorsement of Forestry Certification as it applies to hardwood forests.
- Students stand by objects in the room and by means of questioning can arrive at the sources and disposal options of each object.
- The Dyson box can be hired free of charge from the company's education service. Students can disassemble snap-fit or screw-fixed parts, which are injection moulded out of one thermosoftening, recyclable plastic. Parts can be ABS or PP or PC but each is a monomaterial.
- The BayGen wind-up radio was designed to help people in rural areas hear health education broadcasts. The one laptop per child scheme aims to equip schoolchildren in poor countries with wind-up computers (laptop.org 2007).
- PET drinks bottles are thermosoftening plastic, so are recycled into cooking oil containers, which are then recycled into fleeces.
- Child labour is an issue in garment manufacture; examples looking at fair trade can be found online (labourbehindthelabel.org 2006; stepin.org 2007).

## Conclusion

The immensity of technology allows teaching materials and projects to draw on a wide variety of sources. The understanding of its impact on human civilization can be revealed to students in fascinating ways. The need for students in rural, mono-ethnic schools to appreciate the contributions of other cultures is just as important as it is in cosmopolitan inner-city schools. By bringing contributors from the workplace in to speak to students and by taking students outside to consider and evaluate technology around us, links are built with the local community.

Community links are a key to students' success and involve the whole school, from senior management to individual departments. Strong links with parents/carers and the wider family are a recurring theme in studies of schools, which have raised the achievement of traditionally excluded groups, and much research from the US reveals the benefits of an inclusive curriculum.

# References

Archer, L. Bruce (1978), 'Design education in schools'. Paper presented at the conference Design Education and Industry, organized by the Regional Advisory Council for Technological Education, London and Home Counties, 10–14 July.

Archer, L. Bruce (1980), 'The mind's eye: not so much seeing as thinking'. *Designer*, January 1980, 8–9.

Archer, L. Bruce (1982), 'Cognitive modelling, rational thinking, language, designerly thinking and imaging'. Internal paper, Royal College of Art, Design Education Unit. London: RCA. http://www.batikguild.org.uk/history.asp (accessed February 2008).

Beach, D. N. (1980), *The Shona and Zimbabwe*. New York and London: Africana Publishing Company and Heinemann Educational Books. http://www.blackinventor.com/pages/garrettmorgan.html (accessed February 2008). http://www.blackinventor.com/pages/lewislatimer.html (accessed February 2008).

Blair, M. and Bourne, J. (1998), *Making the Difference: Teaching & Learning in Successful Multi-Ethnic Schools*. Sudbury: DfES and Open University Press.

Bleach, K. (ed.) (1998), *Raising Boys' Achievement in Schools*. London: Trentham Books.

Booth, T. and Ainscow, M. (2002), *The Index for Inclusion*. London: Centre for Studies on Inclusive Education, Lambeth Research and Statistics Unit. http://www.british design.co.uk/index.php?page=newsservice/view&news_id=4170 (accessed February 2008).

Bronowski, J. (1974), *The Ascent of Man*. London: BBC.

Bullock. A. (1975), *Language for Life* (Bullock Report). London: DES/HMSO. http://www.cadinschools.org.uk (accessed February 2008).

Campbell, C. (ed.) (2002), 'Developing inclusive schooling: perspectives, policies and practices'. London: Institute of Education.

Chant, C. and Goodman, D. (1999), *Pre-Industrial Cities and Technology*. London: The Open University and Routledge.

Chidgey, J. (1994) 'A critique of the design process', in Banks, F. (ed.), *Teaching Technology*. London: The Open University and Routledge, pp. 89–92.

Christner, B.C, Morris, C. E, Foreman, C. M, Cai, R., Sands, D.C. (2008), 'Ubiquity of biological ice nucleators in snowfall'. *Science*, 319, (5867), 1214.

Coenraads, R. R. and deBon, C. C. (2000), 'Lapis lazuli from the Coquimbo region, Chile'. *Gems & Gemology*, 36, 28–41.

Coleman, A. (ed.) (1999), *Millennium: A Thousand Years of History*. London: Transworld Publishers.

Conway, R. (1990), 'Values in technology'. *The Times Educational Supplement* (28 September).

Cresswell, L., Lambert, B. and Goodier, A. (2003), *Product Design*. Oxford: Heinemann.

Cross, A. and McCormick, B. (eds) (1986), *Technology in Schools*. Milton Keynes: Open University Press.

Daniel, K. (ed.) (2007), *The Sustainability Handbook for D&T Teachers*. Bourton-on-Dunsmore, Rugby: Practical Action. http://www.defra.gov.uk/environment/statistics/supp/spkf03.htm (accessed February 2008).

Derrington, C. and Kendall, S. (2004), *Gypsy Traveller Students in Secondary Schools*. Stoke-on-Trent: Trentham Books.

Derry, T. K. and Williams, T. I. (1993), *A Short History of Technology*. New York: Dover Publications Inc.

Dollinger, A. (2000), An Introduction to the History and Culture of Pharaonic Egypt: Reshafim. Available at http://www.reshafim.org.il/ad/egypt/index.html?sort=alpha &action=search (accessed February 2008). http://www.esrc.ac.uk/ESRCInfoCentre/facts/UK/index58 (accessed February 2008). http://www.everychildmatters.gov.uk (accessed February 2008).

Geer, S. (2005), The ACE Project: working successfully to raise the attainment of African-Caribbean boys', in B. Richardson (ed.), *Tell It like It Is: How Our Schools Fail Black Children*. London: Bookmarks Publications and Trentham Books, pp. 201–205.

Griswold, P. A., Cotton, K. J. and Hansen, J. B. (1986), *Effective Compensatory Education Sourcebook. Volume I: A Review of Effective Educational Practices*. Washington, DC: U.S. Department of Education.

Hall, J. (2005), 'What can teachers do? What can parents do?', in B. Richardson (ed.), *Tell It like It Is: How Our Schools Fail Black Children*. London: Bookmarks Publications and Trentham Books, pp. 206–213.

Hamdun, S. and King, N. (eds) (1994), *Ibn Battuta in Black Africa*. Princeton, NJ: Markus Wiener.

Henry, A. and Williams, M. (2007), *Black Scientists and Inventors Book One*. London: BIS Publications.

Hrbek I. (ed.) (1992), *General History of Africa III: Africa from the Seventh to the Eleventh Century*. Berkeley, CA: UNESCO and University of California Press. http://www.independent.co.uk/environment/dumped-electrical-goods-a-giant-problem-467840.html (accessed February 2008). http://inventors.about.com/library/blwomen inventors.htm (accessed February 2008). http://inventors.about.com/library/inventors/blGilbreth.htm (accessed February 2008). http://inventors.about.com/library/inventors/blkevlar.htm (accessed February 2008). http://inventors.about.com/library/inventors/bllamar.htm (accessed February 2008).

Jones, A. (2002), in G. Owen-Jackson (ed.), *Teaching Design and Technology in the Secondary School*. London: The Open University and Routledge, pp. 82–3.

ki-Zerbo, J. and Niane. D. T. (eds) (1997), *General History of Africa IV: Africa from the Twelfth to the Sixteenth Century*. Berkeley, CA: UNESCO and University of California Press. www.labourbehindthelabel.org (accessed February 2008). http://laptop.org/laptop/design/ (accessed February 2008).

Levitzion, N. and Hopkins J. F. P. (eds) (1981), *Al-Bakri in Corpus of Early Arabic Sources for West African History*. Cambridge: Cambridge University Press.

Lucas, A. and Harris, J. R. (1962), *Ancient Egyptian Materials and Industries*. Chatham, UK: W. & K. Mackay & Co Ltd. http://www.macworld.co.uk/news/index.cfm?RSS&NewsID=14915 (accessed February 2008).

McClellan, J. E. and Dorn, H. (1999), *Science and Technology in World History*. Baltimore, MD: John Hopkins University Press.

McCormick, R. (2002), in G. Owen-Jackson (ed.), *Teaching Design & Technology in Secondary Schools*. London: The Open University and Routledge, pp. 96–7.

McKenley, J., Power, C., Ifhani, L. and Demie, F. (2003), *Raising Achievement of Black Caribbean Students: Good Practice in Lambeth Schools*. London: Lambeth Education.

McPartland, J. M. and Slavin, R. E. (1990), *Increasing Achievement of At-Risk Students at Each Grade Level* (Policy Perspectives Series July). Washington, DC: U.S. Department of Education.

Meyer, C. and Bir Umm Fawakhir (1997), 'Insights into ancient Egyptian mining'. *JOM*, 49, (3), 64–8. Available at http://www.tms.org/pubs/journals/JOM/9703/Meyer-9703.html#R2 (accessed February 2008).

Ofsted (2002) *ICT in Schools: Effect of Government Initiatives, Secondary Design and Technology*. London: Ofsted.

O'Hanlon, C. and Holmes, P. (2004), *The Education of Gypsy and Traveller Children*. Stoke-on-Trent: Trentham Books.

Owen, J. (2008), 'The governor: We need to know who our Gypsy pupils are'. *Guardian* (11 March).

Parker, A. and Neal, A. (1977), *Molas: Folk Art of the Cuna Indians*. Barre, MA: Barre Publishing.

Patera, C. (1995), *Mola Techniques for Today's Quilters*. Paducah, KY: Collector Books.

Penfold, J. (1988), *Craft, Design & Technology: Past Present and Future*. Stoke-on-Trent: Trentham Books.

Penny, V. (1998), 'Raising boys' achievement in English', in K. Bleach (ed.), *Raising Boys' Achievement in Schools*. London: Stoke-on-Trent: Trentham Books, pp. 81–106.

Pugh, R. (2007), 'Travellers tales'. *The Times Educational Supplement* (30 November).

Riad, H. (1981), 'Egypt in the hellenistic era', in G. Mokhtar (ed.), *General History of Africa II: Ancient Civilisations of Africa*. Berkeley, CA: UNESCO Heinemann and University of California Press, pp. 184-207.

Salend, Spencer J. (2000). *Creating Inclusive Classrooms: Effective and Reflective Practices*. Upper Saddle River, NJ: Prentice Hall. http://www.sda-uk.org/materials (accessed February 2008).

Sewell, T. (1997), *Black Masculinities and Schooling: How Black Boys Survive Modern Schooling*. Trentham Books: Stoke-on-Trent.

Sizemore, B. A. (1987), 'The effective African-American elementary school', in G. W. Noblit and W. T. Pink (eds), *Schooling in Social Context: Quantitative Studies*. Norwood, NJ: Ablex, pp. 175–202.

Spendlove, D. (2002), 'Raising boys' attainment in design and technology', in G. Owen-Jackson (ed.), *Teaching Design and Technology in the Secondary School*. London: The Open University and Routledge, pp. 252–3. http://www.standards.dfes.gov.uk/secondary/keystage3/downloads/sec_pptl042704u4lessoninclus.pdf (accessed February 2008). http://www.standards.dfes.gov.uk/specialistschools/faq (accessed February 2008). http://www.statistics.gov.uk/cci/nugget.asp?id = 192 (accessed February 2008). http://www.stepin.org. (accessed February 2008).

Sutton, J. E. G. (1983), 'West African metals and the ancient Mediterranean'. *Oxford Journal of Archaeology*, 2, (2), 181.

Swan, B. (1998), 'Teaching boys and girls in separate classes at Shenfield High School, Brentwood', in K. Bleach (ed.), *Raising Boys' Achievement in Schools*. London: Trentham

Books, pp. 157–172. http://www.teachernet.gov.uk/wholeschool/behaviour/
tacklingbullying/homophobicbullying/ (accessed February 2008).

Tentscher, W. (ed.) (2004), *Ten Years of Biogas Development in China*. Berlin: Naturgas
Handels GmbH.

Tyler, C. (ed.) (2004), *Traveller Education: Accounts of Good Practice*. Stoke-on-Trent:
Trentham Books.

Wai Andah, B. (1981), 'West Africa before the seventh century', in G. Mokhtar (ed.),
*General History of Africa II: Ancient Civilisations of Africa*. Berkeley, CA: UNESCO
Heinemann and University of California Press, p. 611.

Waxman, H. C. (1989), 'Urban black and Hispanic elementary school students:
perceptions of classroom instruction'. *Journal of Research and Development in Education*,
22, (2), 57–61.

Wesler, K. W. (1998), *Historical Archaeology in Nigeria*. Trenton, NJ: Africa World
Press.

Chapter 7

# English

## Valerie Coultas

The view of the author of this chapter is that teachers who value talk for learning in English lessons will create inclusive classrooms. I believe that talk in small groups and in whole-class discussion can allow all students to develop as more confident language users.

However, such teaching strategies require teachers to feel confident, self-motivated, and able to collaborate and share good practice, willing to experiment with teaching and learning. 'Coaching' from above is not the best way to import such teaching strategies into the classroom. These strategies have to be developed through teacher collaboration and shared discussion about how students learn and how teaching approaches need to be adapted and changed in different contexts.

The argument about talk and teacher empowerment has been made before but it gains a new relevance in the current context of another revision of the secondary curriculum. For while the new English secondary curriculum appears to be more flexible, the new English GCSE has been influenced by the demands of the back to basics lobby, and the 'delivery' of that still top-down English curriculum has to be analysed alongside new forms of social control of students and teachers in the data driven, permanent testing, performance management culture promoted by the government.

In discussing English and equal opportunities three questions will therefore be considered. First, what effect has the National Curriculum and new policy developments had on equal opportunities in English teaching? Second, what is the relationship between English, oracy and equal opportunities? Third, how should this understanding – that talk is central to equal opportunities in English teaching – impact on classroom practice?

# What Effect Has the National Curriculum and New Policy Developments Had on English Teaching?

As English teachers experience yet another change in the secondary English curriculum (QCA 2007a), the problem of trying to control and prescribe the teaching of English is highlighted. For English, as a language and as a subject in schools, never stands still. New words and expressions are always being invented and new texts, technologies and genres are altering reading habits and methods of communication. New pedagogies are developing as students are able to both analyse, reproduce and transform these new multi-modal modes of communication and produce their own texts, for example PowerPoint presentations, moving image texts, digital photographs, creating a website or radio pod cast, communications through MySpace. English teachers need to be able to give children access to a rich variety of spoken, literary and media texts to ensure that learning in schools keeps pace with these developments in language and communication. But the history of the past decade represents a highly prescriptive, reactionary era for English teachers in secondary schools.

## The English National Curriculum – a compromise

The English National Curriculum (DES 1990) represented a compromise with several different views about English teaching. These differing views were acknowledged by the chair of the committee reporting for the government at the time. Cox (1991) suggested that the final document was a compromise between these differing views.

While the National Curriculum did not fully recognize the role that talk plays in thinking and learning across the curriculum, it did acknowledge the importance of the spoken word in English as a subject and speaking and listening became, formally, first among equals as attainment target one (Coultas 2007).

The uneasy compromise that the National Curriculum represented between different strands of thinking meant that, while no one was completely happy with the outcome, the document could be interpreted in different ways. This therefore left teachers some room for manoeuvre to promote inclusive teaching, despite the Coxian literary canon privileging the English Literary Heritage above the literature of 'other' cultures and Standard English being a continued focus for debate (Moss 2000).

## The arrival of prescription

It was with the arrival of the SATs in 1993, the imposition of a prescriptive list of texts in the 1995 Dearing review and the establishment of the Literacy

Task Force in 1996, that the options open to English teachers began to close down. The KS3 SATs always represented the most conservative view of English teaching with their unseen pre-twentieth-century texts for reading and comprehension exercises and their imposed 'literary' study of Shakespeare as a piece of prose rather than a drama text (Coles 2003). These tests matched most closely to the view of English articulated, for example, by John Marenbon (1994), who was highly critical of the 'child-centred' English teaching of the 1970s and 1980s when comprehensive education began.

These exams were always out of place with the real development of language and communication in schools and society and have had a particularly negative effect on equal opportunities in the KS3 English curriculum. English as an Additional Language (EAL) and SEN students inevitably struggled with tests that had a strong cultural bias, that placed no value on collaboration or speaking and listening and imposed a one-shot approach to writing. The SATs, even more than the GCSE, have always looked backwards to a type of English teaching that was inaccessible and elitist. As the exams became established and the pressure on schools to 'raise standards' increased, the effect of these tests on the curriculum become more damaging.

## The standards agenda and school improvement

The Language in the National Curriculum (LINC) project, established in 1990 (Carter), was designed to develop teachers' subject knowledge in English. The research activities of the National Oracy Project, established in 1986 (Norman 1992), assisted teachers with inclusive practice by helping them to value language experiences of all children and plan for, record, evaluate and assess children's talk in purposeful situations.

But the government closed these agencies down in the 1990s and instead adopted the centralizing and directive framework of school improvement and school effectiveness promoted by those such as M. Barber (2001), deciding to set targets for schools and authorities in the drive to raise 'standards'. The government launched the National Literacy Strategy (DfEE 1998), and the Key Stage 3 Strategy (DfEE 2001) with the aim of raising 'standards'. These initiatives marked a decisive shift in education policy, taking the power to decide what to teach and how to teach it away from English teachers.

## A deficit model

The National Curriculum told teachers what to teach, which texts to use, and now the new policy documents told teachers how to teach or more importantly how to 'deliver' the appropriate objectives each term with a strong emphasis on the explicit teaching of grammar. The Key Stage 3 strategy: Framework for Literacy (2001), building on the Literacy Hour in primary schools, advocated the four-part lesson with 'interactive' starters, an introduction, independent work and the plenary moving from word-level work, to sentence-level work, then to text-level work 'where research and study skills are placed before reading for meaning', where progression is 'from the part to the whole' (Bousted 2003). Rigour in English teaching was interpreted as inflexibility. The word 'literacy' replaced 'English' and this denoted an emphasis on improving 'reading and writing'.

Inevitably, the policy-makers had begun to take a deficit view of the students who could not meet the standards and targets and therefore focused on what they found difficult, and this informed the emphasis of the 'literacy' framework. Although some ideas were non-controversial, such as promoting literacy across the curriculum, the documents had very clear priorities, for example to teach essay writing and non-fiction texts in particular and to identify the discrete writing skills required through exposure to and analysis of different genres. This basic skills approach to improving 'literacy', reading and writing, where teachers were asked to target underachievers, was explicitly counterposed to the more child-centred, whole-language approach of the English teaching of a previous era.

## English teachers disempowered

The literacy framework therefore disempowered the classroom teacher and promoted a new didacticism in the English classroom: the imperative of raising standards in reading and writing among those who were seen as 'weak' readers and writers rather than 'developing' readers and writers. The transmission mode of teaching was reinforced; for example, a highly teacher-centred form of shared writing was particularly apparent in the training videos (Hunt 2001). There was resistance to these ideas from some English teachers (Coultas 2007). As Myra Barrs pointed out in a speech at the 2006 London Association for the Teaching of English (LATE) conference, 'the authoritarian, teacher-centred view of how to teach reading and writing in the literacy frameworks did not see form as an expression of content'. The objectives put emphasis on defining linguistic form, particularly naming parts of speech, rather than first focusing on the meanings in a text or the context of language use. Writing was not viewed as a way of encouraging the pupil to make meaning. A large number of predetermined objectives imposed a narrow view of reading and writing where the 'text's meaning is fixed and determinate' (Bousted 2003).

## Reader response, discussion and interpretation downplayed

This meant that within the literacy frameworks, reader response, discussion and interpretation was given less emphasis. Many of the genre theorists (Martin 1985, cited in Myhill 1999) were critical of the whole-language theories that linked reading and writing with speaking and listening. While there are some obvious differences between reading and writing, the genre advocates were keen to draw a very sharp distinction between them and to separate them from speech. They disagreed with the views of those such as James Britton (1970), who had suggested that the first resource for children's writing (and children new to English) will be personal and expressive modes because these are most like speech. They also did not see the reading of whole texts as essential to good writing; they did not acknowledge the 'reader' in the 'writer' in the way in which previous writers had suggested (Barrs and Cork 2001). This meant that less emphasis was placed on the enjoyment of reading and writing (Thomas 2001) and that the newly established equal status of oracy and literacy was threatened.

## Exploratory talk undervalued

An increasingly prescriptive and centralized curriculum, an insistence on target-led, teacher-centred teaching had to lead to some casualties. And among these casualties were not only reader response but also inevitably exploratory and investigative talk. Wyse and Jones (2001) point out that talk takes on 'a functional quality' in the Literacy Hour 'a means by which reading and writing may be enhanced'. Talk has little value for itself. In the KS3 Strategy, speaking and listening was placed in the last column (Bousted 2003; Coultas 2007, Chapter 2).

## A new dawn?

Many teachers have therefore welcomed some of the changes in the new documentation. There is a recognition made of the study of a broader range of texts that students will now be officially allowed to read 'on paper and on screen' (QCA 2007a), the rebirth of the idea of creativity and inclusivity in English teaching and the renewed focus on speaking and listening, that regains its place as the first strand, and the recognition that drama and media texts can promote student self-confidence as with reading classic texts, for example. The opportunities for cross-curricular work and the reference to the use of contexts outside the classroom, made possible by the revised Programmes of Study (which allow for common approaches in different subjects), and the wider recognition of the role of formative assessment, create a little more space for teachers to negotiate the curriculum. The abolition of the KS3 SATs will also allow teachers more freedom to design their own curriculum.

But despite the English 21 (QCA 2005) debate, the discussion around Every Child Matters (Coultas 2008), QCA's attempts to adapt the curriculum and make it appear more forward looking, there is still little fundamental change and no real coherence in the new approach for English teachers. Taking all the changes together there is still continuity with some of the elitist traditions of the original documentation for those perceived as 'more able' students and a renewed and reductive emphasis on basic skills for all but particularly for those labelled 'the less able' (for arguments for a rejection of the concept of 'fixed ability', and the promotion of 'Learning Without Limits', see Hart *et al.* 2004; see also Cole 2008a; 2008b; Yarker 2008).

## The canon

The list of writers, the canon, chosen for pre-twentieth-century literature and for twentieth-century literature is still highly contentious and essentially elitist. Why should this list be there? Who should determine what a 'high-quality' piece of literature is? Cannot English teachers and their students in the twenty-first century be trusted to choose to read high-quality literature without having to still refer to a list drawn up by civil servants in a government department?

## Functional skills

The renewed emphasis on basic skills is dressed up as 'competence', signalling the development of the functional skills agenda. The pilot functional skills programme in English, maths and science began in 2007 as a response to the pressure of 'industry' to address the poor levels of literacy among employees. A pass in functional skills at level 2 will be a requirement for gaining grade C in English, maths and science by 2010 (QCA 2007b). Some have argued (e.g. Ainley and Allen 2007) that the skills 'deficit' is a false construct as increased levels of exam performance (60 per cent five A–Cs) far outstrip the technical demands of the workforce.

'Functional' English is a contentious term and many have questioned what is meant by this reductive terminology. But functional skills signals a real threat to inclusive English teaching as this exam has the potential to open up the old CSE/O level divide in a new form. New inequalities are emerging in the government's interpretation of 'different pathways' for 14–19 year olds (Allen 2007) and it is possible that some students who follow the two days in FE diploma option could be deprived of the opportunity of studying English or English literature. Some schools are already considering replacing the SATs with the functional skills tests for most pupils in Year 9, but those that find the tests more difficult may be placed in separate groups to retake them as they provide a vital link to the five A–C 'gold' standard.

Vocational pathways should not close down opportunities for personal development through the study literature or other texts. As John Hodgson argues (2005), 'critical, cultural and creative literacies should be an entitlement' for all. While many schools and teachers will always try to be creative with new curricula, once again the obsession with meeting superficially 'higher' literacy targets could end up dumbing down the English curriculum and damaging the overall quality of some students' educational experience.

## The abolition of coursework will lead to less choice

GCSE coursework in English will become a thing of the past as the new GCSE exam is introduced in 2009–10. Controlled assignments will now replace the coursework component of the English and English literature exams. Coursework allows the teacher to treat writing as a process, to allow pupils to plan and draft an assignment and get feedback from an audience. It places writing in a more realistic context. The new exams will make all written work for the GCSE of the one-shot variety; even if there are some opportunities for discussion before writing, the choices open to students will be more limited and determined by the examiners without teacher or pupil input. From a 100 per cent coursework in the 1980s, we have now moved to an exam that is more like the old O level. Pupils with SEN and EAL, who often make particularly good progress in writing during the production of GCSE coursework, will inevitably face new obstacles here.

## Data collection – the new testing obsession?

The abolition of the KS3 tests will open up the curriculum but it does not necessarily mean an end to a testing regime in secondary schools. Some teachers fear that we may be moving into a period of even greater bureaucracy and a culture of permanent testing where the new single-level tests and data collection, for example RAISEonline, will be used to inform a more rigorous form of performance management. Assessment for Learning initiatives have been welcomed by schools and given some power back to teachers but even here, Assessing Pupil Progress schemes (DCSF 2009) can become a burdensome and overly bureaucratic approach to the measurement of pupil progress. The obsession with accountability through data collection each term, now in secondary schools, continues to put pressure on school leadership teams, particularly in the most disadvantaged areas, to focus resources on ' underachievers' and leave 'no hopers' with fewer resources (Hart *et al.* 2004).

The government has not yet followed the Welsh example and developed a new form of portfolio moderation and support that empowers teachers to make their own judgements (ACCAC 2000).

## Looking back

Despite its limitations, the English National Curriculum reflected some of the good practice of the previous era, where comprehensive education was on the rise. It allowed some space for English teachers to incorporate equal opportunity practices into English teaching through promoting personal responses to literature, critical literacy and giving more prominence to drama, media texts and speaking and listening.

But the SATs exams and the KS3 strategy drastically narrowed that space. These exams changed the English curriculum, narrowing what was taught to what was tested – a narrow and traditional form of 'literacy', unseen reading comprehension and writing. While the emphasis on a whole-school approach to literacy did build on good practice, the detailed guidance about the planning of 'literacy' lessons in the KS3 strategy and the literacy frameworks marked a decisive break with good practice in English teaching and failed to build on many of the gains that had been made in previous decades. These approaches, despite their intentions, have made English teaching less inclusive. They run alongside changes that have begun to increase testing, target-setting and selection both in and between schools (Coultas 2007).

## Looking forward – teachers must take the lead in assessment

We have seen that, despite some of the aspirations of the new English curriculum, the changes to the GCSE and the introduction of functional skills tests will place limits on inclusive practice in secondary schools. The present form of data collection and possible separate pathways for summative testing at 16 will also have a restrictive impact on classroom practice.

Teachers' planning and assessment, however, should be going in a different direction, particularly in the area of speaking and listening, as the National Association for the Teaching of English (NATE) suggested in their submission to English 21: 'The curricular and social demands of 2015 are likely to include evidence of collaborative as well as individual working ... Drama, speaking and listening should be foregrounded as a key mode of teaching and assessment' (NATE 2005, p. 000). Such assessments, that should involve individual and group presentations, portfolios, practical productions and performance as well as the more traditional written forms, have to be informed by teachers' judgements.

The Welsh documents (2000) show that teachers are being encouraged to assess the four core subjects (Welsh, English, maths and science) across the curriculum at KS2 and KS3. Assessment for Learning initiatives have opened up the debate on what constitutes useful assessment, and but only if forms of formative and summative assessment are developed in consultation with classroom teachers, with reference to best past and present practice (Coultas 2006a; Coultas and Scott 2008), will all children's needs be addressed. This is the way forward for inclusive practice.

## What is the Relationship between English, Oracy and Equal Opportunities?

Oracy is fundamental to learning. Andrew Wilkinson (1965) described it as 'not a subject' but 'a condition of learning', a 'state of being in which the whole school must operate'.

As many English teachers know, students' language is an easily available resource ready for use in any classroom. Learning and language acquisition are closely associated and the teacher's role is to frame the learner's experience to create forms of social activity in the classroom that allow students to collaborate, explore and articulate their thoughts and feelings. This involves 'using the social situation in the classroom to the best advantage' (Cook *et al.* 1989, p. 8) so that the children learn naturally, giving the fullest acknowledgement to the affective domains of learning. A wide range of educational thinkers (Barnes *et al.* 1969; Vygotsky 1986; Wells 1987; Grudgeon *et al.* 1998; Corden 2000; Mercer 2000; Alexander 2001) have all asserted that small-group talk and classroom dialogue are vital to develop thought and to empower students as language users.

In discussing equal opportunities in English teaching I have therefore chosen to highlight the role of oracy because it is the bedrock from which all children can progress. Talk is a great equalizer, encouraging collaborative learning, yet it also allows students make an individual contribution. Equal opportunity approaches in teaching start by acknowledging what children bring to the classroom. The teacher must recognize and value the rich and varied cultural and language experiences that children bring with them from their homes and communities to be able to build on these in the classroom and create an environment and an ethos where students want to learn together.

Exploratory talk in small groups allows students to deepen understanding and develop thinking, to compare what they already know with something new, in an intimate and informal setting. This creates a context in school that is closer to the natural learning that takes place in the home and the world outside school. Talk allows students from different cultural backgrounds greater freedom to express themselves and bring their values, knowledge and experience into the classroom (Coultas 2007). It allows for unanticipated outcomes and gives more space for students to challenge the dominant middle-class values inherent in the school system and for youth to contest or at least interrogate the authority of the adult.

Lessons that promote small-group learning allow for a different approach to inclusion and equal opportunities. No talk task is ever exactly the same because students and teachers always bring unique experiences to a discussion. Such lessons go beyond the superficial, target-led interpretations of personalized learning. For rather than identifying students' 'weaknesses' and planning for separate tasks based on a narrow concept of ability, they create opportunities for children to share knowledge, rehearse spoken language and develop thinking skills together. Such an approach represents a radical break with a deficit 'catch-up' model of disadvantaged students.

This approach to lesson planning and oracy also treats the class as a unified group where common themes and interests are identified and knowledge about language is built upon. A key facet of such an approach is making connections between the teacher's knowledge and the experience, imagination and interests of all the students in the classroom.

This construction of learning as a collective experience, in small groups and as a whole class, through planning for active learning is developed by Hart *et al.* (2004), who focus on the hidden messages and ethos of the classroom. They refer back to Brian Simon writing in 1953, who understood that the progress of the whole group conditioned the progress of the individual child. He emphasized the need for the teacher to, first, 'weld the class together', concentrating 'on the interests the children have in common' and allowing for a variety of individual contributions that 'enliven the class as a whole'. Hart *et al.* (*ibid.*, p. 261) explain that the teacher's role, rather than dividing students up, is to make everybody in the class 'feel important' that inclusive teaching and learning has to be a shared experience, suggesting that 'diversity is achieved by what both teachers and young people do and contribute'. Both teachers and students are forming or developing their identities in such a process.

An English teacher who is able to successfully promote meaningful small-group learning and classroom discussion and dialogue will automatically create an inclusive classroom. Talk helps you get to know your students as individuals on a human level. You will send out an inclusive message by the way you talk to the students and allow them to talk with you, both as a class and as individuals; the choice of open-ended questions and tasks; the planning for collaborative and exploratory talk; the space you allow for thinking, reasoning and evaluating learning. If you truly value the students' voices and give them opportunities to speak and listen in a range of contexts, including to different audiences and in different languages where appropriate, teaching them how to construct knowledge together, you will be able to establish good relationships and work well with any class you are given.

Oracy, although valuable in itself in an inclusive classroom, also has to underpin and support all other strands of English. Oral rehearsal, drama and small-group and whole-class discussions can support and enrich reading and writing. In fact, active approaches to reading are essential to maintain the interest, enthusiasm and engagement of lively young adolescents of all abilities. Techniques such as choric reading, reader's theatre, jigsaw reading, group dramatic readings and drama (see Coultas 2007) need to become a basic part of a secondary teacher's repertoire to prepare students to read texts critically and promote personal response. ICT-based English lessons are also strengthened by activities that allow students to collaborate onscreen (Dimitri and Hodson 2006). The reading and analysis of media texts requires students to elaborate their ideas, compare different genres and to work together to produce media artefacts. Oral activities and outcomes, particularly sustained oral activities that encourage extended discussion (Coultas 2006b), can help to make students more cogent and confident readers and writers.

As I argued earlier, the deficit model underpinning the Key Stage 3 strategy (DfEE 2001) drove document writers away from understanding the significance of the oral language skills students bring to the classroom, and therefore led them to undervalue the speaking and listening strand and the importance of tentative discussions. It is therefore often necessary to reassert the importance of oracy today even among English teachers.

But oracy has never been simply an adjunct to reading and writing. It has great, intrinsic value in itself: for exploring feelings, clarifying ideas, checking errors, extending thinking, formulating and expressing opinions. All these processes require exploratory talk in small groups and presentational talk to wider audiences. Such forms of teaching build trust and self-esteem among all students of all ages and they are particularly valuable in contexts where students require extra support for language development (Coultas 2007). As suggested here, talk is also vital for helping students to understand and respond to what they read and for preparing writing. For equal opportunities in English (and other subjects) well-structured talk is therefore fundamental and opportunities for a wide range of talk repertoires should be planned for across the school.

# How Should This Understanding Impact on Inclusive Classroom Practice?

## Social class

Despite the philosophy of mainstream 'school improvement' that ignores social class and will accept 'no excuses' for underachievement (Barber 2001), a discourse that tries to outlaw discussions of social class and social disadvantage as a reason for lower achievement in English and other subjects, the statistics still tell the same story. Class is still a major indicator of high achievement (Moss 2000). According to Terry Wrigley (2006, p. 18), 'Britain, alongside the US, has one of the widest social divisions in educational attainment'. Wrigley quotes David Taylor (2003), who suggested that working-class boys have become the 'unwitting casualties' of the testing regime, as they are most likely to be labelled as 'failures'. As noted earlier, the SATs at 11 and 14, where girls outperform boys particularly in the writing papers, tested a very narrow and traditional part of English and did not focus on areas where working-class boys often do best – drama, speaking and listening, the study or production of media texts, for example (Coultas 2006b).

In criticizing teachers for inflexibility, the HMI report on English teaching (2005) fails to analyse how, in stark contrast to the days of the Inner London Education Authority (ILEA), where teachers working in the inner city often led innovative practice (Davidson 2004), the schools in the poorest areas are now placed under the most pressure to 'raise standards', drilling working-class students for the exams to meet the targets (Maguire 2006), while schools serving the better off often have more liberal regimes and the teachers are therefore able to be more flexible, creative and adventurous in their teaching. Middle-class and, to some extent, white flight from urban comprehensives to more established 'good schools', as back door selection grows, has also widened the gaps between schools.

School culture is predominantly a middle-class culture. As students rise up the school and higher education system, a higher value is placed on being 'literate', being able to read and write, and less value is placed on oracy. As suggested earlier, the English education system has always seen oracy as the inferior partner to literacy, defined as reading and writing (Alexander 2001).

But working-class culture is different. As Willy Russell (1991) explained, 'kids from working class families are part of a culture that has not literacy at its heart, but oracy'. This means that jokes, anecdotes, quizzes, word games, storytelling, drama, circle time, investigations of spoken language and different dialects, popular culture often provide more natural modes for working-class students and they will succeed in classrooms that give recognition to these forms of pedagogy and create opportunities to speak and think aloud in different contexts. Where students are engaged with the subject matter, they can all develop their argument and the formality of their speech through debate and discussion (Richmond 1983). If they are discussing a subject where they are experts, have become expert through group discussion, or they are knowledgeable about that speech genre, or topic, they will express themselves cogently and more formally. If they are well prepared, through a device such as role on the wall or some form of rehearsal (Coultas 2007) for hot seating, for example, many students will be able to make sustained contributions. These methods and stimuli are the best ways of allowing all students to develop a rich variety of speaking and listening skills and to use talk for learning. Such approaches also support the development of a wider range of reading and writing skills for all students.

## *Standard English*

Some of the sharpest controversies around social class are revealed in the debate on Standard English. The new curriculum suggests that 'students should be able to speak Standard English fluently' and suggests that teachers should bear in mind non-standard usages such as formation of adverbs 'come quick' and verb agreement 'they was'. The implicit advice is that teachers should correct non-Standard spoken English rather than celebrate different dialects. Such a 'correction' approach is at odds with the idea of valuing the linguistic resources of all children and empowering students to become more confident language users. Standard English is one form of dialect and its usage varies according to both the period, and the country in which it is spoken. Regional dialects have their own grammar and are different from Standard English but are equally effective forms of communication.

An inclusive approach to English allows teachers to create opportunities for the use of Standard English, where it is appropriate, but that does not mean 'correcting' students' speech in the classroom or demeaning the language of their home or community (Davies 2000). By allowing students to compare different forms of dialect, accent and discuss colloquialisms, slang, insults and new forms of language, English teachers can engage students in knowledge about language and celebrate diversity.

## Gender

An awareness of gender socialization is essential in promoting equal opportunities in English teaching, for example the ways in which boys often demand a greater degree of attention in class than girls and can dominate debate and discussion. The teacher will need to use a variety of strategies to encourage both genders to participate fully in different forms of discussion

such as ensuring turn-taking in class discussion through establishing ground
rules, creating a variety of roles within groups, evaluating the process of talk
(Coultas 2007).

The furore surrounding Ofsted reports on boys' 'underachievement' in
English (Daly 2000) has oversimplified the debate on gender in several
different ways. First, it has promoted a deficit view of boys' ability in English.
Second, it has helped to screen some of the differences between different socio-
economic groups, and third, it has meant that government reports have failed
to discuss gender discrimination in education against girls and the continued
underachievement of some girls. Finally, like so many aspects of government
policy, it lacks a historical perspective and fails to draw on evidence from the
past in contrasting boys' and girls' performance over time (Epstein *et al.*
1998).

Elaine Millard (1997) challenges the deficit view and discusses how boys
are differently literate and sometimes strong in different areas of English to
girls. She points out that boys' experience of school English is influenced by
their cultural practices outside school and that 'while girls currently appear to
be doing better', boys' social practices may be preparing them more
effectively for 'developments that are redirecting attention from the page to
the screen, from the pen to the mouse, and from a well-structured essay to a
well-organised website' (Millard 1997 cited by Daly 2000).

Research by Goodwyn (1995) supports the view that the majority of
teachers and students see no 'essential difference' in ability between boys and
girls in English – only a difference in attitude towards the subject. While girls
do not mind being good, 'boys want to be funny all the time'. Tying in with
the earlier feminist research some (e.g. Paechter 1998) have suggested that
boys seek to control others – teachers, girls and other boys – while girls seek to
control their environment by controlling themselves.


## From gay liberation to queer theory

New Labour has now repealed Clause 28, which outlawed the promotion of
homosexuality in schools – a response by the Thatcher government to the
work carried out on positive images by the ILEA. But homophobia is still a
mainstream issue when it comes to bullying in schools. Boys to other boys use
'gay' as a universal insult. School cultures act to re-enforce 'normality' and I
have heard male teachers in all-boys schools call groups of boys 'girls', just for
fun – and, of course, to assert their masculinity. Any teacher who is willing to
discuss issues of sexuality can find themselves labelled as deviant unless the
discussion is placed within a carefully thought out, established sex education
programme.

Given that such programmes are now rare in schools, it is often during the
English lesson, in discussions around literature or personal writing, that a

space is created for students to raise issues about identity and sexual orientation. This discussion exists as part of the hidden curriculum all the time in schools and students are often eager to raise questions about sexuality and sexual orientation. Literature allows students and teachers to discuss issues of sexual orientation and moral judgement in a shared reading experience. In such settings, English teachers can allow for independent, curious or even queer readings of texts as Viv Ellis (2000) suggests when commenting on a character in Poppy Z (Brite 1992) who has a very interesting interpretation of the Ralph/Jack relationship in *Lord of the Flies*.

## Students with English as an Additional Language

Oral rehearsal and scaffolding spoken English are central issues for students with EAL. The spoken word is vital for acquiring our native langue and is therefore essential for those who are developing linguistic skills in an additional language. Teachers need to value different starting points in English and recognize that diversity in culture and language enriches English teaching.

Peer collaboration is crucial as it is the motor force of acquiring language for school age children. Small-group learning and peer collaboration allows children with EAL to become involved at the level they choose. They might use body language or speech to join in or just listen to models of language use (Cinamon 1994).

But, in addition, the teacher also needs to understand the importance of creating opportunities for dual language use. Just imagine if speakers of English were in schools where they had to learn all their subjects at secondary level in a foreign language. How would we long to relax and find an opportunity to speak our own language?

The whole school needs to develop a positive approach dual language use and adopt strategies for successfully promoting this. Opportunities need to be created for using home languages with others who share these in group discussions, pair work and storytelling. Students should be allowed to code switch from one language to another and teachers should create contexts where they can talk about their own personal and educational experiences. Students with EAL should be encouraged to write in their home language and books and tapes can be provided in different languages. Members of the local community can be invited into classrooms to tell or read stories with the class.

## Multicultural, black and world literature

The English curriculum is naturally multicultural because it potentially includes literature and language from all cultures and communities. But the

English literary canon challenges this view and suggests that one literary tradition is superior to others.

Many teachers will want to go much further than the new curriculum in exploring multicultural literature, black literature and world literature and texts in translation. In exploring black literature and poetry it is important that teachers make aesthetic judgements and not simply use this literature to explore the sociological aspects of different cultures (Coultas 1989). The oral tradition in poetry lends itself to public reading and performance. Modern Caribbean poetry, for example, can be read aloud and studied for the clarity and resonance of the poet's voice, and such readings can highlight the way in which poets like John Agard and Valerie Bloom use humour and dialect so successfully to expose the contradictions of racism and other forms of human behaviour (Coultas 2007).

## Special educational needs

Physical difficulties do not always mean that a student will have a learning difficulty. However, children with sight and hearing difficulties will need special measures, such as larger scripts, audiotapes or extra visual stimuli. Helpers may also need to scribe for these students.

Children with dyslexia, who may have cognitive difficulties with English in relation to reading, writing and spelling, will benefit from a wide range of different teaching strategies, including use of visual prompts, mind mapping and ICT.

All children with SEN benefit from using talk to learn. The child on school action, or school action plus, with emotional and behavioural difficulties or low levels of cognition, literacy or speech and language difficulties, will respond well not only to visual stimuli but also to drama, and other non-verbal forms of communication. Informal talk, small-group discussion and pair activities with clear outcomes and extra adult guidance that involve, for example, expressing personal experiences and preferences or sequencing, matching and re-arranging text can also support these students. It is the affective mode of learning that often captures the interests of these pupils. While regular routines, rewards and clear ground rules establish a secure environment, oral exercises and non-verbal modes of communication with clear outcomes can boost children's self-confidence, sense of group identity and unlock their imagination and creativity (Coultas 2008).

## We Must Celebrate What Children Can Do

While I have written about identified groups of children and their particular needs, it is important to underline the remarks made earlier in this chapter.

The teacher's role is to establish common bonds and common interests in the classroom to help shape and develop a collective identity and sense of purpose. Talk is a very effective way of doing this. Teaching should be a shared experience where children are involved in personally and socially significant experiences. Diversity can then be 'achieved by both what teachers and young people contribute' (Hart *et al.* 2004). As much as possible the teacher should then be in a position to reward and praise the whole group.

The 'school improvers' make the mistake of focusing with such hard-headed managerial strategies on 'targeting underachievement' that they fail to understand and celebrate what children can do and what really motivates them to learn. These managerial approaches are often very top down and target driven, and fail to understand not only what children bring into the classroom but also the unquantifiable aspects of teaching. They fail to place value on the ethos of a classroom and the role that talk can play in establishing such an ethos or the way in which good practice can be spread from the bottom up. The cult of 'the individual' promoted through the 'advanced skills', 'excellent' and 'fast track' training schemes and the constant restructuring of urban schools have introduced new forms of social control that cut against a collectivist tradition in teaching, a tradition where learning takes place through team teaching, intellectual enquiry and sharing good practice among groups of staff that see themselves as equals. As Lionel Warner (2008, p. 90) suggests, the 'education industry is managed in a distinctly Fordist way, with a steep hierarchy of power, sharp divisions of labour and centralised "quality control"'.

In classrooms where student talk is valued and active engagement and intellectual curiosity is encouraged, the students will learn to work with each other, to listen to, and value each other as well as the teacher. They will learn how to disagree, or come at things from different angles, and value difference but see learning as a shared experience where knowledge is co-constructed.

Some of the ways in which schools can promote speaking and listening involve taping and evaluating teaching in a secure context; sharing good practice through team teaching; asking students to evaluate their learning; recording pupil talk and drama; planning for debates, panels, prizes, presentations, performance, recitations, readings and plays that celebrate all children's oral skills. These are the real pupil voices that should be celebrated in schools and when student councils meet they should be listened to, where possible, not simply used as another managerial 'consultation' device.

Well-structured talk helps to create a positive classroom and school ethos and an intellectual self-confidence that is of lasting benefit to all students. Oracy and literacy are natural allies and student-led, collaborative talk must be at the core of our work if we wish to promote equal opportunities in English teaching.

# References

ACCAC (Qualifications, Curriculum and Assessment Authority for Wales) (2000), *Using Speech for Exploring Ideas Unit 3: Consistency in Teacher Assessment*. ACCAC.

Ainley, P. and Allen, M. (2007), *Education Make You Thick – In it?* London: The Tufnell Press.

Alexander, R. (2001), 'Talk in teaching and learning: international perspectives' QCA Seminar.

Allen, M. (2007), 'Getting personal?' *Teacher to Teacher* Autumn 2007 Supplement to *The Teacher*. London: NUT.

Barber, M. (2001), 'The National Literacy Strategy – recognition of success'. *Literacy Today* 26.

Barnes, D., Britton, J. and Rosen, H. (1969), *Language, the Learner and the School*. Harmondsworth: Penguin.

Barrs, M. (2006), Speech to the LATE conference.

— and Cork, V. (2001), *The Reader in the Writer: Case Studies in Children's Writing*. CLPE.

Bousted, M. (2003), 'English or literacy? That is the question'. *English Teaching: Practice and Critique*, 2, (3).

Brite, P. (1992), *Lost Souls*. Dell Publishing.

Britton, J. (1970), *Language and Learning*. Harmondsworth: Penguin.

Carter, R. (ed.) (1990), *Knowledge about Language in the Curriculum: The LINC Reader*. Hodder & Stoughton.

Cinamon, D. (1994), 'Bilingualism and oracy', in S. Brindley (ed.), *Teaching English*. Routledge and Open University Press.

Cole, M. (2008a), '*Learning Without Limits*: a Marxist assessment'. *Policy Futures in Education*, 6, (4), 453–63. Available at http://www.wwwords.co.uk/pfie/content/pdfs/6/issue6_4.asp (accessed 27 February 2008).

—(2008b), 'Reply to Yarker'. *Policy Futures in Education*, 6, (4), 468–9. Available at http://www.wwwords.co.uk/pdf/validate.asp?j=pfie&vol=6&issue=4&year=2008&article=8_Yarker_PFIE_6_4_web (accessed 21 December 2008).

Coles, J. (2003), 'Alas, poor Shakespeare: teaching and testing at Key Stage 3'. *English in Education*, 37, (3).

Cook, J., Forrestral, P. and Reid, J. (1989), *Small Group Learning in the Classroom*. Chalkface Press.

Corden, R. (2000), *Literacy and Learning through Talk: Strategies for the Primary Classroom*. Open University Press.

Coultas, V. (1989), 'Black girls and self-esteem', *Gender and Education*, 1 (3).

— (2006a), 'Thinking out of the SATS box'. *EnglishDramaMedia* (NATE magazine), (January).

— (2006b), 'Investigating talk in challenging classrooms – boys enjoy the power of talk. *English in Education*, (Summer).

— (2007), *Constructive Talk in Challenging Classrooms*. London: Routledge.

— (2008), *Every Child Matters: Unlocking the Voice of the SEN Child – The Alien Coat Game* (unpublished paper for BERA).

Cox, B. (1991), *Cox on Cox: An English Curriculum for the 1990s*. Hodder and Stoughton.

— (1996), *Cox on the Battle for the English Curriculum*. Hodder and Stoughton.

Daly, (2000), 'Gender difference in achievement', in J. Moss and J. Davidson (eds), *Issues in English Teaching*. London: Routledge.

Davidson, J. (2004), cited by A. Shepherd in 'ILEA planted a passion in me'. *The Times Educational Supplement* (7 May).

Davies, J. (2000), 'Correct or appropriate?', in J. Davidson and J. Moss (eds), *Issues in English Teaching*. London: Routledge.

DCSF (2009), *Assessment and Progression in Speaking and Listening*. Available at http://nationalstrategies.standdards.dcsf.gov.uk/node/21060?uc (accessed 10 February 2009).

DES (1990), *English in the National Curriculum* HMSO.

DfEE (1998), *The National Literacy Strategy Framework for Teaching*. DfEE.

— (2001), *Key Stage 3 National Strategy Framework for Teaching English: Years 7, 8 and 9*. DfEE.

Dimitri, Y. and Hodson, P. (2006), 'Putting the C into ICT', in P. Hodson and D. Jones (eds), *Unlocking Speaking and Listening*. London: David Fulton.

Ellis, V. (2000), 'What has sexuality got to do with English teaching?', in J. Davidson and J. Moss (eds), *Issues in English Teaching*. Routledge.

Epstein, D., Elwood, J., Hey, V. and Maw, J. (eds) (1998), *Failing Boys? Issues in Gender and Achievement*. Buckingham: Open University Press.

Goodwyn, A. (1995), *English and Ability*. Open University Press.

Grudgeon, E., Hubbard, L., Smith, C. and Dawes, L. (1998), *Teaching Speaking and Listening in the Primary School*. London: David Fulton.

Hart, S., Dixon, A., Drummond, M. J. and McIntyre, D. (2004), *Learning Without Limits*. Maidenhead: Open University Press.

HMI (2005), *English 2000–5: A Review of the Inspection Evidence* (Crown copyright). Ofsted.

Hodgson, J. (2005), 'Crisis? What crisis?' *The Times Educational Supplement English Special* (Autumn).

Hunt, G. (2001), 'Talking about reading', in P. Goodwin (ed.), *The Articulate Classroom*.

*Language in the National Curriculum DVD* (2007). University of Nottingham

Maguire, M. (2006), *Socialist Teachers Alliance (STA) Bulletin*.

Marenbon, J. (1994), 'The new orthodoxy examined', in S. Brindley (ed.), *Teaching English*. Routledge in association with The Open University.

Mercer, N. (2000), *Words and Minds*. Routledge.

Millard, E. (1997), *Differently Literate*. Falmer Press.

Moss, J. (2000), 'Literacy and social class', in J. Davidson and J. Moss (eds), *Issues in English Teaching*. Routledge.

Myhill, D. (1999), 'Writing matters: linguistic characteristics of writing in GCSE English Examinations'. *English in Education*, 33, (3), NATE.

NATE (National Association for the Teaching of English) (2005), *Submission to English 21*.

Norman, K. (ed.) (1992), *Thinking Voices: The Work of the National Oracy Project*. Hodder and Stoughton.

Paechter, C. (1998), *Educating the Other*. Falmer Press.

QCA (2005), *English 21*. QCA.

— (2007a), *Review of the Secondary Curriculum* (Draft for Consultation 05/02/07). QCA.

— (2007b) *Functional Skills Bulletin Edition Three* (updated 05-09-07). QCA.

Richmond, J. (1983), 'Talking about race'. *The English Magazine*. The ILEA English Centre.

Russell, W. (1991), in V. Hughes, *Literature Belongs to Everyone* London: Arts Council.

Vygotsky, L. (1986), *Thought and Language*. Cambridge, MA: MIT Press.

Warner, L. (2008), '"The freedom to frame questions worth asking" ... or three stories and three (other) fragments of research'. *English in Education*, 42, (1), (Spring).

Wells, G. (1987), *The Meaning Makers*. London: Hodder and Stoughton.

Wilkinson, A. (1965), *Spoken English*. Birmingham: University of Birmingham.

Wrigley, T. (2006), *Another School Is Possible*. London: Bookmarks.

Wyse, D. and Jones, R. (2001), *Teaching English, Language and Literacy in the Primary School*. Routledge & Falmer.

Yarker, P. (2008), '*Learning Without Limits* – a Marxist assessment: a response to Mike Cole'. *Policy Futures in Education*, 6 (4), 464–468.

# Chapter 8

# Geography

## Maurice Nyangon

This chapter focuses on the barriers to all students achieving their full potential that are rooted historically in the disparate understanding of geography itself. How the subject is delivered is scrutinized from both a historical and a pragmatic perspective but, importantly, the link between past and present is highlighted as key if the subject is finally to be embedded as a cohesive, mainstream subject that allows students to fully understand the realities of their world.

## The Past

For over a century geography has been under scrutiny from school inspectors who expected more from the subject than 'A dreary recitation of names and statistics, of no interest to the learner, and of little use except perhaps in the sorting departments of the Post Office' (Thomas Godolphin Rooper, Bradford Inspector of Schools, *The Geography Teacher* 1901).

Historically, geography has long had a rocky road (begging a great deal of fieldwork) to its current curriculum incarnation. The subject has been fraught with internal disputes and ideological spats that amuse other educationalists who cheerfully label geographers as 'paranoid and frequently insecure' (McLaren 2003). Nothing in the geography curriculum has been stable; reform and innovation are the buzzwords rather than consolidation and entrenchment (Williams 1997, p. 25). It is the most 'chameleon' of subjects, with '57 Varieties' (Goodson 1993). Geographers' disparate voices have, for a hundred years, drowned out, in deeply masculine tones, those of the students: their histories, roots and experience. The subject's potential to empower socially those students, an empowerment that potentially is at the very heart of the subject, is lost. The curriculum, after all, is not neutral but can serve to perpetuate the status quo or to create dreams and visions for a better world (McLaren 2003).

Very possibly a major key to the conundrum of success and failure at school lies in the collision between antecedent curriculum structures and students' cultural capital – school subjects are most commonly seen as at best beneficial at worst neutral elements – in fact through their form and content they are deeply active in determining the distribution of life chances. (Goodson 1993, p. xxvi)

Consequently, large numbers of students are failed if either implicit or explicit (or both) impetus is given to the Western status of cultural capital in which 'select' knowledge, as determined by white, male, heterosexual geographers, becomes sacred. For a century, the lust for academic status and the fear of subject dissipation led to factionalism between regional – 'old' (physical, patriarchal and quantitative), 'new' (environmental and qualitative) and fieldwork geographers that did not serve the subject well and continued to resonate at the birth of the National Curriculum and beyond. What the subject should 'be' has been the source of bitter contention and dispute. From its late nineteenth-century conception as a subject in its own right, geography was fraught with criticism and lack of cohesion. In its late Victorian infancy, it was taught reluctantly by non-specialists and its reputation for rote learning (still robustly defended by those who determinedly decry source-based learning) soon established 'An unintelligent oral cram, which [pupils] were compelled, under penalties to take in and retain till the examination was over' (E. G. A. Holmes, ex-Chief Inspector of Schools, *What Is and What Might Be*, 1912).

Geography was legitimized on the grammar school curriculum by 1904 in the Secondary Regulations (that ironically almost identically mirrored the National Curriculum subjects listed in 1988 (Goodson 1998, p. 156). The Empire itself was cited as key to the subject's importance for students:

Travel and correspondence have now become general; the British dominions are to be found in every clime and these facts alone are sufficient to ensure that the subject shall have an important place in the school timetable. (The Hadow Report: 'The Education of the Adolescent', HMSO 1927)

The nature of geography lessons had been established and changed little post-war. Committing to memory the facts and figures of those 'dominions' was a lesson staple coupled with a descriptive study of the local environment. There were neither attempts to enable students to understand geographical processes nor a holistic understanding of the links between the environment, the elements and people's lives. This notion of geography was labelled, in the 1960s, as 'old geography' and students were disaffected with a subject that seemed to have no relation to post-war Britain. Half a century of Inspectors' criticisms found an answer in a flurry of 'new geography' models incorporating links between landforms and those that worked that land, a qualitative, socially 'scientific' approach. Fieldwork too had to change. Its prevalence in universities had strengthened its position in schools but relied on description rather than analysis and became another point of contention and dispute. Rather than perceive this as natural subject development, battle lines were drawn up:

> Better that Geography should explode in an excess of reform than bask in the watery sunset of its former glories; for in an age of rising standards in school and university, to maintain the present standards is not enough – to stand still is to retreat, to move forward hesitantly is to fall back from the frontier … This is the teaching frontier of Geography. (Chorley and Haggett 1967, p. 377)

What was taught in one class vacillated between schools, and even classrooms. This gulf persists, with some geographers deeming academic rhetoric as 'real' geography, disparaging visual arguments in preference to the textual – giving quantitative data inherent credibility. Equally discouraging, a twenty-first-century geographer can, theoretically, be as passively reliant on artefacts as in the nineteenth century, when lantern lamps – projecting maps, diagrams and photos – were criticized as vehicles for political agitation or missionary propaganda; both substituted passive sensation for knowledge (Driver 2003, p. 228). In the nineteenth and first half of the twentieth centuries, artefacts were used as divisively as text to entrench imperialistic perceptions of indigenous peoples and their relationship to white men. Neither methodology is free from associations of racism and manipulation. The gulf between the 'old' and 'new' geography – of received knowledge and rhetoric, artefact and environment – still must be bridged and contextualized with the geography teacher at the centre of the material (Roberson 2004).

An obsession with academic kudos, seeking confirmation of status from the acceptability of geography as an Advanced (A) level subject by the universities (Goodson 1993), held at bay 'pretenders' such as environmental studies. The loss was the students', and any gain was transitory and ultimately illusionary. Only 20 years ago the National Curriculum imposed a reluctant, uneasy, ceasefire and the inevitability of offering vocational subjects means leisure and tourism was established in geography departments that, 30 years before, resisted environmental studies vociferously. There was a 'siege' mentality approach to protecting the 'academic' nature of the subject perceived as a 'Cinderella' subject by the 1960s in the independent and grammar schools, with students who were not considered able to access the academic rigour of the classics or science being offered geography as a 'softer' option (Goodson 1998, p. 158). This propensity to focus on the 'academic' is still a feature of our twenty-first-century classrooms and to the disadvantage of the subject holistically. At Key Stage 3 (11–14 age groups), geography suffers in its delivery due to the perceived need to develop a Scheme of Work to match specifications chosen for Key Stage 4 (14–16 age group) and Advanced level (post-16 age group) rather than engage and motivate the younger students. Ironically, but unsurprisingly, this leads to many students losing interest in a subject that has little meaning for them as citizens of the world they are studying.

It remains the case that attainment is higher in examination classes, particularly post-16, sometimes reflecting this relative neglect of innovative teaching at Key Stage 3. Examination work continues to be better planned by more expert teachers with higher expectations of students (Ofsted 2005; 2008). Holmes' criticism in 1912 that geography was an 'unintelligent oral cram' still echoes in the opinion of his fellow Inspectors over a century later. Unfortunately, relatively few geography departments have considered the ways in which pedagogy and subject content can be integrated into a coherent and relevant teaching and learning programme that develops students' understanding and skills in geography systematically rather than merely imparting information. This emphasis on coverage of content particularly inhibits the opportunity to develop enquiry-based work and there continues to be a reliance on 'project' investigations resulting in pages of downloaded information from the internet (Ofsted 2005), displayed as meaninglessly in folders and on walls as the copied maps displayed in pre-First World War classrooms.

## The past is not just another country

### 'Race'

British imperialism inevitably cast its racist shadow over the subject; the superiority of the paternalistic Englishman, the natural 'master' over the indolent, childlike 'native', was explicit in early twentieth-century textbooks (Cole and Blair 2006). Yet how far do geography specifications and textbooks courses unpick these prejudices of the past in the study of developing countries? The shadow still hovers in our classrooms but has ceased to be a 'fact' to be explored. Students from developing or Eastern European countries study their birthplaces or countries of origin in an abstract way that is disconnected from the historical and geographical links that existed and exist between Europe, Asia and Africa for so many years. Immigration, emigration and migration are taught in population studies in isolation from the specific student experiences, the personal 'push and pull' factors that have brought them from all over the world into British geography classrooms. The complexities of what 'race' means in modern Britain and why those meanings have been 'constructed' from their imperialistic roots are not explored (Cole and Virdee 2006). Of equal importance is that the attitudes and experiences of all students in the classroom are taken into account and that teachers make no presumptions about student assumptions or prejudices but work towards planning lessons that enable reflection and discussion, enquiry and discovery (Schlesinger 1994).

Geography is taught by teachers who, during their Bachelor of Education (BEd) degrees, Bachelor of Art (BA) degrees followed by Qualified Teacher Status (QTS) or Postgraduate Certificate of Education (PGCE) courses, are very unlikely to have studied the legacy of colonial attitudes on their subject, their classrooms and, essentially, on their own attitudes to the subject (Cole and Blair 2006). Moreover, their primary school geography lessons are likely to have been delivered by a non-specialist whose own image of the subject may have been embedded at the end of Key Stage 3 and not necessarily revised. There is clearly a need to explore explicitly images of teaching and learning so that student teachers' experiences, as learners of primary geography education during PGCE, can be directly related to those as teachers of geography during their school experience. This is important, as it is possible that, as student teachers coping with the demands of classroom control and organization, they fall back on their image of *teaching*, formed from their long period of experiential learning as students, which may be stronger than their brief experience as trainee teachers. Whether, during a one-year postgraduate course, it is possible to develop students' images of geography in ways that are more helpful to them as teachers is another question (Martin 2000, p. 233).

## Gender

Not only is geography a historically racist subject, it is also a historically sexist subject. The renowned Victorian female geographers, Martha Krug-Genthe, Ellen Semple and Clémence Augustine Royer (Robic 2008), and explorers such as Mary Kingsley in West Africa, Marianne North travelling through North America and Isabella Bird voyaging up the Yangtze, had wide contemporary fame and prestige. They have, however, been erased from the curriculum and geographical landscape (Rose 1995, p. 414). Geography has been dubbed by feminist geographers a 'Master Subject', that celebrates the objective, exclusive and dualistic rather than its differences, reflection and situational nature (Rose 1993, p. 72). As if a Trojan Horse (Desbiens 1999, p. 181), female geographers enter the dominant masculinity of the subject with studies of family and female experience that shifts the perceived knowledge of a century in its contention that geography is not objective but subjective.

Established traditions were male, paternalistic and exclusive; traditional cultural geography and geographers regarded the landscape as simply the scene within the range of the observer's vision and it was the male observer who constructed his own particular relationship between society and land. His gaze was both gendered and contradictory; his attempts at objectivity marked by desire and fear. Landscape as a way of seeing is bound to class divisions. For instance, eighteenth- and nineteenth-century merchants commissioned paintings of their holdings, sometimes with them in it. Their beautifully dressed wives and daughters, however, appear as a part of the holding of the master while peasant women were depicted within the landscape to stress their 'natural' position in society (Rose 1995, p. 414).

The notion of fieldwork as a 'Boys' Own' adventure: romantic, alluring and empowering the observer, was described with rapture by James Kirkland Wright, the President of the Association of American Geographers in 1946:

> In the course of fieldwork ... we have all climbed a mountain and gazed over uninhabited and unfamiliar country ... In the contemplative mood that the mountaintops induce, we have brooded over the view ... and experienced a pleasurable sense of the mysterious – perhaps even felt a touch of the sinister. We have heard the Sirens' voices. (Wright 1947, cited in Powell 2002, p. 269)

The dislocation between the observer and the observed led to the neglect of the full range of spatial, material and corporeal practices that should naturally link physical and human geography – the 'Unity Debate'. In the 1980s, this raged over the links between the environment and its inhabitants (Powell 2002, p. 265). Feminist geographers, however, perceived this as further paternalistic 'colonialism' of the subject. Field trips are perceived as tough and heroic, as students confront nature in the name of scientific knowledge and an understanding of 'other' societies; 'geographical masculinities in action' (Rose 1993, p. 69).

Just as with 'race' and its troubled history, the very nature of fieldwork historically should be part of current geography teaching. The notion of the geographer on Wright's mountaintop, lured by the sirens of further exploration and 'discovery', should be an acknowledged part of our understanding of what geography was but cannot be in the twenty-first century.

### Sexual orientation

Perhaps more than any other humanities subject, geography has historically assumed a heterosexual norm and, in so doing, has obliterated alternatives. Neither gender nor sexuality has been regarded as part of the central agenda of human geography, but regarded as peripheral, private and personal. What after all could possibly be geographical about such intimate personal subjects as gender and sexuality? By the 1980s, however, there was a clear emphasis on the issues of class, gender and globalization, progressing in the 1990s to more emphasis on sexuality and sexual politics (England 1999, p. 95). The importance of heterosexuality in maintaining and reproducing geographical order has been recognized, particularly in attempts to elucidate the importance of domestic space in maintaining the 'family values' which lie at the heart of hetero-normality (Hubbard 2000, p. 217).

Space is fundamentally shaped by the dynamics of human sexuality and the way the world has been traditionally mapped mirrors the patriarchal construction of masculinity that geographers are beginning to recognize, and, to a lesser extent, that teachers are beginning to teach. Neither hetero-sexuality nor patriarchy is a natural product of a biological urge to reproduce, but is socially produced and maintained – or not. The heterosexual mapping of cities is the context that coordinates most contemporary Western living, supplies the order and organization that automatically links otherwise unrelated sexualized bodies. From such a perspective, urban sexual geography – in the sense not just of simple location, but of where sexual identities are deemed appropriately to belong – appears crucial to any understanding of heterosexual relations. For instance, Vancouver's 'skid-row' can be taught as a space of abject poverty and destitution where the figure of the derelict symbolizes masculine failure and the deteriorating landscape casts a grim shadow over the ideal of the mythology of heterosexual suburbia (*ibid.*, p. 201). The complex relationship between heterosexuality, family and housing has been explored in Nast and Wilson's (1994) deconstruction of housing projects in Kentucky, where heterosexuality is promoted through suburban building codes, development regulations and aesthetic frameworks enacted through the 'paternal law of the state' and maintained through state surveillance. Even in a housing project designed primarily for single mothers, they show that women are moved from housing unit to housing unit on the basis of their (and their children's) reproductive status, a policy designed to maintain the illusion of heterosexual moral order even when the idealized nuclear family no longer remains the dominant household type.

Similar examples can be cited in England by examining aggressive community protests against street prostitution in a number of British 'red-light' districts, notably Balsall Heath, in Birmingham. Community protesters took to the streets in an attempt to displace street prostitutes and kerb-crawlers from 'their' neighbourhood (Hubbard 1998, p. 61). A further example is that of Knowsley, a deprived outer suburb of Liverpool, known as 'Single Mother City', with accompanying tabloid rhetoric, describing the descent of the area from that of a 'peaceful, rural place with solid values' to 'a place with no moral compass where girls expect the state to provide their children with designer clothing' (Hubbard 2000, p. 209). All examples ironically expose the dichotomy between society and its iniquities and the myths of suburbia and iniquities of street life; this dichotomy should be at the heart of students' learning if teachers address heterosexuality as a political and economic system in which gender is socially, politically and economically (and, to a certain extent, biologically) constructed.

By emphasizing power relations, these discussions can illustrate how heterosexuals are privileged relative to homosexuals and how heterosexual men are privileged relative to heterosexual women. Teachers acknowledging the existence of heterosexual hegemony, while teaching against heterosexism and homophobia, can restore a balance to our geographical past. In doing so the existence of geographers, teachers and students who are not themselves heterosexual can be acknowledged (England 1999, p. 98).

### Social class and capitalism

Geographical balance is not only an equation involving gender and sexual orientation, but also an understanding of the pivot of class and economic power that underpins not only our historical pasts but also our geographical present. Geography has the capacity to explore, explain and examine moral landscapes and journeys. Ultimately, the subject has the power to create a more equitable map in which the morally arbitrary contingencies of good or bad fortune are, if not eliminated, at least exposed and acknowledged as the consequence of exploitation and imperialism (Smith 2000, p. 14).

Just as geography has roots in imperialism and patriarchy that must be recognized, the world we live in is shaped by the highs and lows of capitalism, poverty and environmental crisis, often (usually) determined by chance of circumstance and social situation rather than a matter of individual hard work and volition (Williams 1985, p. 185). However hard some people have worked and however much they have wanted to live and work in a more prosperous and just society, the circumstances they live in shapes the world in which they live and too often they are powerless to change it. In a study of human or economic geography, the morality of capitalist foundations and structures should go hand in hand with the study of natural resources and import–export relationships: 'Disadvantages in resources for social advance-ment are associated with generally inferior economic situations. It is as if the gamblers with the least funds were also dealt the fewest cards' (Miller 1992, p. 228).

Place in its geographical sense is readily added to the argument from arbitrariness in that so much of what people achieve is a matter of being in the right place at the right time, of having good luck in family, teachers, friends and circumstances (Baker 1987, p. 60). This is all part of the undeserved inheritance. No one earns the 'right' to be born to a family living in American affluence rather than Kenyan slums but the enormity between these life chances does not negate the same innate capacities and the same willingness to try (Miller 1992, p. 240). The desire for a better life may be the same but the opportunity to achieve it not so (Nett 1971, p. 215). How capitalist countries determine citizenship and the right to apply for that citizenship is disparate and disheartening at the same time, mapping the world's population with rules and regulation, the modern equivalent of feudal birthright privileges (Carens 1987, p. 262).

Geography teaching should recognize that while equality has not yet in any economic sense been achieved, what can be worked towards is equalization – where social and economic inequalities can be arranged to the conscious advantage of the most disadvantaged through the planned distribution of needs:

> Justice in modern industrial societies requires a societal commitment to meeting the basic needs of all persons ... If persons suffer material deprivation of basic needs for food, shelter, health care, and so on, then they cannot pursue lives of satisfying work, social participation, and expression. (Young 1990, p. 91)

Human geography incorporating the exploration of social justice or, in too many cases, injustice, and its effect on the development, past and present, of the world we live in, can deepen students' understanding of globalization, poverty and need. The gaps between 'them' and 'us' may be described in geography lessons but will only be narrowed if analysed morally:

> There is such a thing as moral progress ... in the direction of greater human solidarity ... the ability to see more and more traditional differences (of tribe, religion, race, custom, and the like) as unimportant when compared with similarities with respect to pain and humiliation – the ability to think of people wildly different from ourselves as included in the range of 'us'. (Rorty 1989, p. 71)

All students need to understand the interconnections of cultural formation rather than the boundaries between places and people (Powell 2002, p. 268).

> Teachers have a major role in preparing young people for adult life; this means life in a multicultural, multilingual Europe, which, in its turn, is interdependent with the rest of the world. It is a world in which the roles of men and women are changing and both sexes are likely to have dual responsibilities for home and work. (National Curriculum Council 1990, cited in Arora 2005)

Equality of opportunity is not only about access to the curriculum for all our students. It is also about content, methodology and relevance to today's world. Geography has to justify its role and relevance in education. Geography that is implicitly and historically rooted in a capitalist, white heterosexual, male past will not embed or develop tolerance nor celebrate differences between cultural groups (Gonzalez and Gonzalez 1997, p. 117).

### Geography for learners with special educational needs

There is evidence that geography is more successful and popular in 'academic' schools and that students perceive the subject as more difficult than other options due to the coursework load and analysis required (Weeden 2006, p. 4). There is, therefore, an even greater imperative to ensure that all learners, including those with special educational needs (SEN), are included in exciting geography lessons. The QCA suggests that some parts of the Key Stage 3 Programme of Study, such as national and international contexts, may be too demanding for some students (or perhaps for some teachers to deconstruct). It may be more appropriate to teach the more demanding parts of the Programme of Study for the earlier Key Stages. Key Stage 3 should maintain and reinforce the knowledge, skills and understanding introduced during the earlier stages by applying these in different areas before introducing new learning. Flexibility, imagination and creativity are encouraged. Lesson planning ideas to support SEN students in geography include visiting zoos and botanical gardens, the use of lighting, making artefacts, freezing water, making and using fans, tying on national costumes and eating a range of foods from other countries. (QCA 2003). This is a very different classroom landscape from that described in the Geography in Schools: Changing Practice Report:

> Many pupils interviewed during inspections describe Geography at Key Stage 3 as 'boring' and lacking relevance. In part, this may be due to its neglect ... Dull teaching is also associated with the continuance of schemes of work that are heavy in content and lack relevance to modern Geography. Some schools use the QCA's schemes, but these tend to be used as 'bolt on' additions rather than being adapted properly to meet the school's needs as was intended. Sometimes, too, the scheme of work is driven by those textbooks which are available and a limited range of resources. (Ofsted 2008)

Of equal importance are the challenge, excitement and learning outside the classroom. Escaping the classroom and participating in fieldwork, now theoretically a requirement for all students, was a move forward into 'hands-on', 'real' geography for those long ago post-Empire building schoolboys seeking adventure, but twenty-first-century classroom doors are more likely to remain locked due to the recent decline in fieldwork provision in schools. Although Lord Adonis, Parliamentary Under-Secretary for Schools and Learners, has robustly refuted any decline in fieldwork (Hansard 2008), claiming there is no evidence to suggest fieldwork has declined in schools, Ofsted found otherwise. The Inspectorate attributes reducing the amount and effectiveness of fieldwork to perceptions of risk among teachers and the litigious world we inhabit, the 'curriculum time' fieldwork takes up, poor expertise and budget constraints. Fieldwork motivates students and enhances their interest in geography, as reflected in the better take-up at Key Stage 4 in schools with an exciting fieldwork programme, yet, two-thirds of schools do not meet the statutory requirements. Students who have had limited fieldwork experience before GCSE can rely only on the teacher for guidance, resulting in – again, history repeating itself – unimaginative, heavily structured learning that fails to enhance their understanding of geographical concepts (Ofsted 2008).

All students – including those with all levels of SEN – have the legal right to access the full curriculum and geography departments must consider each overarching component in order to facilitate access to both the formal and informal curriculum. Key is the discussion of appropriate arrangements and expectations taking place with full knowledge on both the part of the whole staff team and all students. Considering whether that activity is the only, or even the best, way of achieving the disciplinary knowledge might suggest alternative exercises for all or some students. Offering students a degree of choice in the fieldwork, so that their particular needs can best be matched, is good practice. To go beyond this, the need for physical accessibility (in all of its manifestations) needs to be put higher up the planning framework for deciding on locations and activities. Sometimes it may be possible for large departments to offer a range of fieldwork to all students, so they can choose the most suitable one for their SEN or financial situation. For individual elements of assessment, a different type of activity may be made available. Other strategies include peer support learning using a team approach, which draws on the individual team member's abilities (Geography Discipline Network (GDN) 2001).

Teamwork might include the use of ICT and technological innovation with all students contributing in differing ways and therefore responding to the needs of all students – not only those with SEN – in all their learning activities. Ongoing discussion between the fieldwork organizer and the students to establish what is critical, important and unimportant for successful fieldwork is vital at every stage. It is important that this negotiation process is built into planning and that all staff responsible for coordinating or organizing field visits see their role as overcoming barriers to any experiences that could be perceived to be discriminatory, even if unintentionally. Equally important are the attitudes of peers, which may impede effective participation by SEN students – they may be overprotective or do too much of the work for them. These peer attitudes, however well intentioned, are further barriers which SEN students face. Where SENs are visible or audible (through wheelchairs or walking frames, hearing aids, facial expression or speech impairment), these can lead to students being faced with exclusion, infantilization, being patronized or stigmatized. The team-based approach to fieldwork should therefore include discussion to anticipate and plan for these responses, psychologically overcoming barriers prior to the visit. The issue is how will the team respond and react, not the individual. Enhanced public understanding of inclusion SEN is clearly an issue for everybody, not just participants in fieldwork, but the particular nature of geography teaching with its, ideally, emphasis on the relationship between people and environment means that the planning should be part of learning itself (*ibid.*).

SEN students, however, may not share the same value systems as the majority of participants in the fieldwork experience, whether staff or fellow students. They may not feel that personally ascending a high peak, walking through a complex labyrinth of small passageways in an old town or observing the detail of soil or vegetation coloration in a river valley is either a valuable part of the fieldwork or a legitimate expectation. From this perspective, there may potentially be a conflict of views with the teacher where the intended learning outcomes for such experiences are spelled out in non-differentiated terms that fail to characterize the development of skills or understanding that is expected as a learning outcome of the activity. Inclusive practice must be embedded in all aspects of teaching – materials, planning and outcomes.

One approach that theoretically may meet the needs of SEN (and the needs of teachers who wish to save money and cut down on filling in risk assessments) is by providing access to fieldwork through virtual fieldwork courses or environments. Many are available and an instant classroom resource that, used creatively, can complement actual fieldwork. Before embarking on fieldwork students can explore its virtual environment and once there can more easily analyse data and relate it to wider data sources. Similarly, on return, further analysis is possible and can be shared with students who were absent. Locations and experiences that would never be possible are open to all students and classroom teaching enriched. What virtual fieldwork should not be, however, is a substitute for fieldwork itself. They are an addition to classroom learning, not a substitute for all the benefits of 'real' fieldwork – a rationale for excluding students from fieldwork on the grounds of SEN or cost or onerous paperwork. At a cost of between £300 and £3,000, depending on the extent of the licence, schools can purchase software to access a Learning Objects Repository that incorporates a collection of 500 realistic interactive learning objects that demonstrate and simulate scientific phenomena, a multilingual portal and an offline player.

Again, there is a thin line to be drawn between exciting, engaging learning, and materials that take students away from the very fabric and reality of geography that makes it the subject that it is – or at least should be.

## Geography for All Learners: Ensuring the Future is Another Country

*There is not one single thing, which stands so much in the way of social and international advance as a lack of knowledge of Geography. The function of Geography in school is to train further citizens to imagine accurately the conditions of the great world stage, as so help them to think sanely about political and social problems around.*

(Fairgrieve, Geography in Schools (1926), cited in Kent 2000, p. 113)

If Fairgrieve's great claim for geography, made in another century, other lifetimes ago, is to finally come to pass then the statistical decline of geography at Key Stage 4 (Weeden 2006; Ofsted 2008) has to be reversed. Research literature on students' perceptions of subjects and their reasons for choosing subjects is limited, especially for geography, but it appears that the learning process and the quality of the teaching are far more influential than subject content in making geography interesting. Students' preferred ways of working in Geography include multimedia, field trips, producing maps and diagrams, map/atlas work, project work, discussion, practical work and making posters – a variety of learning and learning styles. What teachers may perceive as innovation, for instance the use of ICT, can be no more stimulating than mundane searches of the internet with little thinking about the learning and engagement of the students. ICT should be an exciting tool for learning. Used to generate maps from aerial photographs, build up three-dimensional structures of towns, draw maps with symbols and construct a variety of graphs to illustrate survey results, ICT can both facilitate learning, exploration and creativity (Ofsted 2008). Physical processes – the why and how – are important, rather than the factual 'what' of the 'old' rote learned geography. Of all the humanities, geography has the greatest potential to be taught holistically; not compartmentalized into areas, fact and features.

Students respond negatively to writing ('working through endless booklets and worksheets'), copying, book work, tests, homework, big projects (too long) and drawing maps and diagrams. They reject being mere passive recipients of knowledge and 'technical terminology' through copying terms and definitions, particularly in certain physical geography topics (Weeden 2006; Ofsted 2008). A didactic approach is no more appropriate at A level than at Key Stage 2 (7–11 age group) and should not dominate our classrooms whatever the age of the students (Schlesinger 1994, p. 82).

Geography is, after all, alive; not dead on the page. At Key Stage 3 the non-statutory Programme of Study should be moved and shifted to reflect the world we are living in, the here and now; for instance, using hurricane weather reports as they occur to track the paths of storms and investigate their effects – sometimes even in real-time – printed off during a lesson to give a dynamic feel to the learning experience. Personal testimonies from communities affected by specific hurricanes, or other events, can be easily accessed as well as newspaper reports from a range of perspectives. Indeed, a study of Hurricane Katrina can make links between 'race', class and gender (see Cole 2006). This ability to download current news reports from anywhere in the world, which would otherwise be unavailable, when studied alongside geographical data – flat on the pages of a textbook – provides a 'real' resource for learning. Population census data is also available and allows students to construct graphs using the latest government statistics, building on the information in their textbooks, giving students a first-hand experience of the reality of geography (Hayes 2005, p. 29).

Students' understanding of how they prefer to learn in geography, rather than what they prefer to learn, suggests that their conceptions are unclear (Weeden 2006; Ofsted 2008). Geography departments need to think again about their subject, its place in the wider curriculum and the teaching and learning styles that are most likely to enthuse and engage students, such as group work, fieldwork, individual enquiry and addressing relevant and topical issues. This implies a less formal teaching approach in the classroom with flexibility rather than rigid adherence to a content-driven programme (Ofsted 2005; 2008). The QCA maps Key Stage 3 Geography succinctly and idealistically. The non statutory Programme of Study aims to offer opportunities to stimulate students' interest in their surroundings and in the variety of human and physical conditions on the earth's surface, foster students' sense of wonder at the beauty of the world around them and help them to develop an informed concern about the quality of the environment and the future of the human habitat. They thereby enhance their sense of responsibility for the care of the earth and its people (DCSF 2008). These are aspirational aims – inclusive, embracing and life affirming. The evidence, however, points to lessons that fail to inspire students to take the subject beyond Key Stage 3 as, amid its internal spats and spalls, geography as an academic subject declines in popularity. Between 1988 and 2004 the average number of entries for GCSE Geography was around 270,000 but has fluctuated between a high of 305,000 in 1988 to a low of 227,832 in 2004. There has been a steady and significant fall since 1996, when numbers reached 302,298. Similarly, at A level numbers have fallen from a high of 46,680 in 1992 to a low in 2004 of 34,215. While geography remains one of the most popular subjects at both GCSE and A level, there has been a steady decline in the numbers opting for it over time (Weeden 2006; Ofsted 2008).

Students' perceptions of the subject and the way it is taught clearly influence option choices. The days of students being offered a three-way humanities choice with the 'freedom' to choose between history, Religious Education and geography now belong to another century. All subjects have to 'sell' themselves as relevant, pertinent and stimulating. Students who have failed to be excited, challenged and inspired by Key Stage 3 Geography will simply not opt for it at GCSE.

The Assessment and Qualification Alliance (AQA) GCSE Geography specification aims to incorporate historically the disparate elements that fractured the subject – the human and the physical – and has been structured to provide students with a course that develops a sound understanding and knowledge of geographical themes, issues and skills with, importantly, a people-environment theme adopted to highlight the importance of this interaction. The use of examples and case studies is fundamental in the delivery of the specification detail in order to achieve meaningful understanding of themes, studied in differing environments including areas at various stages of economic development (AQA 2001). The 'Importance [of] interaction', with 'meaningful understanding', are phrases that imply students participating in a learning experience that goes beyond the 'rote' of those dull turn-of-the-twentieth-century lessons, relying on innovative, creative (inclusive) teaching that is still not the norm in our classrooms.

## Future Landscapes?

In 2006, in response to years (a century!) of critical reports and falling numbers of GCSE and A level students choosing to study geography, the government launched, at a projected cost of £2 million, an Action Plan for Geography (APG) with an implementation framework of 2006–10; divided into two phases: 2006–08 and 2008–10. The Action Plan aims to improve dramatically the quality of teaching. It consists of three interlinked and mutually reinforcing activity programmes, within which are eight two-year projects within three areas: communication, support and development. There is a designated website, Geography Teaching Today, 'Ambassadors' for geography and more Geography Advisers have been appointed. Among the key objectives of the plan are that it should improve for *all* students the quality of the educational experience through geography, enthusing young people with the relevance of the subject to employment and citizenship to raise its profile in the education sector. The plan aims to embed in particular its central contribution to address several national policy concerns such as sustainable development, global dimensions, cultural and social inclusion, using and understanding technology and in imparting a wide range of skills sought after by employers (APG 2006). The jury on the effectiveness of the plan, is, literally, still out. The interim report can only conclude:

> Qualitative evidence suggests that the professional development is meeting this outcome but clearly in relation to deeper impacts this needs further research. Some of the ideas that teachers have been challenged with will need to be adopted and adapted in different contexts and this process will take some time. (APG 2007)

So more time is required to do what Inspectors, following disappointing inspections and observations, have demanded for a century. Geography has, therefore, not yet completed its pedagogic journey begun at the turn of the last century and still struggles to be firmly established in the school curriculum as a unified, cohesive and inclusive discipline. To compete on the twenty-first-century curriculum geography has to re-root itself firmly in a world that has shed its imperialist, capitalist, patriarchal past while at the same time robustly acknowledge its existence and impact on our present. Positioned at the heart of a world of human creation and experience, geography attempts to comprehend and change that world (Smith 2000, p. 17). Geography will then finally become the shifting, contextual study of the here and now, not the past and then, that it has always had the potential to be.

# References

Action Plan for Geography (APG) (2007), Interim Evaluation. Available at http://www.Geography.org.uk/news/actionplanforGeography (accessed May 2008).

AQA (2001), GCSE Geography Specification A. Available at www.aqa.org.uk/qual/gcse/geo_a.php (accessed May 2008).

Baker, J. (1987), *Arguing for Equality*. London and New York: Verso.

Carens, J. H. (1987), 'Aliens and citizens: the case for open borders'. *The Review of Politics*, 49, 251–73.

Chorley, R. and Haggett, P. (1967), *Models in Geography*, London: Methuen.

Cole, M. (2006), '"Looters and thugs and inert women doing nothing": racialized Communities in capitalist America and the role of higher education'. *Journal for Critical Education Policy Studies*, 4 (1) Online at http://www.jceps.com/index.php?pageID=article&articleID=64 (accessed May 2008).

— and Blair, M. (2006), 'Racism and education: from Empire to New Labour', in M. Cole (ed.), *Education, Equality and Human Rights: Issues of Gender, 'Race', Sexuality, Disability and Social Class* (2nd edn). London: Routledge, pp. 70–88.

— and Virdee, S. (2006), 'Racism and resistance: from Empire to New Labour', in M. Cole (ed.), *Education, Equality and Human Rights: Issues of Gender, 'Race', Sexuality, Disability and Social Class* (2nd edn). London: Routledge, pp. 43–69.

DCSF (2008), *The Standards Site: Geography at Key Stage 3*. Available at www.standards.dfes.gov.uk/schemes2/secondary_Geography/ (accessed May 2008).

Desbiens, C. (1999), 'Feminism "in" geography, elsewhere, beyond and the politics of paradoxical space'. *Gender, Place and Culture*, 6, (2), pp. 179–185.

Driver, F. (2003), 'On geography as a visual discipline'. *Antipode*, 35, (2), 227–30.

England, K. (1999), 'Sexing geography, teaching sexualities'. *Journal of Geography in Higher Education*, 23, (1), 94–101.

Geographical Association (2006), The Action Plan for Geography, 2006. Available at http://www.Geography.org.uk/news/actionplanforGeography (accessed May 2008).

Geography Discipline Network (GDN) (2001), Available at http://www2.glos.ac.uk/gdn/disabil/overview/toc.htm (accessed May 2008).

Gonzalez, B. and Gonzalez, E. (1997), 'Equal opportunity and the teaching of Geography', in D. Tilbury and M. Williams (eds), *Teaching and Learning Geography*. London: Routledge, p. 117.

Goodson, I. (ed.) (1993), 'School subjects and curriculum change'. *Studies in Curriculum History*. (Vol. 3). London: The Falmer Press.

Goodson, I. (1998), *Subject Knowledge: Reading for the Study of School Subjects*. London: Falmer Press (accessed May 2008).

Hadow Report, The (1927) 'The Education of the Adolescent', HMSO in *The Journal of Geography*, 31. American Geographical Society of New York, p. 123.

Hansard, (2008), Available at www.theyworkforyou.com/lords/?id = 2008-01-22a.124.3.

Hayes, J. (2005), 'Using the internet to invigorate lessons'. *ICT across the Curriculum*, File 1, p. 29.

Homles, E. (1912) 'What is and What Might Be', BiblioBazaar (repr. 2008) p. 111

Hubbard, P. (1998), 'Sexuality, immorality and the city: red-light districts and the marginalisation of female street prostitutes: gender'. *Place and Culture*, 5, 55–72.

— (2000), 'Desire/disgust: mapping the moral contours of heterosexuality'. *Progress in Human Geography*, 24, (2), 191–217.

Kent, A. (ed.) (2000), *School Subject Teaching: the history and future of the curriculum*. London: Kogan.

Martin, F. (2000), International Research in Geographical and Environmental Education, *Postgraduate Primary Education Students' Images of Geography and the Relationship between these and Students' Teaching* 9, (3), 223–44.

McLaren, P. (2003), Foreword in I, Goodson (ed.), *School Subjects and Curriculum Change: Studies in Curriculum History* (Volume 3). London: Falmer Press.

Miller, R.W. (1992), *Moral Differences: Truth, Justice and Conscience in a World of Conflict*. Princeton, NJ: Princeton University Press, pp. 228, 240–41.

Nast, H. J. and Wilson, M. O. (1994), 'Lawful transgressions: this is the house that Jackie built'.:*Assemblage*, 5, 48–55.

National Curriculum Council (1990), 'The Whole Curriculum', in R. K. Arora (2005) *Race and ethnicity in education*. Ashgate, Hants: NCC, p. 7.

Nett, R. (1971), 'The civil right we are not ready for: the right of free movement of people on the face of the earth'. *Ethics*, 81, 212–27.

Ofsted (2005), *Geography in Secondary Schools: The Annual Report of Her Majesty's Inspector of Schools, 2004/5*. London: Ofsted.

— (2008), *Geography in Schools: Changing Practice*. Available at www.ofsted.gov.uk/publications (accessed May 2008).

Powell, R. C. (2002), 'The Sirens' voices? Field practices and dialogue in Geography', *Area*, 34, (3), pp. 261–72.

QCA (2003), *Learning Difficulties: Geography*. Available at http://www.qca.org.uk/qca_1897.aspx.

Roberson, I. (2004), 'Beyond illustration: visualization as a mode of argument and a form of creative performance in the discipline of geography'. *Space and Place*. Online at http://interactive-worlds.blogspot.com/2007/12/welcome.html (accessed May 2008)

Robic, M. C. (2008), 'Sirens within the IGU: an analysis of the role of women at International Geographical Congresses (1871–1996)'. *Cybergeo*, Epistemology, History, Teaching, Article 14. Online at http://www.cybergeo.eu/index5257.html (accessed May 2008).

Rooper, T. G. (1901) 'Selected Writings of Thomas Godolphin Rooper: Edited with a Memoir by R. G. Tatton' (1948) *The Study of Geography* IV. London: Blackie and Son Ltd.

Rorty, R. (1989), *Contingency, Irony, and Solidarity*. Cambridge: Cambridge University Press.

Rose, G. (1993), *Feminism and Geography: The Limits of Geographical Knowledge*. University of Minnesota Press, pp. 9, 65–87.

—(1995), 'Tradition and paternity: same difference?' *Transactions of the Institute of British Geographers* (New Series), 20, (4), 414.

Schlesinger, A. (1994), 'Using curriculum material and teaching methods to reduce prejudice and maintain academic standards in an A level human geography course', in B. R. Sing (ed.), *Improving Gender and Ethnic Relations*. London: Cassell Education, pp. 76–99.

Smith, D. (2000), 'Moral progress in human geography: transcending the place of good fortune'. *Progress in Human Geography*, 24, pp. 1–18.

Weeden, P. (2006), 'Pupils' perceptions of geography: a literature review'. University of Birmingham School of Education (commissioned by RGS-IBG), pp. 1–5.

Williams, B. (1985), *Ethics and the Limits of Philosophy*. London: Fontana Press and Collins, p. 185.

Williams, M. (ed.) (1997), *Teaching and Learning Geography*. London: Routledge, p. 25.

Young, I. M. (1990), *Justice and the Politics of Difference*. Princeton, NJ: Princeton University Press.

Chapter 9

# History

### Ian Woodfield

This chapter provides both an overview of the development of history as a National Curriculum subject and an exploration of the ways in which history can be used in the classroom, both as a vehicle to explore patterns of inequality in Britain's past and as an opportunity to discuss the implications of that shared past with regard to modern prejudices and assumptions. The case is made that without an adequate knowledge of our past we are unable to challenge prejudice and overcome discrimination. It is the contention of the author that the study of history inevitably leads students to fundamental questions of social justice. The informed citizen, he believes, is well aware that history can be used and abused by politicians and commentators, while the uninformed remain in ignorance of our shared past and as a consequence are easily misled by those who wish to exploit isms/phobias.

## History in the National Curriculum

*It is not the waning of faith in reason among the intellectuals and political thinkers of the English-speaking world which perturbs me most, but the loss of the pervading sense of a world in perpetual motion ... change is no longer thought of as achievement, as opportunity, as progress, but as an object of fear.*

(Carr 1964)

When I first read Carr's *What Is History* in the early 1970s I was a student, training to teach history. As I return to Carr's words I am struck by a sense of period, but also paradoxically by the contemporary relevance of his comments. To live in Britain in the 1960s and early 1970s was to live in a country still deeply divided along lines of class, gender and ethnicity. This was still a time when the possession of wealth and privilege guaranteed entrance to the best schools, the best universities and the best jobs; whereas those who suffered any form of physical 'disability' or learning difficulty were almost inevitably isolated from the mainstream of social life. Homosexuality was illegal for men up to 1967, thereafter being legal for consenting males over 21 only in private (it was not until 2000 that the age of consent for homosexual and heterosexual sex was equalized at 16). Despite the decades that have passed and the progress made towards a more just and equitable society, inequalities remain. Social class remains the heart of a continuing pattern of social inequality within our society. To be young and working class in Britain *today* is a fate that embraces an extraordinary range of challenges that only the most fortunate seem likely to overcome. While for those of our young people who experience learning difficulties we know that for many 'inclusion'[1] has failed, despite the best efforts of those professionals who have committed their careers to this approach. At the same time, paradoxically the subject best suited to place both our achievements and our shortcomings as a society in proper perspective – the study of history – is actually less secure now in many of our schools than at any time since the introduction of the National Curriculum.

When I emerged from 'teacher training' (as it was then called) in the 1970s it was to the sure and certain prospect that history – in many state schools, at least – was officially 'dead' as a discrete subject. The 'future', we were confidently told by our lecturers, lay in the new 'social studies'. Our work in schools was all going to be about cross-curricular themes, teaching would take place in 'classrooms without walls' and timetables would be replaced by the 'integrated day'. Little did we know at the time that these radical transformational ideas were to be brought to a shuddering halt within the next decade or so by the re-election of Margaret Thatcher in 1987 and ultimately, in 1991, by the final and full publication of the National Curriculum (DES 1991). However, it would be unfair of me to criticize the original framework without discussing some of its undoubted strengths. For the first time in my teaching career there was in place a coherent 'grand plan' for the school curriculum. There is a lot of criticism today, much of it justified, emphasizing that the removal of creative freedom from teachers has led to a narrow academic focus to the curriculum. What is perhaps less fashionable is the concept of 'entitlement' as enshrined by the original framework of the National Curriculum. Whatever its many flaws, the original framework assumed that history's place in the education was secure; *all* students, it was obviously intended, would receive at least an introduction to the 'big picture' of our national story, establishing for students Britain's place in the world and, at least at an elementary level, providing some focus on the skills and debates of the historical community.[2]

However, the National Curriculum had at its inception, and continues to have today, two fundamental faults. First, it enshrined the concept of 'core' (by implication more important) and 'foundation' (by implication less important) subjects, effectively banishing a large section of the curriculum to permanent second-class status. This is not to question the importance of literacy and numeracy, but the very fact of a hierarchically divided curriculum gave many of the increasingly distinct managerial class in our schools the opportunity to squeeze the foundation subjects of that most precious resource, time. For the second fundamental flaw in the National Curriculum was the complete and abject failure to consider at any meaningful level the number of hours in a day and the number of school weeks in a year. As a consequence the actual content of the curriculum in schools was much less prescriptive than originally intended, a reality recognized by the publication of the Dearing Report (1994), which called for a significant reduction in prescriptive content. Moreover, the increasing emphasis on comparing the relative performance of students served to further marginalize its importance: SATs[3] testing would, it was decided, not apply to foundation subjects like history, but this imperative to measure everything has served to drive schools slowly but inexorably down a path where the requirement to test something that has been taught, and hopefully learned, becomes far more significant than any other claim it may have to some form of educational 'value'.

Ultimately, I remain convinced that history will continue to serve its primary educational purpose, not to contribute to the statistical profile of a school's relative performance, whatever value that may have in the 'real world', but rather to stimulate, inform and enlighten future generations of students. To encourage a deeper understanding of our shared past as more than 'infotainment', the purpose of history is, in Starkey's (2006) words, to provide 'a map of time', a sense of 'where we stand in the universe of time'. It is my contention that the study of history inevitably leads students to fundamental questions of social justice: to consider, for example, Britain's part in the Slave Trade and of the contribution that it made to racist ideology; to appreciate the seductive dangers of simplistic political creeds like Nazism and of the causes and consequences of the Holocaust. Furthermore, I would suggest that no student studying the impact of the Industrial Revolution could fail to appreciate the human and environmental costs of unfettered capitalism. To know, understand and communicate such knowledge should never be the sole preserve of the intellectual elite, for ignorance in a democracy is no defence. The informed citizen is well aware that history can be used and abused by politicians and commentators; the uninformed remain in ignorance of our shared past and are as a consequence are easily misled by those who wish to exploit isms/phobias (see Chapter 2 of this volume).

The latest version of the National Curriculum in History (QCA 2007, pp. 110–19) establishes a list of skills and processes that are designed to help KS3 students' progress in their course of study, including historical enquiry, the use of evidence and communicating about the past. It also focuses on a

number of 'key concepts' that underpin the individual student's understanding of the subject:

1. Chronological understanding
2. Cultural, ethnic and religious diversity
3. Change and continuity
4. Cause and consequence
5. Significance
6. Interpretation.

The second of these key concepts (cultural, ethnic and religious diversity) has
particular resonance for the purpose of this chapter and indeed of this book,
for it *requires* students and their teachers to work towards the development of
an understanding of the 'diverse experiences and ideas, beliefs and attitudes of
men, women and children in past societies and to develop an appreciation of
how these have shaped the world' (*ibid.*, p. 112). To put it more simply, this is
the closest we have yet come to the overt inclusion of social justice as a central
concept in the teaching of history in the National Curriculum. However, this
is certainly *not*, as some might claim, a recipe for a content-free skills-based
curriculum and indeed in general terms the subject-specific content of the
revised curriculum remains – in its broad outline – remarkably familiar.
Unfortunately, the licence given to schools to 'disapply' the National
Curriculum for some students and to reinvent the thematic integrated
curriculum structures of the 1960s and 1970s reopens old debates about the
quality of history provision available to many students in the twenty-first-
century state school.

## History in Action: Promoting Equality in the History Classroom

The following examples are intended to illustrate the ways in which students
at KS3 and KS4 can be brought to confront issues of social justice and
equality within the history classroom. I have suggested particular topics that
would seem to offer appropriate opportunities within the latest version of the
National Curriculum for history, either for conventional classroom-based
study or for a thematic 'project-based' investigation. At KS4 I have suggested
where opportunities occur within existing GCSE courses for students to
consider equality-related issues. These units can be used flexibly in a range of
possible curriculum structures. They could, for example, form the basis of a
module of work within a conventional classroom setting, or alternatively as
the basis of a research project or even part of a thematic approach involving
cross-curricular links and the suspension of the traditional subject-based
timetable.

Traditionally teachers have relied on text-based resources, but increasingly they and their students are able to make use of ICT as a resource and as a pedagogic tool.[4] However, a word of caution is needed in this respect for those who champion ICT as the predominant vehicle for teaching and learning in the twenty-first century. It is vital that students are made to demonstrate their understanding of both the advantages *and* limitations of the medium. A generation of 'cut and paste' students are making their way through the education system, frequently confusing quantity of information (regardless of issues regarding the accuracy and validity of such data) with quality of understanding.

## Sexual orientation and gender

Simon Forrest (2006, p. 129) reminds us that, in Redman's (1994) phrase: 'sexuality is everywhere and nowhere' in school. Young people are inevitably interested in these issues and yet teachers may find themselves constrained not by repressive laws such the notorious and now repealed 'Section 28', but rather by their own uncertainty and lack of training in how to confront potentially controversial issues in the classroom. Much of the published guidance and staff training in the area of gender and sexuality has primarily focused on personal, social and health education (DfES 2004). However, given that it is inevitable that in exploring gender-related issues in lessons not specifically labelled as PSHE teachers will encounter questions relating to sexual behaviour, there is an obvious need for teachers to confront these issues and to respond appropriately. It is also apparent while studying historical case studies – the persecution of minority groups in Nazi Germany as part of a GCSE course, for example – that students may well be confronted by the mistreatment and imprisonment of homosexuals. It is important to remind students that any discussions of such issues should take place within a responsible framework of mutual respect, with a clear direction from the teacher to avoid inappropriate disclosure and of the limits to confidentiality. All schools must have established guidelines on child protection and a published framework for dealing with any matters of concern that may be brought to the attention of teaching staff. However, that being said and while the primary focus of the history lesson may be found elsewhere, the very fact that such issues are dealt with in an open and matter of fact way should make a significant contribution to the development of tolerance and understanding among the student population.

The study of gender-related issues in history creates obvious opportunities for students to confront the long history of inequality and of the efforts of pioneers for 'women's rights' such as Mary Wollstonecraft and the Pankhurst family. Moreover, it also encourages a consideration of the nature of historical stereotypes. The view that women in history were largely powerless and victims of an entirely oblivious patriarchy can be challenged by reference to the lives of strong and independent women, such as Elizabeth, Countess of Shrewsbury and various members of the Tudor dynasty. It is also important to remember that the lives of many ordinary working-class women are as hidden from history as the lives of ordinary working-class men; the glimpses we have of these day-to-day lives are partial fragments, but when revealed they tell a richer and more complex story regarding human relationships than a perfunctory whistle-stop version of the curriculum can ever effectively offer. For example, it is possible that students who explore historical material on gender differences may well encounter references to sexuality that they wish to discuss and in this respect it is important for teachers to encourage open and sensible discussion and for students to appreciate that moral codes change over time. That being said, given the secretive and often illegal status of homosexuality in the past it is unlikely that the KS3 researcher will encounter appropriate resources that focus on such issues; on the other hand, for KS4 students and teachers this may well become a more significant issue.

Mass education in Britain has long harboured policies and practices based on perceptions of the *differences* between men and women. Indeed, it can be argued that recent reforms encouraging 'different pathways' through secondary education are reinforcing not only social class divisions but also gender divisions within our society. Students who study a KS4 curriculum 'suited to their needs' are frequently being directed towards forms of vocational education that remain rooted in ideas about the nature of 'suitable' employment opportunities dominated by particular gender groups. Despite any lip service paid to equality of opportunity any objective consideration of the take-up of vocational courses readily reveals gender stereotypes that are alive and indeed flourishing. The gradual erosion of the KS3 National Curriculum through a liberalization of the statutory frame-work may paradoxically serve to undermine the work of teachers who have sought to confront isms/phobias and by so doing have encouraged their students to adopt an egalitarian view of the possibilities of life.

## Unit title and target age group

The changing status of women in British society, intended to form part of a KS3 Programme of Study.

## Resources

- http://www.bbc.co.uk/history/british/tudors/
- http://www.derbyshireuk.net/hardwick.html
- http://www.channel4.com/history/microsites/H/history/e-h/elizabeth1.html
- http://www.womenandequalityunit.gov.uk/women_work/index.htm

- http://www.channel4.com/history/microsites/H/history/guide16/part09.html
- http://www.bbc.co.uk/schools/famouspeople/standard/seacole/index.shtml
- http://www.bbc.co.uk/schools/famouspeople/standard/nightingale/index.shtml
- http://www.bbc.co.uk/history/historic_figures/garrett_anderson_elizabeth.shtml
- http://www.open2.net/thingsweforgot/thesuffragettes.html

### Learning outcomes

At the end of this unit students should be able to describe and explain why and how the status of women has changed in British society; they should be able to place these changes within a chronological framework; and they should be able to make links and comparisons across time.

### Teaching and learning focus and suggested activities

- Marriage and family life in Tudor times. Students can be asked to draw up a marriage contract emphasizing arrangements including the exchange of property (land or money) rather than the modern concept of 'romantic love'.
- Henry VIII and his six wives. Students can research reasons for both Henry's various marriages and the fates of his six wives.
- Biography: Elizabeth I and Elizabeth, Countess of Shrewsbury – 'Bess of Hardwick'. Students can be asked to compare the lives of these two powerful women in an age dominated by men.
- Witches and wise women. Students could arrange a 'mock trial', recognizing that in reality many of the women tried for the crime of witchcraft were frequently either traditional 'healers' or confused, elderly, poor and alone.

Comparisons can then be made with the lives of women in nineteenth- and early twentieth-century England. Students could research the following:

- The 1882 Married Women's Property Act. Students could prepare a role-play illustrating the husband's right to all property brought to a marriage prior to 1882.
- Elizabeth Garrett's struggle to become the first woman to qualify as a doctor in Britain. Students can prepare a role-play with male students protesting that a woman should not be allowed to attend medical lectures.
- Biography: Florence Nightingale and Mary Seacole. While both women were involved in caring for the sick and injured during the Crimean War they came from very different social and cultural backgrounds. Students

can compare and contrast the lives of these two women and their treatment by British society.

- Research into mortality rates among women in the early part of the nineteenth century can be used to raise questions regarding women's health (with particular reference to the dangers of child-bearing).
- The Suffragette movement and the campaign for the vote. Students can be asked to prepare a PowerPoint presentation on key figures within the movement such as the Pankhurst family and events such as the 'Cat and Mouse Act' or the death of Emily Wilding Davison. Students can also be asked to explore the reasons why women were eventually granted the right to vote after the First World War.

Finally, students can complete their study by researching the impact of twentieth-century reforms:

- The Equal Pay Act (1970)
- The Sex Discrimination Act (1975)

This research should raise questions regarding the current status of women in British society; for example, women are still likely to be in lesser-paid and lower-status jobs than men. Students can be asked to debate the question of whether women are truly equal in Britain today and to explore the links between gender inequalities and social class, for example the continuance of class-based inequalities in education and employment that cut across the gender divide.

## Social class, age and disability

While the suggested unit of study below focuses on social class, the broader study of nineteenth- and early twentieth-century Britain, and of modern world history at KS4, also clearly lends itself to a consideration of the treatment of the elderly and those with physical and mental disabilities. At KS3 a consideration of the New Poor Law and the Workhouse system will inevitably lead students to the fact that many such institutions survived as 'hospitals' into the twentieth century, largely to serve the needs of the elderly poor. Rieser (2006) provides a useful summary of the historical treatment of disability and of the exemplification of the 'perfect body' and the 'healthy mind' from ancient times until the modern world. Furthermore, he reminds us that a belief in 'eugenics' was once widespread and fashionable and not the sole preserve of Nazi extremists; witness these remarks from a letter written by D. H. Lawrence:

If I had my way, I would build a lethal chamber as big as Crystal Palace ... then I'd go out in the back streets and main streets and bring them in, all the sick, the halt and the maimed; I would lead them gently, and they would smile me a weary thanks. (*ibid.*, p. 148)

The study of Nazi Germany, either as part of a GCSE in Modern World History or as a Schools History Project 'depth study', must involve a consideration of policies for euthanasia (including the secret murder of disabled children) and of the compulsory sterilization of those deemed to be 'mentally defective'; such a study is truly a 'warning from history' for those who continue to cling to simplistic beliefs regarding the lives of those who are unable to meet idealized criteria for physical and mental 'perfection'. GCSE courses such as the Schools History Project include 'Medicine through Time' as a development study allowing students ample opportunity to explore the changing treatment of those with mental health problems; for example, the treatment of 'shell shock' in the First World War can be compared and contrasted with the treatment of the 'madness' of George III in the eighteenth century.

### Unit title and target age group

Social class, wealth and poverty in nineteenth- and early twentieth-century Britain, intended to form part of the KS3 Programme of Study.

### Resources

- http://www.channel4.com/history/microsites/C/countryhouse/edwardian-life/politics.html
- http://www.wynnesdiary.com/diary_layout/intro_page/intro.html#
- http://www.qualidata.ac.uk/edwardians/about/introduction.asp
- http://www.spartacus.schoolnet.co.uk/poverty.htm
- http://www.historyonthenet.com/Titanic/titanicmain.htm
- http://www.bbc.co.uk/history/british/britain_wwone/titanic_01.shtml
- http://www.bbc.co.uk/history/british/britain_wwone/titanic_01.shtml
- http://www.bbc.co.uk/history/worldwars/wwtwo/election_03.shtml
- http://www.poverty.org.uk/summary/key%20facts.shtml
- http://www.movinghere.org.uk/

### Learning outcomes

At the end of this unit students should be able to describe and explain the differences between the lives of the upper and middle classes and those of the working class in Britain during the nineteenth century and early twentieth century, and they should be able to place these different experiences of life within a chronological framework and be able to make links and comparisons across time. As a subsidiary aim they should also be introduced to technological and social change, including the impact of uncontrolled capitalism on the environment and public health with particular reference to living conditions in the towns and cities of the period. They should also be able to make comparisons with the modern world and to link their study of contemporary environmental issues in geography or citizenship, with examples from the past.

## *Teaching and learning focus and suggested activities*

- Comparing the lives of the middle and upper classes with the working class, during the nineteenth century and early twentieth century. Students should be encouraged to compile two imagined 'autobiographies', one of their probable life experiences as a wealthy individual and one as a member of the working classes. They can use the data available on the internet and from text-based source material to construct a picture of the life and times of an individual alive at this time: topics covered could include education, diet and health, life expectancy, opportunities for travel, housing and employment. Past experience with this type of work has shown that encouraging students to use their own identity (rather than an invented alter ego) helps to avoid the use of inappropriate stereotypes and to encourage reflection and empathetic understanding. This work can be presented in the form of diary entries, letters and collections of photographic images from the period to represent particular aspects of different experiences of life.
- Students could then be encouraged to place the families of their two imagined autobiographies on board the RMS *Titanic* in 1912. Exploring the wealth of data available on the ship serves to highlight not only the obvious differences in status and income of first- and third-class passengers, but will also enable students to explore technological changes and the different motives for travel during the period (many of the wealthy passengers on the Titanic travelled for business or pleasure, while third-class passengers were frequently immigrants seeking a better quality of life). Students will inevitably confront the technological limitations of the 'unsinkable' *Titanic* but will also be led to consider their chances of survival depending upon their wealth, status, gender and age; with a little research students should easily discover that the chances of a first-class passenger surviving the sinking were far greater than that of a third-class passenger whatever his or her age or gender and regardless of the convention 'women and children first'.
- Students could then be asked to investigate the extent to which the lives of ordinary working people have improved in British society since these events took place; positive developments such as the introduction of the

Welfare State can be balanced against continued inequalities in education and health to produce a 'balance sheet' of positive reforms and continued inequalities. They may also be encouraged to explore questions regarding the motives of people emigrating to improve the quality of their life and to create better opportunities for their children. This understanding can then be used to challenge the popular demonization of 'economic migrants'.

## Ethnicity

Through the study of history at KS3 students should begin to appreciate that the origins of much that is least admirable about present day attitudes towards 'race' and identity in Britain today have origins that lie half-forgotten in the history of the Slave Trade. On the other hand, while there is no evidence to support the simplistic conclusion that 'they were all racists in the past' it is also worth reminding those who might seek to denigrate the contribution of history to the school curriculum that it remains equally true that racism cannot simply be ignored as a problem *of the past* with no relevance to the Britain of today, nor that it should be seen as a topic of study 'best avoided' because it may cause controversy or friction between groups of students (both arguments for avoiding or 'downplaying' this topic were put to me in the 1980s by senior school managers). Similarly, one of the best counters to the accusation that the school history curriculum at KS4 carries too much reference to the Nazi period is by reference to the continued relevance of this period as a 'warning from history' of the consequences of racism and of the horrors of genocide.

### *Unit title and target age group*

The Slave Trade, intended to form part of the KS3 Programme of Study.

### *Resources*

- http://www.blackhistory4schools.co.uk/slavetrade/
- http://www.spartacus.schoolnet.co.uk/USAslavery.htm
- http://www.liverpoolmuseums.org.uk/ism/slavery/
- http://www.brycchancarey.com/equiano/
- http://www.bbc.co.uk/history/historic_figures/wilberforce_william.shtml
- http://www.maryseacole.com/maryseacole/pages/

## Learning outcomes

At the end of this unit students should be able to describe and explain the operation of the Slave Trade, they should be able to place the trans-Atlantic trade within a chronological framework, and be able to make links and comparisons across time. They should also be able to investigate links between the Slave Trade and the origins of contemporary racist attitudes and should be made aware of modern forms of 'slavery' such as the economic exploitation of children in the developing world.

## Teaching and learning focus and suggested activities

- The study of the Slave Trade is best approached by encouraging students to undertake a series of investigations focusing on a number of key areas. These should include: the reasons why Britain became involved in the trade (the economics of the Slave Trade Triangle and the existence of slavery prior to the trans-Atlantic trade); the experience of slavery (the Middle Passage and life on the plantation); reasons for the abolition of slavery (the work of humanitarians and economic and social change, including the impact of slave revolts and rebellions); the consequences of the Slave Trade (establishing links with racist attitudes in the modern world and modern forms of 'slavery' such as the economic exploitation of children and women in the developing world).

- The contribution of individuals to the abolition of the trade can be explored through a series of recorded or videotaped interviews, using whenever possible the words of the individuals involved. Students can be encouraged to collaborate in pairs or small groups to produce these interviews. A good starting point would be Olaudah Equiano and John Newton (both individuals wrote vividly of their experiences and their words are readily accessible as transcripts on the internet).

- Before embarking on any investigation of present day attitudes and beliefs students could be asked to investigate evidence for and against the idea that Victorians were racist. This could be presented in the form of a 'mock trial' of a representative 'Victorian'; evidence for the 'prosecution' could be presented to show that the abolition of the Slave Trade was not immediately followed by the abolition of slavery and that the standard of living of many of the descendants of the slaves imported to the British colonies in the West Indies remained very much inferior to that of white landowners and imperial officers. Evidence for the 'defence' could include the campaign for abolition and the life story of Mary Seacole (a much celebrated if forgotten heroine of the Crimean War).

## Concluding Remarks

In a recent series of regional conferences designed to introduce the revised National Curriculum in History to teachers,[5] a briefing paper from the Historical Association (2008) suggested a four-step programme for teachers seeking to revise their curriculum offer:

1. What role should history play in the life of your pupils and school?
2. How does current provision support your new rationale for history and the revised concepts, processes and content?
3. What new areas of content can you choose to support both the rationale of history in your school and the progression of historical skills and concepts in your pupils?
4. What do you want your pupils to have gained from their study of history at KS3? What would be your ideal end result?

While there is much to recommend this approach, there remain a number of concerns with regard to the place of history in the new National Curriculum: first that the expectation that students in British schools will study a common core of history cannot be easily married with the view (in the words of one keynote speaker) that 'thousands' of different versions of the history curriculum might well emerge from this review process. For while it may be entirely right and proper that students should have the opportunity to explore issues of relevance to their local community, the realities of the school timetable and the allocation of curriculum time within those structures will inevitably raise the pragmatic question of how much of that precious resource they should devote to such a Programme of Study? Second, the new curriculum structures that are often championed as the 'solution' to the overcrowded curriculum are in fact remarkably similar to structures first experimented with thirty years or more ago. The problem then and the problem now is that a thematic approach can have a 'polarizing' effect on the curriculum, removing in the case of history any real sense of the broad sweep of events and replacing this contextual knowledge with a fragmented locally determined version of the history curriculum. It is perhaps a matter of some regret that it is for isolated professionals in their own schools to try to achieve an appropriate balance between the local, national and international, and to make forcefully the case for the continued inclusion of a significant element of history within the KS3 curriculum against the competing demands of subjects that are frequently perceived as more 'significant' in terms of the performance measures that may be applied on a particular school by external agencies such as Ofsted.

    While recognizing these concerns, this is not to say that teachers of history should resist attempts to establish cross-curricular links with other subjects, as the ever-sensible 'In a Nutshell' column in 'Teaching History' comments:

Helping pupils to make connections across disciplines is vital and long overdue. But there are both sensible and crazy ways of doing it. Think how wonderful it would be to have top set Year 9 thinking hard about how the concept of evidence in history DIFFERS from the concept of evidence in science ... cross-curricularity is exciting but its starting point has to be the intellectual structure of each discipline and an understanding of what different disciplines contribute. If your starting point is that each just contributes a pile of 'content', we get nowhere. The only 'skills' required become 'information skills'. (Teaching History 2007)

Unfortunately, as the column also recognizes, some senior managers are largely ignorant of the true nature of good history teaching and of the need for students to 'make the human connection of a mature historical thinker with a novice historical thinker' (*ibid.*).

The vision of a 'skills-led' curriculum which dispenses with the agency of teachers who possess specialist knowledge, and creates structures whereby students apparently simply acquire knowledge from information technology without the need for human contact, is in my view profoundly misguided. It is a vision that completely misinterprets the concept of 'skills' and the potential fertility of approaching a topic from a *variety* of specialist perspectives. At the regional conference I attended the model of a thematic curriculum that 'brokered' relationships between subject disciplines was proposed. Consider the model of potential thematic links in Figure 9.1.

The model postulates a rich and complex learning experience, developing rather than forcing links between various subject disciplines. The potential of history as a subject that can act as a foundation stone of education has long been recognized; but it is perhaps a case that has been forgotten in some schools:

There is nothing that gives unity to all the other [subjects] so much as history. It is a subject above all catholic ... it is as wide and various as life. Nor does it only provide the best common meeting ground for all the separate [disciplines]; it gives them the best and most fruitful junction with the natural sciences. (Rowse 1971, pp. 111–12)

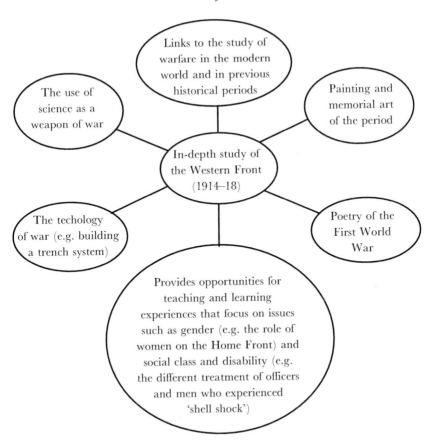

**FIGURE 9.1**

# Notes

1  This is the policy of including students with SEN in mainstream schools.
2  David Starkey (2006) refers to the view that the collective noun for a group of historians should be a 'malice'. In something of this spirit he describes E. H. Carr's seminal work quoted at the start of this chapter as 'truly dreadful'. There is, I believe, behind this remark a serious point regarding the false dichotomy between skills and content. The need to lead students through the repertoire of skills required to study history (or any other subject for that matter) is not an argument for a content free curriculum. At the end of the day *what* students are asked to study matters every bit as much as equipping them with the necessary skills to successfully complete their studies.
3  Standard Assessment Tasks in core subjects continue to be used in England to compare the performance of students at Key Stages 1–3. This approach remains

central to the government's continued insistence on performance league tables for English schools.

[4]  At the time of publication the need to provide resources for the revised National Curriculum and the new specifications at GCSE will inevitably generate a variety of new course materials; in the past materials produced under the auspices of the Schools History Project (publisher Hodder Murray) have provided excellent models of best practice. With regard to web-based resources experience indicates that inevitably website addresses change and sites will appear and disappear. However, using a keyword search will generally produce a range of relevant sites although care must of course be taken to ensure that these sites are monitored for inappropriate content and/or links. Similarly, there is a wealth of material available on film for use in the classroom.

[5]  New Secondary Curriculum Subject Specific Support Programme (2008).

# References

Carr, E. H. (1964), *What Is History?* Harmondsworth: The Penguin Press.

Dearing, R. (1994), *The National Curriculum and Its Assessment: Final Report*. London: SCAA.

DES (1991), *History in the National Curriculum (England)*. HMSO.

DfES (2004), *PSHE in Practice*. Nottingham, DfES Publications.

Forrest, S. (2006), 'Straight talking: challenges in teaching and learning about sexuality and homophobia in schools', in M. Cole, (ed.), *Education, Equality and Human Rights: Issues of Gender, 'Race', Sexuality, Disability and Social Class* (2nd edn). London: Routledge, pp. 111–133.

Historical Association (2008), 'Starting point: creating a departmental vision'. Conference paper, June 2008, Reading..

QCA (2007), *History: Programme of Study*. Available at www.qca.org.uk/curriculum (accessed July 2008).

Redman, P. (1994), 'Shifting ground: rethinking sexuality education', in D. Epstein (ed.), *Challenging Lesbian and Gay Inequalities in Education*. Buckingham: Open University Press.

Rieser, R. (2006), 'Disability equality: confronting the oppression of the past', in M. Cole (ed.), *Education, Equality and Human Rights: Issues of Gender, 'Race', Sexuality, Disability and Social Class* (2nd edn). London: Routledge, pp. 157–179.

Rowse, A. L. (1971), *The Use of History*. Harmondsworth: Pelican Books (first published in 1946 by The English Universities Press).

Starkey, D. (2006), 'What history should we be teaching in Britain in the 21st century?' Conference paper presented at the Institute of Historical Research, June 2006.

Teaching History (2007), 'In a nutshell: arguing the case for keeping history at Key Stage 3'. 129.

Chapter 10

# ICT

Maurice Nyangon

This chapter focuses on the barriers to all students achieving their full potential in Information Communication and Technology (ICT). The transformational power of ICT is explored pragmatically while its failure to be harnessed is identified as an ongoing political issue that further disempowers the already vulnerable. Students with English as an Additional Language (EAL) or Special Educational Needs (SEN), those from non-white backgrounds, who live in poverty or are Looked After Children (LAC), are at risk of falling into the chasm of the Digital Divide, a late twentieth-century educational apartheid. Of equal concern, the widening gender gap in ICT is analysed as female students, despite their academic dominance, fail to opt for the subject beyond Key Stage 4. The software, learning styles and gender stereotypes in relation to ICT teaching and learning, central to inclusive pedagogy, are critically examined to expose the cracks in a subject area that promises so much. Unless teachers are aware of its limitations as a social leveller, ICT can exacerbate the division between those that have and those that have not.

## Introduction

*A grand vision of an educational system in which technology is used not in the form of machines for processing children but as something the child himself will learn to manipulate, to extend, to apply to projects, thereby gaining a greater and more articulate mastery of the world, a sense of the power of applied knowledge and a self-confidently realistic image of himself as an intellectual agent.*

(Seymour Papert, *Professor Emeritus, MIT 1980*)

Equality and empowerment in ICT entails an aspiration to work towards a society in which all students are able to fulfil their potential and live fulfilling lives. Papert, perceived as the 'father' of ICT who invented the Logo programming language incorporating Piaget's constructivism learning theories of education, clearly has a vision of ICT as empowering students. This vision, however, should not rest on terms defined and determined by a Western, patriarchal technological agenda, where the dominant are in a position to ensure that their particular way of being is recognized as universal and the definition of excellence charged with masculine implications (Bourdieu 2002). Papert's semantics – the casual use of 'himself' and 'master' – set a tone that still resonates in the world of ICT: from the gendering of 'reality' computer games, to our classrooms and beyond into the world of work, careers and industry. That ICT itself is embedded in a heterosexual, middle-class, able-bodied white male culture has created a barrier to all students being able to access the level playing field that should be the most egalitarian of all classroom landscapes.

The National Curriculum in England and Wales aims to expose all students to computing across the school curriculum developing knowledge and understanding of ICT. Its history is brief although its roots in its simple function as a teaching aid go back to the world of magic lanterns and reel-to-reel tape. Visionary practitioners, led by Papert, perceived the value of computers in developing the logical skills that underpin computing to resonate throughout education and beyond. Yet the relative expense, despite some major initiatives (The Microelectronics Education Programme and the Micros in School Scheme), still saw their use confined to enthusiasts. Others could see their potential but given the paucity of software, the poor reliability of the equipment and complexity of configuration, they remained confined to a certain 'nerdy' type of teacher until the introduction of the National Curriculum at the start of the 1990s. This was the first official recognition of a role for IT – as the fifth Attainment Target in the technology curriculum with a few references elsewhere in other subjects' Programmes of Study (Davies 2005). Despite this inauspicious start, by 1995 IT had evolved through the Dearing review into a core entitlement for students. The unanswered question was, who was to teach this new subject and in what time?

Information technology presented schools with four challenges: to accommodate a new subject; to provide a robust infrastructure; to develop a coherent scheme to teach IT skills; and to embrace the technology to improve learning and teaching across the school. The problem of fitting IT into an already crowded timetable led to a compromise that was to have an impact on IT delivery and use for some years – it could be taught 'across the curriculum'. This 'cross-curricular' model largely failed in terms of developing core IT skills in an effective manner. Nonetheless, where it was well organized it exposed a wider layer of specialists to the pedagogical challenges of both teaching and using IT. Again, the pioneering enthusiasts were at the fore, working with a disparate range of hardware and software as early networks in schools slowly drove IT forward. Networks equalled sharing and for the pioneers the benefits were obvious, although for others IT seemed to equate much pain for often little educational gain. While the rhetoric at government level proclaimed the importance of IT, funding was not provided to lay a robust foundation on which teachers could build. Various initiatives were started and often stopped just as the results had created a scaffold skeleton. Only a decade ago funding for IT remained largely at the discretion of the individual school and this led to great variance in provision until the Stevenson Report (Independent ICT in Schools Commission 1997). It aimed for 'basic confidence and competence', for both teachers and students in a plea for stability in policy, concluding:

> If the next government does not take steps to intensify the use of information and communications technology in our schools, a generation of children – and a generation of adults as teachers – will have been put at enormous disadvantage with consequences ... that will be difficult to reverse. (Stevenson Report 1997)

Its impact, and the development of The National Grid for Learning in 1998, cannot be overstated. All subjects had to teach ICT (QCA 1999) and the first serious funding filtered into schools in 1999. Consequently, whole-school networks emerged offering benefits within a classroom that could be multiplied across a school. The internet arrived in schools in the mid-1990s, but it was only with whole-school internal networks that access became a possibility for many students at once. Regional Broadband Consortia have since worked to make multiple sustained access a reality but the internet is more than the web – it opens up many new forms of communication: blogs, forums, chat, video conferencing, learning platforms, virtual learning environments and email.

The QCA website makes powerfully emotive claims for ICT:

> ICT capability is fundamental to full participation in and engagement with modern society ... ICT opens up a wealth of information to pupils and allows easy communication and collaboration with others across the globe. This encourages them to understand, respect, value and engage with not only their own cultures and traditions but also those of others and to develop a sense of their own place in the world. (QCA 2007)

The degree to which these ideals are embedded in our classrooms is questionable. Has ICT done what Papert envisioned? Or has it actually created its own conundrum, a new barrier to equality and a further glass ceiling to the educational meritocracy that is the blue sky vision all teachers should share?

# Gender

ICT is a man's world and, whether or not it is 'easier to put a man on the moon than to get more women to enter computer professions' (Wendy Hall, President of the British Computer Society 2007), in most of Europe women remain a minority in the ICT industry (Truth *et al.* 2003). Multiple and diverse masculine organizational and social cultures and behaviour alienate women from ICT by the attitudes and beliefs they hold about this culture, particularly an image of, 'nerdyness' (Webster 2005), a world not only male dominated but dominated by a 'hacker' subculture. Joy, play, fun and love – life itself – are wrapped up in a singular focus on computing (Margolis *et al.* 2000). Female students have significantly negative attitudes attributed to experiences rather than gender, as is the female students' stronger preference for social contact (Proost and Lowyck 1997). Rather than empower the lives of women, there is therefore a danger that ICT will further increase the gender divide (World Bank 2002).

There has been an increase in the opportunities for all students to have access to computers in schools in recent years yet gender differences are still prevalent both within and beyond school, and female students fail to participate in a technological world 30 years after the 1975 Sex Discrimination Act (Clegg *et al.* 2000). While students have equal opportunities offered to them as option choices at the end of Key Stage 3, statistically choices still reflect stereotypically gender-orientated subjects: scientific and technical subjects attract more male students and languages and the arts more female students (Ofsted 1996; *Daily Telegraph* 2007). Of the 15 per cent of women in the UK who work in the ICT industry, less than 20 per cent hold a computing degree (Webster 2005) yet female students outperform male students in ICT academically at Advanced (A) level. In 2007, out of 13,360 A level ICT students, 63 per cent were male (2.3 per cent of the total A level cohort) and 37 per cent female (only 1.1 per cent of the total cohort), yet the female students achieved a higher percentage of A–C grades at 59.2 per cent, while male students achieved 49.3 per cent A–C grades. At GCSE level, where participation is more equitable, female achievement again superseded their male peers in 2006 at a ratio of 7.1:4.9 per cent achieving A* grade, 16.2:12.4 per cent achieving A grade and 19.7:17.4 per cent achieving B grade (*The Times* 2006). Despite their superior academic performance, female students perceive themselves as less able in ICT. Even professional women in the ICT industry believe that ICT competence is linked to interest and thus men will inevitably be both more competent and interested (Sefyrin 2005).

The Theory of Planned Behaviour (TpB), propounded by Isaac Ajzen (1985), provides an insight into the experiences of female students successfully studying ICT at either GCSE or A level and their proceeding option choices. Reporting their experiences is a positive move to attract female students into

ICT examination classrooms and beyond. Investigating classroom organization and learning styles that create more positive attitudes in female students studying ICT is pragmatic action research that can impact upon learning. In the masculine world of ICT female students are supposed to learn it the way men see it. Men have imposed conceptual schemes on the experience of female students that do not help make sense of their experiences; but extinguish experience (Flinders 1997). Intelligence is not a shared unitary construct but rather a multiple construct. According to Gardner, there is not one intelligence, but eight 'multiple intelligences'. These are relatively independent (Gardner 1997) and impact upon the learning styles that engage and motivate students in the classroom. Key to breaking through barriers to ICT participation is research on learning styles regarding group work in ICT. Female students will be uncomfortable in a learning environment that seems to encourage highly focused, obsessive behaviour (Frenkel 1990; DeClue 1997). They are alienated from the subject when ICT use is coupled with competitive or individual tasks, as they prefer, and benefit from, working together (Opie 1997). Some researchers argue that female students perform better in all-female groups, others in mixed groups, but there is consensus in that female students often find the ICT environment hostile, preferring activities where social interaction is encouraged, although collaboration is often discouraged in computer science (Moses 1995). Most assessment takes place competitively, a methodology that females prefer to avoid (Howell 1993; Moses 1995). They are ill at ease in a field that encourages obsessive behaviour (Frenkel 1990). Consequently, female students may feel isolated and this attitude will affect their intent and behaviour: the behaviour to opt out of ICT participation post-GCSE.

While there are statistically few female ICT teachers, girls are also less likely than boys to have ICT confident role models at home. Their mothers and sisters may be using ICT with aplomb in the workplace, but they are not as likely as fathers, uncles and brothers to be playing games or surfing the net at home. The ICT male dominance in the classroom is mirrored at home and in the wider world. Where is the Bella to rival Bill Gates? Even in cross-curricular ICT, it is often men who are in charge of organizing access to hardware and networks (Harris 1999). Just as female students are less confident than male students in using computers, studies have consistently found male teachers to be more self-confident in using ICT and female teachers to rate their knowledge and skills lower on a self-assessment scale (Volman and van Eck 2002).

Closing the gender gap in female participation in ICT beyond GCSE is clearly not about competence; that female students are as competent as male students is not in dispute. It is about complementary activity. Technology itself should support gender differences in work-style preferences to reduce the gender divide (Gracia-Luque and Stein 2005) but for this to occur teachers need to recognize what gender-based learning styles are and embed them into their planning. Single-sex group work can enhance female students' intrinsic interest in ICT in their engagement with each other as they define their learning issues and decide for themselves what is relevant for their learning (Dolmans *et al.* 2001).

Outside the environment of the classroom, the games children play, provide them with 'virtual' role models that influence real lives. There is no doubt that software style also affects students' attitudes to ICT. There are two issues: first, the extent to which software exhibits gender bias, stereotypes and the effect this has; and second, the scarcity of educational software that has been specifically designed to appeal to all students' interests and counteract the impact of computer game stereotyping. As we interact and rely more on software it becomes all the more important that the software systems themselves reflect the ideals of interactional rules that society rests upon; a society free from class, cultural, 'race' and gender bias. Yet given the prime impetus for software development has come out of the United States and its dominant cultural norms of construction (white, male and conformist) it will follow that a mass of cultural and gendered stereotypes will integrate into all forms of the media and media education (Greysen 2005).

Only a glance at Lara Croft and her Tomb Raider adventures reveals what male games designers deem as appealing to girls: a stereotypical erotic male fantasy feeding the mass media. The Angelina Jolie lookalike action figure was theoretically created to motivate and engage girls yet on every level disengages them, distancing them from the targeted learning objectives and lowering their comfort levels and self-esteem. There have been attempts to challenge perceived stereotypes (Drees and Phye 2001) but at the same time other stereotypes are perpetuated – that men work well in teams but do not deviate from their 'traditional' roles as frequently as women do.

## Sexual Orientation

If a child does not fit into a heterosexual mould then role models are even harder to find. There are no comparable role models to Lara Croft for students who question their sexuality. The world of the computer game is as heterosexual and male dominated as that of the computer lab. Where they do exist, non-heterosexual characters are shadowy and ambiguous. Quina Quen from Final Fantasy IX is ungendered but gamers are able, comically, to marry 'him' to the apparently male Vivi. Many fighting games have ambiguously gay characters but rather than challenge traditional gay stereotypes they embody effeminate traits that make them stand apart from their tough, masculine fellow warriors. Their very existence is fragile too. In 1994 Sega made changes to the violent Streets of Rage 3 from the original

Japanese counterpart. The 'boss' was originally the explicitly homosexual Ash, replete in Village Peoplesque garb, but he was deleted as a key character, becoming only an optional playable figure (Thompson 2004). These sidelined gay characters and narratives do not feature in marketing strategies. Young, white heterosexual males drive the industry forward economically and are the target 'gamer'. While they have responded positively to Lara Croft, despite her creator, Toby Gard, bemoaning computer-games makers 'are regarded as being about as hip and cool as abattoir workers', it remains to be determined if a straight male would be willing to play an open gay or transgender character (Howe 2001).

The hugely popular Sims virtual lifestyle 'game' – a twenty-first-century doll's house – unusually broke advertising new ground in 2001 in releasing a TV commercial where an attractive twenty-something male rejected a woman for a man in a nightclub scenario. This was an overt attempt to attract the 'pink' gay gamer dollar. The child-targeted Nintendo Game Boy Advance and DS versions, however, have had the same-sex 'romance' interactions deleted, effectively removing homo/bisexuality from the games (Thompson 2004). This is doubly problematic: first, the extent to which software exhibits gender-biased stereotypes; and second, the extent to which software has been specifically designed to appeal to the interests of anyone other than heterosexual young males. The role that teachers play in challenging perceptions created by gender- and heteronormatively biased software is critical. Left unchallenged, these perceptions may be one factor in the complex process whereby students learn from an early age not only that the world of computers is associated with dominant masculinity but also that academic success is dependent upon sexual approbation. The norm is defined by the way heterosexual young males work with ICT, delivered by male teachers. Their dominance will be secured as the male way of being if perpetually left unchallenged in the classroom and the definition of excellence charged with masculine implications (Bourdieu 2002).

## Social Class

The division between stereotypes on students' PC screens in their bedrooms (or under their desk) plays out for the digital 'haves' in a world where the 'have nots' are as needy as in a Dickens novel:

> Social mobility and equality of opportunity have once again become issues of political and social concern in the recent past ... Education has been often seen as a route to greater intergenerational mobility. So it is natural to ask what role education has in the recent decline in mobility in Britain. (Sutton Trust 2005)

The gap in achievement between rich and poor has become greater in post-war Britain, and working-class children are more disadvantaged now than 50 years ago (Gregg and Machin 2005). This underachievement of working-class students of both sexes is a cause for concern (Bell 2004; Ofsted 2004). As taught in British schools ICT reinforces class power imbalances of the past and present (Volman and van Eck 2002). Underachievement in ICT is endemic in the effect this underachievement has upon the most vulnerable (Bell 2004; Ofsted 2004).

The National Curriculum in England and Wales aims to expose all students to computing across the school curriculum and to develop students' knowledge and understanding of ICT. The DfES introduced the Key Stage 3 National Strategy, based on four key principles (expectations, progression, engagement and transformation), in 2000. It was designed to improve the education of 11 to 14 year olds in England by strengthening teaching and learning across the curriculum, and raising standards in the Key Stage by developing cross-curricular skills, such as literacy, numeracy and ICT, particularly helping students who enter Year 7 with attainment below level 4 in the National Curriculum to make faster progress. Ironically there is growing evidence that the underachieving (statistically) students who come from less prosperous homes economically are falling behind even further despite the strategy. Thus, the students whom it was primarily designed to support may be most likely to be further alienated (Barnes *et al.* 2003). At the same time government policy over the past decade has not done enough to tackle disadvantage in urban schools that face challenging circumstances (Bell 2004). Effective use of ICT in teaching subjects across the curriculum is increasing but good practice remains uncommon (Ofsted 2001–2).

While the Digital Divide narrows as the number of households with ICT access increases overall, the divide with the socio-economic groups without ICT access – single parents, the over 55s, minority ethnic groups and non-English speakers – becomes wider (Becta 2001). The main reasons why households have not purchased a computer are related to cost. This cost factor is most likely to be mentioned by those in social groups D and E. Students least likely to achieve academically at school are in the lowest economic social groups: the very students without ICT access.

For some students multiple factors affect the gap between what they could achieve and what they are likely to achieve. Subscription rates for digital TV are greater in the highest income groups (31 per cent) than they are for those in the lowest (14 per cent). There are differences in the type and quality of hardware and software in households that may exacerbate inequalities further, with children from higher-income backgrounds using home computers for a much wider range of activities than those from lower-income families, and in those homes, ICT is less likely to be fully understood or effectively used. Over twice as many employed people are 'online' than there are unemployed, and 71 per cent of employed compared to 32 per cent of those not working were found to have a computer at home. Households with two adults and one or more children have internet access rates of up to 35 per cent, while single-parent families access rates range from 7 to 11 per cent (*ibid.*).

The government does acknowledge the problem. In 2007 the then Schools Minister, later Minister of State for Schools and Learners, Jim Knight promised to ensure the

> so-called digital divide cannot be allowed to create and reinforce social and academic divisions ... With more than 800,000 children restricted to access at school [who] could be isolated and left behind. There is no sense in asking every school to provide a learning platform to support children at home if some – likely to be the ones who might most benefit – are cut off from that platform. Today, I want to talk further about our aspiration for universal home access and how that might be made a reality ... We need to come up with a sustainable solution which will work for future generations ... rather than looking for a quick fix. (Knight 2007)

What the 'sustainable solution' can be is less apparent although Computers for Pupils, a £60 million, two-year programme has helped some of the most disadvantaged secondary school students improve their education and life skills by putting a computer into the home. The scheme has provided 200,000 home computers for students identified by their schools. The impact and success of the scheme, whether students in most need were being provided with ICT support and all it entailed, was reviewed in 2008. As schools are at various stages of establishing their learning platforms, the impact is likely to be varied and, as always, dependent on individual teachers or school pastoral systems that have to be vigilant in ensuring all students have equitable access, making no presumptions.

Economics is not the only factor to contend with. Free School Meals are not a catch-all universal determinator of need; the Digital Divide also manifests itself in the growing elderly population. The over-65s represent almost 20 per cent of the population but are the group least likely to be connected to the internet or to subscribe to digital television. Internet use drops from 14 per cent among the 64–75 age group to 4 per cent for those aged 75 or over. Retired households are least likely to have internet access. Those over 55 are significantly less likely to own or use a PC and have fewer current or desired computer skills. A large proportion of older 'non-acceptors' report having no aspiration to use a computer at all (Becta 2001). Looked After Children (LAC) who live with grandparents or, frequently, older carers may be unlikely to have qualified financially for the Computers for Pupils programme but nevertheless could fall into the chasm of the 'Divide' due to the lack of pragmatic support in the home.

In May 2006, the DfES published *Outcome Indicators for Looked-After Children in England*. This depressing snapshot of children's experiences during the 12 months to September 2005 showed that 36 per cent of LAC in Year 11 were not entered for any GCSE or equivalent exams. Only 11 per cent of LAC in Year 11 achieved at least five GCSEs at grades A*–C or the equivalent (up from 9 per cent in 2004), compared with 56 per cent of all Year 11 students. Not surprisingly, 14 per cent less LAC stayed in education beyond Key Stage 4 than the national average (DfES 2007). These statistics show how crucial it is that schools support LAC both emotionally and academically. Skills in ICT can only enhance academic achievement and job opportunities yet these students who, arguably, most need the skills are least likely to access them. In the UK, approximately 20 million people deploy ICT to perform their job roles. The ICT workforce is predicted to grow between 1.5 and 2.3 per cent per annum throughout the next decade, with an estimated additional 179,000 ICT professionals to join the workforce over the next ten years (E-skills/ Gartner 2004). At the end of 2008, there was over 1.3 million new technology workers, and by 2010, 65 per cent of the economy will be based on technology (Mitchell 2005). LAC without the qualifications to allow them entry into this economy will spiral further into the Digital Divide, perpetuating poverty, disempowerment and capital disinvestment (Bourdieu 2002) with the world they inhabit. A very different world from that which Gordon Brown aspires to: 'A Britain therefore where effort is rewarded, ambition fulfilled, potential realised, a Britain of high aspirations and a Britain of all the talents' (Gordon Brown, University of Greenwich 2007).

## 'Race'

Just as LAC and the poor struggle to have their talents recognized, so our multicultural classrooms also fail to create a level playing field academically. In 2004 Chinese students were the most likely to achieve five or more GCSE grades A*–C in England, with 79 per cent of Chinese girls and 70 per cent of Chinese boys respectively doing so but the lowest levels of GCSE attainment were among Black Caribbean students, particularly boys. Only 27 per cent of Black Caribbean boys and 44 per cent of Black Caribbean girls achieved five or more A*–C grade GCSEs. Students from the Black African, Other Black and Mixed White and Black Caribbean groups had the next lowest level of attainment and correspondingly had the highest rates of exclusions in 2003–4, up to three times the rate for White students (14 students per 10,000) (National Statistics Online 2005). While these disparate statistics have multifaceted causes and consequences, it is inevitable that the Digital Divide will play its part in the disaffection and underachievement of some students from non-British white backgrounds.

Many deprived neighbourhoods have high proportions of minority ethnic communities, who have less access and ownership of ICT due partly to economic factors. Additionally, barriers exist to those whose first language is not English, as the majority of training, content and operating systems are in English. To benefit from ICT, a certain level of literacy is necessary, and factors relating to culture – for example, expectations and norms relating to gender roles – impact upon its use. Students with English as their first language perform better than students with English as an Additional Language (EAL) in each Key Stage. For example, in Key Stage 3 science, 70 per cent of students with English as their first language achieved the expected level, compared to 55 per cent of EAL students. At the end of Key Stage 4 the difference in performance narrowed but there was still an average 3.1 percentage points differentiation in achieving five A*–C GCSEs. The difference in the percentage of students achieving the expected level in mathematics and science becomes wider with each Key Stage when comparing EAL students with English as their first language (*ibid.*). Targeted ICT support would narrow this gap. There are large variations in attitudes, use and experiences with ICT between groups from various cultural backgrounds although there is, as yet, little research into this area of classroom practice (Becta 2001). The potential ICT has to widen participation for all students is, however, vast if teachers analyse and exploit the cultural dimension of the hardware and software currently available (Robinson 1993).

Written Computer Mediated Communication (CMC) encourages EAL learners to ask more questions and use different language functions more frequently. Email exchanges appear to encourage language that is less narrative and descriptive but more personal, expressive and argumentative. Participants in an email exchange do not share a physical location, so much of the context needs to be made explicit rather than assumed, but the register is more speech-like and less formal than other forms of writing. Communication through email may therefore support EAL learners to move from speech to text. Similarly, the preparation of electronic multimedia communication may allow learners to extend their communicative output through the support of graphics, sound, video and presentational elements. Research indicates that this does not necessarily lead to a focus on what some may see as peripheral, less important, aspects of communication, but that it can give students the opportunity to begin to express linguistically complex ideas more successfully. The advantage of CMC, and ICT more generally, is not only that it provides more opportunities to create more output in different forms, but also that it supports EAL learners to be less self-conscious of their language use and more willing and able to develop their output collaboratively. Evidence suggests CMC provides learners with the opportunity to refer to limitless models of similar output to enhance and improve their work. EAL student-creating web pages is an excellent vehicle for developing collaborative writing, involving not only known peers, but also unknown readers and authors (Davies 2005).

Although much has been written about the importance of 'recognizing and valuing' linguistic diversity, very few examples are given of how this might be encouraged in practice, particularly in situations where few learners or teachers have a common language. One of the major advantages of using e-translators is the recognition of learners' home language in a high-status context resulting in clear social advantages for the student and often enhanced confidence (Davies and Lama 2007). Unfortunately, not all languages are available – some African dialects have not as yet been added to the software and the success of the translators is dependent on teacher support and ICT availability. That this lacks cohesion even within schools themselves and is underfunded is inevitable as schools remain, disappointingly, unaccountable, in our league table governed world, with regard to the achievements of students from multicultural backgrounds.

The Race Relations (Amendment) Act 2000, arising from the Stephen Lawrence Inquiry, theoretically attempts to force public institutions to give real consideration to 'race' equality, including requiring schools to take 'reasonable steps' to make available the results of its monitoring. For instance, it is statutory that all racist incidents be reported to the Local Education Authority. However, the QCA and the Teacher Training Agency (TTA), the key educational bodies, are largely absolved from responsibility (Gillborn 2006). Until Ofsted makes it statutory to give a centrally defined provision for non-British White and EAL students their success is often left to chance. Enriching ICT software to support EAL learning is improving by the term but there is certainly no equanimity in this area, nor are differing social and cultural multicultural backgrounds necessarily going to impact on routine lesson planning.

## Special Educational Needs

The support of students with special education needs (SEN) or additional educational needs (AEN) is reported specifically by Ofsted, who found SEN students generally not well supported and a significant challenge for teachers (Ofsted 2004). Theoretically, throughout the education sector, ICT can help students widen their horizons whether they are 'special needs' or not but for SEN students a computer can be both friend and foe. Teaching does not always cater for the wide range of students' capability in ICT. As an aid to communication, a correctly adapted PC can facilitate access to the curriculum, promoting independence and integration when recording, reporting, retrieving and presenting work may pose problems using traditional methods. Conversely, computers are used constantly as a learning tool across the curriculum and therefore students who cannot access the information or data they require with the available equipment will immediately be at a disadvantage. Thus, a disability can appear to make computer use difficult or even unachievable. The limitation in a student's abilities is consequently assumed to be unavoidable (Waits 2005). More often than not it is not the individual that is the limitation, but the design and implementation of the interface to the computer itself. Computer suites almost uniformly have identical computers, with standard keyboards, mice, monitors and desktops. Unfortunately, the size, needs and abilities of each end-user are not as uniform.

While a computer is an immensely flexible tool, and there is a wide range of adaptations and alternatives that can be used to fit the computer to the user, implementing simple and powerful solutions to facilitate ICT use – changes to fonts, audio and handling the mouse – are frequently inadvertently prevented by the school itself. If the computer system is 'locked down', students are effectively barred from changing any settings in the control panel. Even when they can customize the machine to meet their requirements, their settings are lost after each session. Yet systems can be adapted to accommodate the use of 'roaming profiles', which will retrieve students' settings no matter which computer they log on to, or a log-on can offer a selection of generic profiles to choose from, as appropriate for the most commonly encountered problems among the student population.

Inclusion is a key issue in schools and they should be constantly looking at new ways of improving access to systems and information for all students. For some, a computer can provide access to additional forms of media that are otherwise inaccessible, as in the scanning of traditional texts using Optical Character Recognition (OCR) software to create an onscreen version of the text, to be read back to the user. This means that students can become less dependent on a learning support assistant for all their needs. How can students progress, increase their autonomy, associate with their peer group, produce their own work and participate fully in the classroom environment when they are always accompanied by an adult? ICT should, and has the potential to, be a great 'leveller', minimizing peer differences – so important during formative years, when all students crave to blend in with their contemporaries. By adopting a more inclusive perspective to both teaching and learning materials with ICT, students with specific learning difficulties can benefit both educationally and socially. In addition, greater flexibility in the use of ICT can reveal new ways of working which may have a wider application and pay dividends to the whole class.

A key challenge for schools, therefore, is to ensure that the needs of all students have been taken into account when embedding ICT into the curriculum. For any school to be truly able to say that it has done so, it must have adapted hardware and software so that all students can benefit when learning, not just those for whom the technology is readily accessible. Computers have a two-fold role to play in most discipline areas – as both a learning tool and an aid to communication. The ideal is a premise that technology has the power to promote independence and achievement among all students including those with SEN. This principle is neither universally acknowledged nor implemented, despite the importance that it undoubtedly merits. The successful application and incorporation of adaptive computer technology in a classroom setting requires a degree of strategic planning for which many teachers are ill-equipped, lacking the necessary knowledge, experience, expertise and funding for the task (Liddle 2006).

## Conclusion

When exploring pedagogical issues in ICT teaching, differentiation is essential to create access for all students to the benefits ICT should offer. The question is not how do students learn but how do different students from different backgrounds and cultures, with different needs, learn differently, and what teachers need to do to create a revolving door rather than a closed one to study ICT (Michaelson 2005). Too little attention has been paid to the difficult and fundamental issue of how best to design effective learning experiences which integrate ICT successfully. The government has invested large sums of money in its Curriculum Online initiative (DfES 2001), which aims to bring high-quality online materials into every classroom from Key Stage 1 to Key Stage 4. While this is commendable the issue is how to finance and use materials to maximum advantage to enhance learning for all students, taking the learner and learning styles as its focus. ICT provides the tools to facilitate this, promote rapid dissemination and subsequent discussion, but its successful implementation is in the hands of the teacher (Goodison 2003). Consequently, targeted interventions are necessary to address particular aspects of inequality and raise comfort level and thus motivation. The ICT questions asked, the software used, who teaches students and how lessons are structured all need to be addressed.

It matters at every level if the 'puppet masters' of computer technology are mostly white, heterosexual, able-bodied, middle-class males who create a 'clubhouse' with very restricted entry. Within the 'club' computing salaries are comparatively high, jobs are relatively plentiful and entrepreneurship opportunities unbounded – the very students; young women, those with SEN and those falling within the Digital Divide should be given the (virtual) key to its door. Furthermore, a command of ICT is a crucial asset in many contexts outside the field itself, and the over-representation of white, middle-class men is a 'frightening' discrepancy (Gurian 2002). Teachers need to listen hard, recognizing that a competitive, combative culture rather than collaborative working relationships will alienate many students (Letherby 2003). It is not enough simply to accept the dominant version of success, encouraging all users to accommodate the values, structures and systems created by the dominant culture (Aveling 2002). One of the challenges is to conceptualize computer skills other than those that dominate classrooms and computer labs as real computing and to ask what is 'wrong' with computing rather than what is 'wrong' with users who do not conform to the current stereotype of successful ICT students (Clegg and Trayhurn 2000). This entails an aspiration to work towards a society in which students are able to meet their potential and lead fulfilling lives but not on terms defined and determined by a patriarchal technological agenda, as is the case today. There should be no need to participate in the ICT industry on only male terms, suppressing the instinct to facilitate, support and empower in favour of competition and hierarchy (Pritchard and Deem 1999).

The role that teachers play in challenging these perceptions is therefore critical as, left unchallenged, teachers' attitudes in the classroom, both in their methodology and in relationships with students' learning, are factors in the complex process whereby students learn from an early age that the world of computers is associated with dominant masculinity (Opie 1997). Life must be equitable and teachers are in a key position to ensure that ICT is used to its full potential to support equality in our classrooms. Computing, after all: 'Is not about computers any more. It is about living' (Nicholas Negroponte, founder and chairman of the One Laptop per Child non-profit association).

# References

Ajzen, I. (1985), 'From intentions to actions: a theory of planned behaviour', in J. Kuhle and J. Beckman (eds), *Action Control: From Cognition to Behaviour*. Heidelberg: Springer, pp. 11–39.

Aveling, N. (2002), ' "Having it all" and the discourse of equal opportunity: reflections on choices and changing perceptions'. *Gender and Education*, 14 (3) pp. 265–280.

Barnes, A., Venkatakrishnan, H. and Brown, M. (2003) *Strategy or Straitjacket? Teachers' Views on the English and Mathematics Strands of the Key Stage 3 National Strategy*. London: The Association of Teachers and Lecturers.

Barnes, D. and Todd, F. (1977), *Communication and Learning in Small Groups*. London: Routledge and Kegan Paul.

Becta (2001), 'The digital divide: a discussion paper'. Available at www.becta.org.uk/page_documents/research/digitaldivide.pdf (accessed April 2008).

Bell, D. (2004), 'Stemming the downward spiral of deprivation: 10 years on has performance in urban deprived schools improved?' *Curriculum Management Update* 42, pp. 6–8.

Blanden, J., Gregg, P, & Machin, S. (2005) Intergenerational Mobility in Europe and North America: A Report Supported by The Sutton Trust. Durham: The Centre for Economic Performance, p. 9.

Bourdieu, P., Accardo, A., Balazas, G., Beaud, S., Bonvin, F., Bourdieu, E. (2002) *The Weight of the World: Social Suffering in Contemporary Society*. Cambridge: Polity.

Brown, G. (2007) 'Gordon Brown sets out his vision for education'. The University of Greenwich: New Labour for Britain: http://www.labour.org.uk/home (Accessed April 2008).

Clegg, S., Trayhurn, D. and Johnson, A. (2000), 'Not just for men: a case study of the teaching and learning of information technology in higher education'. *Higher Education*, 40, (2), pp. 175–185.

*Daily Telegraph* (2007) 'A-level pass rate rises for 25th year'. Online at http://www.telegraph.co.uk/news/uknews/1560422/A-level-pass-rate-rises-for-25th-year.html (Accessed April 2008).

Davies, N. (2005) 'Not just how but why: EAL and ICT in the multilingual classroom'. Luton: National Association for Language Development In the Curriculum. Online at http://www.naldic.org.uk/docs/resources/documents/Not-justhowbutwhy.pdf [Accessed April 2008]

— and Lama, D. (2007), 'It's too slow. It doesn't make sense. I'll ask my friend to help me – it's better! Using e-translation in the classroom'. *NALDIC Quarterly*, 4, (2) Online at www.naldic.org.uk/docs/resources/documents/NQ4.2.10.pdf (Accessed April 2008).

Davies, R. (2005), 'The history and development of ICT in schools'. *ICT across the Curriculum* (ICTAC), 1, 16–18.

DeClue, T. (1997), 'Academic computer science and gender: a naturalistic study investigating the causes of attrition' (unpublished doctoral dissertation, Southern Illinois University, Carbondale).

DfES (2001) 'Curriculum online – a consultation paper'. Online at http://www.dfes.gov.uk/consultations (Accessed April 2008).

DfES (2007), *Looked After Children: The Struggle for Stability*. Available at http://findoutmore.dfes.gov.uk/2006/10/lookedafter_chi.html.

Dolmans, D. H. J. M., Wolfhagen, I. H. A. P., van der Vleuten, C. P. M. & Wijnen, W. H. F. W. (2001) 'Solving problems with group work in problem-based learning: hold on to the philosophy', *Medical Education*, 35 (9) September 2001, pp. 884–889.

Drees, D. and Phye, G. (2001), 'Gender representation in children's language arts computer software'. *Journal of Educational Research*, 95, (1), 49–55.

E-Skills/Gartner (2004), 'IT insights: trends and UK Skills Implications Report'. Available at www.e-skills.com/register (accessed April 2008).

Frenkel, K. A. (1990), 'Women and computing'. Communications of the ACM, (November), 34–46.

Gardner, H. (1997), *Frames of Mind: The Theory of Multiple Intelligences*. New York: Basic Books.

Gillborn, D (2006) 'Citizenship education as placebo: "Standards", institutional racism and education policy', *Education, Citizenship and Social Justice*, 1: pp. 83–104.

Goodison, T. (2003), 'Integrating ICT in the classroom: a case study of two contrasting lessons'. *British Journal of Educational Technology*, 34, (5), 549–566.

Gracia-Luque, R. & Stein, J. A. (2005) 'Mainstreaming as highlighting or neutralising? Ex/Inclusivity of Gender in ICTs from a European perspective'. Paper for presentation at 3rd European Symposium on Gender & ICT: Working for Change (1st February, 2005) Manchester.

Gregg, P. and Machin, S. (2005), *Comparative Work on the Findings of the National Child Development Study of 1958 and the Cohort Study of 1970*. London: The Sutton Trust.

Greyson, K. R. B. (2005) 'An Initial Investigation of Students' Self-Construction of Pedagogical Agents', in J. Archibald, J. Emms, F. Grundy, J. Payne & E. Turner (eds) *The Gender Politics of ICT*, London: Middlesex University Press, pp. 53–69.

Gurian, M. (2002), *Boys and Girls Learn Differently!* San Francisco: Jossy-Bass.

Hall, W. (2007), 'An interview'. *Emerald Engineering*. Available at http://engineering.emeraldinsight.com (accessed April 2009).

Harris, S. (1999), 'Inset for IT: a review of the literature relating to preparation for and use of IT in schools'. Slough: NFER.

Howe, S. L. (2001), 'Gaystation'. *XY Magazine* (Jul/Aug 2001), 78.

Howell, J. M. (1993), 'Transformational leadership, transactional leadership, locus of control, and support for innovation: key predictors of consolidated business unit performance'. *Journal of Applied Psychology*, 78, (6), 891–902.

Knight, J. (2007) 'The Digital Divide', Speech Delivered to the British Education Technology Show (Bett) January, 2007: www.dcsf.gov.uk/speeches/media/documents/betttechnology.doc (accessed April 2008).

Letherby, G. (2003) *Feminist Research In Theory and Practice*. Buckingham: Open University Press.

Liddle, J. (2006), 'ICT and lesson planning for students with disabilities'. *ICT across the Curriculum* (ICTAC), 4, 8–11.

Margolis, J., Fisher, A. and Miller, F. (2000), *Caring about Connections*: Gender and Computing: School of Computer Science. Pittsburgh: Carnegie Mellon University.

Michaelson, R. (2005), 'Gender mainstreaming in FP6: experiences from an IST project', in J. Archibald, J. Emms, F. Grundy, J. Payne and E Turner (eds), *The Gender Politics of ICT*. Heondon: Middlesex University Press, pp. 79–94.

Mitchell, S. (2005) 'What does Tech have to do with Women's Rights?', Digital Divide Network, August, 2007: www.digitaldivide.net/ (Accessed April 2008).

Moses, L. (1995), 'Where have the women gone and how do we keep them from going?' (panel session) Technical Symposium on Computer Science Education, proceedings of the twenty-sixth SIGCSE technical symposium on Computer science education (March 1995), Nashville, Tennessee, United States.

National Statistics Online (2005), Available at http://www.statistics.gov.uk/ (accessed April 2008).

Ofsted. (1996), *Gender Differences in Secondary Schools*. HMI. Online at http://www.ofsted.gov.uk/ (Accessed April 2008).

— (2001–2), *Information and Communication Technology in Secondary Schools*. HMI. Online at http://www.ofsted.gov.uk/ (Accessed April 2008).

— (2004), *The Key Stage 3 Strategy: Evaluation of the Third Year*. HMI. Online at http://www.ofsted.gov.uk/ (Accessed April 2008).

Opie, C. (1997), 'Whose turn next? Gender issues in information technology', in A. Clark and E. Millard (eds), *Gender in the Secondary Curriculum: Balancing the Books*. London: Routledge, pp. 80–95.

Papert, S. (1980), 'Teaching children thinking: the computer in school', in R. Taylor (ed.), *Tutor, Tool, Tutee*. New York: Teachers College Press, pp. 204–210.

Pritchard, C. and Deem, R. (1999), 'Wo-managing further education: gender and the construction of the manager in the corporate colleges of England', *Gender and Education*, 11, (3), 323–342.

Proost, K., Elen, J. and Lowyck, J. (1997), 'Effects of gender on perceptions of and preferences for telematic learning environments'. *Journal of Research on Computing in Education* (Summer), 29, (4), 370–84.

Robinson, B. (1993), 'The cultural dimension of information technology', in A. S. King and M. J. Reiss (eds), *The Multicultural Dimension of the National Curriculum*: Falmer Press, pp. 25–53. Online at http://arjournals.annualreviews.org/doi/abs/10.1146/annurev.psych.54.101601.145237?cookieSet = 1&journalCode = psych (Accessed April 2008).

Sefyrin, J. (2005), 'Understandings of gender and competence in ICT'. Paper presented at 6th International Women into Computing Conference University of Greenwich (14th–16th July 2005). Online at http://www.miun.se/upload/Institutioner/ITM/IKS/SI/publikationer/sefyrin_WiC.pdf (accessed April 2008).

Stevenson Report (1997), Information and Communications Technology in UK Schools, *An Independent Inquiry*. London: Independent ICT in Schools Commission.

*The Times* (2006) 'A-Level and GCSE Results'. Online at http://www.times online.o.uk/tol/life_and_style/education/a_level_gcse_results/ (accessed April 2008).

Thompson, C. (2004), *The Game Of Wife – Gay Marriage Comes To Video Games*. Slate. Online at http://slate.msn.com/id/2098339/ (Accessed April 2008).

Truth, E., Nielsen, S., Beekhuyzen, J. and von Hellens, L. (2003), 'Women talking about IT work: duality or dualism?' Special Interest Group on Computer Personnel Research Annual Conference Proceedings of the 2003 SIGMIS conference on computer personnel research: Freedom in Philadelphia – leveraging differences and diversity in the IT workforce. Philadelphia, PA, April 10–12, 2003.

Volman, M. and van Eck, E. (2002), 'Gender equity and information technology in education: the second decade'. *Journal of Educational Research*, 71, (4), 613–634.

Waits, A. (2005), 'Embracing the ICT needs of all learners across the curriculum'. *ICT across the Curriculum* (ICTAC), 1, 22–24.

World Bank (2002), 'Equitable access to information and communication is fundamental for maximising the impact of ICT'. *The Gender and Development Group*. Online at www.worldbank.org/ (accessed April 2008).

Chapter 11

# Music

## Martin Milner

## Introduction

This chapter aims to provide a conceptual compass with which to navigate the various approaches open to classroom music teachers and those who work with secondary age students in schools – teachers, visiting artists, creative partners, community musicians (or 'music leaders').[1] It traces recent developments in music education both in and outside of schools, noting how practices derived from the community music scene have been imported and adapted in mainstream education. Recent national and regional interventions have done much to change the nature of music education, among them the creation of the National Foundation for Youth Music (YM) in 1999 with its 2004 offshoot Music Leader (ML), the government-backed Music Manifesto, the Paul Hamlyn Fund's Musical Futures (PHF-MF), and other projects that have grown from community music practices. This involves a brief explanation of 'community music'.

The current Programme of Study for music in the National Curriculum (KS3) provides many opportunities to promote equality among secondary age students. Those who work in schools have access to a range of proven strategies for meeting the needs of the curriculum that can also serve to actively promote equality. However, there are still gross inequalities in society, reflected and reproduced in classrooms. There are also persistent modes of thinking about what music is and who it is for which reflect and protect these inequalities.

## What Is Music and Who Is It For: Consumer or Participant?

In the latest version of the Programme of Study for music in the National Curriculum (KS3) the stated aim is for teachers to ensure that listening, and applying knowledge and understanding, are developed through the interrelated skills of performing, composing and appraising

and the explicit hope is that students will show

increasing understanding of musical devices, processes and contextual influences. They work individually and in groups of different sizes and become increasingly aware of different roles and contributions of each member of the group. They actively explore specific genres, styles and traditions from different times and cultures with increasing ability to discriminate, think critically and make connections between different areas of knowledge.

This provides a clear framework built on performing, composing and appraising and leaves room for interpretation or variation in terms of delivery in the classroom. It does not indicate a hierarchy of styles, or dictate the study of core pieces or specific musicians, and in this respect enables the teacher to work to the strengths and interests of the students. In my opinion it chimes with the judgement of Christopher Small:

The big challenge to music educators today ... [is] not how to produce more skilled professional musicians but how to provide that kind of social context for informal as well as formal musical interaction that leads to real development and to the musicalizing of society as a whole. (Small 1998, p. 208)

This suggests a shift away from seeing music as a product made by professionals and towards seeing it as a social activity, a process. It means a society where no one utters the words 'I'm not musical', a society where it is taken for granted that music-making is as natural as walking or talking, a society where people come together to have 'a game of music' as naturally as they might play sports in the local park. Or, as Andrew Peggie put it:

We've got to get it out of our heads that the only valid music is that which is either recorded, published or broadcast. There's no direct relationship between degree of dissemination and degree of aesthetic or social value. (Peggie in Walters 2002)

Music teachers and those who work in secondary music have an opportunity to help shift this perception towards one that promotes music-making as a positive social activity rather than a commodity. However, it requires a conscious decision by the teacher to challenge persistent notions of absolute value residing in the Great European Canon – Mozart to Mahler, all those dead white European males still held up in some quarters as the pinnacle of musical endeavour – and simultaneously to challenge the more pervasive contemporary commoditization of music as product.

Community Music as it has developed since the 1960s – and especially through the work of improvisers such as John Stevens and colleagues in the 1980s – has typically placed process at least as highly as the finished product. The way in which music is made is at least as important as the result and can make the difference between engaging participants and turning them off, perhaps forever. As Berendt says, 'composed music says "I"; improvised music says "we". The improviser listens primarily to the people improvising with him/her. The improviser is part of a community' (Berendt 1984, cited by Paton 2000, p. 5).

## Wealth Inequality: The Social Context

Schools have the ability to (but do not, on the whole) work as engines of social mobility. Existing inequalities in society are being preserved and replicated rather than redressed by the structures and ideologies dominant within the education system.

In terms of wealth, and the ability of poor children to overcome poverty, little progress, if any, is being made towards a harmonious resolution. In UNICEF's 2007 report into child poverty in 21 rich countries, the UK comes bottom of the table in nearly all six 'dimensions', including educational and material well-being (the US also scores badly; the Netherlands comes top overall). According to Save the Children Fund (2006) at least 1 in 4 children in the UK (3.6 million) live in poverty; almost 1 in 10 (1.4 million) live in severe poverty. What this means is 3.6 million children who have little hope for the future because they have no reason to expect an improvement in their lot.

Let me repeat: 1 in 10 of all UK children live in severe poverty. That means an average of 3 in every class of 30. When confronted with realities like this, the human reaction is to put the finer points of aesthetics aside and try to address the inequalities. It is immaterial to a child stressed out by poverty whether a resolving cadence is perfect when his or her life is not. It is more important that the music made is relevant and has meaning in the lives of those who make it.

Clearly the socio-political system that holds sway is not working for a great many citizens, the gap between rich and poor is increasing and the old challenges to this state of affairs have, since the 'collapse of communism', had little popular support. However, it now appears a valuable baby was thrown out with that bathwater. There is still an important place for an evolved socialism that takes into account new issues of global capitalism and environmental crises (see Chapter 2 of this volume and Cole 2008 references).

## But I'm Just a Music Teacher!

If it is beholden on all citizens to contribute what they can to promote an egalitarian society, how do humble music teachers begin to promote equality in the small amount of time they have with their charges? How does the knowledge of the wider social context impact on pedagogy, on attitude and on assessment? And how might certain unthinking practices inadvertently shore up a capitalist paradigm that *depends* on inequalities between producer and consumer?

The Brazilian educator Paulo Freire has described a 'pedagogy of the oppressed' in which the relationship between teacher and pupils represents and preserves that between powerful and powerless. The teacher knows all and controls knowledge. The pupil knows nothing, and depends on the teacher to fill him or her up like an empty vessel. The teacher deposits knowledge in the pupil like money in a bank. In place of this Freire argues that every pupil brings to this relationship his or her own experience, and that the educative process can – should – honour this. Pupil is there to learn, but the Teacher can also 'learn' from the pupil. The teacher's role is one of *drawing out* from the pupil what is already latent inside him or her and giving the pupil the confidence to explore his or her own potential. Indeed, one of the interpretations of the Latin root of the word education (*educare*) is to 'lead forth' or 'to guide'.

Schools and the education system as a whole can still perpetuate an 'oppressive' relationship, where knowledge is only valuable if it is on the set curriculum – i.e. has been selected by the authorities as appropriate – and can be tested. Such an approach may serve to reproduce and validate what is already known – to *enculturate* students – but does not honour the innate abilities of young people to explore the world and come to their own conclusions because it denies them any autonomy in their own education. It also works to preserve the social status quo as it favours those who have been brought up in households where such knowledge is already established – mostly wealthier homes – while marking down those who have little or no access to the 'right' knowledge – mostly poorer homes.

In terms of music education teachers can either challenge or reinforce inequalities – either consciously or inadvertently – by the values they assign to different kinds of music. For example, by presenting the Western Classical tradition as the apex of musical achievement the teacher devalues all other forms. This is achieved, as argued by Lucy Green (2003), through using the analytical tools appropriate to an individually authored music based on certain assumptions – i.e. 'classical music' – to analyse other musics such as pop, rock, jazz and folk. According to this analysis, the 'best' music demonstrates four essential qualities: 'universality', 'eternality', 'complexity' and 'originality'. Green argues that these qualities – which are anyway not absolutes but cultural value judgements in themselves – are not the only way of valuing music, and furthermore that using them to value non-classical styles will always lead to a higher valuation of classical styles.

This has long-reaching consequences not just for the classroom, or educational attainment, but for society as a whole. Despite being by far the most popular forms of music enjoyed by students, contemporary forms of musical expression such as hip-hop, reggae, rock, rap and pop are deemed to be less valuable when measured against classical music on the terms of classical music. And because personal identity is closely bound to musical choice, if the favoured music of the student is devalued, so too by implication is the student.

Small identifies this 'elephant in the room' in music education when he asserts that

> Schools ... and the music tuition they provide, can contribute to [a] process of de-musicalization. Music teachers too often regard themselves more as agents for the discovery and selection of talented potential professionals than as agents for the development of the musicality that lies within each child. A hidden logical chain, or syllogism, underlies much ... school music practice ... (1) our music is the only real music; (2) you do not like or are not proficient at or are not interested in our music; (3) therefore you are not musical. (Small 1998, p. 212)

This logical chain extends beyond music to the wider world. Such attitudes assign value and precedence to the ideas that support and embody capitalism as it prevails in the UK today: 1. these markers of success are the only important ones (usually material status symbols such as cars, clothes, etc.); 2. you have not achieved them, 3. therefore you are not successful or important.

However, in terms of music education there *are* alternatives. Whereas they may not explicitly embody socialist thinking, they have their long roots in the community arts movement of the 1960s, itself described as a socialist critique of capitalism.[2] I suggest that they offer ways of addressing and challenging inequalities in society by modelling a more egalitarian approach in the classroom. They do this because they promote music-making as an inclusive, non-hierarchical participatory activity that has relevance for the musicians, rather than something only a few highly trained experts or 'signed' pop and rock musicians can enjoy.

The Music Manifesto, with its mission to 'give every child the chance to make music and enjoy the immense benefits it brings', recognizes the value and importance of community music practice in engaging young people. In its Report No. 2 it speaks of a new music education offer where there is

> high quality and *personalised* music-making ... for all children and young people that builds on and enhances the music entitlement in the National Curriculum *and wider offers in non-formal settings*. (italics added)

Even more practically the PHF-Musical Futures (MF)[3] programme demonstrates how such approaches can work in secondary schools and achieve remarkable results both in terms of immediate musical activity of social and aesthetic value, and in take-up of music at GCSE.

The MF programme worked in selected schools to 'devise new and imaginative ways of engaging young people, aged 11–19, in music activities'. It did this by using informal learning models like those developed and used by community musicians, putting the students themselves in the driving seat and allowing them to learn about music by making music. The teachers stepped back to take a supportive role, intervening when asked for help by the students and contributing their own musicality. I strongly advise music teachers to find out about it.

The MF demonstrates a new approach that puts the students – and what the students value – at the heart of music education. Some might say the case is won, but even if that *were* true, it has never been a good reason to stop pushing to keep the agenda alive. What follows is a discussion of specific kinds of inequality and how music in secondary schools is both affected by and can influence them.

## Music and 'Dis/ability'[4]

It has been said that, as far as music goes, to some extent we are all disabled.[5] Apart from (arguably) the voice, music is made through instruments which are 'unnatural' extensions of our bodies. Instrumental technique needs to be learned in the same way that someone with impaired mobility might have to learn how to use crutches or a wheelchair. Anyone trying to learn to control an instrument for the first time is disabled to the extent that it is unfamiliar. However, some approaches to music-making are more problematic than others in this respect.

An approach that demands technical control and knowledge of scales, chords or set rhythms in order to be 'right' disables the players. It requires the players to overcome their disabilities well enough to satisfy the demands of the music. To play many historically or geographically *located* musics – from Baroque concertos to Balinese gamelan – there are conventions and techniques – we can call them *abilities* – that must be learned or acquired.

This challenge is part of the enjoyment of music-making for many people, whether 'dis/abled' or not. It is fascinating in terms of learning about other cultures in time and space through trying to reproduce their music, and it is a requirement of the KS3 music programme. But equally it turns off many others who don't want to defer their enjoyment until they can reproduce the music 'authentically'. This is the way of classical and generic musics all around the world: once you can play a Bach partita or a 12-bar blues or a flamenco *buleria*, *then* you may take part – not before! Even then you expose yourself to the risk of not doing it well, of making 'mistakes', and more so if you have an impairment.

If you haven't acquired these abilities, this doesn't mean you are not *musical*, or cannot produce music of your own. My own experiences have confirmed that people with a range of impairments enjoy making music together, engaging thoroughly with the processes of composition, arrangement and performance.[6] By asking the individuals in the group to contribute 'exactly those skills which each player can bring to them, no more and certainly no less', we produced music that belonged completely to – and reflected – the musicians.

The players first explored a range of sound sources (instruments, voices, found sounds) through improvisations, trying out different combinations and sometimes making associations with character and narrative ideas: this sounds creepy, that sounds exciting, this is a little girl, that a monster, etc. We discussed ways of organizing the sounds and gradually a structure emerged which could be refined, rehearsed and performed. In the process we also devised ingenious ways of working together, signalling changes and cueing breaks, that led to a more cohesive and effective group. A live performance was given to a small audience which served to focus our minds and give us something to aim for. The whole process was a journey during which we grew together as a group and discovered abilities we did not know we had, confirming Peggie's assertion (above) that the social and aesthetic value of music is not proportional to the degree of dissemination.

This approach is not a substitute for others. It is an immediate way in to enjoying the activity of music-making, one that honours the abilities and personalities of each player. It can very easily work alongside other ways of teaching music, including acquiring technique or appraising geographically or historically *located* music.

A word of caution when using improvisation with SEN groups and people who have EDB or MLD.[7] The community-music-derived MF approach allows for the fact that informal learning might be personal and 'haphazard'. Three SEN teachers involved in MF projects in Hertfordshire report that 'students in SEN schools tend to need structure, and to be able to see a clear progression from simple to complex, otherwise they can feel disorientated and demotivated'. And in her case study from Falconer School, Herts, Head of Music Nadya Dyett writes that 'personalised learning has to be taught and learnt. While it might be a desired outcome it does not always lend itself naturally in a highly structured environment'.

Finally, it is good to remember that music education with anyone, anywhere is always a two-way street to some extent, a point that is central to Freire's pedagogy of the oppressed, and echoed by community musician Duncan Chapman:

A lot of people I work with have a different perception of the world. It's very inspiring for us to understand a bit about that. Lots of reasons are given for doing music with people with special needs: increased sociability and so on. But we have loads to gain from them too. (Cited by Healey, in Moser and McKay 2005)

## Gender and Sexual Orientation

Girls play harps, flutes and sing; boys play electric guitars and hit drums. This is a common perception that is also borne out by research. A study by the London Institute of Education (IoE) reveals that, among 5–16 year olds in the UK, 'Some 90% of harpists are girls, as are 89% of children playing the flute. In contrast, 81% of guitarists are boys and 75% of drummers'. This suggests that gender stereotypes are deeply embedded in the social consciousness and linked to certain instruments. Many of these ideas have been adopted by children as young as 6 years old (but, perhaps significantly, not before),[8] and at the point of entering secondary education are firmly held. This makes the task of challenging these assumptions more difficult.

Why should gender stereotypes be challenged at all? There are several reasons:

- to widen the number of experiences available to developing young people, who otherwise may self-limit due to peer-pressure
- to challenge the idea of gender differences being inevitable rather than socially constructed, and
- to address inequalities that appear later in the workplace, especially pay differentials between the sexes and access to certain careers.

However, it is possible to address these inequalities while still honouring the real differences between boys and girls of secondary age. The same IoE report states:

> The way that physical interaction with the instrument occurs may be important. Boys may prefer instruments that are struck or require high levels of physical exertion. The technical difficulty of the instrument and level of persistence required to play it may also play a part, as evidence indicates that boys tend to do less practice than girls.

In terms of biological development, the ages 11–16 are significant as a period when individuals go through profound changes. Puberty and adolescence highlight the sexual impulse. There is a need for many (but not all) boys to demonstrate and test their masculinity through rough play, sporting prowess and other perceived male activities. This also means explicitly shunning anything that is feminine and might expose them to charges of being un-masculine or homosexual.

Lucy Green has shown that boys are not keen to be involved in some musical activities because of their perception as being un-masculine. 'It's sissy' and 'It's weak' were common responses from teachers and students involved in Green's survey. Green concluded:

> both boys and girls tended to restrict themselves or find themselves restricted to certain musical activities for fear of intruding into the other sex's territory, where they may be accused of some sort of musical transvestism. (Green 1993, p. 248, cited in Harrison 2002)

It is an important role for the teacher to hold these facts in mind while challenging them consistently as constructs rather than an inevitable or natural state of affairs. One way to prevent some of these issues getting in the way is to run single-sex groups. At the early stages of learning to play instruments, and from time to time, this can be helpful. However, once some confidence has been established it may be more appropriate to select groups on musical merit or social complementarity, thus demonstrating that gender is not an issue when it comes to having the skills and abilities to make music.

The Ladyfest events around the world since 2000 are organized for and by women and are important because most music festivals are male dominated. There is a sense that female musicians aren't taken seriously or given a proper platform. A specifically feminist initiative, men are welcome because issues such as domestic violence, pay inequality and a fairer society affect everyone.

As for sexual orientation, there is an ongoing role for all teachers to monitor and address developments in the way students deal with this. Students in secondary school are undergoing an intense period of change during which they will explore and experiment with their sexual orientation. Any homophobic comments should be challenged immediately and consistently so as to send a clear message about tolerance and difference. To ignore or allow such comments is to create an atmosphere where students who are exploring their sexuality, or who already know they are gay, will feel intimidated or worse.

Although it is not possible to show that sexual orientation affects the music made, music and musicians through time have challenged all sorts of social boundaries, and sexuality is just one of them. In the 1970s we had (among others) David Bowie appearing as androgynous characters Ziggy Stardust and Aladdin Sane, playing with identities and blurring boundaries. Since then there have been openly gay performers, notably Tom Robinson, Bronski Beat, Frankie Goes to Hollywood, k.d. Lang and more, who have wedged open the closet door in a very public way. But perhaps most powerfully – in terms of challenging male roles at least – two ostensibly macho rock performers came out, to the relief of some and the consternation of others. The lead singers of heavy rock bands Judas Priest and Queen, respectively Rob Halford and Freddie Mercury, both had 'straight' fans who suddenly had to decide what was more important to them: the music or the sexuality of the musicians. The fact that both continued to have successful careers suggests that sexual orientation was not an issue for most fans.

The music teacher might also introduce the music of notable composers who were or are gay or bisexual as a simple way of making the point that sexual orientation is not linked to any particular style of music. One could include here Tchaikovsky, Aaron Copland, Ma Rainey, Michael Tippett, Bessie Smith, John Cage, Billy Strayhorn, Me'Shell NdegeOcello, Samuel Barber, Ani DiFranco and the musical actor John Barrowman.

Other musicians are notorious for promoting homophobic messages, or narrow ideas of what it means to be male or female. It can appear that particular *styles* are rife with such attitudes – gangster rap and some reggae sub-styles are notable here. I argue that it is the musicians as individual authors (and not the style of music) who should be challenged. It should be possible in a school for students to produce rap and reggae that is not homophobic or narrow minded. It will be a challenging task for the teacher to separate the musical elements from the lyrical content, but an important one.

## Ethnicity

The history of music over the past 100 years (and probably more) has been one of blends, fusions, co-minglings and collisions between styles originating from different cultural and geographic places. Jazz – the melting pot of music – recycled folk traditions, African songs and rhythms, classical and marching music, and was in turn drawn on by composers such as Stravinsky and Gershwin, Bartók and Bernstein. In turn these have inspired and influenced others and so it goes and has always been the way. In Britain in the twenty-first century every urban space is alive with styles from around the world, colliding in an infinite number of ways.

But in terms of ethnicity and music there is a conundrum. Music can and does bring people together. It has huge potential as an international 'language'. But it can equally function as a marker of identity for different cultures. 'Traditional' musics are protected fiercely by their 'owners', and used to preserve and promote unique cultural and ethnic characteristics.

As Paton puts it, 'particular musics are encoded with the ethnic flavours of particular groups and the purity of particular traditions may be jealously guarded' (Paton in PESS 1999). One thinks of Ewan MacColl's 'policy rule' in the folk, blues and ballads clubs of the late 1950s, where singers were only allowed to sing songs from their own country in an effort to promote a folk revival that was strong enough to withstand the influx of American folksongs. Even more,

they came to the conclusion that there had to be a correct way of doing things, and in the Critics group they analyzed each other's singing, criticized each other, and tried to find out of what a 'true English style' consisted. (Denselow 1990, p. 26)

Clearly this kind of behaviour would be completely out of place in twenty-first-century Britain. The music teacher at KS3 and KS4 has to acknowledge the breadth of musics listened to by students, and this is one of the reasons why informal and personalized learning has worked so well in projects like Musical Futures. The mistake would be to value or promote one style over another. The student-initiated approach provides more opportunities to address issues of ethnicity and resolve them musically.

## Social Class

Music-making has always generated product, be it broadsheet songs, manuscript or recordings. Today, a huge volume of music is 'manufactured' and sold by huge multinational corporations to make profits. Musicians – at least professional ones – sell their labour and are thus 'working class'. However, thanks to modern music technology, we can now record and produce a finished product, and in some senses own the means of production: the instruments, the computer software and hardware, the creative imagination and the talent.

However, we do not own the means of dissemination, and this is the vital link in the chain because most people still equate social and aesthetic value with popularity or degree of dissemination. The vast fortunes accrued by the Whitney Houstons and Robbie Williamses of this world are due to their companies being able to promote and sell them globally. There are other musicians at least as able as Whitney and Robbie, who make comparable music, but you've never heard of them because they are not marketed and promoted by major media companies. In this analysis it is the corporates, who own the means of marketing and distribution, that are the 'capitalists', and the musicians are the 'working class'.

The corporate-owned mass media companies such as Sky, Fox, Clear Channel *et al.* exert a massive influence on what we hear, and thus control to a significant extent what (we think) we want. Despite reeling from the impact of free downloads from the web, these companies still call the shots. This means certain images and lifestyles are more prevalent than others, and are tied in with films, TV shows, and other products all designed to keep us wanting more. 'Working class' or not, we are all consumers now.

Community music models challenge this passive consumption of music product in favour of participation in music-making, a DIY culture, and local dissemination. It prizes the actual over the virtual, and seeks to validate the music-making and give music back to the participants.

According to Sound Sense, the UK development agency for community music, this practice:

- Involves musicians from any musical discipline working with groups of people to develop active and creative participation in music
- Is concerned with putting equal opportunities into practice
- Happens in all types of communities . . . and reflects the context in which it takes place.[9]

In short, working for a musical society where citizens make the music that suits the time and place, and are less dependent on what the market can offer because they can do it themselves.


# Environment

The environment and the effects of climate change are going to affect everything we do in the twenty-first century, and we need to respond actively if we are to survive the changes. In one sense, we are all equal before environmental problems because famine, flooding and forest fires do not discriminate. But in reality it is the poorest people who will be least able to deal with these problems, not just in the developing world but right here in the UK.

How does this impact on music education and issues of equality? It is useful to ask two other questions to guide our thinking on this: Where does music come from? And where do musical instruments come from?

Music is made by people. It does not exist in a score or in recorded media such as CDs or MP3s. It does not reside in the instruments used to make it. In fact, it refuses to be pinned down: it is not in the software algorithms that tell our computers what to do; it is not in the loudspeakers that convert electrical impulses into changes in air pressure; it is not in our ears that detect these vibrations. It exists only in the moment it is played, be that on a digital player or in real time by real players. And all of it – digitally produced or not – originates in some kind of human interaction. Music is *in people* and is an expression of their humanity.

People can make music without instruments, and often do. People can adapt found objects to serve musical purposes, and often do. Over the course of history this process has given us the instruments we know today. But these instruments have to come from somewhere, from wood and metals and mineral compounds which are transported across the world to be manufactured.

Whereas many instrument makers claim to avoid using wood from endangered species of trees, or boast environmentally friendly packaging, this is only a small part of a bigger and highly complex picture. The carbon footprint of all manufactured goods will increasingly become a vital consideration. The provenance of these instruments is as important as that of any other products. The music teacher in control of a purchasing budget should choose carefully, and perhaps the best options in the future will be those that rely on voices, found objects and junk instruments!

This will be difficult to square with the strong demand for music technology, which depends on complex international manufacturing networks and such scarce resources as silicon and other minerals. Computer technology and the internet have revolutionized music-making as well as dissemination, but there is an environmental cost. According to a United Nations University study in 2004:

> The average 24 kg desktop computer with monitor requires at least 10 times its weight in fossil fuels and chemicals to manufacture, much more materials intensive than an automobile or refrigerator, which only require 1– 2 times their weight in fossil fuels. Researchers found that manufacturing one desktop computer and 17-inch CRT monitor uses at least 240 kg of fossil fuels, 22 kg of chemicals and 1,500 kg of water – a total of 1.8 tonnes of materials. (UNU 2004, newsletter issue 31)

Although computers are getting smaller, there is a growing demand worldwide and they are being replaced more quickly than before, creating a disposal problem too. Students usually care about the environment and may be horrified to discover these problems. While access to music technology is one way that students can develop and express their individual creativity, knowing about the environmental impact might make them more open to music-making that does not depend on technology.

Another consideration that applies to all the issues of inequality discussed above, including the environment, is the role that music – and song lyrics in particular – can play in contemporary society to raise awareness of current issues. While music teachers may want to remain free of any specific political agenda, the power of music to express opinion cannot be denied.

During the late 1970s the Rock Against Racism campaign showed how a grassroots movement could express popular opinion strongly enough to exert a significant pressure on politics, enough to prevent the National Front party winning seats in East London and ultimately inspire events like the 1985 Live Aid concert.[10] The songs 'Free Nelson Mandela' by the Special AKA and 'Biko' by Peter Gabriel raised awareness in the 1980s of South Africa's apartheid policies. Since 2002 the campaign 'Love Music Hate Racism' has picked up the RAR mantle and continues to oppose the racist ideas of the British National Party, a job that still needs doing especially as the BNP have created their own record label for music that promotes their policies.[11]

The power of song in our media-soaked world is strong, and lyrical responses to the climate crisis – and more significantly how our leaders make decisions in the light of it – should not be underestimated. Many young people are fully aware of this and the music teacher, by adopting a student-centred approach, can encourage them to sing about what is important to them and in ways that communicate effectively with their peers.

## Closing Remarks ...

What is it that makes a musician important? Is it in the creation of composition as for performance in concert halls and opera houses for the delectation of those who like, and can afford, to frequent such places? Is it in holding halls full of such people enthralled with performances of past masterpieces? Or is it in using his or her gifts, skills and experience to awaken and to guide the dormant musicality of those whose music has been taken from them? He or she who chooses the latter course will sacrifice the honours and the financial rewards that the first two can bring, and will need not only unusual musical gifts but also courage and integrity of an unusual kind and degree, for the message is not only simple and revolutionary but it is also alarming to those who hold our society's purse strings; once people become aware that music is in themselves and not only in those who have been selected to become musicians, once they take back to themselves the musical act in a spirit of delight and self-affirmation, who knows what else they might insist on reclaiming, and enjoying, of what has been taken from them? (Christopher Small, in *Search and Reflect*, 1985).

We music teachers are ourselves musicians. We have our own favourite kinds of music, and our own personal educational experience whether studying classical or jazz or folk music to a high level. We might have been told, during teacher education, how to pass on the great traditions of music from yesteryear, about how to nurture those with obvious talent in these traditions. However, I believe the job is more about giving music back to the students than filling them up with notions of the great canon.

Music is a practical and social activity that can be made in a variety of ways. Each way reflects certain power relationships and promotes certain value judgements about class, gender, sexual orientation, 'race', the environment, and 'dis/ability'. It is important that the teacher is aware of this and is able to challenge isms/phobias when they arise in the classroom (see Chapter 2 of this volume).

But most importantly, for any of this chapter to make any sense at all, *good music must be made!* It has been claimed that music is a means of creating a magical state. My own experiences as a musician and educator include almost spiritual moments when the players and everyone present simply become one – what in flamenco is called *duende*. In these moments there is a powerful sense of being part of something bigger, as if individual and collective psyches merge. Such experiences, fleeting as they may be, make meaningless any inequalities of class, gender, sexual orientation, 'race' or 'dis/ability' and remind us of our commonality. Such experiences, if made explicit and contextualized within the realities of social and cultural inequalities, also contribute to challenge them. What music teacher would not want to facilitate and be part of that?

# Notes

1   Music activity in secondary schools is no longer the sole domain of teachers, who might be joined at different times by professional performers, creative partnerships, artists and community musicians or 'music leaders'. For the sake of readability in this chapter, when I refer to teachers I will assume this to include these others, unless otherwise stated.

2   For a fuller discussion of this, see McKay (2005).

3   MF was a four-year, £2 million programme of active research that ended in 2007. For more information: www.musicalfutures.org.uk.

4   'dis/ability': Language is constantly evolving and in all cases it is the attitude behind it that really counts. However, in the same way that 'racism' carries inverted commas to signify the complexities and difficulties with it as a descriptor for a wide range of behaviours, so dis/ability needs to be challenged. Most so-called 'disabled people' are in fact extremely able in many ways. Most so-called 'able-bodied' or non-disabled people, conversely, are not 'able' in every respect. To write 'dis/abled' also emphasizes the social barriers which prevent some people from accessing services and activities. For example, it is the steps to the concert hall which dis/able the wheelchair user from performing there, not the person's impairment (see Chapter 2 of this volume for a discussion of the medical and social models of disability and Rieser, 2006 references).

5   For example, Paton in PESS (1999).

6   I was a music teacher on the Performing Arts for Disabled Artists foundation course at the Liverpool Intitute for Performing Arts (LIPA) in the last year before it was cut (2002–3). Students with a range of impairments – including people with cerebral palsy, blind and partially sighted people and at least one deaf person – studied music, dance and drama. As a group we devised and performed music that was exciting, original and authentic, not to mention a lot of fun!

7   Current terminology, short for special educational needs, Emotional and Behavioural Difficulties and Moderate Learning Difficulties. Although still common in education settings, 'SEN' has not been used in social work settings for about 30 years.

8   Victoria Rowe, who has completed a PhD on gender in music, says children don't develop a firm idea about 'male' and 'female' instruments until about 6 years old (cited by Geoghegan 2008).

9   See www.soundsense.org for more information and to join.

10   See Safraz Manzoor's article in the *Observer*, 20 April 2008.

11   Great White Records was set up in December 2005. According to their website, 'it

was established primarily as a patriotic record label … GWR intends to produce a huge collection of popular music intended for distribution to further the cause of spreading positive patriotism … the chief benefactors/recipients of money raised by GWR will be the British National Party (BNP) to help them further their political and cultural objectives' (greatwhiterecords.com).

# References

Denselow, R. (1990), *When the Music's Over: The Story of Political Pop*. London: Faber and Faber.

Freire, P. (1972), *Pedagogy of the Oppressed*. Harmondsworth: Penguin.

Geoghegan, T. (2008), 'Why don't girls play guitar?' Available on BBC Online News Magazine: http://news.bbc.co.uk/nolpda/ukfs_news/hi/newsid_7342000/7342168.stm (accessed 11 April 2008).

Green, L. (1993) in 'Engaging Boys in the Arts', Australian Association for Research in Education Conference (December 4th 2002). Online at http://www.aare.edu.au/02pap/haro2616.htm.

Manzoor, S. (2008), 'The year rock found the power to unite', *Observer* (20 April).

McKay, G. (2005), 'Improvisation and the development of community music in Britain', in *Community Music: A Handbook*. Lyme Regis: Russell House Publishing.

Moser, P. and McKay, G. (eds) (2005), *Community Music: A Handbook*. Lyme Regis: Russell House Publishing.

Paton, R. (2000), *Living Music*. Chichester: West Sussex County Council.

Peggie, A. (1997), *Musicians Go to School: Partnership in the Classroom*. London Arts Board. (See also Peggie in *Bloody Amateurs*, below)

Small, C. (1998), *Musicking: The Meanings of Performing and Listening*. Middletown: CT: Wesleyan University Press.

Stevens, J. (1985), *Search & Reflect: A Music Workshop Handbook*. London: Rockschool.

## See also

Berendt, J.-E., various books including *The Jazz Book, Nada Brahma: The World Is Sound* and *The Third Ear: Music and the Landscape of Consciousness*.

Hill, D. and Cole, M. (eds) (1999), *Promoting Equality in Secondary Schools*. London: Cassell.

International Society of Music Education (ISME): various publications including the *International Journal of Community Music* (2008), www.intellectbooks.com.

*Making Every Child's Music Matter: Music Manifesto Report No. 2*, various authors (2006). London: Music Manifesto, pp. 29–33. See also www.musicmanifesto.co.uk.

Musical Futures: various publications, including *MF and SEN*, MF and the comparative analysis of Secondary KS3 Music Programme and *Musical Futures*, available at www.musicalfutures.org.uk.

Sound Sense, the UK development agency for community music, produces the magazine *Sounding Board*. www.soundsense.org.

Walters, J. L. (ed.) (2002), *Bloody Amateurs*. (unknown publication) 14.

Chapter 12

# Physical Education

## Jo Shire and Jo Hardman

This chapter examines a range of issues (gender, sexual orientation, 'race', disability and social class) related to the promotion of equality in Physical Education. It explores the historical context of PE, and, through a critical analysis of the current National Curriculum framework, discusses the possible contributions and inequities within PE. Current curriculum content is evaluated and analysed with regard to meeting the needs of all individuals. A range of issues related to creating an equitable teaching environment are introduced and considered, and specific strategies related to inclusive practice are discussed.

## Introduction

During the past decade the concept of social inclusion has been high on the political agenda and has permeated Physical Education (PE) policy planning. The Every Child Matters (DfES 2004) agenda attempts to address the current government's commitment to providing an environment that fosters the well-being of children and caters for all. PE and sport could play a central role in the development of this strategy, as the various benefits associated with participation in regular physical activity are well documented. Further, it could be argued that recent strategies are being used by the current government as a means of addressing a number of social issues that exist in today's society (obesity, youth crime, social identity and citizenship). To this extent it is important to question what is PE about and who is it for? At the same time we need to recognize the influential role that certain 'power houses' play in structuring and manipulating current educational practices.

More recently the role that PE and sport can play in the promotion, education and advancement of the personal, social and moral development of young people has been addressed. In September 2002 'citizenship' was introduced as a curriculum area on the National Curriculum, with the aim that students would 'become informed, active, responsible citizens contributing fully to the life of their school communities' (QCA 1999a, p. 126). Laker (2000, p. 92) suggests that PE is a 'subject of expanded boundaries and possibilities' that could in fact contribute 'to the education of a community of global citizens'.

In 2002 the Department for Education and Skills (DfES) and the Department for Culture, Media and Sport (DCMS) launched the national PE, School Sport and Club Links (PESSCL) strategy. One of the aims of the strategy is to 'enable all young people, whatever their circumstances or ability, to take part in and enjoy PE and sport' (DfES/DCMS 2004, p. 1). The PESSCL strategy advocates that all schools should provide high-quality Physical Education opportunities that cater for *all* young people, regardless of gender, sexuality, 'race', disability or social class. All students should be entitled to a minimum of two hours of high-quality PE and school sport per week. The long-term ambition is that by 2010 the PESSCL strategy will offer all students at least five hours of sport every week, which should include at least two hours of high-quality PE (delivered within curriculum time), and the opportunity to participate in two hours or more beyond the school day (e.g. after-school clubs, community programmes, sport and activity clubs).

PE is a powerful instrument that 'has the power to create awareness and challenge individual attitudes, thereby increasing the possibilities for change and prospect for a more equal and just society' (Clarke and Nutt 1999, p. 212). However, we need to question whether PE is being utilized to the best of its ability, so that all individuals have the opportunity to engage and prosper in this process of awareness and change. Research by Wright (1996; 1999), Penney and Harris (1997), Cockburn (1999) and Estyn (2007) indicates that inequalities, in terms of individual experiences in PE, still exist and that not all individuals are being provided with 'a guaranteed, full and rounded entitlement to learning' that will 'foster their creativity' and inspire pupils with a 'joy and commitment to learning that will last a lifetime' (DfEE/QCA 1999, p. 3).

It is the intention of this chapter to examine a range of issues surrounding PE and the promotion of equality through an exploration of the following areas: gender; sexual orientation; social class and capitalism; disability; and 'race'.


## Gender

PE and sport form part of our cultural worlds. The policies and practices that are used to shape them reflect the values and interests of broader society (Jones and Armour 2000). Furthermore, the way in which PE is taught often reinforces the prevalent hegemonic ideology within Western culture, and, therefore, through the medium of PE, we are teaching students the values and morals of the dominant groups in society. In turn this serves to orientate individuals towards an unequal society (Fernandez-Balboa 1993; Hargreaves 2005). Unfortunately, as PE professionals we tend to see ourselves in isolation from the wider context. This is reinforced by Sage (1993, p. 153) when stating that 'we tend to have little sensitivity about how sport, other forms of physical activity, and our own professional lives are linked to the social relations which underlie social class, inequality, sexism, racism, and often types of social injustice'.

What is seen in many cases is a curriculum that continues to focus around traditional games, performance and ability. There is a hierarchy of programming; for example, football, rugby, hockey and netball enjoy central roles whereas dance and cooperative games are often relegated to a 'complementary status' (Fernandez-Balboa 1993, p. 234). Students are often socialized into certain sports according to 'race', social class, physical ability and gender. The current provision in many schools serves to reinforce gender divisions with girls and boys accessing different curricular programmes often based around what have traditionally been considered as 'masculine' and 'feminine' activities. PE departments are often structured around 'boys' and 'girls' departments reinforcing the concept to students that sport for males and females is different (Stidder 2002).

PE is based largely around past cultural traditions (games) and a disproportionate amount of time is allocated to games (particularly team games) activities. Within this focus there is also the domination of competitive team activities, rather than a balance of this with cooperative, individual activities together with an equilibrium between technical and creative experiences. The number of students involved in competitive sports steadily declines after adolescence, and research shows that competition can have a negative effect on students, can create feelings of incompetence, and, socially, can serve to undermine students' relationships with each other (Fernandez-Balboa 1993; Williams and Bedward 2001). This emphasis on competitive team games can serve to alienate both girls and boys from PE, and government policy statements such as 'Sport – Raising the Game' (Department of National Heritage (DNH) 1995) have continued to reinforce for the profession the emphasis within PE of performance and team games. Attempts to support gender differences are often addressed through different curricular content for both girls and boys, for example girls to play football and boys to do dance. While this approach makes attempts to offer equal access, it does not necessarily provide equality; indeed, it can fail to consider individual interests and should not be the sole focus in providing an equitable, relevant and accessible curriculum for all students.

Choi (2000, p. 84) maintains that PE needs to contextualize experiences as meaningful and goes on to argue that 'a more important part of the story is simply that many girls have little use for sport in the process of becoming women'. In relation to this, consideration must be given to how PE can be made more meaningful. Eccles (1999) suggests that girls are less interested than boys in competitive sports and more interested in physical activities such as biking and swimming as these provide ways for them to socialize and have fun with their friends. While recognizing that the priority of PE is not only to provide physical activity experiences for students, attention needs to be paid to the design of curriculum content in creating experiences that are both educational *and* relevant. This is confirmed by Choi (2000, p. 86) when insisting 'girls do not wish to avoid physical activity completely but their activity choices are based on what is meaningful to them and their lives'. Clearly this will impact on their participation and engagement in PE if those experiences become irrelevant. Consideration needs to be given to providing appropriate and meaningful opportunities for everyone.

The issue of kit remains for many girls as influential in their dislike for PE as it did 20 years ago and is highly instrumental in creating an aversion to PE. Kit requirements in many schools (e.g. short skirts, shaped tops, leotards for gymnastics and dance) contribute to girls being self-conscious, embarrassed and cold (when participating outside). This is bound to impact on their motivation and enthusiasm for the subject. Communal showering has also been, and in some schools continues to be, common practice. Girls particularly find this very stressful (Coakley and White 1992). In addition, PE uniform can often serve to marginalize and alienate some students. There is often little sensitivity in some schools to adolescents' concerns about decency and their developing bodies and body image. We need to reflect on the impact of these issues, and in developing a new curriculum framework the following are vital:

- An examination of the social constructs we use to teach PE and a revision of our entrenched traditional notions of how and what is taught through the consideration of different approaches and models, for example Sports Education (see Siedentop *et al.* 2004), Teaching Games for Understanding (see Griffin and Butler 2005) and Sports Peace (see Ennis 1999; Azzarito and Ennis 2003).
- A consideration of our teaching approaches in seeing ourselves as reformers for change not technicians of delivery.
- Those involved in Initial Teacher Education (ITE) to consider how to further encourage trainee teachers to analyse the social purposes of their profession.
- The kit students wear should be appropriate for the activity in allowing movement without highlighting gender differences. Students should be afforded equal access to relevant kit that does not cause embarrassment, nor affect students' willingness to engage in PE.

# Sexual Orientation

Schools as institutions are reproductions of the broader dominant social ideologies within society. This reinforces an experience for young people where heterosexuality is considered 'normal and compulsory' (McCaughtry *et al.* 2005, p. 426). Within this context PE makes a particular contribution to a student's educational experiences because of the focus of learning being through and by the body. The impact of this physicality on a perceived compulsory heterosexuality is made clear by Wright and Burrows (2006, p. 283) when stating 'the body is inscribed with social meaning and bodies can impact on the way in which individuals interact with their world'. Furthermore, when examining how sport and those within it are portrayed by the media, the images project cultural values which can impact on the teaching of PE (Kirk 1992). McCaughtry *et al.* (2005, pp. 426–7) suggest, therefore, that PE teachers and PE serves to control students' ability to express themselves in relation to their sexuality. In exploring the impact of teachers and subject they maintain:

> The result is that physical education teachers often play key roles in the control of lesbian and gay youth – whether knowingly or not. All too often, these teachers and coaches are gatekeepers of acceptable and unacceptable modes of sexual expression and readily deny lesbian and gay youth safe learning environments and sensitive instruction. It is as if PE and sport wield tremendous heteronormative traditions that seem to be the most resistant to change.

In PE when girls' and boys' dress and their activity preferences fall outside the accepted norms, the implicit and explicit assumption is that they are lesbian or gay regardless of their actual orientations. Sport has been dominated by men and the characteristics that have been traditionally associated with it – strength, masculinity, aggression, competitiveness and so on. Consequently, for women and young girls to participate in sport, and, particularly in activities stereotypically perceived as outside the accepted norms for women and girls, they run the risk of their sexuality and 'femininity' being questioned (Hargreaves 1996; Choi 2000). The same applies to boys; for example, boys who do not enjoy competition or those activities considered traditionally male often feel alienated and are often labelled as 'sissy', 'fairy', 'poof' or 'gay'. While much has changed, stereotypical concerns and ideologies around masculinity, femininity, sexuality and physicality still constrain and limit the participation and behaviour of both girls and boys within PE. There is an awareness of the impact of the inequality the design and implementation of the National Curriculum has on girls' engagement with PE. However, less recognized is the limited opportunities for boys who do not wish to participate in those games considered as traditionally male, and also for less able students of both sexes.

The focus on team games and the emphasis on these as aggressive competitive activities reinforce sport as a masculine domain. Identifying these activities with traits considered to be traditionally masculine can cause conflict for some girls in terms of how they think others consider them in relation to their own femininity and sexuality. This can lead to a dislike of team games by girls (Eccles 1999; Wright 1999; Hargreaves 2005). However, we need to be mindful not to oversimplify the dislike of team games by girls in viewing them as a homogeneous group with the same feelings and perceptions; this is a more complex issue. Williams and Bedward's (2001) research, which assessed the impact of policy on the provision for adolescent girls, found that girls are still often not afforded access to football as part of the school curriculum and were in fact frustrated that they were denied the opportunity to play at school. Girl's football has now replaced netball as the most popular female sport in England (BBC Sport 2005; BMRB 2005) and as Williams and Bedward (2001, p. 59) maintain 'it (*football*) still remains excluded from a curriculum which purports to prepare pupils for leisure activity' (italics in the original). There is no doubt that the lack of equality offered to girls and boys can often be attributed to teachers' feelings of incompetence in certain activities, and as students' interests change and develop so teachers need to be provided with the tools with which to provide relevant and meaningful experiences for all students. Careful consideration should be given to the following:

- Providing experiences for all students that are not differentiated by assumptions about gender and sexuality.
- Verbal and physical abuse do not go unchallenged, and diversity and difference are discussed and celebrated.
- Professional development for teachers in meeting the needs of students' activity interests.
- Teachers need to question students' traditional perceptions of activities as 'male' and 'female'.
- How barriers can be broken down through the deployment of staff who teach certain activities, for example male PE teachers teaching dance to both girls and boys and female teachers teaching football to both girls and boys.
- The teaching of activities that are non-gender specific, for example rocketball, ultimate frisbee, handball.

The way in which students are grouped can also impact on their PE experiences. The key principle underlying decisions of grouping must be that all students have the same opportunities to realize their potential and that we are providing experiences that are positive and encourage learning. Often the cultural setting that is provided can serve to distance students from active engagement with the activity and also other students. For example, in single-sex classes, where hegemonic forms of masculinity are emphasized, boys who do not show aggressive or competitive behaviours can be ridiculed and bullied (Wright 1999). The point here is not that either mixed- or single-gender grouping is appropriate in every case but that careful consideration needs to be given to how students are grouped together and on what basis (Ofsted 1995). Included in this is sensitivity to the context of the activity, the ability of the students, the attitudes of the students, the age of the students and so on.

PE should seek to actively question ideologies of masculinity and femininity in providing a curriculum that is inclusive and accessible for all students regardless of sexuality, gender and ability. Azzarito and Solomon (2005, p. 25) maintain that a 'dynamic relational analysis of gender, race and social class' is needed to highlight the interplay between and across them. They emphasize the need to move away from classifying 'girls' and 'boys' as homogeneous groups and remind us that there are clear differences within these groups related to social class, 'race' and sexuality. This calls, in many cases, for a serious reconsideration of a curriculum that is currently structured around activity areas and performance.

## Social Class and Capitalism

Evans and Davies (2008, p. 200) maintain that social class 'is a visceral reality, constituted by a set of affectively loaded, social and economic relationships that are likely to strongly, if not determine and dominate, people's lives'. This illustrates the impact institutions such as schools, and those within it, can have on the young people we teach. Furthermore, social class is central to the inequalities within the educational system which is often reproduced within PE and school sport (Wright and Burrows 2006). While class is not the only identity that matters (as illustrated in the rest of the chapter), class often gives the other identities discussed in this chapter a 'particular edge' (Connolly 2006). This class reproduction through capitalism within education needs to be highlighted in order to redress current inequalities.

Within PE these differences are often highlighted through the way in which PE in elite private schools is valued and resourced. This is reinforced through the emphasis on ability and performance in being 'recognised as having important exchange value in social life beyond school' (Wright and Burrows 2006, p. 276). Buckingham (2000) maintains that the different emphasis between physical activity for health and physical activity as symbolic capital furnishes different life outcomes for children in government schools. In state schools the perception of PE is often that it is an alternative source of success and status for the academically less able (Laker 2000).

However, the current curriculum in state schools also presents a model which emphasizes performance and ability, and, is intended to 'shape the understanding of teachers and produce particular kinds of Physical Education' (Penney and Evans 2004, p. 12). This is reinforced through the application of the four strands of knowledge, skills and understanding and through the activity-specific requirements for the 'breadth of study'. This performative emphasis is further supported through the level descriptors and attainment target used to assess students' achievements. While the structure of the NCPE clearly identifies four strands (outlined previously), much current practice in schools continues to emphasize particularly the first two, which focus on performance and acquisition of skill. While this structure allows for flexibility in relation to structure and pedagogic practice, as Evans *et al.* (1996, p. 7) maintain, the implications of achieving breadth and balance within this framework rely heavily on the 'accident' of teachers' interests and predispositions. It can lead to curriculum reproduction whereby professionals engage in teaching in the way in which, and what, they were taught.

All young people should have access to a programme of PE that covers the Programmes of Study appropriate to their ability, as a curriculum that focuses on performance and competence can serve to exclude students from accessing their entitlement. As subject specialists we can often be highly selective and this can create for students a single contextualized world and one in which many students feel alienated. The current structure of the National Curriculum means children learn to assess their ability in reference to how teachers judge their performances and to externally defined norms, ideals and values. The performative model and culture created by the current framework places an emphasis on the product, i.e. what students can do, rather than the process, i.e. what students have learned, and, as such, serves to estrange many students (Penney and Evans 2004). This does little to encourage all students to engage with the subject and to become physically active. The performative nature of PE can create feelings of incompetence and impact on self-confidence and self-worth. In addition, it can have a negative impact on the socialization of students' relationships with each other (Wright and Burrows 2006). The requirement to provide relevant opportunities for all students is reinforced by QCA (1999b, p. 6) in stating: 'Planning should set high expectations and provide relevant opportunities for achievement for boys and girls, for pupils from all social backgrounds and ethnic groups and for those who are disabled'.

Teacher awareness of the interests, preferences, abilities and backgrounds of students they teach is clearly necessary to provide a curriculum and lessons that are relevant for everyone. The new National Curriculum for PE offers greater flexibility than the current orders and an opportunity for schools to be creative in curriculum design, and it is perhaps at this time that teachers should be taking the opportunity to assess students' interests.

Extra-curricular activities have a particular focus and offer limited opportunities to only a minority of students (Penney and Harris 1997). This provision in many schools continues to be dominated by team games with a competitive focus and maintains the gender separation mirrored in the core curriculum programme. There is a lack of opportunity for students to participate informally and this serves to exclude the less able and those from lower social classes from much extra-curricular activity. However, the introduction of the PESSCL strategy has gone a long way to addressing these issues with the introduction and development in many schools of a much wider provision of extra-curricular activities than previously. The extension and expansion of this provision is often seen through the use of specialist coaches, sports development officers and adults other than teachers with relevant qualifications. Much of this has been possible as a result of the substantial funding provided through the school sports partnerships. Careful auditing, though, of the range of students participating in these additional clubs and activities needs to be conducted to ensure that it is not just the same individuals expanding their experiences but that additional students are attending. The end purpose for such programmes needs to be explicit and the measures of a successful programme should be clear.

## Disability

In a recent study by Atkinson and Black (2006), which examined the experiences of young disabled people participating in PE, school sport and extra-curricular activities, findings indicated that only half of the students surveyed actually received two hours or more of PE a week. Some 90 per cent of these young people had no access to, or awareness of, disability-specific sports; yet one of the main objectives of the PESSCL strategy is to promote active communication channels between school sport and the community. If we, as practitioners, are to actively promote and develop the concept of lifelong physical activity, then a connection needs to be made between what students experience in their PE classes and the opportunities that are provided for participation in the local community.

Teachers have a responsibility to provide all students with the opportunity to access a broad and balanced Programme of Study – that includes and encourages *all* individuals to participate in PE. All young people have the right to participate in appropriate activities that are well designed, planned and delivered, so that the unique needs of each individual are met. The experiences of these young people need to be authentic, meaningful and purposeful, so that a culture of young people is created who, whatever their circumstances, become physically educated individuals. That is, an individual who understands, appreciates and recognizes what it means to be physically active, so he or she employs the skills learned in PE to everyday life.

The atmosphere created by a teacher can play a significant role in the development of an inclusive and equitable learning environment, and ultimately the development of each individual student. Students should feel safe and secure in their PE lessons. The atmosphere created should be welcoming, so that each individual is motivated to participate. The teacher plays a vital role in the development of this positive learning environment, and has a responsibility to be an advocate for the individual learning programme of each student in his or her class.

Students should be provided with the opportunity to participate in PE lessons that capture their attention, stimulate some form of curiosity and ultimately encourage them to want to participate. Each young person is a unique individual, with different needs. Teachers should recognize, value and respect this individuality. Although all students may have the opportunity to access the learning environment, it is still important to ensure that everyone also has the opportunity to enhance individualized learning and fulfil potential. In the case of a student in a wheelchair, for example, one must consider whether his or her physical development needs are being appropriately met if he or she were to be assigned the task of recording the performances of peers in a high-jump lesson.

Effective teachers will recognize the need to plan accordingly so that all students' needs are considered. They will employ a range of teaching strategies and techniques and constantly reflect on their students' (and their own) progress to ensure that differentiation takes place. In the previous case of the high-jump lesson, the teacher could have planned a parallel event where the student in the wheelchair completed a timed challenge to wheel up and over a wheelchair ramp. In this example the teacher has recognized the unique needs of the individual and differentiated the activity. The student is engaged in some form of physical activity and is still working on similar learning objectives to the rest of the class. The opportunity might also arise for other students in the class to recognize the skills involved in the wheelchair task, thus promoting an understanding of different needs and skills.

A teacher who promotes an equitable learning environment that includes all students will care about the children he or she is working with. The teacher will develop a reciprocal relationship with each student in the class, built on the basic principle of humanism, thus promoting concepts of personal meaning, self-esteem and empowerment. According to Kyriacou (1997), to adopt a humanistic approach teachers need to emphasize the development of the 'whole' person, encourage personal growth and awareness, and students need to be provided with a range of opportunities to make responsible choices. PE provides a number of opportunities for the development of cognitive and affective skills, as well as the obvious physical skills. These concepts should be embedded in the learning objectives when developing specific practices and strategies in PE.

How teachers view their students can also affect the teaching climate. Expectancy theory (Rogers 1982) suggests that very often a teacher will make a predetermined assumption about the individual based on first impressions. These expectations can then affect the way the teacher interacts with the student, which in turn can impact the response of the student. How a teacher reacts to an individual can be affected by preconceived perceptions and bogus stereotypes, be they related to a student's gender, 'race' (dis)ability, class, etc. For example, when a PE teacher is told that there will be a child with a disability in the PE class he or she may become so focused on understanding the nature and aetiology of the disability as to forget about the actual person. The student then becomes 'Joe with . . .', rather than being seen for who the individual actually is. The danger here is that the teacher might 'label' Joe too quickly and make assumptions about what he can and cannot do, without giving him a chance to find out what he can do for himself. Vickerman *et al.* (2003, p. 49) stress that if inclusive practice is to be fully embraced then 'the critical success factors are an open mind, positive attitude and a readiness to review and modify existing learning and teaching strategies'. Every child should be provided with the opportunity to perform and excel to the best of their ability. The focus of each lesson should be on what the child 'can do' rather than what they cannot do. High Quality School Leaders should 'recognize what physical education and school sport can achieve for each pupil and the whole school' and they should 'set high expectations of what individuals, pupils and the whole school can achieve in and through physical education and school sport' (DfES 2004, p. 15).

## 'Race'

As well as the socialization of students according to gender, PE can often serve to socialize students into certain sports according to 'race' and ethnicity as a result of continued stereotyping (Fernandez-Balboa 1993; Cahn 1994; Wray 2002; Azzarito and Solomon 2005). For example, Afro-Caribbean children (boys and girls) are often considered 'aggressive' and 'explosive' and encouraged into activities such as basketball and track (sprinting) events (Cahn 1994; Hargreaves 2005), and South Asian girls and young women are often stereotyped as having an innate lack of sporting ability (Hargreaves 2005). This serves to reinforce the socialization of all students into traditional stereotypes and as Azzarito and Solomon (2005, p. 39) recognize that 'by encouraging pupils' participation in specific physical activity and promoting gendered or racialized physical activities (basketball, athletics, dance or football) boys learn to become white or black men and girls learn to become white or black women'.

The cultural diversity of content within schools is often limited and there is an emphasis on ability and performance because of the assessment structure of the NCPE. This has resulted in students learning to assess their achievement in relation to how teachers judge their performances, resulting in some students feeling that they cannot achieve in PE. The current framework and current pedagogical practices within PE can therefore result in individuals feeling that they have no place in the world of PE and sport.

There is often little attention paid to sports, games or other forms of physical activity practices in other cultures. This perpetuation leads to schools ignoring other cultures, as Fernandez-Balboa (1993, p. 235) states: 'schools teach about the Western Cultural values and ideas of the white male dominant class almost exclusively, disregarding other cultures and ignoring student diversity in gender, race, socio-economic status and physical and intellectual level'. In attempting to address the notion of activities from other cultures this mainly occurs when other cultural dance forms are taught; however, this fails to recognize the wider role of PE as an agent for change and as Clarke and Nutt (1999, p. 213) state:

> Young people should be taught to recognise the universality of PE, since much can be learned form exploring and celebrating others' cultural traditions. But, in doing so, care must be taken to avoid 'tokenism' and the portrayal of activities from other cultures as some exotic alternative to 'our'.

Therefore, consideration needs to be given to the activities taught in PE to include and encourage cultural diversity, and makes PE experiences meaningful for all students. Furthermore, there needs to be the inclusion of culturally relevant pedagogy within ITE. ITE programmes are sites of production of the dominant discourses about PE and teacher trainers can change their practices and influence pedagogic approaches by understanding the social and historical production of this knowledge.

In her research on the engagement of Asian women in physical activity Wray (2002) found that Asian women are expected to participate in Western-based exercise regimes that contradict their culturally located feminine identities. Equally this applies to young girls. There are issues of changing in front of others for Muslim girls/women and also of participating in the presence of boys/men. Consequently, Muslim women are more likely to participate in exercise if the facilities and types of exercise do not disrupt their ethnic/religious identity (Wray 2002). This is also applicable when considering girls' participation in PE.

In order to address some of these issues schools allow Asian students to wear tracksuit bottoms, which can make a significant contribution to encouraging participation. However, in their research on student perceptions of the National Curriculum for PE, Williams and Bedward (2001) found that while teachers thought that white students understood this, those students, in fact, felt they were being treated unfairly because they were not allowed to wear tracksuit bottoms. Accordingly, teachers need to be aware of the role kit has to play in relation to equality in order to ensure this does not impact on relationships between students from different ethnic and cultural backgrounds.

## Concluding Remarks

This chapter has recognized that PE and the professionals within it have a responsibility to recognize and provide high-quality PE for *all* students regardless of gender, sexuality, ethnicity, ability and social class. There is a need to recognize the increasing range of students' cultural and social backgrounds and examine more closely how we may contribute to developments within PE that signal a conscious move towards greater equity for all young people. Our pedagogical practices have a powerful impact on the identities and involvement in sport of the children we teach and, as Law and Fisher (1999, p. 36) state:

> Whatever perspective we take of the state of PE at the end of the twentieth century it is clear that an understanding of the frameworks that pupils use to interpret the subject is crucial to teachers' ability to implement an effective curriculum. Most significant would seem to be the need to provide a curriculum that pupils interpret as relevant to them and their lives, one which they feel they can carry forward into the rest of their lives.

## References

Atkinson, H. and Black, K. (2006), 'The Experiences of Young Disabled People Participating in PE, School Sport and Extra Curricular Activities in Leicestershire and Rutland – Final Report'. Loughborough University: Institute of Youth Sport and Peter Harrison Centre for Disability Sport.

Azzarito, L. and Ennis, C. (2003), 'A sense of connection: toward social constructivist physical education'. *Sport, Education and Society*, 8, (2), 179–98.

— and Solomon, M. A. (2005), 'A reconceptualisation of physical education: the interaction of gender/race/social class'. *Sport, Education and Society*, 10, (1), 25–47.

BBC Sport (2005), 'Pivotal year for UK women's football' (18 February).

BMRB (British Market Research Bureau) (2005), 'Taking Part: The National Survey of Culture, Leisure and Sport'. London: British Market Research Bureau.

Buckingham, J. (2000), 'The truth about private schools in Australia'. Issue Analysis No. 13. Available at http://www.cis.org.au (accessed 12th January 2007).

Cahn, S. K. (1994), *Coming on Strong: Gender and Sexuality in Twentieth-Century Women's Sport*. New York: The Free Press.

Choi, P. Y. L. (2000), *Femininity and the Physically Active Woman*. London: Routledge.

Coakley, J. and White, A. (1992), 'Making decisions: gender and sport participation among British adolescents'. *Sociology of Sport Journal*, 9, (1), 20–35.

Cockburn, C. (1999), 'The trouble with girls a study of teenage girls' magazines in relation to sport and PE'. *British Journal of Physical Education*, 30, (3), 11–15.

Connolly, P. (2006), 'The effects of social class and ethnicity on gender differences in GCSE attainment: a secondary analysis of the Youth Cohort Study of England and Wales 1997–2001'. *British Educational Research Journal*, 32, 3–23.

Clarke, G. and Nutt, G. (1999), 'Physical education', in D. Hill and M. Cole (eds), *Promoting Equality in Secondary Schools*. London: Cassell, pp. 211–37.

DfES (2004), *Every Child Matters*. London: HMSO.

— /DCMS (Department for Culture, Media and Sport) (2004), *High Quality PE and Sport for Young people – A guide to Recognising and Achieving High Quality PE and Sport in Schools and Clubs*. London: HMSO,

DNH (Department of National Heritage) (1995). *Sport: Raising the Game*. London: DNH.

Eccles, J. S. (1999), 'Gender differences in sport'. Paper presented at Contemporary Issues in Sport seminar, University of Michigan, 19 November.

Ennis, C. (1999), 'Creating a culturally relevant curriculum for disengaged girls'. *Sport, Education and Society*, 4, (1), 31–49.

Estyn (Her Majesty's Inspectorate for Education and Training in Wales) (2007), *Girls' Participation in Physical Activity in Schools*. Cardiff: Estyn.

Evans, J. and Davies, B. (2008), 'The poverty of theory: class configurations in the discourse of Physical Education and Health (PEH)'. *Physical Education and Sport Pedagogy*, 13, (2), 119–213.

— , Penny, D. and Davies, B. (1996), 'Back to the future: education policy and physical education', in N. Armstrong (ed.), *New Directions in Physical Education: Change and Innovation*. London: Cassell Education, pp. 1–18.

Fernandez-Balboa, J. M. (1993), 'Sociocultural characteristics of the hidden curriculum in physical education'. *Quest*, 45, 230–54.

Griffin, L. L. and Butler, I. (eds) (2005), *Teaching Games for Understanding*. Champaign, IL: Human Kinetics.

Hargreaves, J. (1996), *Sporting Females: Critical Issues in the History and Sociology of Women's Sports*. London: Routledge.

— (2005) 'Feminist perspectives', in *Berkshire Encyclopaedia of World Sport (2)*. Great Barrington, MA: Berkshire Publishing Group LLC, pp. 572–80.

Jones, R. L. and Armour, K. M. (2000), *Sociology of Sport: Theory and Practice*. Harlow: Pearson Education.

Kirk, D. (1992), 'Curriculum history in physical education: a source of struggle and a force for change', in A. C. Sparkes (ed.), *Research in Physical Education and Sport: Exploring Alternative Visions*. London: The Falmer Press, pp. 210–30.

Kyriacou, C. (1997), *Effective Teaching in Schools* (2nd edn). Cheltenham: Stanley Thornes.

Laker, A. (2000), *Beyond the Boundaries of Physical Education; Educating Young People for Citizenship and Social Responsibility*. London: Routledge Falmer.

Laws, C. and Fisher, R. (1999), 'Pupils' interpretations of physical education', in C. A. Hardy and M. Mawer (eds), *Learning and Teaching in Physical Education*. London: Falmer Press, pp. 23–38.

McCaughtry, N., Rocco Dillon, S., Jones, E. and Smigell, S. (2005), 'Sexuality sensitive schooling'. *Quest*, 57, 426–43.

Ofsted (1995), *Physical Education and Sport in Schools: A Survey of Good Practice*. London: HMSO.

Penney, D. and Evans, J. (2004), 'Levels on the playing field: ability and inclusion in level frameworks in health and physical education'. Paper presented at the Australian Association for Research in Education Conference, Melbourne, 28 November–2 December.

— and Harris, J. (1997), 'Extra-curricular physical education: more of the same for the more able'. *Sport, Education and Society*, 2, (1), 41–54.

QCA (1999a), *The National Curriculum: Handbook for Secondary Teachers in England*. London: QCA.

QCA (1999b), *The Review of the National Curriculum in England: Consultation Materials*. London: QCA.

Rogers, C. (1982), *A Social Psychology of Schooling: The Expectancy Process*. London: Routledge & Kegan Paul.

Sage, G. H. (1993), 'Sport and physical education and the new world order: dare we be agents of social change?' *Quest*, 45, 151–64.

Siedentop, D., Hastie, P. A. and Van der Mars, H. (2004), *A Complete Guide to Sport Education*. Champaign, IL: Human Kinetics.

Stidder, G. (2002), 'The recruitment of secondary school physical education teachers in England: a gendered perspective?' *European Physical Education Review*, 8, (3), 249–69.

Vickerman, P., Hayes, S. and Whetherly, A. (2003), 'Special educational needs and National Curriculum physical education', in S. Hayes and G. Stidder (eds), *Equity in Physical Education*. London: Routledge, pp. 47–62.

Williams, A. and Bedward, J. (2001), 'Gender, culture and the generation gap: student and teacher perceptions of aspects of the National Curriculum physical education'. *Sport Education and Society*, 6, (1), 53–66.

Wray, S. (2002), 'Connecting ethnicity, gender and physicality: Muslim Pakistani women, physical activity and health', in S. Scraton and A. Flintoff (eds), *Gender and Sport: A Reader*. London: Routledge, pp. 141–55.

Wright, J. (1996), 'Mapping the discourses of physical education: articulating a female tradition'. *Journal of Curricular Studies*, 28, (3), 331–51.

— (1999), 'Changing gendered practices in physical education: working with teachers'. *European Physical Education Review*, 5, (3), 181–97.

— and Burrows, L. (2006), 'Re-conceiving ability in physical education: a social analysis'. *Sport, Education and Society*, 11, (3), 275–91.

Chapter 13

# Science

## Brian Matthews and John Clay

### Abstract

In this chapter we argue that science is a social and cultural construction which therefore can incorporate different forms of isms/phobias. However, we also contend that a unifying and deep approach is to teach science while also developing students' emotional literacy. This in turn requires a constructivist process that is based in enquiry with student collaboration, resulting, as research has shown, in tackling multifaceted aspects of isms/phobias while at the same time making science more popular.

## Where Are We at Present? Science in Schools

Most of us come into contact with science and technology as a student in school. School science has for over a century been concerned with introducing learners as novices to a set of theories, practices and established knowledge which has become a familiar part of our cultural entitlement. It is normally packaged and presented in such a manner that what is between the covers of a textbook is considered to be the truth. The learner is presented with information often in the form of indisputable facts set out in a sequential manner offering an unproblematic narrative. When the facts are coupled to a set of numbers and a neat formula, this becomes objective, universal, certain and infallible. The more we accept science as certain, the more likely we are to resort to transmission teaching and rote learning, which in turn leads to forms of testing to assess effective transmission. 'Ineffective transmission', reflected in low test scores, can then be blamed on two factors: incompetent teachers or 'inadequate' learners. The National Curriculum orders for science at Key Stages 1–4, the Standard Assessment Tasks (SATs) that remain, and the General Certificate in Secondary Education (GCSE) at 16 are all part of this 'package deal'.

This model of learning and testing then becomes part of the technology for producing a hierarchy of learners: knowers vs non-knowers, experts vs non-experts, sheep vs goats. The selected minority can then possibly continue through hard work and perseverance to become future high priests of the faith. This approach to screening out the majority of learners considered to be unsuitable future scientists is hugely wasteful. As opposed to this perspective, science can be viewed as an intensely human activity, as a cultural construct with a clear social dimension. The birth of 'modern science' and the history of its development need critical examination and re-evaluation. The Mertonian concept of the scientific community working to and within the four principal norms of universalism, communality, organized scepticism and disinterested-ness has helped to portray science as acultural, objective and unfettered by the messy contradictions that pervade other forms of knowledge construction. This view of science also colludes in the separation of science from technology.

## Where Do We Go from Here?

In the report 'Primary Horizons' published by the Wellcome Trust in 2006 the authors state that:

> Children's early years are key to shaping society's attitudes towards science. By the time children reach secondary school, they will have experienced seven years of schooling and will have well-developed attitudes to science. While this could be of great benefit where attitudes are positive, several recent studies ... suggest that children's attitudes towards science are declining in the later primary years. In an age of rapid advancement in science and technology, such a trend is clearly worrying, not just because of the need to ensure a continuing supply of highly trained and competent scientists but also ... because of the importance of equipping young people to understand the impact of science on their lives and to take decisions based on this understanding.

Hence, it can be argued that we have to challenge the view that there is only one form of scientific literacy and move away from an autocratic view of scientific literacy, and argue for ways of knowing that are both democratic and accountable to society. This must take account of the social and cultural consequences of applications.

Therefore, different models of 'scientific literacy' can be critically examined and promoted, to educate students in schools to cope with an increasing plurality of views and visions, and to develop a globally equitable, socially just and ecologically sustainable economy and technology.

## What's Happening in the World?

In a project undertaken for the Organisation for Economic Co-operation and Development (OECD) in 1996 the editors reported on 23 curriculum projects from 13 countries around the globe. The case studies represent what the education policy-makers in the participating countries considered to be particularly innovative. The motives for reform stem from a general dissatisfaction of the education received by students in science, mathematics and technology. The pressures for the changes were grouped into concerns around:

- a concern about the competitiveness of the national economy
- the need to prepare twenty-first-century citizens to the emerging economic, social, cultural and environmental challenges
- the need for greater inclusiveness and equity, and
- the desire to promote new conceptions of learning and to ensure that teachers play a central role in conceiving and shaping reforms.

What the OECD team also found was three broad trends or themes common to all the innovations in the respective countries. First, all the case studies stressed the importance of practical work for learners as being crucial; second, the connections between the sciences and between science and other areas of study were emphasized; and third, the need for science and mathematics to be seen as ways of knowing how to make sense of the world we inhabit. These themes took place at a time when the science education provision in England was becoming very narrow and prescriptive in terms not only of the curriculum but also in classroom pedagogy.

As teachers of science we can ask what we would ideally like students to develop as a result of doing science in school. We would want students to leave school being interested in science and wishing to continue to take an interest in it as well as having developed an understanding of the basic principles. Also we would want them to see science as a set of complex 'contextualized truths' that are at times contradictory and have varying degrees of uncertainty. They would also realize how powerful science is and that it is one of the major forces that are changing the world and affect how societies function. Hence they will be equipped socially and emotionally to consider issues such that they will be able to engage with discussions on the future directions of science and how it should be used to further societies. This implies that they would have the emotional development to de-centre, consider the conflicting demands of others and to have some sort of vision of society. They would be open to changes in scientific and political thinking and have the emotional resilience to not be threatened by them. Since science is a complex set of 'contextualized truths' we can see how it can be permeated by aspects of sexism, racism, homophobia, disablism and issues of social class. These isms/phobias (see Chapter 2 of this volume) are often treated separately as they manifest themselves in different ways. However, in this chapter we will take a deeper and unifying theoretical perspective that we regard as underlying most forms of discrimination, namely the absence of emotional literacy. Taking this approach will enable science teachers to understand how an emotionally literate approach helps in challenging a broad range of discriminatory structures and practices. Additionally, it will help teachers in seeing that inequalities are not uni-dimensional. Understanding inequality arising from particular factors needs to be clearly understood and dealt with where appropriate in the school science curriculum. This would help children and young people to engage in learning in ways that will help them change society to be more empathetic, concerned with confronting inequality and desire to achieve greater social justice.

## Emotional Literacy and Equality

There has been an increasing trend in society to recognize the importance of the emotions in life and in promoting empathy in schools. Goleman argued that people who did very well academically at school often did not go on to use their abilities in society. He said:

> What factors are at play when people of high IQ flounder and those of modest IQ do surprisingly well? I would argue that the difference quite often lies in the abilities called here *emotional intelligence*, which include self-control, zeal and persistence, and the ability to motivate oneself. And these skills ... can be taught to children, giving them a better chance to use whatever intellectual potential the genetic lottery may have given them. (Goleman 1996, p. xii, italics in the original)[1]

There is now a movement to improve students' emotional literacy: the term literacy is used more consistently in Britain and has the advantage that it avoids the connotations with cognitive intelligence (Matthews 2006). In England the Social and Emotional Aspects of Learning (SEAL), which is a government funded project, is being used in about 80 per cent of primary schools and is now in secondary schools (DfES 2007). This project defines emotional literacy as having the following five components.

1. self-awareness
2. managing feelings
3. motivation

4. empathy
5. social skills

The definition of emotional literacy used by SEAL is similar to Goleman's but neither addresses, directly, issues of equal opportunities or social justice. Each goes towards defining emotional literacy, but makes no reference to the variation between individuals and between groups – such as gender, faith, sexual orientation, disability, social class and ethnicity – and whether or not any particular attributes develop differently depending on the nature of the group in which the interactions take place. It is almost as if emotional literacy develops in a social vacuum (Matthews 2006).

Here is an attempt made by one of us, based on research to enable boys and girls to develop their understanding of each other, to define the relationship between emotional literacy and equality:

> Emotional literacy ... is both an individual development and a collective activity and is both about self-development and the building of community so that one's own sense of emotional well-being grows along with that of others ... Emotional literacy involves connections between people and working with their differences and similarities while being able to handle ambiguity and contradiction. It is a dynamic process through which the individual develops emotionally and involves culture and empowerment. For example, it includes understanding how the nature of social class, 'race' and gender impinge on people's emotional states to lead to an understanding of how society could change. Hence it incorporates an understanding of power exchanges between people and a challenging of power differentials. (*Ibid.*, p. 178)

Enhancing emotional literacy is considered here as a group enterprise, involving the interplay of power and empowerment. This contrasts with much of what occurs in schools where in many cases the education taking place operates to assess students for ranking purposes. They are in an *individual-in-group* situation in classrooms where they are (either) communicating (or not) with others to express ideas and to learn. Taylor (1994) argues that people have to 'recognize' each other at a variety of levels, otherwise:

> Mis-recognition can cause people damage, especially when a demeaning picture of themselves is reflected back to them from other people. This is because people gain a sense of themselves in dialogical relationships with other people 'sometimes in struggle *against* the things our significant others want to see in us'. (p. 33)

## 'Racism' and emotional literacy

We would argue that the concepts of equality and emotional literacy should be seen as complementary. What matters is that teacher strategies will enable students to interact and engage more deeply with thoughts, feelings and actions. For example, sometimes in nearly all-white schools teachers say that there is little racism and that the children just 'get on' with each other. However, when you explore deeper the underlying racism often emerges. Similarly, students can appear to get on because they only talk to each other superficially on topics in science that are deemed factual and therefore value-free. Emotional literacy can enable individuals to develop the capacity to understand the complexity of taken-for-granted assumptions and to consider issues of racism and the dynamics of power.

There are many ways that racism can be tackled in the classroom. These include, for example, the use of foods from a wide range of countries when studying nutrition (Gill and Levidow 1987); showing how other cultures have contributed to science, such as the history of iron smelting (Reiss 1993); and Abu Ali al-Hasan Ibn al-Haytham, who discovered how the eye worked (QCA, nd). Teachers have also gone over how scientists from different cultures have helped discover things, such as Latimer and light bulbs (BlackInventor, nd; Queen's University, nd; Henry and Williams 1999). Others have included lessons to look at the ways that science itself has supported racism, and that 'race' is not a scientific concept (Gill and Levidow 1987; Thorp 1991; Thorp *et al.* 1994; see also Chapter 2 of this volume).

Another approach has been to ask students to draw a picture of scientists – although it is better to ask them to draw two scientists as more information can be gained; these normally include a preponderance of white male scientists. The drawings can be discussed along with showing scientists from all over the world (Harrison and Matthews 1998; Matthews and Davies 1999). As a result, students' perceptions can be changed.

However, while these approaches are all important they only look at science and its relationship with racism. If we are to tackle racism between students at a deeper level, we need to look at student–student interactions and their emotional literacy. This can be done in the classroom where students work in groups and are given time to discuss how well they got on together and how to improve their social and emotional behaviour (Matthews 2006).

Here are some quotes from that research in which students indicate how their views have changed because of approaches to emotional literacy in the science classroom:

> Group work with members of other races is an *excellent* idea, since it allows open discussion on otherwise 'racist' remarks. This way it can be discussed openly without insult. Helps understanding incredibly. (Female, background unknown)

It made me feel more confident to work with other girls ... my respect for them has grown. I have experienced no racial attacks from group work, and I have experienced racial attacks disappearing as a result of group work in mixed groups during my secondary school group projects. (Male, Bengali)

Yes because you get to meet different people and get to know them and some times people have a lot more in common but they don't know it. (Male, white) (Matthews and Sweeney 1997, p. 34)

It is also evident in some of the quotes that gender and ethnic discriminations are not seen as totally separate from each other and that students comment on both. The student's identity is made up of a complex integration of many factors.

The ability to accept uncertainty, contingency and challenge preconceptions are also the prerequisites for a good science education that wishes students to engage with science, recognize that it has its limits, and that the knowledge produced is always uncertain. In other words, scientific literacy and emotional literacy are connected and so it will help science teaching if both are tackled together.

## Gender, science, thinking skills and emotional literacy

The model of science that is essentially mechanistic as shaped and driven by Cartesian logic was refined by René Descartes – the separation of mind from body; this helps establish the object/subject divide and can be seen as a contributory factor in girls being put off science. The mechanistic view of science has been critiqued by scientists such as Evelyn Fox-Keller (1985), who has said that:

The most immediate issue for a feminist perspective on the natural sciences is the deeply rooted popular mythology that casts objectivity, reason, and mind as male, and subjectivity, feeling and nature as female. In this division of emotional and intellectual labor, women have been guarantors and protectors of the personal, the emotional, the particular, whereas science – the province par excellence of the impersonal, the rational, and the general – has been the preserve of men. (p. 7)

Francis Bacon talked about science as we know it in terms of a clearly gendered language when he distinguishes the method he advocated from its 'ineffective' predecessors by its 'virile' power, its capacity to bind Nature to man's service and make her his slave. In this positivist tradition, natural phenomena, it was felt, could be analysed into its constituent parts and then arranged according to causal laws. It is like looking at an old-fashioned watch with cogwheels which eventually turn the hands of a watch. The mechanistic view of the world led to everything being measurable, quantifiable and expressible as a formula. This has led to the process of atomization and specialization and a point of view that an expert understanding of the constituent parts will enable us to put together a new whole that would be an improvement on the old whole. The school science curriculum remains impervious to the critiques against the traditions of reductionist science.

Feminist science should not be equated with the feminization of science, such as girl-friendly science in the context of school, considered essentially a matter of choosing a softer content, or finding a context that is seen as more appropriate to the concerns of females, for example doing cosmetic science or, where possible, a biological angle or approach. This only trivializes the issues and perpetuates the stereotypes relating to soft sciences for the girls and hard sciences for the boys. Masculine and feminine are categories defined by culture, not by biological necessity. Women, men and science are created, together, out of a complex dynamic of interwoven cognitive, emotional and social forces. Despite the dangers inherent in the 'feminization' of science, science is more than simply a 'way of doing' or a body of cold, indisputable facts. It is not merely a cognitive endeavour but can be a deeply personal as well as a social activity. However, accepting that science is a social and cultural activity means that it can be permeated with racism, sexism and other isms/phobias. Hence, teaching science should be cognisant of this. There are many ways that gender issues can be raised in the science classroom and some of these overlap with approaches to racism. For example, the 'draw two scientists' described above brings out as much about sexism as racism, and the contribution of female scientists can also be discussed. These help girls to see themselves as scientists as role models are provided. However, it is clear that one of the ways that girls can be encouraged to take up science is to make it more social and relevant to them. There are many ways of doing this but the way we focus on here is to make the classroom more social through developing thinking skills. This also provides an ideal opportunity to develop the student's emotional literacy.

The Qualifications and Curriculum Authority (QCA) have published the Personal, Learning and Thinking Skills (PLTS) to provide a framework for describing the qualities and skills needed for success in learning and life (QCA 2007). They say:

The PLTS framework embraces: social and emotional aspects of learning, employability, responsible citizenship, enquiry skills and creativity, self-direction and independent study, reflection on learning (learning to learn and assessment for learning).

The framework comprises six groups of skills:

- independent enquirers
- creative thinkers
- reflective learners
- team workers
- self-managers
- effective participators.

This framework has much potential for developing education and contains a move away from the simple rationalistic model. Overall the PLTS are the sorts of skills scientists need and that they are now central to the curriculum is very useful for science teachers.

When the students are in a group and asked to 'collaborate with others to work towards common goals' (PLTS) they have to communicate and get on with a range of other students. Hence, for science in schools to be effective and meaningful, it would be necessary to recognize the importance of emotional literacy in order to help students enter into dialogue. This could also enable them to develop the skills of having some control over their personal development and would also centrally involve students having to confront all aspects of prejudice. They can be engaged in discussions with students of differing academic abilities, sexes, 'races' and social classes. Clearly, to be fully implemented this requires a commitment to fully co-educational multiethnic comprehensives with no public schools.

Since developing thinking skills requires collaboration, the students' emotional literacy can be developed. If this is done in mixed-sex groups, sexism can be tackled at the same time. In the research the boys and girls worked together and had to comment on how well they got on and to discuss their social and emotional interactions, while the control groups covered exactly the same curriculum without these interventions (Matthews 2006). An important finding was that the students were more likely to continue with science as a subject (Table 13.1).

**Table 13.1**

|                                                                          | Research                     | Control                      |
| ------------------------------------------------------------------------ | ---------------------------- | ---------------------------- |
| Percentage that indicated that they were likely to continue with science | Boys: 85%<br>Girls: 85%      | Boys: 71%<br>Girls: 76%      |

The boys' and girls' attitudes to science benefited from doing the collaborative group work with the feedback discussions. Part of the reason for this was that the development of emotional skills meant that the girls and boys helped teach each other (Matthews *et al* 2002, pp. 109–10):

Yes, we all helped each other learn (girl)

Funnily enough, Liam taught me about solar power (girl)

Yes, I taught John (girl)

[You learn science] because you get to know their [*sic*] people's views (boy)

The connection between the social aspects and learning science was expounded by the students:

Sometimes it [group work in science] makes you get on better with people but sometimes they disagree but I think that is good for girls to work with boys and boys to work with girls because it will probably help you to understand the other sex and race. (girl)

I think that in life it is very important because as we grow we will come across many different people and it's good to get along with them at an early age. (boy)

At first they were really annoying, but now there [*sic*] fine. (girl)

You get more confident talking to boys. (girl)

I get on better with the girls as we do more. (boy)

I think people don't like other people because of what they see. Doing group work can make them see what the other person can do. (boy) (Matthews 2006 p. 108)

Developing emotional literacy in the classroom can therefore make a contribution to tacking sexism, while at the same time enabling boys to realize that girls can not only achieve at science, but also teach them, and vice versa. The more this happens the more the stage is set for girls to become scientists.

## Sexual orientation

Students who are developing emotionally will be increasingly able to be empathic, self-reliant and emotionally resilient. One of the advantages of addressing aspects of emotional literacy is that it enables students to learn about and understand each other, irrespective of their sexual orientation. It is common for students to taunt each other about being gay such that students feel they cannot relate to others. The development of emotional resilience and understanding allows students across different sexualities to understand each other such that, should a student feel secure enough, he or she can raise such issues openly. By that time the students are in a better position to understand that there are a wide range of ideas of femininities, masculinities and sexual orientations with no set definitions or ways of acting out sexually. They will be more able to accept ambiguity and contradiction and deal with uncertainty. As a result they should be able to see the differences (and similarities) between people and sexualities as an asset and not a threat and hence equality can become part of an authentic education. They will also be able to reflect on their own and others' actions, and the limits of their knowledge. Hence they will be more able to accept contingency and so be open to new information and feelings that may change their minds. Since science, especially the physical sciences, has traditionally been seen as a masculine subject it can be defined as a male (heterosexual) activity as is pursued in ways that are relatively devoid of emotion and with the male dominating nature. This is very slowly changing, with female scientists available for role models. However, while teachers are gradually drawing on such information for females there is a dearth of non-heterosexual scientists that can be used. As a result other ways of educating about such issues have to be found. The moves to incorporate PLTS, and in particular personal development, within the curriculum can be used to counter the mechanistic view of science. Similarly, as can be seen from the quotes above, incorporating emotional literacy enables students to make the social and emotional connections with science by themselves. In this work students have to learn to work with, and to get on with, *all* their classmates as the groups are changed regularly. Hence students of a variety of sexualities, although usually hidden, learn together and gradually build up empathy and trust. This can avoid misrecognition and, over a period of time, even recognition of what one can see in others that which one is struggling with, within oneself.

It is worth stressing how important this is in forming an emotional and social base from which to work when problems arise. Similarly, students see for themselves that other students can help them learn science, irrespective of sexual orientation; it enables the stereotype of science being a masculinist project to be challenged and overturned.

## Special educational needs

Because of time and resources it is difficult for the teacher to be able to help those students who are labelled as SEN. Effective differentiation in the classroom is something that most teachers grapple with, with varying degrees of success. While differentiation and providing support is essential, peer support is an element that can be used effectively. One of the features this research brought out was the extent to which students helped each other learn. All of the classes were in mixed-ability groups and as a result students with varying scientific knowledge worked and helped each other. In the following, quotes – all names changed – are from interviews with an external evaluator of the research. Darren is a student with little achievement in science and Ms Jones is a support teacher.

| | |
|---|---|
| Darren: | I'm not the cleverest, but I do try in science and not a lot of people get under 50%, they're all up high. The highest I've got is about 72%. |
| Evaluator: | I wonder if that is because you've been doing the group work or not? |
| Darren: | It probably is because you've been discussing them, before the test you can work it out with other people, they give you their answers and you remember and you give them your answers. It sticks more. |

Later on in the interview they discussed working with other students of different attainment in science:

| | |
|---|---|
| Darren: | Group work … it's helpful and sometimes it can't be helpful because sometimes there could be very clever people in the group that are like 'Oh I'll do this and do this', and say if I was in Jonathan's group, but if he was like, 'go away I don't need you', which he's not, it would be pretty unfair for the person who hasn't got that much ability. But if you are working in group work, it can work. |
| Darren: | Sometimes she mixes us all up. She puts at least two people that are brainy with two which hasn't [*sic*] got the best of ability, so the two who is [*sic*] very good at science could help them out. |
| Jane: | She doesn't do it like that, like two disability [*sic*] and two clever people, cos that wouldn't be really fair, but the groups we do have, some of them we have like, if I've got a newcomer in my group, I remember that group because I've had them quite a few times. |
| Darren: | Yeah that's because we're working well together, so that's why she hasn't changed the groups so much. Me, Sally and Mark aint the cleverest of people, but Annuka is, but we all get on well together, cos Mark has like a helper, Ms Jones, and she likes group work as well, cos when Mark's in our group, she gets involved in our group work which is good. |
| Darren: | The reason he does know about science is cos he works in his group more often, because if he didn't work in a group and he |

just worked on his own with Ms Jones, Ms Jones is not a
science teacher, she works in every lesson and he wouldn't
benefit from what he's got now, so working in a group has
helped him get the answers.

Connie:        But he's quite shy as well. And I think group work helped
him socialise with other people more and build up his
confidence to actually speak what's on his mind and show
how clever he really is.

These quotes illustrate how students in mixed-ability settings with the
feedback and discussion mechanisms used in the classroom can be helped to
support each other. This structure can help to combat the notion of fixed
ability as it assumes that all students can learn with each other's help (Hart *et
al.* 2004). This is not to say that all students react in this positive way; some do
not like to work in groups at all, and some will not help others, but most do
and with skilful teacher interventions classes will be very supportive of each
other (Matthews 2006; Morrison and Matthews 2006). These quotes also
show how students themselves come to question the idea of fixed ability (Hart
*et al.* 2004); see last sentence by Connie, as she indicates that Mark has
ability.[1]

## Science and social class

Gender is only one factor that affects schooling, achievement and measured
attainment. Other factors such as class and ethnicity are stronger
determinants of educational achievement. Gillborn and Mirza (2000) argue
that:

> of the three best-known dimensions of inequality ('**race**', class and
> **gender**) the latter, **gender**, and in particular boys underperformance,
> represents the narrowest disparity. In contrast to the disproportionate
> media attention, [our] data shows **gender** to be a less problematic issue
> than the significant disadvantage of '**race**', and the even greater inequality
> of **class**. (bold in the original) (p. 23)

The attainment gap between the highest and lowest social classes has
widened. The ways in which social class affects educational opportunities are
multiple and complex: some factors lie outside the school; others operate
through institutional processes that disadvantage particular groups of
students. The familiar association between class and attainment can be seen
to operate within each of the main ethnic groups. The majority of boys and
girls from socially advantaged backgrounds do better in all subjects at GCSE
than the majority of girls from disadvantaged families.

In 2007, through the Department for Children, Schools and Families (DCSF), the UK government funded a two-year project aptly named Narrowing the Gap. This ambitious project set out to narrow the gap in outcomes between vulnerable and excluded children and young people and the rest of their peers against the context of generally improving outcomes for all. In a comprehensive data mapping and analysis exercise undertaken by the National Foundation for Educational Research (NFER), published in 2008, it was found that poverty and social class were still the most significant factor in determining the outcomes and trajectories of children and young people. The findings showed that:

- Despite all efforts, the UK has one of the strongest links between circumstances into which a child is born (socio-economic group) and their adult outcomes.
- The lower the social economic group, the higher the risk of poor outcomes.
- 'Poor' circumstances, leading to poor qualifications, transmits poverty across generations.

For science teachers there are two immediate ways of raising awareness in students. First, one aspect of social class is the psychological way it impacts on perceptions and power such that others can view those with wealth with a certain deference. With the exercise of power can come a confidence that can go unchallenged. However, it can be confronted as people gain the confidence to empower themselves by understanding the processes involved. As pointed out above:

> [emotional literacy] includes understanding how the nature of social class, 'race' and gender impinge on people's emotional states to lead to an understanding of how society could change. Hence it incorporates an understanding of power exchanges between people and a challenging of power differentials. (Matthews 2006, p. 178)

At a simple level power is made explicit through the mechanisms used above and to be explained below. For example, one pupil who was running a discussion on the dynamics of the group while learning science stated: 'Do we include you [the teacher] in the sheet [analysis] as you talked in the group as well as us?' Developing emotional literacy enables the development of self-belief and emotional resilience, and understanding of social class issues is a factor in challenging class structures.

Second, science teachers can develop cross-curricular work to show how science can protect class structures. One example is in the Green Revolution, where farmers in countries like India were helped to produce more crops. However, this was done through the use of fertilizers and mechanized methods (brought from the West) and as a result only the richer farmers could afford them, and poorer farmers could then not compete with the produce prices (Gill and Levidow 1987; Thorp *et al.* 1994). Another example is in the science of surveillance and information technology which operates to reinforce class divisions (Lyon 2002). Surveillance is used to protect the property of those who are wealthy while controlling people from lower social classes (Davies 1996; Norris and Armstrong 1999; Peissi 2003). When computers were introduced into the workplace the manufacturers made it quite explicit that the main reason was to control the workforce, give managers greater control and to bring intellectual labour under increased control (Cooley 1987; Matthews 1992; 1996). It can be argued that the more one moves to a technocratic society, the more social relationships are changed to make an instrumentalist rationalist society with hierarchical control possible. Part of this is an ideological debate about the nature of 'intelligence' and the extent to which it is possible for machines to have 'intelligence', which is impacting on the use of 'intelligence' in education (Matthews 1996). Further, teachers can do all they can to avoid the creeping surveillance of students (and of teachers) that threaten their emotional development and promote the acceptance of stratified social control (Kelly 2003; Epic 2005; Matthews 2006). These debates would be ideal material for a cross-curricular exploration of science and social class.

## What does equality and emotional literacy mean for the teacher?

The active and participatory model of the classroom has implications for the role of the teacher. There is a shift from a *teacher-centred* model to a *learner-centred* approach (CCEA 2007) where the teacher becomes more of a facilitator to encourage students to think. This practice is based on research, like the Children's Learning in Science Project (CLISP) (Scott 1987), into how students learn which has shown that they construct their ideas based on experiences that they have already had. The findings have been consistent with a **constructivist** view of learning where it is accepted that:

- Learners have views and beliefs about the world. These can be accurate or based on misconceptions.
- Learning involves the construction of meaning through experience and language.
- What is learned depends on the knowledge and experiences of the learner as well as the context of the learning situation and the materials presented.
- This construction of meaning is an active process.
- What is learned may not be what the teacher intends. (Driver 1983; Brookes and Brookes 1993; Bennett 2003)

The connections between emotional development, language and learning are evident in Vygotsky's work, which points out that teaching and learning develop through collaborative group work with dialogue. Vygotsky argued that 'Every function in the child's cultural development appears twice ... First *between* people (*interpsychological*), and then *inside* the child (*intrapsychological*) ... All the higher functions originate as actual relations between human individuals' (Vygotsky 1978, p. 58, italics in the original). Cole (1996, p. xii) argues that the 'mind emerges in the joint activity of people and is in an important sense coconstructed'. Hence schools can play a significant role through enabling students of all backgrounds to interact in a safe environment while forming their identity. These arguments resonate with the changing views on science as a social construction and where the knowledge that is found has a relationship with the society in which it is produced (Hodson 1998). Hodson (1998) argues for a personalized approach to science education where the teacher can be seen as a co-learner.

This type of pedagogy will aid the development of thinking skills and emotional literacy as they set the students in a situation where they are confronted with ideas and have to engage their minds. Students can work together collaboratively, actively listening and so be participatory learners. Hence, their social and emotional skills can be developed at the same time as learning cognitively. Students should take more responsibility for their own learning and reflect on what they are achieving. However, emotions, feelings, values and morals are not the same as thinking skills and require different approaches from the teacher to enhance them. We tend to contrast the development of emotions, in which thinking skills are an important part, with the development of 'wisdom'. In order to know what to do with the knowledge learned, how and what to apply it to, one needs to have an understanding of people, how different groups in and across societies have different needs, and how to relate to them. In other words, a developed emotional literacy is required to convert knowledge into wisdom. Table 13.2 expresses some aspects of this and how issues of gender, ethnicity, social class, disability and sexual orientation could be integral to education.

Clearly a change in pedagogy plays a significant part in effecting changes in students' isms/phobias. Science lessons, with practical work and discussions of issues in science and how ideas affect them (University of York Science Education Group and Nuffield Curriculum Centre 2006), is an ideal place to engage students in dialogue and to raise their emotional literacy and awareness of social justice. Because science is seen as central to solving many of the world's problems, developing some understanding of scientific concepts is required for engaging in these debates. Hence teachers are able to capitalize on this inherent interest in science to engage students to develop a critical scientific literacy (Sjøberg and Egil 1997; Hodson 1998; Sears and Sorensen 2000). With all the opportunities for enhancing students' emotional and

**Table 13.2**

| Schools now tend to be: | Enabling educator:<br>If emotional literacy were a key aim: |
|---|---|
| Based on cognition | Based on emotions and cognition |
| Largely based on achievement measured, a 'thing' achieved | A process variable with context. Never achieved |
| Individualistic | Individual in group |
| Often reductionist; based on knowledge and skills | Holistic |
| Equal opportunities separate from learning | Equal opportunities and social justice central to developing emotional literacy |
| 'Space/time' filled up with things to do | Space/time to reflect |
| Little space for students to think about themselves | Space where they as a person matter |
| Unconscious not considered | Unconscious plays a part |
| Single causes and effects | Multiple causes and effects |
| Most learning takes place in school | Many experiences undergone that form the basis of self- and emotional development take place outside of school and so school must take account of that |
| Emotional literacy development for better cognitive success; attendance and behaviour | Emotional literacy vital in its own terms to help people have more fulfilling sexual and non-sexual relationships, companionship, friendship and emotional resilience |

scientific literacy science teachers are ideally placed for helping in developing education that can be transformative. Jenkins (2007) argues:

> School science education thus faces a number of challenges. It needs to reflect important philosophical, conceptual, and methodological differences between at least the basic sciences and to develop pedagogical strategies that present scientific inquiry in terms that accommodate the creative and imaginative as well as the logical. It must provide an opportunity for students to engage with a range of personal, social,

economic, or political issues that stem from the role the sciences have come to play in society and to understand the uncertainties and ignorance associated with their role in the realm of practical action. (p. 275)

It is beyond the scope of this chapter to detail how this can be done in the classroom, but the students are placed and work in collaborative activities in, as far as possible, mixed groups. Here are some principles to help their social and emotional development: students can communicate with each other in a safe environment, think and reflect on the social processes and feelings that occur in collaborative learning. Then they should be able to communicate (through writing and talking) what the interactions meant to them and compare this with what other people thought had gone on (understand that there are different perceptions of the same discourse). Hence they will have some evidence about different feelings and can discuss their perceptions so that they come to understand their own and each other's emotional and cognitive viewpoints. In this way they can learn about each other and empathize with each other. This is both individually and across groups. The students can become aware of power differences across and within groups. They can also learn to understand the subject and become aware that it involves social interactions and is not just a solitary pursuit (Matthews 2006).

## Environmental concerns

Similarly, science education can play a part in promoting a sense of social citizenship (Maiteny and Wade 1999; Cross and Fensham 2000; Lawton *et al.* 2000; Ratcliffe and Grace 2003). Ratcliffe and Grace (2003) argue that for science education to serve wider purposes including citizenship, teachers also need to change their pedagogy in similar ways to those indicated above, namely to be confident about their understanding of the nature of science, be a facilitator, open and dialogic, develop reasoning skills and to find authentic activities (p. 159). They put forward different forms of pedagogy and propose that the knowledge and understanding of the teacher should include understanding of aspects such as the nature of citizenship, ethical implications and about sustainable development.

# Conclusion

We have indicated that science is a social and cultural construction that is world related. We would argue for models of school science that acknowledge and promote critical scientific literacy. A form of literacy that contributes to the development of skills, knowledge and attitudes in learners that enables them individually and collectively to play an active part in reducing gross inequalities and in creating the conditions for promoting social justice and greater environmental sustainability. A prescriptive curriculum that sees science in schools as the preparation of future professional scientists has the inevitable consequence of disenfranchising the majority at the expense of a small minority. It fails to acknowledge the social and emotional engagement of learners with learning and creates exclusionary discourses and practices that leave science to 'experts' and officials. This can lead to a democratic deficit that can have unintended consequences for society at large and for the planet as a whole.

For science educators to tackle inequalities we have argued that approaches to emotional literacy in the classroom can act as an underlying and unifying theme to help combat inequalities; emotional literacy can be the engine of equity (Matthews 2005). One important aspect of classroom practice is that it is enquiry based, and constructivist approaches to learning explored. The approaches described above are also of direct importance for other subject areas wishing to tackle equity issues. It is an exciting time for science educators and students.

## Note

[1] For arguments against the whole notion of fixed ability, see Hart *et al.* (2004); for Marxist responses to the Learning Without Limits (LWL) project, see Cole 2008a; 2008b; Yarker 2008.

## References

Bennett, J. (2003), *Teaching and Learning Science: A guide to recent research and its applications*. London: Continuum.

BlackInventor (n.d.), 'Lewis Latimer'. Available at http://www.blackinventor.com/pages/lewislatimer.html (accessed June 2008).

Brookes, J. and Brookes, M. (1993), *In Search of Understanding: The case for constructivist classrooms*. Alexandria, VA, USA: Association for Supervision and Curriculum Development.

CCEA (Council for the Curriculum, Examinations and Assessment) (2007), *Active Learning and Teaching Methods for Key Stage 3*. Belfast: PMB Publications. Available at http://www.nicurriculum.org.uk/docs/key_stage_3/ALTM-KS3.pdf. (accessed July 2009).

Cole, M. (1996), *Cultural Psychology. A Once and Future Discipline*. Cambridge, MA: Harvard University Press.

— (2008a), '*Learning without Limits*: a Marxist assessment'. *Policy Futures in Education*, 6, (4), 453–63. Available at http://www.wwwords.co.uk/pfie/content/pdfs/6/issue 6_4.asp (accessed 27 February 2008).

—(2008b), 'Reply to Yarker'. *Policy Futures in Education*, 6, (4), 468–9. Available at http://www.wwwords.co.uk/pdf/validate.asp?j = pfie&vol = 6&issue = 4&year = 2008& article = 8_Yarker_PFIE_6_4_web (accessed 21 December 2008).

Cooley, M. (1987), *Architect or Bee? The Human Price of Technology*. London: Hogarth Press.

Cross, R. and Fensham, P. (eds) (2000), *Science and the Citizen*. Victoria, Melbourne, Australia: Arena.

Davies, S. (1996), *Big Brother: Britain's web of Surveillance and the New Technological Order*. London: Pan.

DfES (2007), *Social and Emotional Aspects of Learning (SEAL) for SECONDARY schools*. Available at http://nationalstrategies.standards.dcsf.gov.uk/secondary: Department for Education and Skills (DfES) (accessed July 2009).

Driver, R. (1983), *The Pupil as Scientist*. Milton Keynes: Open University Press.

Epic (2005). *Children and RFID Systems*. Available at http://www.epic.org/privacy/rfid/children.html Electronic Privacy Information Center (accessed March 2005).

Fox-Keller, E. (1985), *Reflections on Gender and Science*. London: Yale University Press.

Gill, D. and Levidow, L. (eds) (1987), *Anti-Racist Science Teaching*. London: Free Association Books.

Gillborn, D. and Mirza, H. S. (2002), quoted in J. Clay and R. George, 'Equality and Diversity', in V. Ellis, (ed.) (2007), *Learning and Teaching in Secondary Schools* (3rd edition). Exeter: Learning Matters.

Goleman, D. (1996), *Emotional Intelligence: Why It Can Matter More than IQ*. London: Bloomsbury.

Harrison, L. and Matthews, B. (1998), 'Are we treating science and scientists fairly?' *Primary Science*, 51, 22–25.

Hart, S., Dixon, A., Drummond, M. J. and McIntyre, D. (2004), *Learning Without Limits*. Maidenhead: Open University Press.

Henry, A. and Williams, M. (1999), *Black Scientists and Inventors. Book 1*. London: BIS Publications.

Hodson, D. (1998), *Teaching and Learning Science: Towards a Personalised Approach*. Buckingham: Open University Press.

Jenkins, E. (2007), 'School science: a questionable construct?' *Journal of Curriculum Studies*, 39, (3), 265–82.

Kelly, P. (2003), 'Growing up a risky business? Risks, surveillance and the institutionalized mistrust of youth'. *Journal of Youth Studies*, 6, (2), 165–80.

Lawton, D., Cairns, J. and Gardner, R. (eds) (2000), *Education for Citizenship*. London: Continuum.

Lyon, D. (ed.) (2002), *Surveillance as Social Sorting: Privacy, Risk and Automated Discrimination*. London: Routledge.

Maiteny, P. and Wade, R. (1999), 'Citizenship education', in S. Bigger and E. Brown (eds), *Spiritual, Moral, Social and Cultrual Education: Exploring Values in the Curriculum*. London: David Fulton, 36–48.

Matthews, B. (1992), 'Towards an understanding of the social issues in information technology: concerning computers, intelligence and education'. *Journal of Information Technology for Teacher Education*, 1, (2), 201–13.

Matthews, B. (1996), 'The politics of information technology: some implications for schools'. *Education 3 to 13*, 24, (2), 42–4.

Matthews, B. (2005), 'Emotional literacy as the engine of equity'. *Emotional Literacy Update*, 3, (21), 10–11.

— (2006), *Engaging Education: Developing Emotional Literacy, Equity and Co-education.* Buckingham: McGraw-Hill and Open University Press.

— and Davies, D. (1999), 'Changing children's images of scientists: can teachers make a difference?' *School Science Review*, 80, (293), 79–85.

—, Kilbey, T., Doneghan, C. and Harrison, S. (2002), 'Improving attitudes to science and citizenship through developing emotional literacy'. *School Science Review*, 84, (307), 103–14.

— and Sweeney, J. (1997), 'Collaboration in the science classroom to tackle racism and sexism'. *Multi-cultural Teaching*, 15, (3), 33–6.

Morrison, L. and Matthews, B. (2006), 'How pupils can be helped to develop socially and emotionally in science lessons'. *Pastoral Care in Education*, 24, (1), 10–19.

NHM (2008) *Slavery and Science.* Available at http://www.nhm.ac.uk/ (rest in press) (accessed June 2009).

Norris, C. and Armstrong, G. (1999), *The Maximum Surveillance Society. The Rise of CCTV.* Oxford: Berg.

Peissi, W. (2003), 'Surveillance and security: a dodgy relationship'. *Journal of Contingencies and Crisis Management*, 11, (1), 19–24.

QCA (nd), 'Abu Ali al-Hasan Ibn al-Haytham and optics'. Available at http://www.qca.org.uk/qca_7930.aspx (accessed June 2008).

QCA (2007), *A Framework of Personal, Learning and Thinking Skills.* Available at http://curriculum.qca.org.uk/uploads/PLTS_framework_tcm6-1811.pdf?return=http%3A//curriculum.qca.org.uk/skills/plts/index.aspx%3Freturn%3Dhttp%253A//curriculum.qca.org.uk/skills/index.aspx (accessed March 2009).

Queen's University (nd), *Multiculturalism in Science*, Available at http://educ.queensu.ca/~science/main/profdev/mcpdng02.html. (accessed June 2009).

Ratcliffe, M. and Grace, M. (2003), *Science Education For Citizenshi: Teaching Socio-Scientific Issues.* Maidenhead: Open University Press and McGraw-Hill.

Reiss, M. J. (1993), *Science Education for a Pluralist Society.* Buckingham: Open University Press.

Scott, P. (1987), *A Constructivist View of Teaching and Learning in Science (Children's Learning in Science Project).* Leeds: Centre for Studies in Science and Mathematics Education, University of Leeds, Leeds, LS2 9JT.

Sears, J. and Sorensen, P. (eds) (2000), *Issues in Science Teaching.* London: Routledge/Falmer.

Sjøberg, S. and Egil, K. (eds) (1997), *Science, Technology and Citizenship: The Public Understanding of Science and Technology in Science Education and Research Policy.* Oslo: (NIFU) Norsk Institutt for Studier av Forskning og Utdanning.

Taylor, C. (1994), 'The politics of recognition', in A. Gutman (ed.), *Multiculturalism: Examining the Politics of Recognition.* Princeton, NJ: Princeton University Press, 25–74.

Thorp, S. (ed.) (1991), *Race, Equality and Science Teaching. An Active INSET Manual for Teachers and Educators.* Hatfield, Herts: ASE (Association for Science Education).

Thorp, S., Pratap, D. and Edwards, C. (eds) (1994), *Race, Equality and Science Teaching A Handbook for Teachers and Educators.* Hatfield, Herts: ASE (Association for Science Education).

University of York Science Education Group and Nuffield Curriculum Centre (2006), *Twenty-First Century Science*. Oxford: Oxford University Press.

Vygotsky, L. S. (1978) *Mind in Society: The Development of Higher Psychological Processes* (eds M. Cole, V. John-Steiner, S. Scribner and E. Souberman). Cambridge, MA: Harvard University Press.

Wellcome Trust (2006), 'Primary horizons: starting out in science'. London: Wellcome Trust

Yarker, P. (2008), '*Learning Without Limits* – a Marxist assessment: a response to Mike Cole' *Policy Futures in Education*, 6 (4), 464–468.

Chapter 14

# Personal, Social and Health Education

Gillian Hilton

## Abstract

This chapter discusses the role of Personal, Social and Health Education (PSHE) Economic Wellbeing and Financial Capability at KS3 and KS4 in promoting equality. It is clear that this aim is severely hampered by the uncertain nature of PSHE provision within secondary schools and the chapter argues for the subject to be made statutory in the curriculum, with specifically trained subject teachers provided to work in schools in order to fulfil the aims and objectives of PSHE laid out by QCA and reported on by Ofsted. The controversy of the need to provide compulsory Sex and Relationships Education (SRE) partly within PSHE is also discussed as this is an area of great concern for the health and prospects of young people. PSHE can do a great deal to help with disaffection particularly in problem areas such as teen pregnancy and drug and alcohol addiction, which blight the lives of many young people. However, the chapter argues that until the subject is taught by enthusiastic, knowledgeable, well-trained teachers, it will not be able to achieve its stated aims. There is great potential here for the promotion of equality which at present is not being realized. This chapter presents an analysis of the rise and effects of the subject in the curriculum and its ability to promote equality. This is an area of education that has for many years been on the fringe of the curriculum in many schools and due to its non-statutory status is still considered by some as the 'Cinderella' of the curriculum.

The history of PSHE is linked to the public schools' concept of pastoral care: developing and caring for the whole child, not just academic output. Sporting prowess, honesty, loyalty and strength of character were prized. The house system was eventually perceived as a way of providing emotional support to pupils, who were far from home. This concept of pastoral care was adopted by the state system including the notion of 'houses' to which pupils were loyal and where competition was fostered. In state schools the need for PSHE, delivered in a formal manner for some children, came with the advent of the large comprehensives, many of which mirrored the house system of public schools. Taught sessions on personal and social or health education on an ad hoc basis arose during the 1960s, 1970s and 1980s. There was no formal set curriculum and many schools did not provide such lessons, seeing this area of education as the family's concern. At the same time there was increasing discussion about the need for sex education and whether schools should be involved in this area. Government intervention in 1986 resulted in the issuing of the Circular 4/86, which put sex education formally on the agenda but not as a compulsory subject. In 1988 the National Curriculum was introduced but PSHE did not feature among the listed subjects. At the same time Home Economics, which had often covered many topics related to relationships, health and personal finance, was subsumed into design and technology, removing from the curriculum the wider concepts of health, healthy eating, parenting and budgeting, part of good Home Economics programmes.

In 1990, however, the Conservative government realized that the National Curriculum was missing essential wider concepts and so the cross-curricular themes were introduced. These were to permeate all the subject areas and included health education and economic and industrial understanding. However, though the Brunarian curriculum model used for the health education document was considered a good one by many teachers, the cross-curricular themes sank without trace beneath the over-burdened, content heavy, statutory curriculum subjects. By the time Dearing reviewed the curriculum for 1994 the themes had virtually disappeared. Added to this were the comments made by the then Chief Inspector of Ofsted (established in 1992) Chris Woodhead, that the notion of pastoral care and PSHE was anti-academic and unnecessary; all that was required was good subject teaching.

During discussions for the rewrite of the National Curriculum in the late 1990s the Labour government set up a committee, Preparation for Adult Life (PAL), which pressed for the introduction of PSHE as an additional subject in the new curriculum. As a result the revised curriculum issued in 1999 saw PSHE included as a non-statutory subject for all Key Stages. PSHE is the 'taught, planned programme of teaching and learning that promotes pupils' personal and social development and their health and well being' (QCA 2005a, p. 1).

Careers education was seen as an essential part of PSHE and was included in the original curriculum plan. However, specific areas have, over the past years, received closer attention with reports and guidance issued by QCA and Ofsted. These, which include Sex and Relationships Education (DfEE 2000; Ofsted 2002), drugs education (QCA 2003), mental health (Ofsted 2005a), financial capability (QCA 2005a) and parenting education (Ofsted 2007), have been promoted within the PSHE curriculum and have received comment and reports from Ofsted and QCA over the past few years. The framework for PSHE, which is applicable to all Key Stages, is defined in three strands which relate closely to each other, namely

1. developing confidence and responsibility and making the most of their abilities
2. developing a healthy lifestyle
3. developing good relationships and respecting the differences between people. (QCA 2005a, p. 1)

In 2007 the rewrite of the secondary curriculum resulted in the production of two separate sections in PSHE, namely personal well-being, linked to the outcomes of *Every Child Matters*, and economic well-being and financial capability. These two areas have similar aims but different key concepts and processes.

The increase in subject area content came at the same time as citizenship as a subject (non-statutory at primary, statutory at secondary level) was being introduced, resulting (Ofsted 2005b) in some teaching time previously allotted to PSHE allocated to citizenship, thus reducing the teaching time available. Though many of the subject topics in the two areas are similar, the approach to them needs to be distinct. PSHE is concerned with the social and personal development of individuals and their health and well-being; citizenship is about becoming active citizens and considering issues that affect society in general: 'PSHE is concerned at a micro-level with qualities, attitudes, knowledge and understanding, competencies and skills in relation to oneself and others' (Griffiths and Jones 2004).

Ofsted (2005b) has demanded that PSHE must have planned, explicit delivery and not just be added to work in other subjects areas, though opportunities can be provided in assemblies, tutorial programmes, work experience, special projects, set-aside days and subject areas as an addition, and QCA (2005a) supports this approach.

PSHE underpins and can contribute to many of the wider areas related to the development of the individual and so, with the third point in the QCA (*ibid.*) framework cited above, help to promote equality and understanding. In article 12, The United Nations *Convention on the Rights of the Child* (1989) provides schools with the legal support to encourage children to express views and make decisions, which is at the heart of PSHE intentions. This can also be the springboard for involving all children in consultations on the content and process of PSHE in the school. This is closely supported by the Department for Children, Schools and Families (DCSF) and Ofsted, who gave this as a reason for PSHE being non-statutory in the National Curriculum. However, it is by no means common practice in many schools.

The National Healthy School Standard (NHSS) was launched in October 1999 (DfEE/DoH 1999). The concept of health here is a wide one and QCA believe it should support the PSHE framework and enable schools to become healthier places (QCA 2000). The government wants all schools to aim to meet the targets set by the standards for the four themes of the NHSS (healthy eating, physical activity, emotional health and well-being) through a whole-school approach. PSHE can contribute to all these areas. Ostensibly therefore PSHE can help in a small way to reverse the disadvantages of a deprived upbringing.

The Children Act (2004) requires all schools to contribute to the five national outcomes for children and good PSHE cover can provide a sound base for these, namely being healthy, staying safe, making a positive contribution, enjoying and achieving and economic well-being. PSHE therefore has a big part to play in the education of students, not only by making a contribution to their all-round development, but also by increasing self-esteem and self-knowledge and empowering students to make well-informed decisions about life choices. Good personal development and a feeling of well-being can have a positive impact on academic achievement. The *Every Child Matters* (DfES 2003) agenda, which formed a basis for the Act, points to the importance of PSHE in achieving the desired outcomes for children through developing good relationships, learning how to resolve conflict, taking responsibility and supporting others. This echoes the aims of the Education Act (2002), which calls for the involvement of children in decisions made about them.

The concept of inclusion underpins current government policy and PSHE is seen as potentially a major contributor to this area. QCA (2005a) include a section on inclusion and teaching about diversity in PSHE. The guidance given points out that teachers must consider adjusting the material provided for PSHE lessons to meet the needs of students with learning difficulties 'Every effort should be made to maintain entitlement and equality of opportunity' (*ibid.*, p. 25). It adds a further section on the requirement to teach about diversity, viewing difference in a positive light and taking into consideration students with English as an Additional Language. Blake and Plant (2005, p. 1) agree that PSHE can be a good vehicle for helping students develop the requisite social and emotional qualities that 'can be nurtured to promote inclusion and reduce inequalities'. They firmly believe that PSHE can be highly significant in aiding the development of a sense of worth in vulnerable children. DfES (2004), Blake and Plant (2005) and Ofsted (2007) all agree that student participation in the planning of lessons and school policies is a positive step towards promoting equality, and the whole ethos of PSHE is based on consultation, for example with parents, local health groups, faith groups and the police, thus ensuring a balanced approach. Many areas of the PSHE curriculum address highly relevant issues to students such as bullying and drug use, popular topics in many schools. Lesson provision can be accommodated to meet varying needs such as different learning styles and areas that need particular consideration due to local circumstances, such as high rates of drug abuse or safety issues. Lesson delivery too can be adjusted in Sex and Relationships Education (SRE) to meet the needs of some faith groups for separate-sex teaching. The whole culture of PSHE needs to be taught in a safe environment where students and teachers feel comfortable and able to value and respect differences of opinion about a wide range to topics.

Some faith groups dislike the present SRE curriculum as it can appear to promote safe sex and assume that all people outside of marriage are sexually active, a conclusion offensive to some groups. This can be used as a reason for withdrawing students from SRE in PSHE. However, this also removes learners from important information about local health services, sexually transmitted infections (STIs) and discussions about the need for equality in sexual relationships that lies at the heart of good SRE teaching. It is essential therefore that a wide variety of opinions about sexual relationships and behaviour are addressed in class, not just the safe sex message. Students need to discuss ideas such as the belief that sex is for marriage and should not be for casual relationships, and the reasons why some groups believe that this is the correct approach. It is essential that all students realize that others may have different opinions from themselves and that they learn to respect those opinions. In order to help schools with this the government's Healthy Schools have appointed an Asian SRE specialist to aid in producing culturally acceptable, inclusive approaches to SRE (Healthy Schools 2007). As in all lessons, resources need to be checked for bias and reflect the multicultural nature of our society. The DFEE (2000) guidance is rather vague in this respect as they merely mention that unsuitable resources should not be used, leaving this decision to the discretion of teachers.

Education about disability is not a major element of the PSHE curriculum, but the whole ethos of the subject should be underpinned by the belief that all individuals should be respected and valued for their contributions to society; part of the QCA PSHE curriculum guidance points to the need for students to be taught to respect the differences between people (QCA 1999). This is where support from local organizations and even contributions from individual pupils can be used to promote better understanding and challenge prejudice. For example, it is possible to give students the opportunity to experience what it is to have partial sight by the use of aids provided by charities for the blind. This type of practical experience is highly valuable, promoting better empathy and challenging prejudice. Using people with disabilities to discuss with students how their lives are affected, in particular by their acceptance or non-acceptance in society, will encourage the communication and interpersonal skills which are at the heart of PSHE learning. If this is impossible, then good research by students followed by role-play can be used to highlight how discrimination affects the lives of people with disability, especially those whose disabilities are hidden or whose physical appearance is affected. Information from the media and portrayals of disabled people on television or on film can also be a valuable starting point for discussion. Asking students to record how often the disabled are present in popular soap operas or seen presenting programmes on television can produce a lively discussion and the hidden nature of disability and subsequent discrimination debated.

With regard to gender equality it is important for teachers of PSHE to accept that students arrive in school with strong beliefs and value systems related to gender, masculine and feminine behaviour and accepted roles. These beliefs are affected by their upbringing, cultural mores and the influences of media portrayals of men and women. PSHE provides a safe place in which to question and challenge these givens, and aspects of gender expectation and cultural differences can be discussed in an open, respectful environment. Gendered perceptions will influence students' responses to aspects of PSHE such as adolescence and relationships and these perceptions will be altered by a student locating him/herself as straight or gay. The relationship between biological sex and socially learned gender needs to be addressed. Teachers have to accept that in certain areas girls are more prepared and better informed than boys, who may feel their masculinity threatened by discussions on feelings. By sensitive handling stereotypes and accepted prejudices about gender expectation and behaviour can be addressed and students made more aware of the inequalities in society, such as the differences in earnings between men and women. The whole culture of PSHE needs to be one that encourages students and teachers to feel comfortable and able to value and respect differences of opinion about a wide range of topics. However, there can be problems with a too accommodating approach to some issues; for example, gender equality laws in this country need to be stressed and the rights of women to choose their own partners and to have equal access to education and training as men. The practice of female circumcision should be covered in SRE and students informed that in this country it is against the law.

The consideration of 'race' and promotion of 'race' equality is entwined in PSHE with the development of the individual and his or her respect for individual differences. At its best PSHE provides a platform for the simulation of social processes which students may meet elsewhere in society, enabling them to challenge prejudice. Role-play, if well managed, can be a valuable tool to allow students from a variety of backgrounds to attempt to put themselves into lives experienced by others and be able to discuss their feelings when on the receiving end of others' prejudices. Individual work can enable students to reflect on their own attitudes to others and group work can examine society's responses to and prejudices about 'race', particularly stereotypes favoured by media. Most young people now see Britain as a multicultural society and are positive about that fact, but it is important for them to understand that the way people perceive themselves and are perceived by others with regard to their ethnicity can have a major impact on their lives.

However, it is social class and the inequalities that it brings that has more impact than ethnicity or gender on the future lives of students (Gillborn and Mirza 2000). The main element here is the inequality of income, which results in children being raised in poverty. Much of this is related to low educational qualifications accompanied by a lack of self-belief together with exploitation by employers paying low wages. PSHE in its concentration on the individual can be used as a way of raising self-esteem and also promoting ambition and the wish to achieve. Careers education here has a part to play in challenging stereotypes of job suitability, educational attainment and university graduation and informing students of their rights as workers, though this can also be dealt with in citizenship education. It is essential that students are offered a wide view of possible routes to success in later life, including entrepreneurship, and shown that a good education is essential to such success. PSHE has to help students address media portrayals of success such as being 'discovered' or becoming 'a celebrity', the strongly held beliefs of many adolescents, as a route out of a deprived social situation, and the stereotyped expectations on achievement related to social class. The lack of social mobility now available to individuals can make a good discussion point for PSHE lessons and link well to citizenship.

The controversy surrounding the teaching of SRE is a relevant area in which to consider the ability of PSHE to promote equality. SRE is taught in schools in the current context of worries over risk-taking behaviours in young people, namely unsafe sex leading to sexually transmitted infections, alcohol abuse and as mentioned above teen pregnancy. Worryingly, Ofsted (2002; 2005a; 2005b; Hilton 2003; Evans and Evans 2007) all point to the lack of expertise and specific training of many teachers whose responsibility it is to teach this area. Schools must make and keep up-to-date policies on SRE and the school governors and heads are responsible for deciding on the curriculum and when it will be taught within the spirit of the DfEE (2000) guidelines. They have to inform parents as to time and content of the lessons and that they can withdraw their children from SRE in PSHE lessons. The whole is underpinned by the Learning and Skills Act (2002), which ensures that school must present SRE with due consideration to the importance of marriage and family life. This presents problems for teachers, as the concept of family varies widely and now many children do not live in the nuclear family. Originally, stable relationships had been added to this part of the guidance, but was removed as a result of parliamentary objections (Monk 2001). The question then arises, if schools have such control over SRE and parents allowed to withdraw children from the aspects of SRE in PSHE, can then equality of access to requisite information and discussion of rights and responsibilities be available to all children? Problems too arise with complaints of students that material is too oriented towards the needs of girls, and boys feel that this area of the curriculum has little to offer them.

Further controversy in this area has existed over the 'promotion of homosexuality', forbidden by Acts in the 1980s directed towards Local Authorities. Fear among teachers resulted in consideration of sexual orientation having no place in the curriculum in most schools and the challenging of homophobic behaviour which should be at the heart of PSHE not occurring. Despite therefore the more recent DfEE (2000, p. 13) advice for teachers to 'deal honestly and sensitively with sexual orientation, answer appropriate questions and offer support', it also warns teachers that there should be 'no direct promotion of sexual orientation'. Adams *et al.* (2004) report inconsistencies in approaching this topic and that sexual orientation was mentioned in only two-thirds of equal opportunity polices in the 13 schools surveyed, but was not mentioned specifically in anti-bullying polices in the same schools. This fudge was mirrored in Ofsted's (2007) report that schools have not received sufficient help with teaching about sexuality and that homophobic behaviour among pupils still goes unchallenged as do sexist attitudes. Indeed, Stonewall's *School Report: The Experiences of Young Gay People in Britain's Schools* describes homophobic bullying as being 'almost endemic' in Britain's schools and that homophobic insults are commonplace (Hunt and Jensen, nd, p. 2). All these issues point to the lack of emphasis on relationships education and the need to be tolerant of others' beliefs, sexual orientation, and ideas which good PSHE can provide. Research by the UK Youth Parliament showed that more than half of the 20,000 young people questioned claimed that their SRE in school was inadequate and that relationships education was severely neglected, most aged over 17 years claiming that they had received no instruction in this area (UK Youth Parliament, nd).

One of the most troublesome areas is assessment in PSHE where Ofsted (2002; 2005b) have reported subject knowledge being covered, but little emphasis made on bringing changes to attitudes and behaviours. This is to some extent ironic and teachers' obsession with content knowledge can be founded in the content-heavy NC, where knowledge acquisition and retention have become paramount. PSHE assessment here is to some extent challenging the statutory testing system. The problem is compounded by the lack of status of PSHE. Students see it as unimportant as it is not a GCSE subject which is assessed throughout Key Stages 3–4 as is the other new subject of citizenship. The attitude of some schools to PSHE, with regard to the time allotted and the teachers involved, demonstrates to students its apparent lack of importance in the curriculum. Lessons taken by form tutors with little assessment in place, students show little interest in the work and little progress is made (Ofsted 2005b), seriously undermining the ability of PSHE to promote equality.

Can PSHE therefore promote equality? Possibly, but only if it is adapted to the needs of students, available to all, taught by well-trained enthusiastic teachers and has a high profile in the statutory school curriculum. Sadly, at present, these requirements are not totally fulfilled and therefore equality does not exist. Ofsted, in various PSHE subject reports, have acknowledged that PSHE teaching is not consistent across the sector and some schools are still not delivering PSHE through taught lessons set aside weekly for the purpose. Ofsted point out that this position is 'untenable' (Ofsted 2005b, p. 1; 2007).

PSHE deals with many controversial areas thereby giving students the possibility to make reasoned informed choices about their behaviour. This is not an easy task for teachers as issues such as drugs and sex education present constant challenges, but in the eyes of many, more problematic are the non-statutory status of the subject, the lack of specifically trained teachers and the rights of parents to withdraw children from parts of SRE as mentioned. This can lead to inequality of provision across the country. The question of the status of PSHE and the lack of statutory Programmes of Study have been causing concern since the introduction of the subject into the National Curriculum in the 1999 rewrite. Most vociferous has been the Independent Advisory Group on Teenage Pregnancy, whose yearly reports (IAG 2003; 2004) have constantly called for PSHE to become statutory, thus ensuring that all students will receive good comprehensive SRE. The government has been concerned for a considerable time about the high rates of teen pregnancy in this country, compared to those in Europe and the soaring rates of STIs in young people. Finally in 2006 IAG issued a discussion document calling strongly on the government to make PSHE and therefore SRE statutory in the NC. This was followed by a petition organized by the National Children's Bureau and supported by many other organizations and individuals to the DCSF, again reiterating the need to make PSHE statutory. Government response, however, was disappointing. Despite confirming the government's commitment to the teaching of PSHE in schools, the response was:

> Currently there are no plans to change the statutory status of PSHE. The government does not believe that making PSHE a foundation subject will automatically lead to improvements in teaching and learning. (Pm.gov.uk 2008)

The argument seems again to be resting on the need for flexibility in the curriculum but one must wonder if the real reason here is worry about the reactions of some right-wing parental pressure groups and from certain faith groups. This sits oddly with the Social and Emotional Aspects of Learning (SEAL) initiative begun in primary schools and now being introduced in the secondary sector (DfES 2005). PSHE is considered to play a strong part in SEAL yet Ofsted still comment that some schools are not delivering PSHE at all. PHSE has the potential to make a major contribution towards preparing children for adult life and developing work-related skills through careers education. However, though work placements are now mandatory and vocational routes post-14 are coming on stream, employers constantly complain about the lack of a workforce with the requisite skills of self-responsibility, teamworking and decision-making, all of which can be enhanced by a good PSHE programme. The IAG (2006) point to a review by the Teenage Pregnancy Unit, which demonstrated that strong PSHE in a school aids the reduction in teen pregnancy rates so wished for by the government. Teen pregnancy adversely affects young mothers in their future ability to study and work. The IAG report also points out that good PSHE aids schools to meet targets for 'race', equality and inclusion. Finally, in 2008 the government, responding to the report of the Sex and Relationships Education (SRE) Steering Group, agreed that PSHE should become statutory in the new secondary curriculum (DCSF 2008). However, the right of parents to withdraw children from SRE lessons in PSHE appears to be intact.

Achieving the outcomes for PSHE as stated by QCA (2005a) and thereby providing equal provision and promoting equality is additionally severely handicapped by the lack of properly trained subject teachers. In their advice to new secondary teachers NCB (nd, p. 2) state 'whatever your subject specialism you will almost certainly deliver personal social and health education in your teaching career'. Sadly, this is all too true, even though successive Ofsted reports have constantly affirmed that PSHE is far more successful when delivered by a specialist team. Where form tutors do the job, lessons are far less satisfactory and that schools recruit few teachers with a PSHE specialism (Ofsted 2005b). This is hardly surprising as there are few opportunities to train as a PSHE specialist during initial training. Evans and Evans (2007) undertook a study of the Graduate Teacher Training Registry website and discovered that no providers offer PSHE as a specialist subject. Hardly surprising therefore is Ofsted's repeated plea for specialist teachers. Many students in Initial Teacher Training (ITT) receive only a few hours' input on this subject, due to PSHE's non-statutory nature, as secondary teachers are trained in specific subject areas. Citizenship, introduced in 2000, immediately resulted in the Training and Development Agency (TDA) allotting training places for that subject in secondary ITT programmes. Not so for PSHE. Hardly surprising that Ofsted (2005b) reports that many newly qualified teachers (NQTs) and others in the school system lack confidence in delivering PSHE lessons because of poor training. In their standards for qualification to teach, the TDA assume that if Qualified Teacher Status (QTS) is reached then trainees have met the required standards related to aiding the personal development of students. This, however, does not cover the lack of subject knowledge in this area that newly qualified teachers bring to their first appointments. How many students, and parents, are aware that controversial issues such as drugs and SRE are taught to them by teachers with little specific training? This does still occur in some schools and certainly if a statutory NC subject is taught by poorly or untrained staff, parents generally complain. Hilton (2003) found that boys responding to questions about PSHE assumed that all teachers were specifically trained in the subject.

Government has responded to concerns expressed by many teachers and organizations about the lack of specific-subject specialists by introducing the Certification for the Teaching of PSHE to be undertaken by subject coordinators. However, the questions remain. Can the training of one coordinator in a school inform the form tutors, still so commonly used to teach this material? Will the students receiving input from a trained person not be better equipped in their social and emotional relationships than those who receive lessons from a disinterested form tutor forced into the role? Hilton (*ibid.*) found that boys hated embarrassed form tutors working in this area and considered that science and maths teachers did not have the right teaching skills to deal with PSHE through active teaching methods. These skills required to promote active learning, coupled with secure subject knowledge, must be provided for all students in order that an equal experience of PSHE learning occurs.

As a result of the lack of these specialist teachers many schools use outside resources and organizations to teach the more challenging areas of the PSHE curriculum. This is a practice encouraged by all the regulatory bodies, but results are mixed. Experts, such as the police working in drug prevention, school nurses or local health providers, may have subject knowledge, but may find teaching more of a challenge; particularly in classroom management. Bad behaviour in classrooms is often a challenge to many PSHE teachers, as the subjects addressed can cause embarrassment resulting in students not taking lessons seriously. However, in reality students dislike teachers who cannot control classes and Hilton (2007) found that boys resented teachers who could not keep PSHE classes in order as this ruined their own chance to express their opinions and to learn.

The learning outcomes for PSHE (Ofsted 2005b) clearly demonstrate that at the heart of the subject is the promotion of equality, respect and consideration for others. The subsections of developing confidence, careers education and guidance, developing healthy lifestyles, developing good relationships and respecting the differences between people, SRE and drugs education, if well taught in a supportive environment, where students can explore attitudes, beliefs and feelings, should allow them to develop into balanced tolerant adults, whose decisions are made after considering various opinions and a careful review of the facts. Financial education can aid in understanding how to control personal budgets, resist advertising and reject peer pressure to spend money which is not available. However, all this requires expert teaching and time neither of which is a 'given' in secondary schools at present.

Drawing on evidence from the Organisation for Economic Co-operation and Development (OECD) Programme for International Student Assessment (PISA) and the World Health Organization's (WHO) survey of Health Behaviour in School Age Children, Unicef has recently reported that children in the UK are at the bottom of a league table of 14 countries for well-being (bbc.co.uk 2007). Children here are tested more than in any other country, start school earlier and experience more family breakdown resulting in unhappiness, risk-taking, poor health, poor relationships and low expectations for the future. This is resulting in a too high number of students being disaffected in school and opting out of the established rules of society. Disaffection with regard to education among school students has been a concern of successive governments as it results in a high number of young people who are not in education, training or employment. The House of Commons Select Committee on Education has also examined this phenomenon and reported in 1998 (House of Commons 1998) a list of those young people most likely to be affected including those with special needs and those looked after by Local Authorities. Stone *et al.* (2000) produced a report for the Social Exclusion unit of DfEE about young people outside of education and employment. The main findings showed that dysfunctional families, personal and behavioural difficulties, lack of confidence and traumatic life experiences lay at the heart of anti-social and disaffected behaviour. Participants identified many barriers which prevented re-engagement including drug addiction, racism, prejudice, lack of support or information and debt. In all these areas good PSHE provision could make a difference to the lives of these young people. It is not a cure-all for the ills of youth, but it could and should make a valuable contribution to their transition to adulthood. PSHE cannot provide equality in family income, or control the time parents give to their children. However, other issues that worry children such as relationships with peers, families and teachers, finding work they enjoy, drug problems, making decisions about behaviour, preventing too early pregnancy and staying healthy, can all be addressed in a well-taught PSHE programme. PSHE cannot help the disaffected who are already playing truant or have been excluded from education, but it can help children to understand their own feelings and help them to express them in an acceptable manner. Time in PSHE lessons can be given to allow children to practise saying no to risk-taking behaviours, without losing face with peers, and self-esteem and self-confidence can be boosted. In this way PSHE can to some extent alleviate disaffection and students' rejection of school and society.

To be successful and to promote equality needs a holistic approach, as yet not apparent in the provision for PSHE in secondary schools. Strong leadership is required from headteachers and governors, through middle management to all staff. Only by this whole-school approach will PSHE be taken seriously by students. There needs to be a commitment to the aims of the subject from all those involved in teaching it. Without this what NCB (2006, pp. 12–13) describe as the 'four cornerstones for developing PSHE namely, Participation, Partnership, Policy Development and Practice (curriculum) Development and Professional Development' will not occur. The IAG (2006) firmly believes that there needs to be a closer link between the areas in the children agenda now at the forefront of government attention. Therefore, the strands of PSHE, citizenship, NHSS, SEAL, Religious Education and SRE must come together with the support of specialist services. A holistic approach needs to be undertaken if PSHE is to help promote equality for students, especially if it is to help those from deprived backgrounds or with special educational needs, those looked after by Local Authorities and the disaffected, who are rejecting education in ever-increasing numbers. Of course, PSHE cannot solve all of schools' and society's problems but it could do far more than at present is being achieved. To realize these aims then, PSHE, and SRE within it, must be statutory with a well-planned curriculum available to all, whatever their beliefs and culture. It must be provided in separate curriculum time up to the proposed new school leaving age and in colleges for students aged 16 to 19. Patchy provision for post-16s has been consistently noted. Teachers need to be properly trained in this as a specialist subject area and no teacher who does not want to work in this subject should be forced to do so. All teachers need to have awareness of the role that PSHE can play in developing students' lives while in school and when they reach adulthood. A whole-school approach needs to be developed to ensure that PSHE can promote better health and a greater sense of well-being in our young people (Rivers *et al.* 1999, in NCB 2006). If these problems are not addressed, PSHE provision will remain patchy and inadequate in many schools and the chance to improve the lives of young people will be lost to the detriment of society and their individual future lives.

# References

BBC (2007), 'UK is accused of failing children'. Available at http://newsvote.bbc.-co.uk/mapapps/pagetools/print/news.bbc.co.uk/1/hi/uk/6359363.stm (accessed 15 February 2008).

Blake. S. and Plant, S. (2005), *Addressing Inclusion and Inequalities through PSHE and Citizenship*, London, NCB.

Children Act (2004). London: The Stationery Office.

DCSF (2008), *Government Response to the Report by the Sex and Relationships Education (SRE) Review Steering Group*. London: DCSF.

DfEE (2000), *Sex and Relationships Education*. London: DfEE.

— /DoH (Department of Health) (1999), *National Healthy School Standard Guidance*. London: DfEE.

DfES (2003), *Every Child Matters*. London: DfES.

DFES (2004), *Working Together: Giving Pupils a Say*. London: DfES.

DfES (2005), *Excellence and Enjoyment: Social and Emotional Aspects of Learning*. London: DfES.

Evans, C. and Evans, B. (2007), 'More than just worksheets? A student of the confidence of Newly Qualified Teachers of English in teaching personal social and health education in secondary schools'. *Pastoral Care*, 25, (4), 42–50.

Gillborn, D. and Mirza, H. (2000), *Educational Inequality: Mapping Race, Class and Gender*. London: Ofsted.

Griffiths P. and Jones, M. (2004), 'Inspecting PSHE' training conference. London, Ofsted, March.

Healthy Schools (2007), 'Welcome to the Sex and Relationships Mini site'. Available at www.nottinghamhealthyschools,org,uk (accessed 25 February 2008).

Hilton, G. L. S. (2003), 'Listening to the boys: English boys' views on the desirable characteristics of teachers of sex education'. *Sex Education*, 3, (1), 33–45.

Hilton, G. L. S. (2007), 'Listening to the boys again: an exploration of what boys want to learn in sex education classes and how they want to be taught'. *Sex Education*, 7, (2), 161–74.

House of Commons (1998), *House of Commons Select Committee on Education and Employment: Fifth Report Session 1997-8 (1998)*. Available at www.publications.parliament.uk/pa/cm/199798/cmselect/cmeduemp/498v/ee052.htm (accessed 12 February 2003).

Hunt, R. and Jensen, J. (nd), *The School Report: The Experiences of Young Gay People in Britain's Schools*. London: Stonewall.

IAG (Independent Advisory Group on Teenage Pregnancy) (2003), Annual report 2002/3. London: Independent Advisory Group on Teenage Pregnancy.

— (2004), Annual report 2003/4. London: Independent Advisory Group on Teenage Pregnancy.

— (2006) *Time for Action: Personal Social and Health Education (PSHE) in Schools*. London: Independent Advisory Group on Teenage Pregnancy.

Monk, D. (2001), 'New guidance/old problems: recent developments in sex education'. *Journal of Social Welfare and Family Law*, 23, (3), 271–91.

NCB (National Children's Bureau) (nd), *Spotlight: Meeting the Standard in PSHE. Briefing 3. Teaching PSHE in Secondary Schools*. London: NCB.

— (National Children's Bureau) (2006), *A Whole-School Approach to Personal Social and Health Education and Citizenship*. London: NCB.

Ofsted (2002), *Sex and Relationships*. London, Ofsted.

— (2005a), *Healthy Minds: Promoting Emotional Health and Well-Being in School*. London: Ofsted.

— (2005b), *Personal Social and Health Education in Secondary Schools*. London: Ofsted.

— (2007) *Time for Change? Personal Social and Health Education*. London: Ofsted.

Pm.gov.uk (2008), PSHE campaign: petition reply. Available at http://www.pm.gov.uk/output/Page14157.asp (accessed 7 January 2008).

QCA (1999), *The National Curriculum: Handbook for Secondary Teachers in England*. London: QCA.

— (2000), *Personal Social and Health Education at Key Stages 3 and 4*. London: QCA.

— (2003), *Drug, Alcohol and Tobacco Education: Ccurriculum Guidance for Schools at Key Stages 1-4*. London: QCA.

— (2005a), *Sex and Relationships Education, Healthy Lifestyles and Financial Capability*. London: QCA.

— (2005b), *PSHE Key stages1-4: Guidance on Consulting, Recording and Reporting*. London: QCA.

Stone, V., Cotton, D. and Thomas, A. (2000), *Mapping Troubled Lives: Young People Not in Education, Employment or Training*. London: Social Exclusion Unit/DfEE.

Strange, V., Forrest, S., Oakley, A. and Stephenson, J. 'Sex and relationships education for 13–16 year olds: evidence from England'. *Sex Education*, 6, (1), 31–46.

UK Youth Parliament (nd), United Kingdom Youth Parliament report on sex and relationships education. Available at www.ukyouthparliament.org.uk/campaigns/ sre/AreYouGettingglt.pdf (accessed 21 February 2008).

United Nations (1989), *Convention on the Rights of the Child*. Adopted by the General Assembly of the UN, 20 November 1989. Geneva: United Nations Children's Fund.

Chapter 15

# Mathematics

Mark Boylan and Hilary Povey

## Abstract

In this chapter we discuss four current features of mathematics classrooms which militate against working for equality: setting and assessment practices; a closed and restricted curriculum; closed and restricted teaching and learning practices; and restrictions on teacher autonomy. We look at the policy contexts which have produced these features and explore how each of them works to produce inequity. We then consider some recent changes which have opened up possibilities for action for a more socially just mathematics and consider examples of practices that promote equality and can be enacted in today's mathematics classrooms.

## Introduction

One view of mathematics is that it is a neutral subject and that it involves the study of timeless and universal truths. On this view it might be difficult to see the relevance of issues of equality and social justice to the teaching and learning of mathematics in schools. However, we argue here that what is taught in mathematics classrooms, how it is taught and the way mathematics teaching and learning are understood, are all profoundly interconnected with promoting equality and social justice (Cotton 2001).

Beyond the classroom, mathematics continues to be central to industrial society and capitalist economics. Above all other subjects, it is used to rank students; and lack of success in mathematics is an important barrier to individuals joining high-status, high-earning occupations. The mathematically successful are more likely to hold positions of power in society. Mathematics is also essential to being able to 'read the world' (Gutstein 2006) and to act upon it. For example, increasingly, people's lives are affected, often negatively, by the consequences of a global finance system using ever more complex financial products based on complicated mathematical algorithms. Alternatively, to be able to participate fully in debates about global warming requires an understanding of risk.

Over the past decade the political and ideological nature of mathematics has become less hidden. The first National Curriculum and its successors prescribed the curriculum content and the testing regime and the linked league tables ensured that it was followed closely in schools (Dowling and Noss 1990). The early 1990s continued the trend that began in the 1980s of greater control by government over teachers, teaching and pupils. There was a 'back to basics' move to rebrand mathematics as numeracy leading to the introduction in primary schools of the National Numeracy Strategy that covered the whole of the mathematics National Curriculum (DfEE 2001). The National Numeracy Strategy – a complex set of contradictory elements that can support more progressive practices in terms of equality but which can also legitimize practices that are profoundly damaging (Boylan 2000) – was extended into secondary schools as the National Framework in 2001. The framework was focused not only on what was taught but also on how it was taught. The stated intention was to raise achievement; the framework documentation was issued by the 'Standards and Effectiveness Unit'. One justification for the 'standards agenda' was a concern for those socially disadvantaged – the talk was of social inclusion – but this was inextricably linked up with the market approach to education, to technocratic thinking and to the need to compete economically with other countries. Thus talk of social inclusion and raising standards hid the links between inequality, poverty and social injustice. Concern for international competitiveness has extended into comparisons between mathematics attainment in the UK and that in other countries, for example in the government-commissioned report on the future of mathematics, *Making Mathematics Count*, which linked international competitiveness to achievement in mathematics (Smith 2004). In addition, the Secretary of State for Education intervened in the internal school practices related to the organization of teaching: 'progressive teachers who refused to divide pupils according to ability were responsible for comprehensives' failure' (Blunkett, quoted by Judd 1996).

Overall, then, we believe that the outcome of various policy changes in mathematics education has been both to make mathematics less equitable and to make promoting equality more difficult. In this chapter we first discuss four key features of the current situation:

1. setting and assessment practices
2. a closed and restricted curriculum
3. closed and restricted teaching and learning practices
4. restrictions on teacher autonomy

More recently, however, there have been changes and possibilities, openings if you will, that are more hopeful for promoting equality in the mathematics classroom. The new mathematics National Curriculum, which was introduced for Year 7 in 2008–9 and which will roll forward with this cohort of pupils in future years, can be seen as a move away from a content-based curriculum, placing greater emphasis on process skills and offering some openings for progressive mathematics teachers in terms of content. Support for changes in curriculum, in the organization of learning and in classroom practices that could help to develop an equality agenda, have also come, perhaps surprisingly, from the Ofsted report into mathematics in schools (Ofsted 2008), a document full of contradictory tensions. At the same time there are signs of greater willingness to listen to teachers and to put the sort of teacher-led professional development that is essential to promoting more equitable practices at the heart of teacher professional development (Watson and De Geest 2008). In this context, we explore what a mathematics curriculum and a mathematics classroom that promoted equity might look like, what openings there are for a more democratic mathematics, and what might be some practical ways forward. We highlight, throughout the discussion, the connections with the key equality issues of gender, sexual orientation, ethnicity, disability, social class, capitalism and environmental concerns.

## Setting and Assessment Practices

In the UK the idea of 'ability', and labelling by ability, is central to the way learning mathematics is thought about. This 'feudal' (Tahta 1994, p. 25) way of thinking about mathematics education is the keystone of current school mathematics practices. It leads to setting, banding or streaming being almost universally adopted in organizing secondary mathematics classes. It is so deeply entrenched in thinking in mathematics education that it is almost impossible to believe that there are other ways of understanding mathematical development or of organizing learning. For a critique of the whole notion of 'fixed ability' and for arguments that learning should be perceived as without limits for all, see Hart *et al.* (2004) and Cole (2008).

We know that the practices of grouping by ability, and the frequency of formal and informal testing that goes with them, are damaging for learners. They damage learners' view of themselves and of what they and others can achieve (Reay and Wiliam 1999; Hardy and Cotton 2000; Solomon 2007), they damage their relationship to mathematics (Boaler 1997a; Bartholomew 2001; Nardi and Steward 2003) and they damage their relationships to other students (Boaler 1997b; Angier and Povey 1999; Boylan 2004).

This helps to reinforce the belief that mathematics is an elite and difficult subject and helps to maintain the role of success in the subject as a gateway to privilege. The use of setting in mathematics is one way in which children are prepared for a world organized by social class with people at the top and bottom of society. Setting itself contributes to reinforcing class positions. There is evidence that working-class students taught in sets in mathematics are more likely as adults to have socially lower status employment than similar students taught in mixed-ability groups (Boaler 2005). Significantly greater numbers of working-class students are placed in lower GCSE mathematics sets than might be expected if setting was done solely on the basis of Key Stage 3 test scores (Wiliam and Bartholomew 2004). This is consistent with many other studies that show that pupils from disadvantaged socio-economic groups and some ethnic groups are more likely to find themselves in lower sets (Ireson, Clark and Hallam 2002), and specifically in mathematics (Gillborn and Mirza 2000). Girls also are under-represented in top sets (Brown *et al.* 2008). The ranking and competition causes many students, often from socially disadvantaged backgrounds or with learning disabilities, to become alienated and disaffected with mathematics: 'the students are unwilling to engage in this hierarchical game' (Nardi and Steward 2003, p. 359). A more limited curriculum and unchallenging work are experienced in the lower sets (Boaler *et al.* 2000; Bartholomew 2001). In general, the few who like competition are male, middle class and confident, and are more likely to be found in the 'top set' (Boaler 1997a; Bartholomew 2001). Setting is inevitably and essentially inequitable. For example, the set in which they are placed has a significant effect on attainment: pupils who have similar levels of attainment but who are then placed in different sets can expect different outcomes (Ireson, Hallam, Hack, Clark and Plewis 2002; Wiliam and Bartholomew 2004). Despite this, all attainment teaching in mathematics has never really featured extensively in the mathematics classrooms in the UK. Even when mixed-attainment grouping was at its height, the proportion of secondary schools which used an ability criterion to group students in mathematics went from 'around 50% in the first year of secondary education to around 87% in the third year: *beyond this point some form of setting by ability was almost universal*' (Ruthven 1987, p. 244, italics added). In addition, 'setting by ability is far more prevalent in mathematics, particularly in the earlier years of the secondary school, than in other subjects' (*ibid.*). When David Blunkett was making the pronouncements about the need for setting quoted above, the past president of the Secondary Heads Association asked, 'Where has he got the idea that we are all ideologically bound to mixed-ability teaching? The idea went out years ago' (Judd 1996).

This is all the more curious when note is taken of strong research evidence that indicates that grouping by ability does not raise achievement in secondary schools generally (Slavin 1990) nor in mathematics in particular

(Boaler 1997b). Where studies have found evidence for some differences in attainment, these show that it is students who attain more highly at the end of primary school who get some limited benefit while students whose attainment is lower make greater progress in mixed-ability classes (Ireson, Hallam, Hack, Clark and Plewis 2002). Further, the benefits for the pupils in the higher sets may well to be due to a range of other factors such as the nature of the curriculum offered and classroom practices used, differences in teachers allocated to teach particular sets and so on (*ibid.*; Wiliam and Bartholomew 2004). International comparison supports this: 'every country that outperforms England in mathematics makes less use of ability grouping' (Wiliam and Bartholomew 2004, p. 291). And we know that a commitment to the idea that all students are capable of achieving more, especially those whose current attainment is lower, produces results (Ollerton and Watson 2001; Watson and De Gees 2005; Boaler 2006).

Setting at KS3 has increased in part through the use of narrowly banded national testing – the SATs – where the curriculum offered to pupils who were entered for the SATs levels 3 to 5 was different from that offered to pupils who were entered for the SATs levels 4 to 6 and so on. 'Teaching to the test' then prompts grouping pupils according to the test that they will take. This, plus the denial of the possibility of getting a grade C on the Foundation GCSE paper, has effectively meant that for an entire generation of school students their mathematical fate in terms of qualification was decided on entry to school in Year 7.

## A Closed and Restricted Curriculum

Over the past decade there has been a significant narrowing of the mathematics curriculum, militating against offering the opportunity for all students to engage with both authentic 'real-world' mathematics and challenging mathematics requiring deep thinking. This is the result of a prescribed curriculum, the associated testing regime, the focus on ranking of pupils, teachers and schools and the inspection regime that goes with this. What is to be taught has become what is to be tested and what can be tested easily are disconnected skills and fragmented content.

The inspection regime requires teachers, in every lesson, to demonstrate student progress, defined as visible increase in the sum of what they know. These advances are prescribed from the beginning of the lesson in terms of specific learning objectives – which must be achievable and measurable – indicating what all, most or some of the students will learn. So, in some school classrooms, the mathematics is broken down and pre-digested by the textbook writer, the producer of downloadable lesson plans, the creator of web-accessed interactive whiteboard screens or by the teacher into 'bite-sized' pieces. Because there is an emphasis on remembering 'how to' rather than on 'why', each small step is encountered separately and practised independently in parts so small that the isolated fragments mostly lose meaning for the learners. Such an approach is not, of course, universal and in other classrooms and in some departments mathematics is offered in a more connected way. Often it is those schools whose students are already socially disadvantaged that are under most pressure from the inspection regime, where teachers have the hardest struggle to find the space to offer a more connected and more meaningful curriculum. However, it is also in those schools that teachers are most likely to understand the need for a critical approach and are thus enabled to find such spaces.

These developments have taken place in the context of a view of mathematics that was already abstract and disconnected from people's lived experiences: 'this kind of thinking, to put it starkly, is destroying our planet and perpetuating domination and oppression' (Walkerdine 1994, p. 74). The policy context supported the traditional view of mathematical knowledge as impersonal and external and as stratified into hierarchies, a view which denies the validity of the perspectives and knowledge of those who are not part of the powerful groups in society (Freire 1972; Giroux 1983; Gutstein 2006). The mathematics experienced by students is thus without history or cultural context and, as far as it is seen to originate anywhere, is understood to come from ancient, European men.

Alongside all this, and associated with the change from mathematics to 'numeracy', it has been suggested that not all students need to access the mathematics curriculum as currently understood. For some, what is needed is functional mathematics, that is, the mathematics to function materially in contemporary capitalist societies. On this view, 'real maths' is only for the high attainer.

## Closed and Restricted Classroom Practices

The educational policy changes introduced in the past twenty years have all tended to reinforce the closed and restricted classroom practices associated with the traditional teaching of mathematics (Dowling and Noss 1990). Such teaching falls within the transmission model of learning where items of content or procedures are 'delivered' to the learner (Freire 1972; Davis *et al.* 1990), the teacher being the sole arbiter of what counts as knowledge (Cobb *et al.* 1992). This traditional style of mathematics teaching – authoritarian, teacher centred, test dominated – tends to encourage a competitive atmosphere in the mathematics classroom (Barnes and Coupland 1990) and these closed and restricted classroom practices are likely to disadvantage students who are not positioned in the structurally social dominant groupings, instead generating 'personal fatalism [and] servility' (Skovsmose 1994, p 189).

In addition, there has been a valorization of 'whole-class teaching', a teaching strategy which often legitimizes and encourages questioning practices that many students find alienating. It is the teacher who asks the question who is expected to know the answer rather than the learner who responds. Such exchanges do not support teachers and students working together to seek for new understandings and new and adapted knowledge. In addition, because replies are evaluated, such exchanges can be a cause for great anxiety (Anderson 2000). Much of the vocabulary used to describe such practices indicates a relationship where the teacher's role is not to support and guide but to catch out and to compete. Questions are part of teachers' 'weaponry', with questions being 'fired' at students who have been 'targeted' to respond (Boylan 2004). Unsurprisingly, many learners find such questioning practices damaging, even more so when they are given little time to think and reflect in order to keep up the 'pace' of the lesson. They are found to be particularly uncongenial to girls (*ibid.*) but also help to construct the mathematics classroom as a space which can support only limited ways of being a boy, particularly boys from the working class (Zevenbergen 2000).

The National Numeracy Framework suggests a three-part lesson of starter, main activity and plenary. This has been interpreted by many schools as if it were a statutory demand with no other lesson model being possible. It is a structure which is best suited to the 'delivery' of content or procedures, leaving no opportunity for more extended projects, such as some topics connected to society or cross-curricular work; nor does it support problem-solving or more creative approaches despite the fact that we know that many students are unwilling to pursue mathematics because of the absence of such ways of working (Boaler 2002). Although there is limited evidence from secondary schools due to a lack of research, the evidence from primary schools is that the classroom practices encouraged by the Numeracy Strategy including the three-part lesson structure may disadvantage the lowest-attaining pupils, with the gap between the attainment of the highest attaining and lowest attaining increasing (Brown *et al.* 2003). Such practices always disproportionately disadvantage those from the less powerful groups in society, those who are the focus of this book.

## Restrictions on Teacher Autonomy

The trend that started in the 1980s to restrict teacher autonomy has continued. By teacher autonomy we mean the ability of teachers to exercise control over what happens in their classrooms. We also mean the extent to which teachers internalize guidelines as directives and feel the need to seek *permission* for professional actions. There is commonly a gap between how teachers experience the restrictions on them and the actual restrictions. The framework is important in this regard in that it created a restriction on how teachers teach. The three-part lesson it advised was discussed above. Although there is a lack of research evidence, anecdotally, it appears that those schools following the government's approach most closely are those who teach the relatively poorer children. An example is the use of learning objectives at the start of lessons. In schools placed in 'special measures' or 'notice to improve' who are subject to frequent Ofsted visits, writing learning objectives on the board at the start of lessons is often mandatory. In schools in more affluent areas there is much less compulsion to do this.

The introduction of the framework also saw a significant change in the nature of teacher professional development. The training and professional development linked to it, like its forerunner in primary, was offered on a cascade model. Numeracy consultants were offered extensive training packages including scripts, overhead transparencies (OHTs) and videos to be delivered to teachers. It is significant that the first part of the decade saw the winding up of, arguably, the most substantial teacher-led professional and curriculum development project – the SMILE scheme. Initial Teacher Education (ITE) continues to be tightly controlled. While working with teachers on school-based collaborative professional development projects we have found that for some schools there are significant restrictions on the amount of time that departments can spend on issues connected specifically to teaching and learning mathematics. Instead, priority is demanded for whole-school responses to government policy initiatives. All this has undermined teacher controlled professional development.

What implications do restrictions on teacher autonomy have for promoting classroom equality? First, as stated above, these restrictions are not uniformly felt; greater restrictions are experienced by those teachers working in schools that are lower in the league tables. Greater restrictions on teachers mean greater restrictions on pupils. A recent Ofsted report identifies that teachers are 'teaching to the test' (Ofsted 2008). Although teaching to the test is not good for any pupils in terms of developing an understanding of mathematics, some groups of pupils can more easily 'make do' with this sort of teaching: this may be either those top-set pupils who are competitive and are already relatively privileged or, as suggested anecdotally, those significant numbers of middle-class pupils who benefit from private tuition, something poorer families cannot afford. We suggest that developing democratic classrooms is important to creating classrooms that support equality. This is more difficult when teachers feel they are not free to develop their own practice independently.

# Openings

We claimed above that recent policy shifts have opened up some possibilities for action, for developing equality, openings rather than restriction. So what might these be? We have criticized aspects of the National Framework. However, we recognize that the framework, and the discussion about teaching and learning practices it has generated, does offer other possibilities. As the Ofsted report *Understanding the Score* illustrates, it is not usually these more positive elements that are taken up in the classroom (*ibid.*). But, against a background of a dominant approach to teaching that emphasizes explanation and practice, some aspects of the strategy can lead to greater pupil engagement if enacted. For example, it encourages the use of 'non-routine problems that require [pupils] to think for themselves' (DfEE 2001, p. 6) and recommends that 'as far as possible, [teachers] present each topic as a whole, rather than as a fragmented progression of small steps' (*ibid.*, p. 46).

The founding of the National Centre for Excellence in Teaching Mathematics (NCETM) has seen a significant change in attitude towards supporting teacher-led professional development. A return to school-based curriculum and professional development can in itself help create the conditions for promoting equality in the classroom and the NCETM has supported a range of such programmes. In addition, a range of projects directly promote more equitable practice. For example, the Learning Mathematics Outside the Classroom project has included activities aimed at Afro-Caribbean and African heritage boys (NCETM 2008a) and teacher-led action research projects to promote girls' attainment have been supported (NCETM 2008b).

The 2008 National Curriculum (QCA 2008) represents a small step away from a content-focused to a process-focused curriculum which we argue below is important to social justice in the mathematics classroom. The introduction to the curriculum recognizes that mathematics is 'essential in public decision making' (p. 139). It also suggests the need for pupils to 'read the world' mathematically (Gutstein 2006), for example by being able to interpret mathematics presented in the media and through advertising (QCA 2008, p. 144). The importance of mathematics as a means of modelling and the consequent limits to models is stated. Examples given include modelling changes in society and the environment. The curriculum opportunities expected include applying mathematics beyond the school mathematics curriculum, both developing cross-curricular themes and looking at contexts outside of school. It also states that it is important to recognize 'the rich historical and cultural roots of mathematics' (*ibid.*, p. 41). For the first time the National Curriculum explicitly states that pupils 'should learn about problems from the past that led to the development of particular areas of mathematics' (*ibid.*, p. 42). This legitimizes and supports introducing into the classroom the sort of activities and approaches – for example, the history of mathematics and mathematics in its cultural context – that are discussed below. The curriculum also includes a number of 'cross curricular dimensions': identity and cultural diversity, healthy lifestyles, community, participation, enterprise, global dimension and sustainable development, technology and the media, creativity and critical thinking. All of these have potential in terms of developing equality themes in the classroom.

The new curriculum also states that pupils should work collaboratively in pairs and small groups and recognizes the importance of discussion; this either directly supports or at least does not preclude approaches to teaching and learning mathematics discussed below that foster classroom practices which promote equality and democracy in classrooms.

In October 2008 the government announced the ending of KS3 national tests. This is a significant policy change; although the ending of the KS3 SATs in mathematics will not in itself end the testing culture that it has helped to embed and deepen nor the setting practices associated with them, it does represent an important if limited rolling back of the testing regime. The time devoted in many schools in Year 9 to preparing for the tests can be used for other purposes and potentially ones that can promote equality in the some of the ways we describe later in the chapter.

We suggest that these changes represent 'openings' which teachers can develop. It is important to recognize that part of the motivation for these changes is a concern with the competitiveness of British capitalism, in terms both of raising the overall attainment in mathematics and of developing a creative and flexible workforce, themes found in both the recent reports commissioned by the government (Smith 2004; Williams 2008). We should expect that those who wish to promote capitalist values, large corporations and so on, would want to provide materials that support their point of view. In addition the place of data handling in the mathematics curriculum is at risk. The Smith report suggested relocating data handling and statistics in other curriculum subjects (Smith 2004) but data handling is a key aspect of mathematics for citizenship and this is a move that should be resisted (Noyes 2007). However, teachers passionate about promoting equality at last have opportunities that have not existed for some time to work with learners to use mathematics to make sense of the world.

There is an established tradition, critical mathematics education, which promotes the view that mathematics education can be and should be linked to goals of social justice (Ernest 2001). Rico Gutstein (2006) identifies three goals for mathematics education in terms of social justice. First, mathematics educators should aim to help learners to 'read the world', that is, help the learner to understand the social and political reality of the world through mathematics. Second, learners can begin to 'write the world': 'writing the world with mathematics means using mathematics to change the world' (*ibid.*, p. 27), that is, using mathematics to engage in action for social change or at least to gain the skills to do this, deconstructing the ways mathematics is used to hide wealth and power inequalities. Third, mathematics can help learners from disadvantaged groups to form stronger social and cultural identities and for these identities to be respected by others. We also draw out a fourth, present in the practices of Gutstein and other critical mathematics educators: inculcating a challenging and problem-solving approach to mathematics, fostering the courage to think independently and to understand how to defend ideas. This critical mathematics tradition has much to say to teachers committed to promoting equality in the contemporary world across all the equity themes identified in this book: gender, sexual orientation, ethnicity, disability, social class, capitalism and environmental issues. In the sections that follow, we explore these overarching ideas and offer specific suggestions for practical ways to exploit the openings envisaged above.

## Promoting equality in practice: setting and assessment

Before the introduction of the SATs it was not uncommon for children to work in mixed-ability groups in Year 7 and even Year 8. Such arrangements reduce inequities due to gender, ethnicity and social class. While ending the SATs may make it easier to argue for all attainment grouping, many mathematics teachers today in secondary schools have little experience of teaching classes in which a wide range of attainment is represented. Introducing all attainment grouping in mathematics can be challenging for teachers who are unfamiliar with this way of working and time and support is needed to develop effective practice (Wiliam and Bartholomew 2004). Nevertheless, the key role of setting and the way the idea of ability is constructed that go with setting practices mean that this is a challenge that mathematics teachers committed to equality need to address. There is evidence that this can be done and there are examples of strategies (see Linchevski and Kutscher 1998; Hart *et al.* 2004).

In addition, there are well-articulated and compelling models for approaches to teaching and learning that lead to high achievement and more equitable outcomes for all, as well as more general personal development and growth for pupils (Boaler 2006; 2008). One source of support is the Association of Teachers of Mathematics working group that meets regularly to help develop successful work with all-attainment mathematics classes; another may be coming from the SMILE project mentioned above where an attempt is being made to make the materials available again and also to offer an opportunity for teachers to work together on curriculum development. One of the schools involved in the Changes in Mathematics Teaching Project re-introduced all-attainment teaching in Years 7 and 8 and examples of their practice appear on the project website (www.cmtp.co.uk). Another approach is to follow up recent initiatives in secondary schools supported by the Gulbenkian Foundation for Human Scale Education. This has promoted Year 7 as a foundation year in which pupils experience a more child-centred and integrated curriculum based on cross-curricular themes and extended project work. Although mathematics has not usually been included in early examples, this has begun to happen in some schools and there is no reason, other than the belief that mathematics needs to be taught in sets, that this should not be done.

Changing setting practices will take time and individual mathematics teachers concerned with social justice may not be able to influence department or school policy easily. Therefore it is important to find ways to at least reduce the damage that setting can do to learners' sense of themselves, of mathematics and to their relationships with each other. One effect of the culture and beliefs about setting is that students labelled as 'low achievers' are offered a restricted and diminished curriculum. This is not necessary and is exceedingly harmful to their learning. Anne Watson and Els De Geest (2005) show that teachers committed to helping such students to engage with mathematical reasoning, motivation and engagement can make a significant difference.

Given the end of SATs there is even less justification for continuing to test children in mathematics with the methods common in schools. How students' mathematics is assessed needs to be reconsidered in classrooms concerned with equity. Routinely, these assessment practices will not be simply summative but will be genuinely and deeply formative; they will avoid practices that adopt the rhetoric of formative assessment but become disengaged performances for pupils and teachers alike or worst ways to reinforce and regulate fixed ranking by ability, for example the way 'traffic lights' are sometimes used. Radical alternatives may be difficult to access immediately but a mathematics classroom predicated on equality needs to generate relevant assessment approaches, ones which allow learners to demonstrate what they can do rather than what they cannot do and which highlight the importance of developing depth of understanding of mathematical processes. Changing assessment practices was a key to developing a remarkably successful school in inner-city New York. Rather than using assessment to rank order students through regular standardized testing, 'assessments were made by panels of experts having long conversations with students and looking at their work' (Mathews 2004).

Mathematics teachers also have a key role to play in using their own mathematical skills to disentangle and counter some of the myths that surround beliefs about testing and the predicting of pupil performance in schools. For example, understanding why narrow setting necessarily leads to a large number of pupils at any one time being placed in the wrong set requires understanding statistical data and mathematical models. Similarly, although SATs have gone, CATs remain in many schools. CATs, or Cognitive Ability Tests, are also used to label pupils in particular ways. These are tests that have been developed as predictors of large populations. However, their use in predicting an individual student's qualification outcomes (and consequently in some instances as a means to set children) is deeply flawed mathematically. Understood from a mathematical perspective, grade predictions are probabilities where often the probability of the headline predictive grade, while having a higher likelihood than any other grade, is less likely than the probability of another outcome.

The doctrine of testing is also used to shore up essentialist and simplistic views of students such as labelling by VAK learning style. Presentations delivered as part of training courses, focused on using pupil information data to raise tests scores and league table positions, make claims that some pupils have low CATs scores because they are 'kinaesthetic' learners. While it may be the case that individuals have a preference for engaging in and/or are able to learn differently from different sorts of learning activities, we take the view that such preferences, like learning itself, are socially constructed. Simplistic correspondences in terms of cause and effect between such data and classroom learning read like twenty-first-century versions of nineteenth-century myths about the relationship between gender, ethnicity and social class and a variety of social practices including ability in mathematics, sporting prowess and so on. Critical mathematics educators have a particular responsibility to help their fellow teachers to themselves 'read the world' mathematically.

## Promoting equality in practice: the curriculum

As we discussed above, there are two forms of mathematics curriculum that work against equality. On the one hand, it may be experienced as impersonal, external, elitist, disembodied, ahistorical; on the other, as bite-sized, fragmented and only 'functional'. But what alternative ways are there for thinking about the curriculum?

There is an extended tradition which identifies the need for students to be able to 'read the world' critically (Gutstein 2006). To be able to participate in democratic citizenship, it is important for all students to have sufficient mathematical literacy to be able to understand the mathematical models being presented to them, to be aware of the ways in which the process of creating mathematical models is not neutral and to understand that the use of mathematical models affects fundamentally the sort of solutions to social problems that are seen as legitimate. As Ole Skovsmose writes, 'mathematics is formatting our society ... perhaps God did not organise the world according to mathematics but ... [it seems] humanity has now embarked on just such a project' (1994, p. 43). He outlines a school project in which the mathematical modelling processes behind the provision of state benefits are interrogated, raising fundamental questions about how, for example, disability is measured; another project investigates energy production and consumption in practical and engaging ways. In addition, mathematics can be used as a tool to uncover injustices and to interrogate the ways in which capitalism works and is reproduced: Marilyn Frankenstein's (1989) work is full of useful examples here. For example, pupils might explore the wage rates per hour of various occupations including the wages of top executives. The problem could be to find how many days different types of worker – nurses, cleaners on minimum wage, council admin workers, builders and so on – would need to work to earn as much as the Chief Executive of a well-known company. This approach of using mathematics to interrogate the real is in contrast to the type of 'realistic' examples used in, for example, National Curriculum tests (and so, by replication, in commercial schemes) that have significant class bias (Cooper 2001).

The current developments to encourage cross-curricular working provide rich opportunities to adopt a collective approach to addressing social justice issues in the mathematics classroom. Rico Gutstein, teaching in the US, describes in detail his work in a school that was predominantly Mexican or Mexican American students (Gutstein 2006). Examples of the ways he encouraged the students to 'read the world' mathematically included analysing data both on local housing costs for different ethnic groups and on unequal distribution of wealth. Such investigations necessarily cannot be confined to only mathematics but include discussion of a wide range of social factors. In *Rethinking School Mathematics* Andrew Noyes (2007) offers examples of other ways mathematics can be linked to citizenship themes, including global citizenship. Examples include investigating public spending, personal finance and environmental issues. An example of what is possible in practice in today's schools can be found in the work of Filton High School. Arising out of a cross-curricular project involving up to 35 teachers, the mathematics department has developed a resource called 'The Human Race – the Migrant Species' (Vernell and Carter 2008). The resource addresses the way in which mathematics has 'migrated' and explores mathematically two anti-immigration beliefs: 'Too many immigrants are coming into the country' and 'Our country cannot afford to help immigrants'. As well as exploring social issues through mathematics and mathematics through social issues, mathematics can be used to bring social issues into the classroom. Developing ideas originating in the SMILE scheme, pupils can investigate the 'arithmetic of disability', for example how their classroom or school spaces might be redesigned to allow full access for wheelchair users.

The new National Curriculum, with its encouragement to recognize the historical and cultural roots of mathematics, has openings for activities promoted by a radical tradition which identifies the mathematics found in the practices and experiences of people, worldwide, who are not members of the most powerful groups. Such study allows critical questions to be asked about 'what constitutes mathematics ... what counts as valued knowledge, and how things came to be this way and how they are sustained' (Johnston and Dunne 1996, p. 61). These questions draw attention to the connections between power and knowledge. They also help to give mathematics a human face: the personal enters classrooms when locating topics to be studied and questions to be addressed within a historical context. A useful source of ideas is *Math Equals: Biographies of Women Mathematicians* by Teri Perl (1978). To recognize that the mathematics that is presented in textbooks was the result of specific human endeavour, that all mathematics has upon it the traces of human hands, that the greatest mathematicians struggled and doubted and changed their minds, that they scribbled and corrected and were sometimes wrong, helps learners to construct themselves also as mathematicians – human, fallible and engaged. Making explicit to students aspects of the history of mathematics can contribute to helping them to understand that mathematics is constructed and that where and when mathematics arises is related to whose interests it serves. Similarly, classroom materials that draw on majority world practices and experiences (e.g. Shan and Bailey 1991; Nelson *et al.* 1993) offer recognition to the knowledge of the less powerful, introduce multicultural resources into the classroom and provide a context in which to raise the critical questions with students that extend multiculturalism into anti-racist pedagogy (Kassem 2001).

This aspect of the new curriculum also legitimates the focus found in the critical tradition which highlights issues of gender and sexuality. Gender issues and the engagement of girls in mathematics has been on the agenda for 30 years and the challenge this equity theme presents to the curriculum has been extensively explored. The cre8ate maths project (http://cre8atemaths.c-seprojects.org/) contains some contemporary examples of a positive approach to gender. Even mentioning sexuality, however, has been taboo. The invitation in the new curriculum to place mathematics in its historical context suggests one possibility for opening up an awareness of unthinking heterosexism: Alan Turing is one of the most significant mathematicians of the twentieth century. He is recognized as one of the founders of computer science and mathematical computing. He was key to breaking the Enigma code during the Second World War. He is an intriguing and exciting historical figure. He was also a gay man. We have experience in a higher education context of successfully including Alan Turing's life and work when studying history of mathematics. Although the mathematics might need to be adapted for a school context, this topic, code and cryptography is one which pupils generally find engaging. This is one example of possible historical study that explicitly recognizes the sexual orientation of mathematicians. There is also much scope to explore statistically the arithmetic of sexual orientation in different societies and cultures. Such an approach helps to undermine an essentialist view of sexual orientation in favour of a socio-cultural view within which there is celebration of difference and choice.

## Promoting equality in practice: the classroom

Just as in the case of the curriculum, so with the classroom: very similar features promote social justice across all the equality themes with which this book is concerned. So, if young people are to learn to think mathematically, to develop as persons and to acquire those democratic competences needed to critique the world around them and to live as citizens – critical consciousness, sustained and sustainable action and cooperation (Moreira 2002) – what sort of places do mathematics classrooms need to be?

Mathematics classroom practices which take social justice issues seriously include: promoting a willingness to share ideas, making space for the ideas of others, supportive listening, and less valorizing of the individual and of individual success (Povey 2003). Such classrooms need to be places in which learners set up productive relationships with the process of coming to know. If we are to generate and support authoritative knowing, that is, to nurture learners who see themselves both as authors and as authorities, our classrooms have to be spaces for dialogue (Alro and Skovsmose 2002) where sometimes learners are in control of both the content and the direction of the talk. Building such a fluid and responsive social space is not easy and is not accomplished quickly, not least because it is so different from many of the accepted practices of school mathematics classrooms. Our questions need to be designed less to elicit information and more to point up relatively complex problems where multiple lines of inquiry are possible and where the expectation is, first, that the teacher does not already know all possible fruitful responses and, second, that responding will take some time. Encouraging discussion in pairs or small groups gives everyone the chance to explore ideas and then rehearse their articulation before presenting them to others. Genuine dialogue is needed to critique meanings and to build shared ones which are based on respect for what the learners bring, striving for a deep ecological democracy that stresses interconnectedness, not just between people but with the planet too.

Tasks which can be approached in a variety of ways, and for which a wide range of tools can be offered as appropriate, provide useful opportunities for learners to see themselves as active, as choosing, deciding, producing arguments for and against, assessing validity and generating questions and ideas. Our curriculum needs to be problem centred: a problem-centred curriculum involves the need to take risks, which is a precondition for imagining a different and more just world (Giroux 1992); and posing and re-posing problems helps uncover the linguistic assumptions hidden in their original formulation. There needs to be intellectual 'room to move' and tasks set will be significant problems requiring time and space to be worked on: there will be a sense of spaciousness (Angier and Povey 1999).

'Spaciousness' can also be a metaphor for the social relationships in the classroom where, we believe, students are asking for more of themselves to be recognized and expected to participate. Some students use the metaphor of family relationships and such a metaphor helps us to understand that 'the emotional qualities of classroom interactions will exert a significant influence on what is learned' (Confrey 1995, p. 39). To promote equality through classroom practice in mathematics means creating space to be human, space to think and space for difference.

Sexual orientation is one of the least developed areas in terms of promoting equality in mathematics, as in schools generally. Mathematics as currently taught valorizes a particular kind of heterosexual masculinity, a masculinity – damaging to all, boys as well as girls, and destructive of the planet – based on competitive hierarchy. Heather Mendick proposes 'queering mathematics' (2006), arguing that currently it is gendered; to do mathematics is to do a certain sort of masculinity. Drawing on queer theory she argues that the closed nature of mathematics calls for an approach that aims to transgress and bring pleasure to the classroom. And opening it up to allow for different ways of being in and doing mathematics can only benefit all pupils who currently do not find images and roles to identify within mathematics. This includes an awareness of, and respect for, disability:

> An education suitable for *all* learners – good for each and good for everyone – requires everyone to take account of the real differences between them, however they are expressed. (Griffiths 2003, p. 37, italics in the original)

We recognize that the description we have given of a mathematics classroom which takes equity as a key principle of practice is a long way removed from what exists in most mathematics classrooms in the UK and one that is difficult to enact in the current educational context. However, such classrooms can be created and developed. For example, Jo Boaler reports on a mathematics department in the US, at 'Railside' school, an ethnic and socially diverse school operating in a context where the politicization of mathematics and the pressure for 'traditional' methods is greater than in the UK due to the 'math wars' in which reform is contested by educational conservatives. This department developed an effective approach to learning mathematics that, in comparison to schools using less equitable approaches, promoted high achievement for all in absolute terms and also reduced differences in achievement relative to social and cultural factors (Boaler 2006; 2008). In addition, the practices in this school also developed pupils' self-respect and autonomy as learners and a positive relationship to mathematics that included understanding the subject as a socially constructed and negotiated enterprise. The increase in these pupils' respect and concern for their peers extended into a more general development of respect for cultural and individual difference. Boaler describes this with the term 'relational equity'. Central to these teachers' practices was a form of structured group work based on 'complex instruction' (Cohen and Lotan 1997). This approach included valuing many dimensions of work by offering open-ended problems that offered many opportunities for success: 'when there are many more ways to be successful, many more students are successful' (Boaler 2006, p. 42). Other aspects of practice included: supporting students to develop and carry out specific roles when working in groups; seeking to affirm the competence of all, especially students who might have lower status in a group; developing students' sense of their responsibility for each other's learning through classroom practices and forms of assessment, including assessing collaborative outcomes; having high expectations of all students; emphasizing that success in mathematics was the product of effort rather than ability and all could succeed; and explicitly reflecting on and outlining the type of learning practices that would help students to learn.

### Promoting equality in practice: teachers working together to develop practice

Promoting equality in the mathematics classroom makes different demands on teachers from teaching in more traditional ways, particularly in an educational environment that is not always supportive of, and often hostile to, the aims of social justice. While we have attempted to point to ways in which individual teachers can make a difference in their own classrooms, many of the examples that we have given have involved groups of teachers working together to develop classroom practices or curriculum materials. In many mathematics departments and beyond there are 'Teachers working for change' (Povey 1995), that is, teachers committed to changing the mathematical experience of learners in a way that promotes equity. Teachers who seek to promote equality in the classroom will be more successful if they work collaboratively with other mathematics teachers and teachers of other subjects who share their aspirations and values. At root, promoting equality in mathematics classrooms means creating a context in which teachers can work together, sharing difficulties and inspiring and energizing change.

## Conclusion

In this chapter we have identified key areas in which the current dominant practices tend to work against the promotion of equality. We have pointed to some ways in which teachers can begin to develop more equitable practices. In this country and elsewhere there exists a rich and vibrant current in mathematics education that seeks to address equity issues through creating a school mathematics which celebrates difference, dialogue, critical awareness and intellectual challenge for all and promotes the role mathematics has in the development of the personal author/ity (*ibid.*) needed for engaged participation (Boylan 2004) in community and society.

For a long time in mathematics education, as in society generally, progressive values and ideas have been marginalized. Recently there have been openings that create space for a range of practices that can promote equality in the classroom. We have pointed to some of the ways in which teachers can develop their own practice in relationship to, and in connection with, that of others who seek to enact such practices. Mathematics has a significant role to play in the reproduction of inequitable outcomes and beliefs that serve to work against social justice in mathematics and beyond. The benefits of developing the instances we have cited of more equitable practices into a stronger current in mathematics education has much to offer to pupils, to teachers and to society. Adapting one of the slogans of the anti-capitalist movement of the early years of the twenty-first century: another school mathematics is possible.

# References

Alro, H. and Skovsmose, O. (2002), *Dialogue and Learning in Mathematics Education: Intention, Reflection, Critique*. Dordrecht: Kluwer.

Anderson, J. (2000), 'Teacher questioning and pupil anxiety in the primary classroom'. Paper delivered at the British Educational Research Association Conference, Cardiff University, September 2000.

Angier, C. and Povey, H. (1999), 'One teacher and a class of school students: their perception of the culture of their mathematics classroom and its construction'. *Educational Review*, 51, (2), 147–60.

Barnes, M. and Coupland, M. (1990), 'Humanising calculus: a case study in curriculum development', in L. Burton (ed.), *Gender and Mathematics: An International Perspective*. London: Cassell, pp. 72–80.

Bartholomew, H. (2001), 'Learning environments and student roles in individualised mathematics classrooms' (unpublished PhD thesis, Kings College University of London).

Boaler, J. (1997a), *Experiencing School Mathematics: Teaching Styles, Sex and Setting*. Buckingham: Open University Press.

— (1997b), 'Setting, social class and survival of the quickest'. *British Educational Research Journal*, 23, (5), 575–95.

— (2002), 'The development of disciplinary relationships: knowledge, practice, and identity', in A. Cockburn and E. Nardi (eds), *Proceedings of the 26th Annual Conference of the International Group for the Psychology of Mathematics Education (PME) 2000*. Norwich.

—(2005), 'The "psychological prisons" from which they never escaped: the role of ability grouping in reproducing social class inequalities'. *Forum*, 47, (2 and 3), 125–34.

— (2006), 'How a detracked mathematics approach promoted respect, responsibility and high achievement'. *Theory into Practice*, 45, (1), 40–6.

— (2008), 'Promoting "relational equity" and high mathematics achievement through an innovative mixed-ability approach'. *British Educational Research Journal*, 34, (2), 167–94.

— , Wiliam, D. and Brown, M. (2000), 'Students' experiences of ability grouping – disaffection, polarisation and the construction of failure'. *British Educational Research Journal* 26, (5), 631–48.

Boylan, M. (2000), 'Numeracy, numeracy, numeracy and ideology, ideology, ideology'. *Proceedings of the Mathematics Education and Society (MES2) Conference 2000*, Montechorro, Portugal.

— (2004), 'Questioning (in) school mathematics: life worlds and ecologies of practice' (unpublished PhD thesis, Sheffield Hallam University).

Brown, M., Askew, M., and Millett, A. (2003), 'How has the national numeracy strategy affected attainment and teaching in Year 4'. *Proceedings of the British Society for Research into Learning Mathematics*, 23, (2), 13–18.

Brown, M., Brown, P. and Bibby, T. (2008), '"I would rather die": reasons given by 16-year-olds for not continuing their study of mathematics'. *Research in Mathematics Education*, 10, (1), 3–18.

Cobb, P., Wood, T., Yackel, E. and McNeal, B. (1992), 'Characteristics of classroom mathematics traditions: an interactional analysis'. *American Educational Research Journal*, 29, (3), 573–604.

Cohen, E. and Lotan, R. (eds) (1997), *Working for Equity in Heterogeneous Classrooms: Sociological Theory in Practice*. New York: Teachers College Press.

Cole, M. (2008), '*Learning Without Limits*: A Marxist assessment'. *Policy Futures in Education*, 6, (4), 453–63. Available at http://www.wwwords.co.uk/pdf/valida-te.asp?j=pfie&vol=6&issue=4&year=2008&article=7_Cole_PFIE_6_4_web (accessed 9 November 2008).

Confrey, J. (1995), 'A theory of intellectual development: part III'. *For the Learning of Mathematics*, 15, (2), 36–45.

Cooper, B. (2001), 'Social class and "real-life" mathematics assessments', in P. Gates (ed.), *Issues in Mathematics Teaching*. London: RoutledgeFalmer, pp. 245–258.

Cotton, T. (2001), 'Mathematics teaching in the real world', in P. Gates (ed.), *Issues in Mathematics Teaching*. London: RoutledgeFalmer, pp. 23–37.

Davis, R., Maher, C. and Noddings, N. (1990), 'Suggestions for the improvement of mathematics education', in R. Davis, C. Maher and N. Noddings (eds), *Constructivist Views on the Teaching and Learning of Mathematics, Journal for Research in Mathematics Education Monograph 4*. Reston, VA: National Council of Teachers of Mathematics, pp. 187–191.

DfEE (2001), *Key Stage 3 National Strategy. Framework for Teaching Mathematics: Year 7, 8, 9*. London: DfEE Publications.

Dowling, P. and Noss, R. (eds) (1990), *Mathematics Versus the National Curriculum*. Basingstoke: Falmer Press.

Ernest, P. (2001), 'Critical mathematics education', in P. Gates (ed.) *Issues in Mathematics Teaching*. London: RoutledgeFalmer, pp. 277–293.

Frankenstein, M. (1989), *Relearning Maths: A Different Third R – Radical Maths*. London: Free Association Books.

Freire, P. (1972), *Pedagogy of the Oppressed*. Harmondsworth: Penguin.

Gillborn, D. and Mirza, H. (2000), *Educational Inequality: Mapping Race, Class and Gender*. London: Ofsted.

Giroux, H. (1983), *Theory and Resistance in Education: A Pedagogy for the Opposition*, London: Heinemann.

— (1992), *Border Crossings*. London: Routledge.

Griffiths, M. (2003), *Action for Social Justice in Education: Fairly Different*. Maidenhead: OUP.

Gutstein, E. (2006), *Reading and Writing the World with Mathematics*. New York: Routledge.

Hardy, T. and Cotton, T. (2000), 'Problemetising culture and discourse for mathematics education research: tools for research'. *Proceedings of the 2nd International Mathematics Education and Society (MES2) Conference* 2000, Montechorro, Portugal.

Hart, S., Dixon, A., Drummond, M. J. and McIntyre, D. (2004), *Learning Without Limits*. Maidenhead: Open University Press.

Ireson, J., Clark, H. and Hallam, S. (2002), 'Constructing ability groups in the secondary school: issues in practice'. *School Leadership and Management*, 22, (2), 163–76.

Ireson, J., Hallam, S., Hack, S., Clark, H. and Plewis, I. (2002), 'Ability grouping in English secondary schools: effects of attainment in English, mathematics and science'. *Educational Research and Evaluation*, 8, (3), 299–318.

Johnston, J. and Dunne, M. (1996), 'Revealing assumptions: problematising research on gender and mathematics and science education', in L. Parker, L. Rennie and B. Fraser (eds) (1996), *Gender, Science and Mathematics: Shortening the Shadow*. Dordrecht: Kluwer, pp. 53–63.

Judd, J. (1996), 'Comprehensives have failed, says Blunkett'. *Independent* (28 February).

Kassem, D. (2001), 'Ethnicity and mathematics education', in P. Gates (ed.). *Issues in Mathematics Teaching*. London: RoutledgeFalmer, pp. 64–76.

Linchevski, L. and Kutscher, B. (1998), 'Tell me with whom you're learning and I'll tell you how much you've learned: mixed ability versus same-ability grouping in mathematics'. *Journal for Research in Mathematics Education*, 29, (5), 533–54.

Mathews, J. (2004), 'Seeking alternatives to standardized testing', *The Washington Post* (17 February). Available at http://www.washingtonpost.com/wp-dyn/articles/A47699-2004Feb17.html (accessed 4 March 2004).

Mendick, H. (2006), *Masculinities in Mathematics*. Maidenhead: OUP.

Moreira, L. (2002), 'Mathematics education and critical consciousness', in A. Cockburn and E. Nardi (eds), *Proceedings of the 26th Annual Conference of the International Group for the Psychology of Mathematics Education (PME) 2000* Norwich.

Nardi, E. and Steward, S. (2003), 'Is mathematics T.I.R.E.D.? A profile of quiet disaffection in the secondary mathematics classroom'. *British Educational Research Journal*, 29, (3), 345–67.

NCETM (National Centre for Excellence in Teaching Mathematics) (2008a), 'Football club maths'. Available at http://www.ncetm.org.uk/Default.aspx?page=13&module=res&mode=100&resid=9335 (accessed 26 October 2008).

— (2008b), 'Our level fives have doubled, but why are they all boys?' Available at http://www.ncetm.org.uk/Default.aspx?page = 41&module = research&research-id = 6849#final%20report (accessed 26 October 2008).

Nelson, D., Joseph, G. and Williams, J. (1993), *Multicultural Mathematics*. Oxford: OUP.

Noyes, A. (2007), *Rethinking School Mathematics*. London: Paul Chapman Publishing.

Ofsted (2008), 'Understanding the score'. Available at http://www.ofsted.gov.uk/Ofsted-home/Publications-and-research/Documents-by-type/Thematic-reports/Mathematics-understanding-the-score/(language)/eng-GB (accessed 20 October 2008).

Ollerton, M. and Watson, A. (2001), *Inclusive Mathematics 11–18*. London: Continuum.

Perl, T. (1978), *Math Equals: Biographies of Women Mathematicians*. New York: Addison-Wesley.

Povey, H. (1995), 'Ways of knowing of student and beginning mathematics teachers and their relevance to becoming a teacher working for change' (unpublished PhD thesis, University of Birmingham), pp. 51–64.

Povey, H. (2003), 'Teaching and learning mathematics: can the concept of citizenship be reclaimed for social justice?', in L. Burton (ed.), *Which Way Social Justice in Mathematics Education*. Westport, CT: Praeger Publishers.

QCA (2008), *The National Curriculum*. Available at http://curriculum.qca.org.uk/uploads/QCA-07-3338-p_Maths_3_tcm8-403.pdf?return = /key-stages-3-and-4/subjects/mathematics/keystage3/index.aspx%3Freturn%3D/key-stages-3-and-4/subjects/index.aspx (accessed 1 October 2008).

Reay, D. and Wiliam, D. (1999), '"I'll be a nothing": structure, agency and the construction of identity through assessment'. *British Educational Research Journal*, 25, (3), 343–54).

Ruthven, K. (1987), 'Ability stereotyping in mathematics'. *Educational Studies in Mathematics*, 18, (30), 243–53.

Shan, S. and Bailey, P. (1991), *Multiple Factors: Classroom Mathematics for Equality and Justice*. Stoke-on-Trent: Trentham.

Skovsmose, O. (1994), *Towards a Philosophy of Critical Mathematics*. Dordrecht: Kluwer.

Slavin, R. (1990), 'Achievement effects of ability grouping in secondary schools: a best evidence synthesis'. *Review of Educational Research*, 60, 471–90.

Smith, A. (2004), *Making Mathematics Count: The Report of Professor Adrian Smith into Post 14 Mathematics Education*. Available at http://www.tda.gov.uk/upload/resources/pdf/m/mathsinquiry_finalreport.pdf (accessed February 2008).

Solomon, Y. (2007), 'Experiencing mathematics classes: ability grouping, gender and the selective development of participative identities'. *International Journal of Educational Research*, 46, 8–19.

Tahta, D. (1994), 'Coming up to Russian expectations'. *Mathematics Teaching*, 146, (March), 25–26.

Vernell, P. and Carter, C. (2008), 'Another education is possible'. *Socialist Review*, (September). Available at http://www.socialistreview.org.uk/article.php?article number = 10510 (accessed 19 September 2008).

Walkerdine, V. (1994), 'Reasoning in a post-modern age', in P. Ernest (ed.), *Mathematics, Education and Philosophy: An International Perspective*. London: Falmer, pp. 61–75.

Watson, A. and De Geest, E. (2005), 'Principled teaching for deep progress in mathematics: improving mathematical learning beyond'. *Educational Studies in Mathematics*, 58, 209–34.

— (2008), *Changes in Mathematics Teaching Project.* Available at www.cmtp.co.uk (accessed July 2009).

Wiliam, D. and Bartholomew, H. (2004), 'It's not which school but which set you're in that matters: the influence of ability grouping practices on students' progress in mathematics'. *British Educational Research Journal*, 30, (3), 279–93.

Williams, P. (2008), *Independent Review of Mathematics Teaching in Early Years Settings and Primary Schools.* Nottingham: DCSF Publications.

Zevenbergen, R. (2000), 'Boys, mathematics and classroom interactions: the construction of masculinity in working-class mathematics classrooms'. *Proceedings of the 23rd Annual Conference of the International Group for the Psychology of Mathematics Education PME)* 2000, Haifa.

Chapter 16

# Religious Education

## Julie Light

In this chapter, I begin by situating Religious Education historically, and go on to look at RE and the National Curriculum. I then consider issues of ethnicity, describing the role that RE can play in challenging racism. Next I look at gender, and suggest that raising student achievement still has more of an emphasis on boys as learners than girls. Moving on to sexual orientation, I examine the attitudes of both students and teachers and conclude that educational establishments fail in their duty as educators to promote equality for all especially when it comes to LGBT issues. I conclude with discussions of social class and special educational needs. With respect to the former, I focus on negative attitudes towards working-class students and how RE could undermine these. As far as SEN is concerned, I address cross-curricular ideas which might promote a deeper understand of SEN students and the discrimination they may face within the education system.

## Introduction

Religious Education is now hitting the headlines. After decades of being pushed to the back of the class there does not seem to be a week that goes by without someone making comments as to what the curriculum of RE should consist of. However, neither the government nor the media seem to have any real sense of the essence of RE. As a Curriculum Leader for RE, I see, more than ever, the need for RE in our classrooms. With a nation that is full of different cultures and faiths, I cannot help but feel I must push for a greater understanding in our quest for diversity. However, the question that has to be asked is, why is change happening now and what consequence will this have for the children we teach?

In secondary classrooms around the country Religious Education is being transformed, in theory at least, into a leader of the diversity in the education world, but in order to understand how and why this transformation has taken place, we have to examine RE's history.

There has been, and still continues to be, a metamorphosis within this subject area in response to a number of events that have taken place within our society at large over a long period. Indeed, these events can be traced back over generations, but it is not unfair to say that the real beginning of change started with a realization that, in order to progress in a multicultural Britain, we had to understand and thus accept the cultures and backgrounds of others.

The multicultural and antiracist movements emerged at a time when people's consciousnesses were at a peak during the mid- and later stages of the 1970s (see Chapter 2 of this volume). These movements, which inspired a rise in Muslim assertiveness and a culture that embraced the wide appeal of black youth culture, rallied against the unfair treatment of minority ethnic communities within society, both by institutions at large, and in the communities in which they lived. In response to struggles by Asian, black and other minority ethnic communities and their white supporters, a certain unity was established which resulted in the anti-discrimination legislation of the Race Relation Acts of 1965, 1968 and 1976.

From the early 1980s there were 'race' riots across the country in retaliation to the 'sus laws', laws dating back to the nineteenth century which effectively permitted the police to stop and search and even arrest, purely on the basis of suspicion, as a crime-prevention tactic, anyone they chose. 'Sus' was specifically directed at young black males. Riots continued over the next decade in different towns and cities across Britain. Responses to these riots, however, were late in coming, with the Conservative Party failing to introduce adequate measures within schools that might have helped ameliorate the growing feeling of separation between ethnic groups in an ever-increasingly multicultural Britain. The Swann Report of 1985 looked at key issues within the learning environment and focused on *tolerance* of minority ethnic communities and their cultures within a white society. What this did was to reinforce the differences between ethnic groups, add to stereotypical views, and exacerbate the ideological differences between the multiculturalists and antiracists of the time, the latter arguing that there was a need for a change within the power structures of institutions themselves, and indeed in society as a whole. What is now apparent is that Religious Education was caught between these two political and ideological poles: the multiculturalists, on the one hand, stressing the importance of issues of cultural and religious representation; and the antiracists, on the other, focusing on the need for an understanding of power and equality in all aspects of life.

The year 1997 saw the installation of a Labour government after 18 years out of power. David Gillborn (2008, p. 75) has described the first four years of the New Labour government as 'naïve multiculturalism' since, although there was evidence of a limited commitment to equity, apart from a decision to set up separate faith schools, and the Stephen Lawrence Inquiry Report

(Macpherson 1999), this commitment was largely superficial, consisting of 'rhetorical flourishes that left mainstream policy untouched' (Gillborn 2008, p. 75).[1]

Gillborn (*ibid.*, pp. 76–80) calls the second period, that is to say, between 9/11 and 7/7 (2001–5), as 'cynical multiculturalism'. It is a period (*ibid.*, pp. 76–7) when the government continued

> its *rhetorical* commitment to ethnic diversity and race equality ... [in] a cynical attempt to retain the appearance of enlightened race politics while simultaneously pursuing a policy agenda that increasingly resembled the earlier assimilationist/integrationist phases ... where the voices and concerns of White people were openly accorded a position of dominance. (cited in Cole 2009, p. 000, italics in the original)

The third period, from 7/7 (2005) up to the present, Gillborn describes as 'aggressive majoritinarianism' (Gillborn 2008, pp. 81–9). On 7/7, a coordinated series of explosions in London killed fifty-two people, and injured a further seven hundred. Gillborn (*ibid.*, p. 81) argues that these attacks heightened 'still further the retaliatory confidence of politicians and the media', and that their mood from one of retaliation to 'aggressive majoritarianism' 'where Whites now took the initiative in promoting ever more disciplinary agendas' (*ibid.*). As he concludes (*ibid.*):

> The rights and perspectives of the White majority were now asserted, sometimes in the name of 'integration' and 'cohesion' (the code words for contemporary assimilationism) but also simply on the basis that the majority disliked certain things (such as Muslim veils) and now felt able to enforce those prejudices in the name of common sense, integration and even security. (cited in Cole 2009, p. 000)

## RE and the National Curriculum

With the changes in the September 2008 National Curriculum, the government has the opportunity to bring RE in from the cold and bring it under the umbrella of the NC. While some RE teachers would not want this, I would argue that the advantages of doing so would have the positive effects of standardizing the content of RE across the country. At the present time, however, the majority of Standing Advisory Councils for Religious Education (SACREs) have started to put emphases on skills rather than religious content. For example, Robert Jackson, director of The Warwick Religions and Education Research Unit, focused his speech at the September 2004 Oslo Coalition on Freedom of Religion or Belief Conference on his belief that

Pupils should be taught skills of interpretation and should be given opportunities for reflexivity, considering the impact of new learning on their own beliefs and values and applying critical judgements in a constructive, rational and informed way. (Jackson 2004, p. 1)

Jackson also argued that the way forward is

for the pupils to be given a role in selecting topics and in designing and reviewing methods of study used, being treated as co-learners with the teacher. There is an increasing amount of research evidence (including evidence from projects on children's dialogue) showing that children and young people are motivated to learn if they are given agency.

Having in the past put this theory to the test I can agree with the positives of this. Of course, it has to depend on the skills a student already has, and the will to learn, but for the majority of students it is a positive form of teaching and learning. My view, therefore, is that RE should be part of the National Curriculum, but that skills of interpretation and critical reflection should be central, with students having a real input on the direction of their learning. It should be stressed that for this form of teaching and learning to be successful, there is a need for adequate finances and resources. On entering the classrooms of many teachers, however, the lack of funding is extremely obvious. Thus, in the present climate, while continuing to agitate for increased funding and resources, most teachers will have to use the provisions they have to promote equality in RE.

Some have argued, for example David Hargreaves, head of the Qualifications and Curriculum Authority (QCA), that RE should be replaced by citizenship (Hargreaves 1986, p. 31). However, there now seems to be a consensus that the subject is not to be replaced by, but should be married to, citizenship.

As James Robson (2007) argued in response to the Government Report on Citizenship by Sir Keith Ajegbo:

Religious Education and Citizenship have often been linked, with a high degree of content cross over and many RE teachers provide the teaching in Citizenship classes. Indeed, the fact that Oxford University is starting an RE PGCE course, with Citizenship as an important element to it, cements the intimate relationship that the two subjects have. Many may then be disappointed that this report misses an opportunity to emphasize the importance of RE when it comes to teaching Citizenship and diversity. (Robson 2007, p. 1)

His sentiments echo those of headteachers up and down the country. One has

274 *Equality in the Secondary School*

only to look at *The Times Education Supplement (TES)* job section to realize
that more and more headteachers and school governors are joining the two
departments together in schools because of the crossovers of topical matters.
There is of course the added advantage of saving curriculum time and money.

RE teachers will continue to press for the separation of the two disciplines,
and for both to be part of the National Curriculum.

On a more general note, in reality the majority of students from non-faith
schools, whether boys or girls, when asked, voice the opinion that they do not
like RE because 'I don't believe in God'. Many RE teachers will dispute the
fact that students dislike RE lessons, as well as every other subject in the NC.
One has only to look at the *TES* staffroom webpage (http://www.tes.co.uk/
section/staffroom) to see this. For most, the teaching of RE is carried out to an
excellent standard but there is a small amount of RE teaching being carried
out by teachers who indoctrinate rather than teach religion from a non-
biased point of view, and by teachers who are not willing to change their
teaching style to suit today's students. Given this scenario, the likelihood of
changing the students' perceptions of RE is dubious for the majority of non-
religious believers. There is the additional factor of RE not being high on
many schools' agendas and teaching staff being drafted in from other
specialist areas into areas where they are uncertain. Of course, it can be
argued that with the opportunities that now exist in Personal Development
Planning (where every teacher should now be given expertise advice in areas
that are a concern for them) all these problems have the potential of being
eradicated.

## Ethnic and Religious Diversity

In a recent speech at the Victoria and Albert Museum (December 2007),
Tony Benn (2007, p. 1) argued that religions have an underlying moral
acceptance of others, but that it is the few who twist these teachings to their
own advantage. It is here, I would argue, that RE can and should play its
part in cultivating equality for all within our classrooms and thus the wider
community. While there are, of course, those who have a negative view of
others' religions, for our part as teachers it is our duty to promote religious
equality.

Given the massive increase in Islamophobia and religious hate crime in the
UK since the events of 9/11 in the US (e.g. Cole and Maisuria 2007; Cole
2008, pp. 000; 2009, pp. 000) and the events of 7/7 in the UK (e.g. Cole and
Maisuria 2007; Cole 2008, pp. 000; Gillborn 2008, pp. 24–5; Cole 2009, pp.
000), RE teachers have a duty to educate all students about the true nature of
religions. All teachers, whether teaching individual lessons or topics in KS 3
or the religion of Islam in KS4, have the opportunity to undermine

Islamophobia at a basic level. With respect to racism more generally, and to xeno-racism (see Chapter 2 of this volume), given topics that range from segregation in the US; apartheid in South Africa; the Holocaust in Germany; through to the personal stories of Martin Luther King, Stephen Lawrence and Ghandi; RE can give the lesson depth and understanding, and install empathy in both students and teachers.

In the two Key Stages, students are taught about the dangers of isms/ phobias (see Chapter 2 of this volume) which can lead to genocide. School trips, visitors to school and (email) correspondence encourages the students to become more susceptible to others on a personal basis as this allows them to have a say in their own educational topics and focuses. Personalized learning allows students to build up knowledge at their own time and pace and can be successful in educating against isms/phobias, since the students do not feel they are having other people's views thrust upon them.

Empathy and thus understanding are further achieved when students are able to look in depth at different aspects of a person's life and come to a conclusion as to that person's contribution to equality. Some well-known people are listed below but these should not be the only people that students look at from a religious standpoint. People within their communities could also be the focus as could individual lesser-known religious people. With respect to well-known figures, students could:

- Listen to stories about the lives of two religious figures, for example **Mother Teresa** and **Martin Luther King**, and compare their different religious viewpoints, philosophies and life histories – the former a staunch conservative Roman Catholic, the latter a Baptist, who became more and more inclined to socialism in his later life (see Cole 2009, pp. 000). Students could collect and present, in a variety of ways, pictures and other information from a range of sources about the lives of these religious figures.
- Add descriptive words to pictures of the religious figures.
- Communicate and collect information about an important event in their own lives that can be related to the life of a religious figure, for example **a special journey**.
- Produce a visual display to show they are aware of something of the lives of religious figures.
- Examine artefacts that link with religious figures and indicate something about their beliefs and lives.
- Respond to, and ask questions about, religious figures.
- Communicate with people who have links with religious figures, for example **people of the same faith**, to find out about their lives.

The work could be linked to work in art, D&T, English, history and PSHE.

Tables 16.1 and 16.2 give examples of two prominent religious figures.

**Table 16.1** Archbishop Desmond Tutu

| | |
|---|---|
| His life story | Born 1931<br>Became a teacher then trained to be a priest.<br>Lived in London and then Johannesburg where he became the first black person to hold the position of Dean of St Mary's Cathedral. In 1978 became the first black General Secretary of the South African Council of Churches. |
| What did he have to fight against? | Fought against apartheid (black and 'coloured' South Africans being forced, often violently, to live separately to white South Africans) in a non-violent way. In 1985 he won the Nobel Peace Prize for this work. |
| How did he do this? | He made the following demands:<br>• equal civil rights for all<br>• the abolition of South Africa's 'pass laws' (which severely limited the movements of the non-white population)<br>• a common system of education for all<br>• the cessation of forced deportation from South Africa to the so-called 'homelands'. |
| What did Tuto do? | Preached against apartheid using examples from the Bible that showed that non-violence was correct and injustice and cruelty were wrong.<br>Chose non-violent protest like marches, boycotts and petitions.<br>Used the Bible and prayer to keep focused on his vision of a South Africa where everyone would live together in peace and harmony. |

**Table 16.2** Martin Luther King

| | |
|---|---|
| His life story | Born 1929.<br>Went to college and became a priest.<br>In 1957 he helped organize the Southern Christian Leadership Conference (SCLC), which formed to coordinate protests against segregation and discrimination.<br>He was arrested a number of times and many attempts were made to kill him. His house was bombed and he was stabbed.<br>In 1964 he was awarded the Nobel Peace Prize, for his non-violent struggle against racism.<br>He was shot dead in 1968 in Memphis, Tennessee. |
| What did he have to fight against? | The use of different services and different living areas which severely disadvantaged black people. |

| How did he do this? | Organized a bus boycott. |
| --- | --- |
| | Used non-violent direct action based on the methods of Gandhi, who led protests against British rule in India. |
| | In 1963 led mass protests against discrimination in Birmingham, Alabama, where the white population were violently resisting desegregation (an end to segregation). |
| | Took part in the enormous civil rights march on Washington in August 1963, and delivered his famous 'I have a dream' speech, predicting a day when the promise of freedom and equality for all would become a reality in America. |
| | In 1965, led a campaign to register blacks to vote. |

# Gender

It has been known for some time that girls outperform boys at GCSE Religious Studies, as much as they do in other academic subjects. Under-achievement by boys in the subject is, and continues to be, a concern for all teachers.

Although in short course GCSE, where schools generally enter the whole cohort, the numbers of boys and girls entered for the examinations are comparable, many more girls than boys take the full course. In both the full and short courses, girls gain most of the A* to A grades while boys predominate in the lowest grades. (HMI 2005, p. 4)

Other important disclosures that came from the Annual Report of 2005, and which are no shock to any good teacher, is that boys tend to be positive about RE, but find that the teaching styles of some teachers do not make the subject inclusive for them. This unfortunately is the case with a high percentage of underachieving boys. Managers and Leading Teachers have been aware of this for a number of years, and in Initial Teacher Education (ITE), student teachers are given advice and suggestions as to how to address the issue of underachieving boys in general. What teachers must do is to use a number of teaching styles and be aware of differing learning styles in order to cater for every learner in the classroom. This is not an easy task because to be successful in exams students have to be able to relay their knowledge in writing and it is this skill that needs to be built upon, but even so, to release the potential of all learners, exam takers or not, this must be carried out. In the Ofsted (June 2007) report *Making Sense of Religion*, it was said that boys enjoyed RE when:

- they could explore interesting topics which mattered to them

- they were finding out what other pupils thought, particularly about social and moral issues
- it provided what they saw as a rare opportunity – denied them in a heavily examination-orientated Key Stage 4 curriculum – for more extended discussion, expressing opinions and developing personal views in relation to controversial human issues
- it involved learning about different beliefs and lifestyles and helped people to get along better with one another and to be more tolerant; RE was perceived to be a key subject in generating this kind of understanding. (Ofsted 2007, p. 15)

At Key Stage 4 students' opinions are more developed than at Key Stage 3. For the first time in RE, they are, in general, ready to answer philosophical and ethical questions, especially if they have been taught 'the religion by religion' approach (which entails looking at different aspects of each religion). An example of this approach is **Hinduism and how to lead a good life**, followed by **Hinduism and beliefs about death**. However, this way of teaching does not allow students to see cohesive similarities and differences between the religious faiths. Students should be able to articulate the world views of different religions, but also to discuss with confidence their own opinions of these world views, and to compare them with other religions. This should add an element of 'self-worth', allowing for the building of confidence.

In my experience, it is often the most 'laddish' of boys who present well-thought-out arguments as to what they feel affects them in their everyday lives, so perhaps teachers who fear behavioural problems should be less reluctant to enter into the arena of debate with their classes. They might like to try to engage the whole class in debate and discussion. When asked, boys tend to state that they prefer debate as a way of learning, although they understand that in order to achieve the aims of the lesson there has to be an understanding of how debating in the classroom works (*ibid.*, p. 9). Other methods of teaching and learning, such as collaborative learning, are also seen as unworkable by some teachers because of behavioural worries, thus hindering the learning of some students. According to the Ofsted report (*ibid.*), there is also a feeling among boys that they could not cope with the fragmented learning of RE where some teachers jump from one religion to another. However, many SACREs are now implementing question-based RE where issues are the main focus and religious views are discussed in order to answer the ethical or philosophical question being asked, which should facilitate boys' learning. Moreover, with the main emphases of many SACREs now being the development of skills, concepts and attitudes rather than the delivery of content, educating the boys should become a positive rather than a negative experience in the RE classroom.

Since I became an educator in the late 1990s one of the main topics has been raising the achievement of boys. At a recent in-school INSET (May 2008), we spoke about this yet again, looking at details of strategies to help the boys. However, once again I found myself thinking about strategies for teaching girls. We know how educators think boys should learn, but when I tried to do a quick internet search on obtaining higher results for girls I was surprised to find very little on the subject. Raising achievements for girls seems to be non-existent in print in the UK, but I feel that it is fundamental that this area should be examined as a matter of urgency, especially in the context of today's street culture where many girls are adopting attitudes that mirror the laddish behaviours of boys.

During KS4 students are given the opportunity to explore their attitude towards gender. Patriarchy within the different religions is addressed in 'The Gender and the Media' Unit of Work in KS 4. Patriarchy exists in one form or another in most religions, In Table 16.3, I present some opposing arguments as to whether or not Christianity is sexist.

---

**The role of women in Christian society**

Pupils should be taught that.
- Sexism is treating people differently because of the gender to which they were born.
- Patriarchy describes how society is controlled by male attitudes and values. Women tend to be disadvantaged.
- Many people think that the Christian Church is sexist and does not treat men and women equally. Others would argue that the Church has begun to follow the teachings of Jesus and is starting to address sexism.

---

**Table 16.3**

| Christianity is sexist | Christianity is not sexist |
| --- | --- |
| Women have had little to do with the power in the Church, even though they have traditionally made up the majority of the members. | Feminist theology is slowly beginning to make the Church think about its male-dominated language and sexist attitudes. |
| God is assumed to be a man. | Some would argue that St Paul's ideas about women were simply typical of the time in which he lived and that he spoke of the different roles that men and women had. |
| In most churches women cannot rise to the highest positions. | |
| Some sections of the Bible are sexist. St Paul: 'Women should remain silent in the | Jesus did not show sexist behaviour. 'He preached to women as well as men' (Lk. 10.38–42) and revealed himself as saviour |

churches. They are not allowed to speak ... If they want to enquire about something, they should ask their own husbands at home; for it is disgraceful for a woman to speak in the church.'
(1 Cor. 14.34–35)

'Now I want you to realize that the head of every man is Christ, and the head of the woman is man, and the head of Christ is God.'
(1 Cor. 11.3)

to a Samaritan woman (Jn 4.7–30).

Jesus had women disciples and after the resurrection appeared first to a woman (Mt. 28.1–10).

Christians believe, and Jesus said, that God created all people equal.

Over the past few years in the Anglican Church the issue of women priests has been very important. It has caused widespread division in the Church with some male leaders leaving the Church.

## Sexual Orientation

Within our classrooms, we as teachers of all subjects should promote equal rights for all. However, in RE there are problem areas because of the religious beliefs that are taught. It is fair to say that we have, outside of these lessons, teachers that fulfil their legal requirements of equality within the legal boundaries, but within certain RE lessons the complete opposite is true. On 1 June 2007 Alan Johnson, then Secretary of State for Education, spoke on BBC Radio 4's *Today* programme:

> Schools cannot discriminate against gay or lesbian pupils or their parents during the admissions process or in lessons. But guidance accompanying the legislation makes it clear that faith schools will not face prosecution for teaching in strict accordance with their religious views.

There are in general mixed views on lesbian, gay, bisexual and transgender (LGBT) issues and thus equality within RE. Double standards within some faith schools and within RE classrooms are a major concern for believers in equal rights for all. How can one promote equality for all and fulfil legal requirements if both staff and students' sexual orientation is questioned and chastised?

When teaching the faiths, there is a commonality that sex outside of marriage is sinful and those who commit these sins will be punished. Homosexuality is viewed in much the same light, as a sin, within lesson objectives and within the real world of the classroom. In non-faith schools, unless a teacher's personal homophobic views enter the teaching, which it should not as indoctrination is not part of RE specification, there is little issue. Teachers tend to teach the issues as part of 'fact' about that particular religion. This way class debate is opened up and issues can be discussed from all points of view.

Within the faiths (Christian and Muslim) schools it is not the mere fact of being a homosexual that is problem for concern but the *act* of homosexuality. In 2005 the Most Rev Peter Smith, Archbishop of Wales, underlined the phobia about this when he said 'homosexuals in relationships should be barred from classrooms because they set a bad example to pupils and staff'. Of course, this view was not held by the biggest Welsh union the NASUWT, who thought his anti-gay views were 'discriminatory'. However, Rev Smith concluded:

> If a homosexual is living an 'active' life, or on a casual basis, that would cause us difficulty as it goes against the whole Catholic ethos. We would have grave difficulty with that as we expect teachers to give a good example. (Baker 2005)

If this is a view that is widespread in some faith schools, then the promotion of true diversity in such schools is not possible. The government has not acted upon such homophobia and has in fact given the green light for this form of discrimination by allowing religious educational institutes to remain outside of British law. How and where that leads some members of the school community needs addressing since, as it stands today, we are failing as educators in our duty to protect and care for all our students and staff.

## Social Class

In this section, I will focus on 'the working classes' in the sociological sense of its everyday meaning. Differences within RE are most apparent within the structure of educational environments, for example faith schools and schools in affluent areas where results are higher than those of schools in working-class and deprived areas. However, the arguments for and against single-faith schools is an ongoing question and cannot be answered within this short chapter. What is apparent is that the government needs to talk to the staff in these schools to find a solution so that in the process of binding their own communities, the faith schools do not alienate others.

We as teachers know very little of the worlds our students inhabit. Family, peers, cultures and, at times, language can all impact on a student's education within school. As a teacher I talk about a number of equality issues with my peers, but the area that is less spoken about is that of classism. Today, the class system is not as straightforward as it once was. Through education and buying property, I personally have proceeded from my working-class background to the new status of middle class. The country itself has become far more stratified in the past 30 years, a situation that has lead to economic unfairness (one only has to think of the north/south divide) and distrust and misunderstanding between groups of people. The students we teach are very aware of the social status of their own peers within the classroom. Dispelling myths and gaining understanding should be encouraged. Classroom discussion allowing students to produce probing questions (within guided boundaries) give students time to reflect on their own experiences and those of others, thus breaking down barriers. This is especially true in schools that cater for a number of students from different class backgrounds.

Lessons that open up class issues are not always easy. The media has played its part in forming untruthful stereotypes. Recently in such a lesson a student said that working-class girls had babies so they didn't have to work. While talking about human rights and the right to an education, another student wanted to know whether 'all teachers at secondary school thought that common kids were going to have a million kids, live on benefit and get a council flat?' He said that he had this said to him and although he said the teachers 'were only joshin [joking]', the statement had made him feel miserable and undervalued.

As a teacher from a working-class background I have found myself angry at my peers for feeling *sorry* for working-class students. This is an area that I have always found extremely patronizing, but I have also found myself angry at those who show no empathy for the students they teach, having little in common with them due to social class differences. Perhaps this is a *self hang-up*, but an area that I feel does need more insight is the notion that some working-class people do not see education as a main priority within their lives. It is true that it is often the case that parents/carers who have disliked their years in school tend to pass this negativity on to their own children, who in turn will pass it on to their own. Breaking this cycle is a whole-school initiative yet within the Religious Education classroom there is ample opportunity to bring personal opinion into the arena making RE open to all. By encouraging all students to participate in debating and discussion, all aspects of social and cultural life can be touched upon thus building up a plurality of understanding of others within our communities.

## Special Educational Needs

With respect to children with special educational needs, it is important to find out the specific nature of the special need(s) of the student and identify how one might plan for such need(s). Class teachers should, of course, be fully aware of school procedures for identifying and supporting children with SEN.

Some of the most common types of SEN are:

- dyspraxia (specific learning difficulty)
- Asperger's Syndrome (on the autistic spectrum)
- Attention Deficit Hyperactivity Disorder (ADHD)
- speech and language disorders and general learning difficulties (the slow learner).

The Learning Without Limits (LWL) Group was set up by the University of Cambridge School of Education in the late 1990s, its purpose being to explore ideas that transformed the learning capacities of students. They are against 'streamed' classes where students are placed in order of academic achievement. The group's view is that many children were (and still are) 'labelled and stifled' and are given little chance of success in education when put into 'ability' groups. However, in 'mixed-ability' classes it is common practice to differentiate for all students. This means that the teaching is supposedly flexible and varied for all students including those with SEN. SEN students will have Individual Learning Plans (IEPs) and Personal Statements, which act as a guide to direct the teacher to the best possible learning for that student. It may mean that working in small groups, working with classroom support from an adult or their peers, or working to specific targets is all that is needed for a particular student or group. Nonetheless, The LWL rejects differentiation and replaces it with 'diversity through co-agency'. Diversity through co-agency is concerned not with the matching of task to student (differentiaton), but with connection – 'achieving a genuine meeting of minds, purposes and concerns between teachers and young people' (Hart *et al.* 2004, pp. 182–3). As Hart *et al.* explain:

> Tasks and outcomes are deliberately left open, or constructed in such a way as to offer choice of various kinds, so that young people have space to make their own connections, to make ideas meaningful in their own terms and to represent and express their thoughts, ideas and feelings in their own ways. (p. 183)

This is an excellent model to follow especially with the emphases today on personalized learning. However, it would remain to be seen if a teacher would be persecuted for taking such an initiative. I have yet to observe a lesson where there has been an open-ended outcome and feel that perhaps this concept would escape those who draw up teaching guidelines. The following may help in today's teaching climate.

### Effective differentiation involves the following

- Setting clear objectives that are achievable.
- Articulating those objectives to the children so that they understand what is expected of them.

- Having a good understanding of the subject.
- Ensuring lessons have suitable content that is accessible.
- Enabling children to learn at their own pace.
- Planning work in meaningful contexts.
- Planning for progression.
- Assessing what the child can actually do, and using that information to identify 'gaps' in learning and inform planning.
- Using teaching approaches that motivate children.
- Catering appropriately for children's different abilities

**Differentiation**

- input (e.g. appropriate use of language, focused questions, targeted information, repetition for specific groups etc)
- tasks (remember, this does not just mean different worksheets! Think how the same objective might be met through different multi-sensory approaches which involve active learning in meaningful contexts)
- resources (e.g. arrangement of the classroom environment, materials to support an activity, visual aids, ICT etc)
- support (e.g. peer support, group work, adult support – including the role of the teacher)
- outcome (e.g. teacher/child expectations for the finished piece of work). (Association of Teachers and Lecturers 2008, p. 2)

As in all classrooms, if the above is put into practice within the RE mainstream classroom, SEN students should progress in terms of levels and knowledge.

There is not a high emphasis on disability within RE at the present time. All inequalities are looked at in general with the main focus on prejudice. However, to help the students understand disability as a whole, they need to be given information that allows them to have a sense of the history of disabled people, including an understanding of the medical and social models (see Chapter 2 of this volume; see also Rieser 2006a; 2006b), as well as an understanding of how laws in the UK have changed. Empathy should be encouraged in lessons to conquer students' fear, ignorance and isms/phobias. A very good introduction and cross-curriculum theme can be found at the British Film Institute (BFI) website, where they look at the following topics. Relevant lesson plans accompany notes of the different areas.

- ways of thinking about disability
- 'medical model' vs 'social model'
- stereotypes
- defying the stereotypes

- disability, diversity and equal opportunities
- developing an equality policy in schools

More information can be found at the British Film Institute website.

## Concluding Remarks

In this chapter I have dealt with issues of ethnicity, gender, sexual orientation, social class and disability. These are only a few of the diversities that people face in their everyday lives and yet, in the process of writing this chapter, it has become more and more apparent that, even with laws and guidance, as a mere teacher of RE, I have little hope of winning alone the battle for equality for all. However, with every child I teach, I have the potential to educate about the wrongs and rights of humankind. Like those involved in the antiracist struggles of the 1970s, I will continue to fight to eradicate something that I believe hinders the basic goodness of humankind. However, unless governments and other influential bodies take the initiative and change their *two-faced policies* then my cause is lost. Religious Education can either promote inequality, or it can be a force for equality for all.

## Note

[1] The following discussion of Gillborn (2008) is taken from Cole (2009). Gillborn writes from the perspective of Critical Race Theory. Cole (2009) is a Marxist response to this.

## References

Association of Teachers and Lecturers (2008), *Effective Differentiation*. London (2007). Available at http://www.new2teaching.org.uk/tzone/Students/essays/sen.asp (accessed January 2008).

Baker, M. (2005), 'Outrage at archbishop's gay teacher views'. *IC Wales* (10 April). Available at http://icwales.icnetwork.co.uk/news/wales-news/tm_objectid = 15386326&method = full&siteid = 50082&headline = outrage-at-archbishop-s-views-on-gay-teachers-name_page.html. (accessed February 2008).

BBC (2007), Interview with Alan Johnson. *Today* programme (1 June).

Benn, T. (2007), 'Tony Benn on slavery, religion and justice'. Socialist Unity website, London (31 December 2007). Available at http://www.socialistunity.com/ ?p = 1444 (accessed November 2007).

BFI (British Film Institute) (2008), 'The history of attitudes to disabled people'. London. Available at http://www.bfi.org.uk/education/teaching/disability/thinking (accessed March 2008).

Cole, M. (2008), *Marxism and Educational Theory: Origins and Issues*. London: Routledge.
— (2009), *Critical Race Theory and Education: A Marxist Response*. New York: Palgrave Macmillan.
— and Maisuria, A. (2007), '"Shut the f*** up", "you have no rights here": critical race theory and racialisation in post-7/7 racist Britain'. *Journal for Critical Education Policy Studies* 5 (1).
Gillborn, D. (2008), *Racism and Education: Coincidence or Conspiracy?* London: Routledge.
Hargreaves, D. (1986), 'Curriculum for the future', in: G. Leonard and J. Yates (eds), *Faith for the Future*. London: Church House Publishing.
Hart, S., Dixon, A., Drummond, M. J. and McIntyre, D. (2004), *Learning Without Limits*. Maidenhead: Open University Press.
HMI (2005), 'Religious Education in Secondary Schools: School Subject Report'. *The Annual Report of Her Majesty's Chief Inspector of Schools* 2004/05 (HMI 2480). London: The Stationery Office.
Jackson, R. (2004), 'Teaching for tolerance, respect and recognition with relationship or belief'. Universiteter I Oslo.September 2004. Available at http://folk.uio.no/leirvik/OsloCoalition/Jackson0904.htm (accessed January 2008).
Macpherson, W. (1999), *The Stephen Lawrence Inquiry, Report of an Inquiry by Sir William Macpherson*. London: The Stationery Office.
Ofsted. (2007), *Making Sense of Religion*. London. Available at http://www.ofsted.gov.uk/assets/Internet_Content/Shared_Content/Files/2007/june/mkngsnsofrlg.pdf (accessed 30 May 2008).
OPSI (Office of Public Sector Information) (2005), *Education Act (1996), Ch 56, Section 375, (3)*. London. Available at http://www.opsi.gov.uk/acts/acts1996/ukpga_19960056_en_36 (accessed January 2008).
Rieser, R. (2006a), 'Disability discrimination, the final frontier: disablement, history and liberation', in M. Cole (ed.), *Education, Equality and Human Rights: Issues of Gender, 'Race', Sexuality, Disability and Social Class* (2nd edn). London: Routledge.
Rieser, R. (2006b), 'Inclusive education or special educational needs: meeting the challenge of disability discrimination in schools', in M. Cole (ed.), *Education, Equality and Human Rights: Issues of Gender, 'Race', Sexuality, Disability and Social Class* (2nd edn). London: Routledge.
Robson, J. (2007), 'Letter for report by Sir Keith Ajegbo'. London (9 February 2008). Available at http://news.reonline.org.uk/headline.php?150 (accessed December 2007).
The Times Educational Supplement Staffroom (2008), 'Why do we have to do RE anyway?' London. Available at http://www.tes.co.uk/section/staffroom/thread.aspx?story_id=2597380&path=/re/&threadPage=8&messagePage=2: (accessed 3 April 2008).

Chapter 17

# Modern Foreign Languages

## Pura Ariza and Debs Gwynn

## Introduction

In this chapter, we show how equality issues can be addressed in the foreign languages (FL) classroom, and we hope to provide motivation for teachers who still understand the enormous potential of education in creating a better world for us all. We look at the experiences of bilingual learners, point out the inequality of provision for students with special educational needs, examine the hype over boys' 'underperformance' and suggest ways in which we can combat homophobia. For each section, we have included suggestions of how to promote equality through the FL curriculum itself.

## A Brief History

The British Education System has always had an ambivalent approach to foreign languages. Until the introduction of comprehensive education, languages were considered the preserve of the educationally deserving (grammar school students) and the privately educated ruling class. These elitist attitudes were further shaped by the racist legacy of the British Empire and as a result foreign languages (FL) were never considered really essential for successful education. The change to comprehensive education in the 1970s brought the promise of greater access and equality, and the introduction of the National Curriculum in 1988 put FL on the school curriculum in parity with (some) other subjects for the first time. Numbers taking FL rose steadily as they were offered to a much wider range of students than ever before. When languages were made compulsory for all students up to 16 in the 1990s, ensuring the same subjects were offered to all mitigated against the effects of social class, gender and teacher-expectations on subject choice (see Davies *et al.* 2008), and numbers studying FL to GSCE, A level and in HE continued to rise (DfES 2002).

The success was short lived, and in 2002 government policy put a stop to this growth in take-up: the introduction of the deceptively titled 'Languages for All' Strategy for England (DfES 2002) removed the requirement for schools to teach FL up to KS4 to all students. In spite of spurious claims about the lack of popularity of FL (Parker and Tinsley 2005) and an explicit criticism of teachers, the rationale for this was clear: languages are needed for future employment and increase employability – but they are not needed by everyone. In making decisions about the KS4 curriculum, schools must 'consider carefully the needs and aspirations of their pupils, and the provision of opportunities which will maximise their future employability' (DfES 2002, p. 26) – and this does not involve offering FL to all. Clearly, studying a language should not be wasted on those who have no need for it. Thus schools are tasked not only with designing a curriculum to meet the needs of business and industry, but also are given a role in predetermining the destiny of their charges.

The introduction of the 'Languages for All' strategy for England (DfES 2002) also signalled a cavalier disregard for the earlier recommendations of the Nuffield Languages Inquiry (2000), which espoused a broader understanding of the role of languages. Its effects were immediately felt, and within a year 75 per cent of schools made FL optional at KS4 (Pachler *et al.* 2007). Study after the age of 14 has once more become a privilege for the few, concentrated in Specialist Language Colleges and marginalized in the lower tier of the 14–19 curriculum (even in subjects such as Travel and Tourism). When the schooling agenda is driven by results instead of pupil need, offering FL study to students who will not gain the magical grades is unlikely to be supported by school managers. Current government policy in FL has sanctioned a curtailment of young people's aspirations. It is part of an education system which is about maintaining inequalities and limiting opportunities, where education is seen increasingly as a training for the world of work, determined by the requirements of business, and tailored to meet the needs of the employer. The role of employers in education continues to grow, with the introduction of the work-based 14–19 curriculum, and the endorsement of business control of the curriculum through the academies programme. In this context, FL provision has lost out, becoming restricted for the working-class majority, who are not destined to use their language skills to rescue ailing businesses, and who are expected to give up language study in favour of something which offers a better return for the state's investment.

It is a policy which has also put language teachers in the extraordinary position of having to justify their subject's place on the school curriculum. As market values seep into our schools, FL teachers are cast in the role of advertisers for their wares who are expected to 'make a case' for including FL on the timetable. It is an exercise which cannot possibly meet the requirements of both school managers and students. The former require only grades and points to score for the school on the league tables. The latter are looking for inspiring, motivating, fun lessons, which even the most heroic teacher efforts will struggle to produce from the outdated, dull and adolescent-unfriendly GCSE syllabus. FL teachers need to break out of utilitarian arguments for FL study, to defy the 'delivery' version of teaching and to reject moves to deprofessionalize them through the increasingly prescriptive control of their teaching.

## Languages, Bilingual Learners and Equality

Attitudes towards languages in the education system and in schools are firmly based on a largely unquestioned inequality: there are 'modern foreign languages' (for which read 'French, German, Spanish and occasionally a bit of Italian or Chinese') and there are other languages. These are the 'home languages', the 'mother tongue' languages or 'community languages' – namelessly grouped together, without context, history, recognition, academic affiliation, teaching or qualifications. While 'modern languages' are given status and curriculum time, 'other' languages are rarely offered freely as a school subject, but are more likely to be taught to students who already speak them, in twilight classes by peripatetic teachers who are not integrated into the school staff. The prescription of the 1999 National Curriculum (DfEE/QCA 1999) that secondary schools must offer one of the languages of the EU before any other only contributed to the relegation of non-European languages to a subordinate position (Gardner 2001).

This divisive attitude to languages may be reinforced by language teachers themselves ('They're all speaking in another language – I don't know what it is!' claimed one Spanish teacher disdainfully; and 'You speak another language, dear, don't you? Is it Hindu [*sic*] or Gujarati?' asked a headteacher who had just been proudly showing off the French provision in her primary school). There is a shocking incongruence here: for the linguist, bilingualism is the ultimate goal – the greatest prize to be won in learning a language; but for bilingual learners in schools, their language skills in an unnamed language have no recognition, use or importance once they enter the school gates. Their linguistic abilities are measured with reference to English only and so found wanting. The deficit model of pupils 'with EAL' effectively steals the accolade of bilingualism from all those pupils with knowledge of languages associated with immigrant communities rather than academic study or potential business links. As Anderson (2000) points out, while sporting skills are likely to be fostered by schools, the language skills of bilingual learners are frequently overlooked.

Perhaps this will change, as more recently the new National Curriculum (QCA 2007) seems to recognize the importance of 'world languages', and has removed the condition that an EU language must be offered first in school. There is some indication of a new attitude, one which recognizes that learning a language may not be an entirely employment-orientated endeavour, and that languages might also be learned for family reasons (or even for enjoyment ...). But references to 'world languages' in the National Curriculum (*ibid.*) are few, and there is still no mention of bilingual learners. In the Key Stage 3 Framework (DfES 2003), bilingual pupils' language skills are entirely obscured within the deficit model of pupils 'with EAL'. When it comes to formal recognition, the range of GCSEs is narrower than the range of languages in the UK, and in spite of much lobbying, a GCSE in Somali is not considered sufficiently profitable. At university the picture is similar; there are, for example, no degree course in Urdu, Gujarati or Punjabi in the UK (although projects such as Routes into Languages (www.routesintolanguages.ac.uk) are working to address this need).

In contrast, we consider the FL classroom the ideal place to promote greater equality between languages. Language teaching should be about celebrating all languages (Datta and Pomphrey 2004) and language teachers are in a particularly strong position to lead this.

## 1. Promoting the use of all languages

Perhaps an obvious place to start would be to extend the traditional emphasis on the use of target language in class to encourage the use of all other languages present. There is an uncomfortable irony in the current situation, where on the one hand FL teachers struggle to persuade their students to use French/German/Spanish in class, while bilingual learners are often afraid to use languages other than English at school (MacGahern and Boaten 2000; Martin 2003). The FL classroom has real potential for challenging this and actively promoting an interest in all languages. I well remember the first time a Spanish word I was teaching gave rise to giggles and 'looks' from the Arabic speakers in the class ... and the benefits and interest generated in all students by our exploration of how and why there were similarities with Arabic. This eventually led to a permanent display of words with shared origins and a brief history of Arabic in Spain written by an otherwise demotivated 15-year-old bilingual. This was extended to all languages represented in the classroom – as well as some which were not as students amazed us all with their insightful comments and knowledge, and their ability to compare and analyse along syntactic, semantic and phonological lines.

For bilingual learners who were new to English but literate in another language, the decision to write vocabulary lists in three languages (Spanish, main language and English) seemed obvious to us as linguists, though the surprise and relief on the faces of the students was touching. This strategy, combined with openly encouraging bilingual learners to talk about their learning in whatever language seemed best, may well have made a wider contribution, as using a language one is confident in is essential for cognitive development and personal growth (Gravelle 2000; Cummins 2001) and can influence not only understanding, but also interest, motivation and involvement (Gardner 2001). Students benefit from discussing their learning with others – but of course this shouldn't be limited to using English only (Conteh 2003). Foreign-language teachers, all of whom have lived abroad, coped with immersion in another language and revelled in the many benefits of bilingualism, may find that this gives them greater confidence with multilingual interactions.

## 2. Teaching about cultures

Teaching about other cultures already forms an essential part of the FL curriculum, but knowledge alone is no guarantee of tolerance, and there is a step to be taken between the liberal hopes of the National Curriculum (1999) that learning about other cultures will of itself make people more aware, and an open challenge to notions of superiority in our understanding of multilingualism and cultural plurality both here and in the Spanish-/ German-/French-speaking countries we study (Byram 2003). However, teaching resources and writing for FL largely ignore bilingualism across Europe. The traditional ethnocentric analysis of 'modern foreign languages' has given rise to a limited, monolithic conceptualization of culture (Broadbent and Oriolo 1991), comparing an undifferentiated 'us' with an equally indiscriminate 'them' in what at times appears to be an obsession with difference and otherness. Supporting citizenship classes, the FL classroom must promote both respect for diversity and an understanding of how both British and European cultures depend on the indissoluble coexistence and comingling of plurality.

For the teacher of French or German or Spanish, this will include attention not only to the actual language taught (perhaps words for a greater range of clothes options, or places around town, or cities to be studied), but also to the atmosphere of the classroom when students are invited to talk about their personal lives, habits and families. We need to be sensitive to the fears of bilingual learners that in order to succeed in Britain they should leave any cultural differences behind them (*ibid.*). Bilingual learners in schools have reported that their feelings of alienation and difference at school were aggravated by the negative comments they received about their families (especially size of family), their clothes and their customs (and in particular regarding food) (Bhatti 1999) – precisely the topics on which school students will be invited to talk in their FL lessons. In our own classrooms, providing a secure and non-threatening context facilitated discussions which gave rise to the unexpected but welcome discovery of the huge number of factors we had in common, as students and the teacher grouped, and then regrouped, finding areas of commonality which bound us at times to some and then to others. There is a tendency in FL teaching to fixate on cultural otherness, but small differences in mealtimes or family membership must not be allowed to mask the unifying potential of teaching about culture (Lawes 2000), or the opportunity for language teaching to challenge stereotypes and racism (Starkey and Osler 2003). It is not living with more than one culture which causes conflict for minority ethnic students, but the fact that one is considered inferior to the other (Gardner 2001) and the racism they experience (Shain 2003). In addressing language inequalities, the FL classroom is contributing to the fight against racism.

## In the classroom

It is important to remember that Britain is a country of many languages, and to put the teacher at the centre of language promotion. This does not depend on there being bilingual learners actually present. An understanding of plurilingualism across the world is equally relevant in schools with monolingual populations.

- Ensure all languages are named. Terms such as 'mother tongue' and 'community language' lack status and convey the idea that the language is only for a reduced set of speakers, not important enough have a place in school and be studied. Ensure that all languages are offered equally to all students, and that heritage languages are not seen as only for members of particular communities or groups. Ensure that all language teachers are members of the MFL faculty.
- Be informed about where languages are spoken and contextualize languages historically, geographically and politically. Use this information to confer status appropriately. Reject reference to nameless 'community languages', spoken by only by minority groups in the UK.
- Demonstrate your linguistic abilities by learning and using greetings, for example, in a wide range of languages. Support non-linguists on the staff who want to do the same. Promote the use of bilingual language support in all subjects (e.g. vocab sheets).
- Support non-bilingual staff in understanding the use of more than one language as a benefit to learning, not as a threat. If appropriate, talk about your experiences of acquiring bilingualism.
- Teach a non-European language for 'Equal Opportunities Week' in the school. Collaborate with a bilingual student. Encourage other staff to bring non-European languages, history and educational culture into their lessons.

- Be aware of the links between greater language awareness and bilingualism and build on these.
- Make displays which draw from a wide range of languages.
- Pay attention to vocabulary taught and avoid ethnocentrism.
- The FL class may be the only area where a student's lack of knowledge of English will not hinder learning – ensure bilingual students are not withdrawn.
- Language learning skills developed in the FL class will support the bilingual's learning of English – ensure bilingual learners are not withdrawn.

## Students with Special Educational Needs and Equality

Historically, students with special educational needs (SEN) have often been denied access to FL lessons in both mainstream and special school settings. It was felt that this group of students would find foreign languages too difficult and that they needed to concentrate on English. In 1992 the National Curriculum introduced compulsory language learning for all secondary school students, but teachers were given little guidance on how to include all groups, and many were worried about how to deliver the new curriculum to students with SEN. They felt under pressure to get results and struggled because of a lack of appropriate materials and the unsuitability of the end-of-course certification (Asher and Chambers 1995). However, after ten years FL became optional at KS 4 and the obsession with performance league tables has led many schools to discourage students with SEN from choosing a foreign language at KS 4.

McColl (2005) questions how the FL teaching programme is devised and whether more could be done to make it accessible to a greater number of students. She points out that students are often grouped without reference to the course they are following and that consequently some students' learning needs are not met:

> the question of whether or not to offer a foreign language programme to certain students has more to do with adult attitudes and expectations, or resource availability, than with the ability of students to benefit. (McColl 2005, p. 104)

Some adults claim that students with SEN should not study foreign languages because they have difficulties with their first language and it will confuse them or because they should be learning other subjects first. However, the opportunities for students to make linguistic and social progress and gain greater cultural awareness through language study cannot be ignored (McColl 2000).

## 1. Promoting inclusion

The reality in schools, however, is more complex as there are often barriers and constraints that make it difficult to secure quality resources and to provide inclusive language teaching for all students. These barriers are often out of the control of the classroom teacher and are a result of school, Local Authority or government policies. The MFL framework has 151 pages and only 5 relate to teaching students with SEN. It suggests that teachers 'take action in their planning to ensure that these pupils are able to take part as fully and effectively as possible in the National Curriculum' (DfES 2003, p. 140). The clear message here is that students with SEN have to fit in with the curriculum, whereas true equity would be a flexible curriculum that adapts to the needs of the learners. The expectation on schools to push its students to achieve externally imposed targets can lead to students with SEN being removed from their languages lessons to attend extra English classes. The justification given for this is that the students will find MFL too difficult, although this argument has no logic, as many students with SEN enjoy FL lessons and feel comfortable in them because they start at the same point as their peers. The importance of the transferable literacy skills which are learned in FL lessons should not be underestimated. In the course of learning a new language students will become more aware of how languages are structured, develop further strategies for reading, for example predicting and selecting, and gain better understanding of sounds and rhythms. Furthermore, students with dyspraxia are likely to find PE difficult, but they are not automatically withdrawn from that subject and we do not tell any student to stop studying because they find aspects of it difficult.

## 2. The effect of marketization

The marketization of education is forcing schools to view students as points which contribute towards their position in the league table. Students with SEN are being directed towards vocational 'GCSE equivalent' courses as they are seen as easier options which carry the same point score as GCSE exams. These courses usually have some element of work placement and yet there is no foreign language input despite many businesses now being part of the global market. The sense of achievement that students with SEN would get if they were able to speak to a customer or supplier in a foreign language, and be understood, cannot be overestimated. Even if they were only able to exchange simple greetings it would be a considerable boost to those students, but current education policy is target driven and focuses on teaching for exams rather than for enjoyment.

The government's drive for standards and its inclusion policy are in conflict and demand different ways of working (Ainscow *et al.* 2006; Wedell

2008). Wedell (2008) argues that for real inclusion to happen the education system would need to be radically overhauled and start by acknowledging the diversity of all learners, not just those with SEN.

This focus on raising standards has centred firmly on the core subjects of English and maths. Schools concentrate much of their curriculum around the two subjects, which means less time for other lessons. English and maths are prioritized for all students but they are seen as even more important for students with SEN, who are often taken out of other lessons, including MFL, in order to study more literacy and numeracy. The entitlement of students with SEN to a 'broad and balanced' curriculum is being eroded and the principle of comprehensive education providing access to the curriculum for all is being sacrificed. The marketization of education is leading to a two-tier system which values academic achievement above all other aspects of education and which threatens to return us to a hierarchical system of grammar and secondary modern schools. Education is not a right that has to be won; students do not need to justify their right to learn. Students with SEN make comparable progress in FL to other subjects and education is not about teaching students who will later become experts.

## In the classroom

- Set clear teaching and learning objectives. You will need to set different learning objectives for different students. Break these down into small, achievable steps. Be very clear about the learning outcomes.
- Have a clear and easy-to-achieve reward system.
- Have clear classroom rules and boundaries.
- Keep to a routine (e.g. showing answers to a listening exercise). This allows them to develop confidence about *what* they have to do, and can allow them to concentrate on *how* to do it. Use games and encourage students to make or suggest games.
- Avoid copying from the board and provide pre-printed sheets where possible.
- Break instructions down to one or two simple directions at a time.
- Teach students how to learn or remember vocab – don't assume they know how already.
- All students must work in all four skill areas (except in exceptional circumstances). Students with special educational needs will need more input, more practice and more rehearsal. Consider different ways for students to show learning: physical responses, using visual support, ticking pictures, etc.
- Make written tasks meaningful and relevant.
- Use language in context – make it meaningful.
- Don't put pressure on students by asking them to speak in the FL in front

of the whole class – use pair/group work.
- Know your students – refer to IEPs where appropriate and talk to the SEN department.


## Gender and Equality

The gender attainment gap is considerably smaller than the gaps associated with ethnic background and social class (DCSF 2007; Ball 2008), but it is this area of difference which has attracted research and comment in the field of foreign-language learning at secondary school. Reflecting a national anxiety, there is hardly an FL- teaching handbook that does not address the 'issue' of boys' 'underachievement', and recommend ways in which teachers should tailor their teaching to meet boys' needs *and preferences* (although there is no clear picture of these). The problem is that rather than questioning and challenging the contribution of education in constructing unequal gender roles, arguments for addressing boys' needs are still formulated on assumed sex differences and stereotypes. In addition, current recommendations for school and classroom action are heavily and negatively influenced by the pressures of hyper-accountability and scoring points for school improvement. We must not allow the relentless pursuit of A*–C grades to hijack a genuine promotion of equality.

The differences in GCSE grades between boys and girls in foreign languages are well documented (see www.cilt.org.uk/research/statistics/education/secondary.htm#secondary4 for the latest figures) although the full picture is not so clear: crude figures of GCSE grades in FL do not explore the within-group differences in boys' attainment (far greater than the gender difference – Ball 2008) and may fail to point out that gender differences in languages exams do not continue at A level (Sunderland 2000; National Statistics Online www.statistics.gov.uk/cci/nugget.asp?id=434 (accessed 18 December 2008)). There is, of course, no evidence that girls are not underachieving, but this is not currently on the agenda. Unidimensional comparisons of boys' and girls' pre-A level grades are currently contributing to national anxieties about boys' attainment and needs, and teachers are told that they must respond.

In a historical context, boys' lower grades are not new: Cohen (1998) offers a fascinating picture of how boys' performance in language learning has, across more than two centuries, been characterized by lower performance, compared to girls'. Crucial to her analysis is an exploration of the *explanations* offered for boys' lack of success, and her conclusion that while their achievements are attributed to an intrinsic boy characteristic – intellect – their failures are, by contrast, ascribed to external factors, such as teaching methods or the content of the curriculum or the nature of the subject.

Conversely, girls' achievements are more likely to be seen as the result of their greater application or dedication. In this way, gendered interpretations of performance lead to explanations which do not question boys' inherent potential, but which detract importance from girls' successes.

Current investigations of boys' underperformance in FL have engaged in useful enquiries into their stated beliefs about FL learning and their preferences for classroom activities (Jones and Jones 2001; Barton 2003), giving learners a rare voice in shaping the education they are offered and demonstrating boys' ability to engage in reflective, thoughtful and insightful comments on their learning experiences. However, investigations of boys' needs will *only* be problematic if premised on an acceptance that boys and girls have different needs in the classroom, since the evidence against sex-determined differences in language learning is quite comprehensive (Raphael Reed 1998; Sunderland 2000). Furthermore, when causes of boys' under-performance are attributed to external factors such as uninteresting teaching (Field 2000) and teachers who do not target boys' needs adequately (Jones and Jones 2001), there are echoes of Cohen's (1998) analysis. It is especially concerning to see the picture of girls which emerges through the shadows of boy-focused investigations: girls are passive learners, more likely to put up with poor-quality teaching, with a higher boredom threshold, who never-theless score higher grades. But this has not given rise to a national anxiety or action plan: the message is clearly that it is acceptable for teachers to provide poor-quality teaching for girls, but not for boys.

There are, of course, rather whimsical claims that the GSCE syllabus is 'girl-friendly' – although any teacher who has risked insomnia trying to find a motivating angle from which to teach GCSE topics such as 'Talking about your holiday ailments' or 'Booking a hotel room' might more usefully ask just how 'adolescent-friendly' the syllabus is – but again this interpretation leads to an unhelpful delineation of gender stereotypes which confirms rather than challenges how education contributes to the construction of sex roles. The implication that there might be more 'boy-friendly' topics is an invitation to write a stereotype. Interestingly, when interviewed, neither boys nor girls felt that foreign languages was a girls' subject (Lee *et al.* 1998; Jones and Jones 2001; Barton 2003) – but the teachers in the same studies did. It is also worth noting that the focus on boys as language learners is currently confirming noticeable within-group variation: some appreciate the use of target language, others don't (Jones and Jones 2001); they prefer solitary work (Barton 2003) and like working with a partner more than girls do (Lee *et al.* 1998); boys benefit from concentrating on form rather than communication (Field 2000) and find the abstract learning of FL difficult (Barton 2003). It is not at all clear that boys have clear, gender-linked preferences which distinguish them from girls.

The focus on boys' separate learning needs has, in the context of hyper-accountability, another dimension. The potential of education as an agent for change has fallen prey to the market-driven agenda of school effectiveness, as measured by Ofsted grades, points in exams and positions in league tables. Boys' underachievement currently has a key place in the measurement of school effectiveness, and as such teachers are required to listen and attend to boys' learning preferences ... or run the risk of being held responsible for an individual's failure to achieve. The pressures on schools (through league tables, targets, inspections, performance pay, etc.) to improve their scores has led to a narrowing of the curriculum and a loosening of the link between exam success and subject knowledge (Mansell 2007), as teachers are finding themselves spending more time teaching students how to score points in exams, and less on teaching the actual subject. In the context of hyper-accountability, we must question whether the concern for boys' 'under-achievement' is driven by a concern for their learning or by the need for schools to score points.

What is needed is teaching which listens and attends to the needs of all its learners, in order to stimulate their interest and learning irrespective of the harmful pressures of school inspections. FL teaching can and should challenge stereotyped assumptions of language-learning success, and question the inequalities and restrictions of gendered socialization. This will not be achieved through the masculinization of the classroom or by pitting boys' interests against girls'. FL teachers should demonstrate that aptitude is not fixed, and that learning in the foreign-language classroom is achievable by all.

## In the classroom

- Encourage debate on sex roles and ascribed characteristics when topics bring this up (jobs around the house/work experience/future plans, etc.). Allow students to explore their developing ideas and to answer each other (from experience, we know how 'expert' interventions from the teacher can kill debate ...).
- Encourage students to explore gender stereotyping from a historical and social viewpoint, looking at differences over time and location – link to the campaign work and struggle of the Women's Movement.
- Overtly challenge and comment on gender-biased assumptions in teachers/materials/policies.
- Dispel myths of GSCE syllabus being 'more appropriate' to one sex; replace with argument that GSCE syllabus is both inappropriate and unstimulating to adolescent learners; seek out and teach topics which your learners will find interesting; demonstrate how interest is not determined by gender.
- Reject the binary opposition of sex-role stereotyping (if something is female, it can't also be male ...).

- Celebrate International Women's Day – use the internet to locate and exploit local material from FL country.
- Use non-sexist language and teach it – los alumnos y las alumnas/nosotros y nosotras/ils et elles/las niñas. Show how a challenge to the established use of the masculine form to indicate all forms was part of women's movement demands across the world – relate to the use of 'he or she', which we now expect.
- Monitor your responses to boys and girls, and time taken interacting with each, including your use of FL. Get someone else to observe you and monitor this. Reflect.
- Be aware that boys may already have a poor self-image as language learners, may already have constructed themselves as likely to fail – challenge this and build the self-esteem of success.
- Be aware of gender and groupings for group work. Monitor and discuss with the students – promote equality.

## Sexuality, Homophobia and Equality

Attitudes to lesbian and gay teenagers (and, to a lesser extent, to bisexual and transgendered teenagers) have undoubtedly improved over the years, largely as a result of the organized activism of lesbian, gay, bisexual and transgender (LGBT) people. This has resulted in increased anti-discriminatory practices and, occasionally, legislation (there is better employment legislation, for example, but it does not apply to transgendered people). Nevertheless, the damaging legacy of Section 28 lives on. Section 28 of the Local Government Act (1988 – available in full at www.opsi.gov.uk) infamously made it illegal for Local Authorities to 'intentionally promote' homosexuality and had a particularly hard impact in schools. In spite of the fact that it was, belatedly, repealed in 2003, its contribution to institutionalizing the homophobia which LGBT school students and teachers endure in schools is still very much in evidence.

The role of schools in constructing (unequal) gender roles and in the creation of a (dominant) male identity has produced an unusual collusion between school authority and students, as 'un-male' expressions are policed and proscribed by both (Mac an Ghaill 1994). Learning how to be a male necessarily requires elements of misogyny and homophobia, and the combined success of school students, the authority of the school and the leftover fear of Section 28 in confirming the bigoted belief that gay relationships are not equal to heterosexual relationships is pervasive. Currently, there is real concern over the insidious use of the term 'gay' to signal negativity, opprobrium and worthlessness in almost any context. Thurlow (2001) has documented how the omnipresent, aggressive use of 'gay' by pupils is a daily assault on the psychological health of young LGBT people. The prevalence of homophobic abuse in schools serves to enforce heteronormativity, and any male students who do not take part in heterosexual normalizing behaviour may be the butt of homophobic insults and 'humour' (Kehily and Nayak 2006).

According to Stonewall (2007), homophobic bullying is 'almost endemic' in British schools: 65.5 per cent of young lesbian, gay and bisexual students have experienced direct bullying – rising to a figure of 75 per cent in faith schools. Only 23 per cent of young gay people at school have been told that homophobic bullying is wrong, and over half of lesbian and gay pupils do not feel able to be themselves at school. Mullen (1999) found that lesbian, gay and bisexual youths were three times more likely to suffer from depression, and young gay men were four times more likely to attempt suicide, compared to their heterosexual peers. He describes the vicious cycle of social exclusion, as heterosexism and homophobia create a climate of fear and shame that encourages silence, reinforcing invisibility and isolation, leaving negative attitudes unchallenged, legitimizing abuse, discrimination, harassment, invisibility, isolation and violence, leading to internalized homophobia, and social exclusion (*ibid.*).

There is an urgent need for schools to address institutional homophobia and transphobia, and to secure the promotion of LGBT equality in line with the statutory promotion of race, gender and disability equality. This is not just about tackling bullying, and mere exhortation to treat LGBT people with respect is not a remedy (TUC 2007). Every Child Matters (www.everychildmatters.gov.uk) states that homophobic bullying is incompatible with the government's objectives, and yet *in this area alone* both individuals and institutions are given the opportunity to opt out of its recommendations. Teachers and schools are at liberty to negatively characterize LGBT people, identity and lifestyle with impunity. Similarly, the DCSF guidance on tackling homophobic bullying (available at www.teachernet.gov.uk) is detailed and well researched but nevertheless does not *require* schools to tackle homophobia (as they are required by law to address racism). Education needs go beyond promoting tolerance; it is the assumed superiority of heterosexuality – and by implication the inferiority of lesbian, gay, bisexual and transgender people – which must be openly challenged. In order to do this, we will need to approach sexual orientation and gender identity as educational issues, not just pastoral ones. Education must contribute towards a greater understanding and awareness of diversity and defy the inequality of heteronormativity.

**In the classroom**

- Challenge students every time they use the word 'gay' in a non-complimentary way. ('Gay? I hope you mean that as a compliment ...';

'There's nothing wrong with being gay. There's a lot wrong with using the word gay as an insult.' Etc., etc.).

- Tackle the collusion of silence by ensuring that there are lesbians, gay men, bisexual and transgender people represented in all topics studied.
- Promote an understanding that all families are different, and all are special. Promote the concept that the key elements of family life do not depend on the presence of one mother and one father. Include same-sex parents and be aware of the growing number of children with gay parents.
- Ensure support and safety for pupils who write their Christmas card 'To my mums'.
- Welcome same-sex couples at parents' evenings.
- Ensure that there are LGBT people in the famous people pupils study – include openly gay and trangender actors/musicians/sportspeople, etc.
- Ensure that there are gay teenagers in topics of generation issues, relationships with parents, money problems, etc. Be careful not to compartmentalize – gay teenagers have many of the same problems as non-gay teenagers.
- Include gay couples in role-plays, for example 'Booking a hotel room'.
- Include LGBT issues in any human rights/social issues studied, for example LGBT rights as an asylum issue.
- Prepare a class comparison of civil partnership rights across Europe and in target language countries (e.g. Spain has full gay marriage, but France does not recognize civil partnerships from the UK).
- Teach gay-specific target language.
- Ensure LGBT month is celebrated in your school.
- Remember LGBT victims of the Holocaust in Holocaust Memorials.
- Teach the history of Gay Rights in the UK in the list of human rights issues studied.

## Useful websites

- www.stonewall.org.uk – LGBT lobbying and campaign group
- www.schools-out.org.uk – working for LGBT equality in education
- www.nooutsiders.sunderland.ac.uk – project promoting LGBT equality in primary schools
- www.lgbthistorymonth.org.uk – history and resources for LGBT history month
- www.andymullen.com – LGBT research and issues
- www.teachers.org.uk – National Union of Teachers: advice for LGBT teachers, and for raising issues in schools

# References

Ainscow, M., Booth, T. and Dyson, A. (2006), *Improving Schools, Developing Inclusion.* London: Routledge.

Anderson, J. (2000), 'Which language? An embarrassment of choice', in K. Field (ed.), *Issues in Modern Foreign Languages Teaching.* London: Routledge Falmer.

Asher, C. and Chambers, G. (1995), *Modern Foreign Languages and Special Educational Needs: A Study of Provision and Practice in a Sample of Mainstream and Special Schools.* London: University of Leeds.

Ball, S. (2008), *The Education Debate.* Bristol: Policy Press.

Barton, A. (2003), *Getting the Buggers into Languages.* London and New York: Continuum.

Bhatti, G. (1999), *Asian Children at Home and at School: An Ethnographic Study.* London: Routledge.

Broadbent, J. and Oriolo, L. (1991), 'Language education across Europe: towards an intercultural perspective', in D. Buttjes and M. Byram (eds), *Mediating Languages and Cultures: Towards an Intercultural Theory of Foreign Language Education.* Clevedon: Multilingual Matters.

Byram, M. (2003), 'Teaching languages for democratic citizenship in Europe and beyond', in K. Brown and M. Brown (eds), *Reflections on Citizenship in a Multilingual World.* London: CILT Publications.

Cohen, M. (1998), 'A habit of healthy idleness: boys' underachievement in historical perspective', in D. Epstein, J. Elwood, V. Hey and J. Maw (eds), *Failing Boys? Issues in Gender and Achievement.* Buckingham: Open University Press.

Conteh, J. (2003), *Succeeding in Diversity: Culture, Language and Learning in Primary Classrooms.* Stoke-on-Trent: Trentham Books.

Cummins, J. (2001), 'Empowerment through Biliteracy', in C. Baker and N. H. Hornberger (eds), *An Introductory Reader to the Writing of Jim Cummins.* Clevedon: Multilingual Matters.

Datta, M. and Pomphrey, C. (2004), *A World of Languages: Developing Children's Love of Languages.* London: CILT.

Davies, P., Telhaj, S., Hutton, D., Adnett, N. and Coe, R. (2008), 'Socioeconomic background, gender and subject choice in seconcdary schooling'. *Educational Research*, 50, (3).

DCSF (2007), Research Brief RB002. Available at http://www.dcsf.gov.uk/rsgateway/DB/RRP/u014850/index.shtml (accessed 18 December 2008).

DfEE/QCA (1999), *The National Curriculum: Handbook for Secondary Teachers in England.* London: DfEE/QCA.

DfES (2002), *Languages for All: Languages for Life. A Strategy for England.* Nottingham: DfES Publications.

— (2003), *Framework for Teaching Modern Foreign Languages: Years 7, 8 & 9.* London: HMSO.

Field, K. (2000), 'Why are girls better at modern foreign languages than boys?', in K. Field (ed.), *Issues in Modern Foreign Languages Teaching.* London: Routledge Falmer.

Gardner, P. (2001), *Teaching and Learning in Multicultural Classrooms.* London: David Fulton Publishers.

Gravelle, M. (ed.) (2000), *Planning for Bilingual Learners.* Stoke-on-Trent: Trentham Books.

Jones, B. and Jones, G. (2001), *Boys' Performance in Modern Foreign Languages – Listening to Learners*. London: CILT.

Kehily, M. J. and Nayak, (2006), 'Lads and laughter: humour and the production of heterosexual hierarchies', in M. Arnot and M. Mac an Ghaill (eds), *The RoutledgeFalmer Reader in Gender and Education*. London: Routledge.

Lawes, S. (2000), 'The unique contribution of modern foreign languages to the curriculum', in K. Field (ed.), *Issues in Modern Foreign Languages Teaching*. London: Routledge/Falmer.

Lee, J., Buckland, D. and Shaw, G. (1998), *The Invisible Child: The Responses and Attitudes to the Learning of Modern Foreign Languages Shown by Year 9 Pupils of Average Ability*. London: CILT.

Mac an Ghaill, M. (1994), *The Making of Men: Masculinities, Sexualities and Schooling*. Buckingham: Open University Press.

MacGahern, D. and Boaten, K. (2000), 'Planning for inclusion: learning at Key Stage 4', in M. Gravelle (ed.), *Planning for Bilingual Learners*. Stoke-on-Trent: Trentham Books.

Mansell, W. (2007), *Education by Numbers: The Tyranny of Testing*. London: Politico's.

Martin, D. (2003), 'Constructing discursive practices in school and community: bilingualism, gender and power'. *International Journal of Bilingual Education and Bilingualism*. 6 (3 and 4), 237–52.

McColl, H. (2000), *Modern Languages for All*. London: David Fulton.

— (2005), 'What? and How?' *Support for Learning*, 20, (3), 103–8.

Mullen, A. (1999), *Social Inclusion: Reaching Out to Bisexual, Gay and Lesbian Youth*. Reading: ReachOUT.

Nuffield Languages Inquiry (2000), *Languages: The Next Generation*. London: The Nuffield Foundation.

Pachler, N., Evans, M. and Lawes, S. (2007), *Modern Foreign Langauges: Teaching School Subjects 11–19*. London and New York: Routledge.

Parker, L. and Tinsley, T. (2005), *Making the Case for Languages at Key Stage 4*. London: CILT.

QCA (2007), *The National Curriculum Statutory Requirements for Key Stages 3 and 4 from September 2008*. London: QCA.

Raphael Reed, L. (1998), 'Zero tolerance: gender performance and school failure', in D. Epstein, J. Elwood, V. Hey and J. Maw (eds), *Failing Boys? Issues in Gender and Achievement*. Buckingham: Open University Press.

Shain, F. (2003), *The Schooling and Identity of Asian Girls*. Stoke-on-Trent: Trentham Books.

Starkey, H. and Osler, A. (2003), 'Language teaching for cosmopolitan citizenship', in K. Brown and M. Brown (eds), *Reflections on Citizenship in a Multilingual World*. London: CILT Publications.

Stonewall (2007), 'The School Report: the experiences of young gay people in Britain's schools'. Available at www.stonewall.org.uk (accessed 13 January 2009).

Sunderland, J. (2000), 'Issues of language and gender in second and foreign language education'. *Language Teaching*, 33, 220–3.

Thurlow, C. (2001), 'Naming the "outsider within": homophobic pejoratives and the verbal abuse of lesbian, gay and bisexual high-school pupils'. *Journal of Adolescence*, 2001, (24), 25–38.

TUC (2007), *Promoting LGBT Equality through Education*. London: TUC Publications.
Wedell, K. (2008), 'Confusion about inclusion: patching up or system change?' *British Journal of Special Education*, 35, (3), 127–35.

# Afterword

## Mike Cole

Contributors to this book have addressed themselves to the promotion of a wide range of equality issues. It needs to be pointed out that such promotion by teachers and other educational workers has been facilitated by the great strides that have been made with respect to progressive equalities legislation in recent years in the UK (see the Equality and Human Rights Commission, 2008). However, while such legislation is to be welcomed by all forward-thinking people, for Marxists the application of equality legislation also serves to give the impression that human rights are comprehensively upheld whereas in fact workers' rights *as workers* are denied in the workplace, including the school and other educational institutions.

While the political system is *formally* democratic (although the reality is the choice of voting for two pro-capitalist parties every five years, both of whom enact anti-worker legislation), the workplace makes no pretence at being a democratic institution. This lack of democracy in the workplace has been exacerbated in recent years by the onslaught of 'new public managerialism' (NPM). As Dave Hill and Ravi Kumar (2009, pp. 20–1) explain, in the context of education, NPM entails the importation into the old public services the language and management style of private capital. This, they go on, has replaced the ethic and language and style of public service and duty. Under NPM, education as a social institution has been subordinated to international market goals.

As Lewis *et al.* (2009) put it:

> This replaces collective collegiality and decision-making (or decision-influencing) with individualistic, competitive, and hierarchical work relationships. There is the siphoning upwards of power to senior management teams – or the senior manager, head teacher, or principal – who may have no educational experience or background at all (as in the United States, and as envisaged in England and Wales). (Lewis *et al.*, 2009, p. 121)

For James Gross (2006) this constitutes a negation of human rights:

> Inducing workers to see the world through their employer's frame of
> reference to legitimize and maintain employer control of the workplace
> without changing the power relationship of superior employer and
> subordinate employee constitutes manipulation that is an affront to
> human beings and human rights. (Gross, 2006, pp. 33–4)

Gross (*ibid.*, p. 23) has further argued that human rights, including
workers' rights, are not negotiable, they are not earned or enacted by
contract, but 'are a species of moral rights simply because they are human'.
For Marxists, the exploitation of workers is the root of all social justice, which
is explained by the Labour Theory of Value (see Cole, 2009, pp. 146–7).
Workers alone create value, but the surplus created is appropriated from
them in the form of profits.

As I write this Afterword, most of the world is in the depths of a major
recession. It is impossible to understand this recession without addressing the
contradictions inherent in the capitalist system. At the same time, rather than
being empowered to think creatively about the possible future directions for
the country and the world, students are being conformed to the current
requirements of national and global capitalism – a flexible workforce,
something openly acknowledged by capitalists and politicians who support
them.

In Chapter 2 of this volume, I noted that no space is provided for a
discussion of *alternatives* to neo-liberal global capitalism, such as world
democratic socialism. I further suggested that discussing socialism in schools
may be seen as one of the last taboos. Now that neo-liberal capitalism has
been shown not to work (remember Margaret Thatcher telling us there is no
alternative, with Tony Blair and Gordon Brown subsequently in full
agreement?), now is the perfect time to move forward. Now is an opportune
moment in history to bring into the classroom discussions of alternatives to
neo-liberalism, and indeed to UK-backed US imperialism in Iraq,
Afghanistan and elsewhere. Such alternatives must include not only an
examination of more humane state-controlled capitalism, but also democratic
socialism (Venezuela is an interesting case in point; see Cole, 2009).
Environmental issues are now firmly on the agenda, but in the context of
no basic changes to the system that sustains ecological destruction. Teachers
and other educational workers who believe in democracy and empowerment
should agitate for the curriculum to also encompass, as an antidote to the
globalization of capitalism, discussions about the globalization of socialism,
and the end of poverty, exploitation, misery and oppression.

# References

Cole, M. (2009), *Critical Race Theory and Education: A Marxist Response*. New York: Palgrave Macmillan.

Equality and Human Rights Commission (2008), 'Key legislation' Available at http:// www.equalityhumanrights.com/en/foradvisers/keylegislation/pages/keylegislation.aspx (accessed 3 February 2009).

Gross, J. (2006), 'A logical extreme: proposing human rights as the foundation for workers' rights in the United States', in R. N. Block, S. Friedman, M. Kaminski and A. Levin (eds), *Justice on the Job: Perspectives on the Erosion of Collective Bargaining in the United States*. Kalamazoo, MI: W. E. Upjohn Institute of Employment Research.

Hill, D. and Kumar, R. (2009), 'Neoliberalism and its impacts', in D. Hill and R. Kumar (eds), *Global Neoliberalism and Education and Its Consequences*. New York: Routledge.

Lewis, C., Hill, D. and Fawcett, B. (2009), 'England and Wales: neoliberalised education and its impacts', in D. Hill (ed.) (2009), *The Rich World and the Impoverishment of Education: Diminishing Democracy, Equity and Workers' Rights*. New York: Routledge, pp. 106–135.

# Index

Locators shown in *italics* refer to illustrative matter.

318 *Equality in the Secondary School*

Thatcher, M. 146
Theory of Planned Behaviour 164–5
Thomas, A. 243
Thomson, P. 49
Thurlow, C. 299–300
Tomlinson report (14–19 curriculum)
    100
transgenders
    marginalization of within art and design
        education 64–5
travellers
    challenges of within design and
        technology teaching 95–6
Troyna, B. 65–6

*Understanding the Score* (OFSTED) 255
United States of America
    role of equality and opportunity in
        education within 3–12
    *see also* schools, US

Vygotsky, L. 45, 48, 225

Warner, L. 123
Wartofsky, M. 45
Watson, A. 258
Watson, R. 59, 60
Wertsch, J. 45
Wesselmann, T. 61
*What Is History* (Carr) 145
Wilkinson, A. 115, 200
Wilson, M. 133
Woodhead, C. 233
working class
    marginalization of by nature of art and
        design curriculum 59–60
    role of RE in enhancing attitudes
        towards 281–2
Wright, J. 132, 196
Wrigley, T. 118
Wyse, D. 111

Young, I. 135

Zenke, K. 38